Cavendish
Publishing
Limited

'A' LEVEL LAW – PAPER II

SECOND EDITION

TITLES IN THE SERIES

LECTURE NOTES

'A' Level Law – Paper I
'A' Level Law – Paper II
Child Law
Civil Liberties
Commercial Law
Company Law
Conflict of Laws
Constitutional & Administrative Law
Criminal Litigation and Sentencing
Equity & Trusts
European Community Law
Evidence
Family Law
Intellectual Property Law
International Trade Law
Jurisprudence
Land Law
Public International Law
Revenue Law
Succession, Wills & Probate

PRINCIPLES OF LAW

Administrative Law
Business Law
Contract Law
Criminal Law
Employment Law
English Legal System
Environmental Law
Law of Tort

Cavendish
Publishing
Limited

'A' LEVEL LAW – PAPER II

SECOND EDITION

Penny Booth, LLB (Hons), LLM, Cert Ed, B Ed
Senior Lecturer in Law
University of Teesside

Jean Holden, MSc, B Ed, PGD Soc Rsch
Senior Lecturer in Law
University of Plymouth

Gordon McLeish, BA, Cert Ed, Solicitor
Senior Lecturer in Law
University of Plymouth

Jill Spencer, PhD, LLB, AKC, Solicitor
Senior Lecturer in Law
University of Plymouth

Edited by Peter Shears, BA, LLB, LLM
Director of Legal Studies
University of Plymouth

First published in Great Britain 1995 by Cavendish Publishing Limited, The Glass House, Wharton Street, London WC1X 9PX

Telephone: 0171-278 8000 Facsimile: 0171-278 8080

e-mail: info@cavendishpublishing.com

Visit our Home Page on http://www.cavendishpublishing.com

'A' Level Law – 2nd ed
Paper II – (Lecture Notes)
1. Law – England 2. Law – Wales
I Shears, Peter
349.4'2

ISBN 1 85941 176 2
Printed and bound in Great Britain

Preface

Studying law at any level can be a daunting process – at 'A' level it can be worse!

There are many 'A' level texts which are written to be broadening, deepening and inspiring books. Some of them achieve some of these goals.

These two texts – 'A' Level Paper – I and 'A' Level Paper – II are different. They are written to cover the syllabuses of the key Examination Boards.

We have considered the published requirements of the JMB, the AEB and the University of London at 'A' and 'Advanced Supplementary' level and we have provided what we believe to be the material required by candidates for these examinations.

Like it or not, the law changes every day. There has been considerable movement in many areas covered by this book since its first publication. In preparing this new edition the authors have been able to incorporate important new material on statutory developments in contract law, the developing tort of negligence, the reform of the crime of murder and significant developments in *mens rea* in criminal law generally, the constantly shifting nature of our civil liberties, and several shifts in family and employment law. Add to this the intriguing prospect of a new government with some different ideas and we seem to be living (and studying) in interesting times.

Of course, we have tried to be interesting, relevant and stimulating too, but the main aim is to tell students what we think you need to know to meet the expectations of the examiners. Each syllabus area has been covered by a subject specialist.

As to the techniques required in the examination room, we have also written a 'Questions and Answers' book to enable candidates to use the knowledge they acquire from these books to the best advantage when faced with the examination paper.

We have stated the law as we believe it to be in the mid-Summer of 1997.

All that remains is to wish you the very best of luck!

Peter Shears

Contents

PART III CRIMINAL LAW

PART IV THE LAW OF CIVIL LIBERTIES

PART VI LABOUR LAW AND THE WORKPLACE

Table of Cases

Table of Statutes

Table of European Union Legislation

PART I

THE LAW OF CONTRACT

Chapter 1

Introduction and Overview

A contract is a legally binding agreement which means that if broken, it may be enforced by the courts. The formation of contracts is an essential part of every day life. Examples of contracts range from the simplest of transactions, such as buying goods from a corner shop, taking a ride on a bus or opening a bank account to undertaking a major construction project, signing up a new player for a football team or buying a house. While most contracts can be formed quite simply, by word of mouth, in writing or by conduct, the law requires that certain types of contract must comply with specified formalities, eg created in the form of a deed or in a written format which contains prescribed details (see Chapter 2, 2.4 below).

1.1 What is a contract?

Modern economies are based upon a high degree of division of labour. This in turn necessitates trade and exchange so that peoples' wants can be satisfied. The transactions involved in this process would be difficult if not impossible to arrange were it not for the existence of a set of rules by which contracting parties' interests are protected and by which they can enforce their rights. Without them there would be no foundation upon which parties could base their conduct or legitimate expectations and no criteria for the enforcement of agreements by the courts. Businesses and private individuals simply could not operate in such a vacuum unless they were prepared to return to a very primitive form of economy and experience a consequent fall in their material standard of living.

1.2 The need for a law of contract

It is often said that 'all contracts are agreements but not all agreements are contracts'. Since the courts will enforce the former but not the latter, it is important to establish the essentials of a legally binding contract. The next chapter on contract law – the formation of contracts – identifies and investigates those characteristics of an agreement which the courts will regard as creating a contract. Firstly an agreement is made when an offer made by one party (the offeror), is unequivocally accepted by the other (the offeree), but a contract is more than an agreement. A simple contract is a bargain. Each party to the agreement acquires rights in return for the commitment to perform obligations, in other words, each party must support the contract with consideration.

1.3 The essentials of a legally binding agreement

Even when these qualities are present, the courts will not enforce the agreement if the parties lacked the intention to be legally bound. In commercial transactions the courts will presume that the parties intend to be legally bound. It is up to the parties to rebut that presumption with evidence of a contrary intention if that is their wish. In social and family agreements, for obvious reasons, the contrary presumption is made.

These then are the elements of a contract – agreement formed by offer and acceptance, consideration in the form of some benefit/detriment moving between the parties and an intention to be legally bound, ie an intention to create rights which can be legally enforced.

1.4	**The contents of the agreement**

Having established that a contract exists it is necessary to consider the terms on which the parties have agreed to be bound. The rights and obligations contained in the terms of a contract are generally agreed and stated by the parties – these are express terms – but there are situations in which the courts are prepared to imply additional terms into a contract. Furthermore, Parliament has provided by statute that specified terms will be implied into certain types of contract, notably contracts for the supply of goods and services.

Contractual terms are not all of the same importance. The relative status of terms – conditions, warranties and innominate terms is considered below. It affects the rights of the wronged party in the event of breach of contract. A wronged party can only treat his obligations as at an end, if he or she so chooses, if he or she is substantially deprived of the benefit under the contract, or if a breach of condition has occurred.

Another type of term is of considerable importance – exemption clauses. These purport to limit or exclude the liability of one of the parties for defective or non-performance of their side of the bargain. It is important to be clear about the effectiveness of such clauses by applying common law rules laid down by judges and controls over exemption clauses provided by statute in the Unfair Contract Terms Act 1977 and the Unfair Terms in Consumer Contract Regulations 1994.

1.5	**Defects in the bargain**

There may exist defects in the bargain and these may prevent its enforcement by the courts.

For example, as is considered below, certain classes of person, notably minors (those under 18), and those who are drunk or of unsound mind may avoid a contract on the grounds of their capacity in certain eventualities.

As a matter of public policy illegal contracts, eg contracts to commit a crime or a tort, are void. Thus, as a general rule, the courts will not allow actions to recover money or goods that have passed under such contracts. However, these rules of non-recovery do not generally apply to other *prima facie* void contracts such as contracts in restraint of trade.

It is a requirement that contracting parties genuinely consent to the agreement, so a party may avoid a contract where there is evidence of misrepresentation, duress, undue influence or, in limited circumstances, where the agreement was made as a result of a mistake.

The doctrine of privity is centrally important in contract law. It has already been stated that a contract confers rights and imposes obligations on the parties. It follows that only the parties to the contract can enforce it. Third parties – 'strangers to the consideration' – are not generally in a position to enforce an agreement, even if it has been made for their benefit. There are exceptions to this general rule and proposals have recently been made for reform.

Contractual rights and obligations will cease when the contract is discharged. This can be achieved in various ways. In most cases the parties simply perform their respective obligations to discharge the contract. Alternatively, the parties may reach some form of legally binding agreement whereby they are released from their obligations.

1.6   Discharge of contracts and remedies for breach

According to the doctrine of 'frustration', the courts will also acknowledge that the contract is discharged when, due to some unforeseeable event, which is not the fault of either party, it is no longer possible to perform obligations. These radically changed circumstances must make the contract an altogether different commercial undertaking from that which had been envisaged when the contract was formed.

Where a party fails to perform contractual obligations or renders a defective performance, on the face of it an action will lie for breach of contract and the wronged party may apply for a remedy. This usually takes the form of financial compensation – damages – which are intended (insofar as money can) to place the parties where they would have been had the contract been properly performed. Damages are a common law remedy and are available as of right. Sometimes, where damages would be an inadequate or inappropriate remedy, the court will award discretionary equitable remedies in the form of specific performance – ordering a party to perform contractual obligations, or an injunction, to prevent a party from breaking the contract.

1.7	**The sources of contract law**	As a common law subject, most contract law can be found in the decisions of judges in cases which have been reported in law reports. At the front of this book there is a list of the cases mentioned in the text with full case references. As many 'A' level' students do not have access to full law reports it is worth bearing in mind that many good contract case books are available. (A brief synopsis of cases can be found in *Briefcase on Contract Law*, 1997, 2nd edn, Cavendish Publishing Ltd.)

Although the facts of a case may be very interesting, it is the *ratio decidendi* – the reason for the decision – which is of greatest importance since it is this legal principle which can be applied to subsequent similar cases and problems.

Some areas of contract law are now regulated by legislation. Of particular importance are the Sale of Goods Act 1979 (as amended), the Supply of Goods and Services Act 1982, the Misrepresentation Act 1967, the Unfair Contract Terms Act 1977 and the Unfair Terms in Consumer Contract Regulations 1994.

When writing essays or answering problem questions it is important to cite authorities (cases or statutes) for any proposition of law. That is, the sources of the legal rules that are stated must be cited.

1.8	**A developing source of law**	Contract law is constantly evolving to meet the demands of new situations. Old decisions may be overruled by subsequent cases. Decisions of courts of first instance may be reversed by the Court of Appeal whose decision may in turn be reversed by the House of Lords. It follows that the most recent decisions are of considerable importance. Current law reports can be found in most quality newspapers.

There are some circumstances for which the law may not yet provide, eg in recent years we have witnessed the development and use of new methods of communication during contract formation. We have case law to refer to when contractual communications are made by telephone or telex but as yet we have not decided cases involving the use of electronic mailboxes. When presented with problems relating to such new developments it is only possible to speculate as to what the law might be, but it must be informed speculation – based upon existing guidelines laid down in previous cases relating to other forms of instantaneous communication.

1.9	**Some basic terminology**	Every discipline has its own language and contract law is no exception. It is important to discover the meaning of new legal words and expressions as they are encountered. A failure to do so will seriously affect comprehension and chances of success.

Here are a few frequently used expressions:

Contracts may be described as 'valid', 'void', 'voidable' or 'unenforceable'.

A valid contract has the attributes of a legally binding contract and may be enforced by the courts.

A void contract is one which will not be recognised by the courts – it has no legal effect, eg a contract may be void for illegality.

A voidable contract is one that can be set aside at the option of the wronged party, eg the victims of misrepresentation, duress or undue influence may choose to avoid the contract. On the other and they may choose to go continue with the contract, despite the defect, and sue for damages.

An unenforceable contract arises when the court will not enforce the agreement for some reason provided by the law, eg if a minor buys 'non-necessaries' on credit the court will not enforce the agreement against him – minors are a protected class of person and do not have full contractual capacity.

Chapter 2

The Formation of Contracts

Agreement is one of the essential elements of a binding contract. To ascertain whether or not agreement has been reached, it must be seen whether one party (the offeror) made a firm offer which the other (the offeree) accepted. If counter proposals are put forward by the offeree it is clear that the parties are not yet in agreement. They are still negotiating. If, finally, the parties come to the point where, by the formula of offer and acceptance, they have reached a *consensus ad idem* (meeting of the minds), agreement exists.

2.1   Agreement

In recent years judges have indicated a willingness to depart from this traditional approach, sometimes in the interests of commercial realities. In *Gibson v Manchester City Council* (1978), Lord Diplock observed:

> there may be certain types of contract, though I think they are exceptional, which do not fit easily into the normal analysis of a contract as being constituted by offer and acceptance.

In the same case, Denning MR expressed the view that the circumstances as a whole should be investigated when attempting to discover whether or not an agreement had come into being. Most recently, Lord Steyn in *Trentham Ltd v Archital Luxfer* (1993) placed emphasis on giving effect to the 'reasonable expectations of sensible businessmen'. In this case both parties to a contract had performed their obligations – the defendants had supplied and installed aluminium windows and doors and the plaintiffs had paid for them. When sued for defective performance the defendants claimed that no binding contract had ever come into being. It was nevertheless held that an executed contract came into existence during performance, even if it could not be analysed precisely in terms of offer and acceptance.

An offer may be defined as a willingness expressed by an offeror to enter into a contract on the terms stated with the person to whom it is addressed. An offer can be made to a particular individual, a group of persons or to anyone who cares to accept it. In *Carlill v Carbolic Smoke Ball Co Ltd* (1893) the Court of Appeal held that an advertisement containing an offer of £100 for anyone who used the company's carbolic smoke ball and who caught 'flu constituted a general offer. The defendants were obliged to pay Mrs Carlill £100 because she had accepted their

2.1.1   Offers

offer by using the smokeball and she had complied with the condition attached to the offer by subsequently contracting 'flu.

Offers can result in 'bilateral' or 'unilateral' contracts, depending upon the way in which they are expressed. In *Carlill's* case above, obligations were imposed upon only one party at the outset – the Smoke Ball Company – who were obliged to pay £100 to any person who fulfilled the conditions of their offer. Nobody was obliged to use the smokeballs but if they did so this amounted to acceptance of the offer. Offers to the world at large, such as reward notices, are usually in the form of an offer in a unilateral contract but such offers can be made to individuals.

In the case of bilateral contracts a bargain is struck at the outset. A promises to do something for B if B promises to do something for A in return. This is the most common form of contract and acceptance must be communicated.

An offer must be distinguished from an 'invitation to treat' which is simply an invitation to do business. An offer is definite both in the terms in which it is expressed and also the intention of the offeror to be bound. An invitation to treat, on close inspection, will be seen to lack one or both of these qualities. The courts will apply an objective test to determine the existence of an offer, ie what a 'reasonable person' would consider to be the true intentions of the parties in the circumstances. This can be difficult in some situations as was illustrated in the case of *Gibson v Manchester City Council* (1979).

In this case the courts had to determine whether or not the following words constituted a firm offer which was capable of acceptance: 'The corporation may be prepared to sell the house to you at the purchase price of £2725 ...'. Although Mr Gibson believed that an offer had been made to him the House of Lords held that these words were not sufficiently firm to amount to an offer. They simply indicated a willingness to consider a sale and purchase in due course.

2.1.2   Displays

Goods displayed in a shop window or on shelves in a self-service store, even with a price attached, amount only to an 'invitation to treat'. The display is intended by the shop to stimulate customers' interest. A request to purchase an item is the offer. It is then up to the shop to accept (or reject) that offer.

In *Fisher v Bell* (1961) it was held that a flick-knife, bearing a price tag, in a shop window was not an 'offer for sale' of an offensive weapon.

Similarly, in *Pharmaceutical Society of Great Britain v Boots* (1953) a display of patent medicines on the shelves of a shop constituted an invitation to treat and not an offer to sell.

Advertisements do not generally contain offers. *Carlill* is, therefore, an extraordinary case in which the wording of the advertisement showed an offer expressed in precise terms and an intention to be bound on the part of the offeror.

Advertisements frequently carry claims of a very general and often exaggerated nature, which are mere 'puffs' or 'hype'. As such they clearly lack the characteristics of an offer. Other advertisements may appear definite in the terms in which they are expressed but circumstances show the absence of an intention to be bound by the advertiser. Thus, price lists, catalogues and circulars issued by traders are merely information for prospective customers and regarded as invitations to treat (*Grainger and Sons v Gough* (1896)).

Even advertisements in newspapers and magazines, which appear specific in the terms in which they are expressed, have been held to lack an intention to be bound and have been classed as invitations to treat since the advertiser would not intend to hold himself bound to sell to everyone who responded to the advertisement.

In *Partridge v Crittenden* (1968) an advertisement in a magazine stating 'Bramblefinch cocks and hens 25 shillings each' was held not to constitute the statutory offence of 'offering for sale' a wild bird.

An auctioneer's request for bids is an invitation to treat. Each bid constitutes an offer. The auctioneer signals his acceptance of the highest bid with the fall of the hammer. Until this point any bid may be withdrawn (*Payne v Cave* (1789) and s 57(2) Sale of Goods Act 1979).

An advertisement that an auction will be held at a certain time and place is merely a statement of intention. It is not an offer to hold the auction which someone can accept by turning up at the appointed time and place (*Harris v Nickerson* (1873)).

'Without reserve' indicates that the auctioneer will sell to the highest bidder and there is no minimum price stipulated by the owner which has to be reached before the auctioneer can 'knock down' the item.

The significance of the words 'without reserve' was considered in *Warlow v Harnson* (1859). It was said *obiter* that this would amount to an offer to sell to the highest bidder, which was accepted when a bid was placed.

There are, therefore, two sets of offer and acceptance. The first is the auctioneer's offer to deal on 'without reserve' terms. This the offeree accepts by making a bid. Second, the bid itself constitutes an offer to buy which the auctioneer is free to accept or reject. If the auctioneer failed to accept the highest

2.1.3   Advertisements

2.1.4   Auctions and tenders

bid an action for damages would lie for breach of the first agreement.

This reasoning was impliedly approved by the House of Lords in *Harvela Investments Ltd v Royal Trust of Canada* (1985) in which it was also held that where the offeror has impliedly requested fixed bids, referential bids are inconsistent with fixed bidding. In this case a bid of $2,100,000 or $101,000 in excess of any other offer was held to be invalid.

Where someone places an advertisement asking for the submission of tenders for the supply of specified goods or services the advertiser is free to select one or none of the tenders. The advertisement is an invitation to treat; the tenders are offers (*Spencer v Harding* (1870)). However, according to the decision in *Blackpool and Fylde Aero Club v Blackpool Borough Council* (1990), if the request for tenders is addressed to particular parties there is an implied offer in a unilateral contract that consideration will be given to all tenders complying with the terms of the invitation. In this case the plaintiffs were invited to tender for the concession to provide pleasure flights from the municipal airport. The defendants were held to be in breach of contract for failing to consider a tender from the plaintiffs which had complied with the requirements of the tender and met the deadline.

| 2.1.5 | Sales of land |

With regard to sales of land the court will look closely to see if there is a definite intention to be bound.

In *Harvey v Facey* (1893) the plaintiffs telegraphed the defendants: 'Will you sell us Bumper Hall Pen? Telegraph lowest cash price.' The defendants replied: 'Lowest cash price for Bumper Hall Pen £900.' The plaintiffs responded: 'We agree to buy Bumper Hall Pen for £900 asked by you. Please send us your title deeds.'

The court held that no contract existed. The defendants' reply was not an offer, merely a statement of their intention. The question 'Will you sell us Bumper Hall Pen?' had not been answered.

Similarly, in *Clifton v Palumbo* (1944), the Court of Appeal held that no offer had been made. The context showed the parties to be at the commencement of negotiations and the plaintiff's statement was merely a preliminary indication as to price. See *Gibson* above.

| 2.1.6 | Acceptance |

For an offer to ripen into agreement there must be acceptance; that is some outward sign by which the offeree communicates to the offeror his assent to the exact terms proposed. Whether this has occurred in any particular case is primarily a question of fact, although there are rules, such as those relating to acceptance sent by post (see 2.1.10 below), which govern the situation.

Acceptance must be unconditional; the precise terms offered must be accepted.

If the offeree 'agrees' but adds a new term or amends a proposal, no contractual agreement has been reached. The parties are still negotiating. The new or amended term is a counter-offer; the original offeror has now become the offeree.

A counter-offer destroys the original offer. In *Hyde v Wrench* (1844) the defendant offered to sell land to the plaintiff for £1,000. The plaintiff made a counter-offer to buy for £950, which the defendant rejected. The plaintiff later purported to accept the original offer to sell to him for £1,000. Held, this no longer existed, having been destroyed by his counter-offer to buy for £950.

On the other hand, a mere request for information will not destroy the original offer (*Stevenson v McLean* (1880)).

Sometimes an offeree 'accepts' but indicates that he does not intend to be bound until some condition is fulfilled. At this stage no agreement has been reached; neither party is subject to any obligations.

It is common to find this occurring in connection with the sale of land. Such a contract must be in writing and signed by the parties (see 2.4.2 below).

It is common practice to agree sales 'subject to contract'. The parties expressly declare they have no intention of being bound until they sign a formal document. Each is able to withdraw until such time as the formalities have been completed (*Winn v Bull* (1877)).

However, if the facts show the parties did manifest a clear intention to be bound, and the formalities required have been satisfied the court will hold that a contract exists (*Branca v Cobarro* (1947)).

Sometimes the counter-offer rule leads to difficulties where the parties are not particularly concerned about details and are anxious for business to commence. In *Brogden v Metropolitan Ry Co* (1877) the appellants had been supplying the respondents with coal for some time when they decided to regularise the arrangement. The respondents' draft contract had minor amendments made to it by the appellants and returned. The document, now technically containing the appellants counter-offer was filed by the respondents' manager. No acceptance of the new terms was made. The parties implemented the arrangement but later a dispute arose between them. It was held that when the respondents ordered and took delivery of coal their conduct amounted to acceptance of the appellants' counter-offer.

| 2.1.8 | Acceptance by conduct | The idea of acceptance by conduct has been applied to 'battle of the forms' situations. That is, where commercial buyers and sellers of goods and services, each having standard written terms on which they intend to do business, purport to 'accept' the other's offer but on their own terms. The battle is likely to be won by the last party to send their terms, the other party then acting upon them and so accepting them (*Butler Machine Tool Co Ltd v Ex-cell-O Corp* (1979)). |

This is not the only possible outcome. The court may decide that negotiations were in progress but that no firm offer was ever made. Payment for performance in such circumstances could only be claimed on the basis of *quantum meruit* (see Chapter 6, 6.2 below). Alternatively, it may be decided, as in *Pagnan SA v Feed Products Ltd* (1987), that a contract has come into existence where the parties have agreed on the essential terms, even though agreement on others remains outstanding.

| 2.1.9 | Acceptance of tenders | The 'acceptance' of a tender does not always result in a binding agreement. If the tender is an offer to supply a definite quantity of goods or services at a particular time or times, its acceptance does indeed constitute acceptance in the legal sense. The tender may, however, contain an offer to supply 'from time to time' or 'as and when required'. An offer to supply in this way is construed as a standing offer. Its 'acceptance' has no legal significance. |

However, each request by the offeree to be supplied with a specified amount of the goods or services is an acceptance of the standing offer confined to that quantity. The result will be a separate contract each time the offeree places an order. The standing offer may be revoked at any time, although orders made must be honoured (*Great Northern Ry Co v Witham* (1873)).

| 2.1.10 | Communication of acceptance | There must be some outward sign by the offeree that he has accepted. Normally, the offeree's decision must also be communicated to the offeror. Mere silence cannot amount to acceptance. |

In *Felthouse v Bindley* (1862) the plaintiff wrote to his nephew offering to buy a particular horse for £3–15s saying: 'If I hear no more I consider the horse mine at the price'. The nephew did not reply but told the defendant, an auctioneer who was selling his stock, to remove that horse from the sale.

The defendant mistakenly sold the horse and the plaintiff sued him for conversion. Held, the plaintiff's claim failed as there was no contract between him and his nephew. He had not become owner of the horse.

In the case of a unilateral contract an offeror may waive communication of acceptance, although he cannot dispense with the necessity of specifying some act on the part of the offeree by which acceptance is to be inferred (see *Carlill*).

Thus, he runs the risk of incurring an obligation without knowing it. However, he may not impose an obligation on an inactive offeree.

A further exception to the rule that acceptance must be communicated concerns acceptance sent by post.

In *Adams v Lindsell* (1818), it was held that acceptance is deemed to have been communicated the moment the letter is *properly* posted, even though it is delayed or even lost in the post. In *Household Fire Insurance v Grant* (1879) the defendant applied for shares in a company. It was held that the letter of allotment posted to Mr Grant amounted to an acceptance although the letter never reached him.

It would seem to follow that an offeree, having posted his letter of acceptance, is unable to revoke the acceptance by some quicker method of communication which arrives first. There is no direct English authority on this matter, but a Scottish case, *Dunmore v Alexander* (1830) gave effect to the revocation of an acceptance by these means.

The postal rules relating to acceptance do not apply:

- where the letter of acceptance was not properly posted (*Re London and Northern Bank* (1990));

- (probably) where the letter was not addressed correctly (*Getreider-Import GmbH v Contimar* (1953));

- where the offeror expressly or impliedly excludes the application of the postal rule; eg in *Holwell Securities v Hughes* (1974) the offeror's statement that an option was 'exercisable by notice in writing' was interpreted by the courts to mean that actual notice had to be received rather than simply posted.

- in the case of instantaneous/electronic communications such as telephone, telex, fax, and the use of answering machines and electronic mailboxes. It is important to note that there are no hard and fast rules for these cases. Each must be judged according to the circumstances.

In *Entores v Miles Far East Corporation* (1955), when considering the transmission of acceptance by telex, Lord Denning stated that: 'the contract is only complete when the acceptance is received by the offeror: and the contract is made at the place where the acceptance is received.' In this case a contract was held to have been formed in England when an English company received an acceptance by telex from a Dutch company. It would follow that acceptance occurs when it is received, rather than at the point of transmission but there is still scope for contention regarding the point at which the acceptance is effectively communicated.

Denning LJ observed that an acceptance made by direct telephone conversation is effectively communicated when the offeror hears the offeree's acceptance.

The answer to the question of time of communication is not so clear when other forms of electronic communication are used as it is necessary to establish whether the communication was 'received' on arrival, when the other party had actual notice of it or the time by which they should have had notice of it. In the words of Lord Wilberforce in *Brinkibon Ltd v Stahag Stahl GmbH* (1983): 'No universal rule can cover all such cases: they must be resolved by reference to the intentions of the parties, by sound business practice and in some cases by a judgment where the risks should lie ... .'

In *Tenax Steamship Co. Ltd v The Brimnes (Owners)* (1975) a telex withdrawal had appeared on the charter's machine within office hours on one day but it was not noted until the following day. It was held that communication in this case was effectively received on arrival because the message appeared within office hours, so the senders could reasonably have expected it to be read on the same day.

It would seem then, that when dealing with the question of when a communication is effectively communicated it is necessary to consider all relevant factors including the nature of the communication, the method of transmission and the time of arrival in relation to the reasonable expectations of the sender.

If an offer prescribes the manner in which acceptance is to be made a different mode will not do (*Eliason v Henshaw* (1819)).

In other cases the general rule is that if some expeditious means of communication is mentioned by the offeror some other, but equally speedy means, will suffice (*Tinn v Hoffman* (1873) and *Yates Building Co Ltd v Pulleyn Ltd* (1975)).

The prescribed method may be waived by the offeror (*Manchester Diocesan Council for Education v Commercial and General Investments Ltd* (1969)).

Except where the circumstances above apply, any reasonably appropriate means may be used provided the acceptance reaches its destination (*Entores Ltd v Miles Far East Corpn* (1955)).

Can a contract result from a situation where the acceptor is unaware an offer has been made? It seems that it cannot. In the Australian case of *R v Clarke* (1927), where a reward was offered in return for information, it was held that the information giver, who had forgotten about the offer of a reward, was not entitled to it. He was in no better position than if he had never heard of it. However, in *Williams v Carwardine* (1833) it was held that so long as the giver of the information had the reward in mind at the time, her motive in coming forward was irrelevant.

2.1.11   Knowledge of offer

A related problem concerns cross-offers. In *Tinn v Hoffinan* (1873) it was said obiter that if each side makes an identical offer to the other and, for example, they cross in the post, there is no contract until one party responds by acceptance of the other's offer, although it is clear the parties are of one mind.

An offer, by being accepted, ends when it ripens into a legally binding agreement.

2.1.12   Termination of offer

Offers which are not accepted do not continue indefinitely. They may terminate in the following ways:

- Rejection

- Counter-offer (see 2.2 below)

- Revocation

  Revoking (withdrawing) an offer is possible at any time until acceptance. Even where an offeror promises to keep his offer open for a specified length of time he is under no obligation unless his promise has been 'bought' by consideration from the offeree (see 2.2 below).

  Revocation is ineffective unless communicated to the offeree. This holds good even where the revocation is sent by post (*Byrne v Van Tienhoven* (1880)).

  It was held in *Dickinson v Dodds* (1876) that revocation may be communicated by someone other than the offeror himself. However, the offeree is not expected to take notice of every piece of idle gossip. Each case must turn on its own facts. The question to be addressed is: did the information come from such a source that a reasonable man would rely upon its accuracy?

The American case of *Shuey v US* (1875) decided that an offer contained in an advertisement could be revoked by another advertisement, even though some offerees had not seen the second one. (Of course, American decisions can never have more than persuasive authority in the English courts.)

A difficult question arises in the case of a unilateral contract where the offeree's act denotes acceptance. Is the offer revocable at any moment until the act is complete? In strict theory the answer would seem to be, 'yes'. This result would be very hard on an offeree who had nearly completed the act in question.

Various suggestions have been made by lawyers for overcoming the difficulty. Rather than engaging in theoretical niceties, the courts have looked at the presumed intention of the parties (*Luxor (Eastbourne) Ltd v Cooper* (1941)). The House of Lords held an offer to an estate agent was revocable.

In *Errington v Errington* (1952) the Court of Appeal held that an offer by a father to convey a house to his son, provided the son paid the mortgage instalments, was irrevocable while the payments continued.

- Lapse

  An offer expressed to be open for a specified period will end when the period expires, otherwise an offer will lapse after a reasonable time.

  What is reasonable must depend on the facts (*Ramsgate Victoria Hotel v Montefiore* (1866)).

  An offer will also lapse if made subject to a condition which is not fulfilled (*Financings Ltd v Stimson* (1962)).

- Death

  If the offeror dies, the offeree may accept provided that:

  (a) he is unaware of the death; and

  (b) the contract is not one dependant on the personal qualities of the offeror (*Bradbury v Morgan* (1862)).

  On the death of the offeree the offer terminates and cannot be accepted by his personal representatives.

2.1.13   Constructing a contract

Despite the hallowed language of offer and acceptance the courts have occasionally been forced to acknowledge the existence of a contract, although the facts have proved difficult, if not impossible, to fit into the traditional formula.

Sometimes a contract has been inferred from conduct (*Clarke v Dunraven* (1897)).

At other times the courts have constructed a 'collateral' contract (*Stanklin Pier Ltd v Detel Products Ltd* (1951)). Here the pier company (plaintiff) contracted with X for X to repaint the pier using paint specified by the company. The defendant manufacturer persuaded them to nominate the defendant's paint, assuring them of its suitability, which the plaintiff did. The paint was purchased from the defendant by X and applied. It turned out to be a costly mistake and the plaintiff spent £4,000 putting things right. It was held that a contract existed between plaintiff and defendant despite the fact that the sale of the paint took place between the defendant and X. The defendant was treated as having offered to guarantee the suitability of their paint for the job if the plaintiff would stipulate its use in the contract with X. The plaintiff had accepted this offer.

The device of the collateral contract has been used elsewhere, for example *Andrews v Hopkinson* (1956) and *Carlill v Carbolic Smoke Ball Co* (1893).

2.2 Consideration

Most legal systems refuse to enforce promises unless there is something to indicate that the promisor intended to be bound.

2.2.1 Function and definition

It is a fundamental assumption of English law that a contract is more than a mere agreement; it is a bargain. If a person wishes to enforce the promise of another he must show that he himself has given or has promised to give something of value in return. English law does not recognise as binding a gratuitous or 'bare' promise. The value, given or promised, is called consideration.

An exception to this fundamental rule occurs in the case of a 'speciality' contract, that is one contained in a deed. This exception, historically much older than the consideration rule itself, allows a bare promise contained in a deed to be legally enforceable despite the absence of consideration.

A 19th century definition of consideration often referred to comes from the judgment of Lush J in *Currie v Misa* (1875):

> '... some right, interest, profit or benefit accruing to one party, or some forbearance, detriment, loss or responsibility given, suffered or undertaken by the other.'

A better definition is probably that of Pollock, approved by Lord Dunedin in *Dunlop v Selfridge Ltd* (1915) which uses the language of sale:

'An act or forbearance of one party, or the promise thereof, is the price for which the promise of the other is bought, and the promise thus given for value is enforceable.'

2.2.2	**Rules relating to consideration**	The rules, evolved by the judges, are useful analytical tools which, when applied, help to determine whether or not bargains exist. Each is concerned with a particular aspect of the doctrine of consideration.

This rule is used to ascertain whether promises made or acts done by the parties are linked to form a bargain.

2.2.3	**Consideration may be executory or executed but must not be past**	Consideration is 'executory' where the parties exchange promises to perform acts in the future. Nothing has yet been done to implement the mutual promises but the parties are legally bound. The deal is made.

'Executed' consideration occurs where one party performs an act in return for the other's promise. For example, in the case of a unilateral contract where a reward is promised (offered) the act of giving the information is both acceptance and the supply of the acceptor's part of the bargain.

If a party makes a further promise, even though motivated by gratitude for the original contract or an earlier act, the additional promise is said to have been made for a 'past' consideration. Strictly speaking, it has not been made for a consideration at all as in the eyes of the law past consideration is no consideration. The subsequent promise and the previous contract or act are not part of a bargain and are thus unrelated.

In *Roscorla v Thomas* (1842) the defendant's promise to the plaintiff that the horse which the plaintiff had already bought was sound and free from vice was unenforceable. The promise was given for a past consideration. Similarly, in *Re McArdle* (1951) brothers and sisters, who inherited a house, promised to reimburse their sister-in-law for having carried out improvements to the house. The Court of Appeal held the promise to be unenforceable.

The position is different if the person performing the act does so at the request of the other and the context shows that both expect payment to be made. For example, in *Lampleigh v Brathwaite* (1615) the subsequent promise to pay a specified amount by the defendant was held to be linked to the initial request and to be part of the same transaction.

It is important to note that the initial request by defendant to plaintiff is not of itself sufficient to link it to the later promise. The circumstances must show that the request for and performance of the act by the plaintiff were done not by way of friendship but business: *Re Casey's Patents, Stewart v Casey* (1892), confirmed by the Privy Council in *Pao On v Lau Yin Long* (1980) where Lord Scarman said:

> 'An act done before the giving of a promise to make a payment or to confer some other benefit can sometimes be consideration for the promise. The act must have been done at the promisor's request, the parties must have understood that the act was to be remunerated further by a payment or the conferment of some other benefit.'

A statutory exception to the rule on past consideration is contained in s 27 Bills of Exchange Act 1882. Any antecedent debt or liability is regarded as valuable consideration sufficient to support the promise to pay contained in the bill.

A promisee is the person to whom a promise is made; someone who wants to take the benefit of another's promise.

2.2.4   Consideration must move from the promisee

The rule emphasises the fundamental concept of a *quid pro quo*, that both parties must contribute to the contract. A person who wishes to enforce another's promise must show that he himself has 'bought' that promise. Someone who is not a party to the bargain cannot sue on it (*Price v Easton* (1833) and *Tweddle v Atkinson* (1861)). The rule is linked to the concept of privity of contract (see Chapter 4).

The courts will not enquire into the adequacy of consideration. A bargain will not be upset because the act or promise supplied by the plaintiff is, in market terms, an inadequate recompense for the defendant's promise. The parties are supposed to be capable of appreciating the value of their own interests. The law will not stop someone entering into, what is for them, a poor bargain in the absence of fraud, misrepresentation or some other invalidating factor.

2.2.5   Consideration need not be adequate

Consideration may be merely symbolic: as in *Thomas v Thomas* (1842) where a promise to pay £1 per annum to occupy a house was held to create a valid contract and in *Chappell & Co Ltd v Nestlé Co Ltd* (1960) where the House of Lords regarded empty chocolate wrappers as part of the consideration payable by members of the public in a 'special offer' promotion.

What is the position where the parties agree to settle out of court a claim which one is bringing against the other?

Originally, it was held that a promise not to pursue a claim which was without legal foundation was not valuable consideration. However, this proved to be impracticable as the case would first have to be tried to see if there was, or was not, a good cause of action.

The consideration is better expressed as being the abandonment, not of a legal right, but of a claim to a legal right. However, safeguards exist. Someone relying on the surrender of a claim to support an agreement to settle must show an honest belief in the claim, and that it is not merely vexatious or frivolous (*Horton v Horton* (1961)).

The position is probably the same where, although there is no actual promise to abandon a claim (a forbearance to sue) such a promise may be inferred from the circumstances (*Alliance Bank Ltd v Broom* (1864)).

Sometimes it is difficult to see where the courts will draw the line between the symbolic and the non-existent.

A 'peppercorn' rent for a lease is regarded as valuable consideration, whereas in *White v Bluett* (1853) a son's promise to stop boring his father with complaints, if the father would pay off the son's debts, was not valuable consideration, as it was too vague.

| 2.2.6 | Consideration must be sufficient or real |

Where the law recognises consideration as of some value it is said to be 'real' or 'sufficient'. However small, there must be some element in the plaintiff's promise or act which can be regarded as the price of the defendant's promise. Thus, to promise to carry out an existing obligation may be to promise nothing at all. This dilemma has proved a fruitful area for litigation in the following situations.

If a person, through operation of the law or because of his status, for example, he is a policeman, is duty bound to act in a particular way, he does not supply consideration by promising to carry out that duty. The plaintiff in *Collins v Godefroy* (1831) failed in his claim to be paid for fulfilling his promise to the defendant to attend court and give evidence. The plaintiff had already been served with a court order to attend (a subpoena) and had, therefore, done no more than he was, at law, already bound to do.

| 2.2.7 | Existing public duty |

On the whole, the courts have been fairly willing to find that a plaintiff has exceeded his public duty and in doing so has supplied consideration. A policeman in *England v Davidson* (1840), in response to the defendant's offer of reward, gave information leading to the conviction of a criminal. He was held to have rendered a service which, on the facts, was beyond the scope of his official duties, thus furnishing consideration.

Police, who provided protection for a colliery from striking workers to an extent which professionally they thought unnecessary, supplied consideration and were entitled to payment for the extra protection (*Glassbrook Bros v Glamorgan County Council* (1925)).

In *Harris v Sheffield United Football Club Ltd* (1988) it was argued unsuccessfully by the club that the police had a public duty to turn out in force for Saturday afternoon home matches as it was well known that crowd trouble was likely. The Court of Appeal held that the club itself had chosen to schedule most of its matches at this time when it was aware that the police presence required could be achieved only by substantial overtime payments. The police authority was entitled to be paid.

A further example of the courts' willingness to uphold an agreement and find consideration present whenever possible is *Ward v Byham* (1956). Here the father of an illegitimate child agreed to pay the mother £1 per week maintenance if she could show that the child was 'happy' and 'well looked after'. The mother was already bound by statute to 'maintain the child'. However, the Court of Appeal held the mother was furnishing consideration in promising to do more than merely maintain the child. (Compare this to the result in *White v Bluett* above and note Lord Denning's view in *Ward* that a promise to perform an existing duty is of benefit to the recipient and should therefore be regarded as valuable consideration.)

No consideration is furnished at all if the plaintiff merely promises to perform what he is already under an obligation to perform for the defendant because of an existing contract between them. Thus, in working a ship home short-handed after two sailors deserted, the remaining crew were doing no more than coping with the problems normally expected on a voyage. They had not furnished consideration to support the promise to pay them extra wages (*Stilk v Myrick* (1809)).

However, where shortages in crew rendered the ship unsafe the others were successful in their claim to additional pay (*Hartley v Ponsonby* (1857)).

Argument as to the presence or absence of consideration in such cases may be clouded by claims of 'economic duress' having been brought to bear on the defendants. That is, in order to extract the promise of extra payment from the defendant, the plaintiff exploited the financial pressures under which he knew the defendant was operating (*North Ocean Shipping Co Ltd v Hyundai Construction Co Ltd* (1978) (and see Chapter 4, 4.3 below)).

The problem was recognised and discussed in *Williams v Roffey Bros & Nicholls (Contractors) Ltd* (1990). Due to bad management and under-pricing, Williams, a sub-contracted

2.2.8   Existing contractual duty

carpenter, ran into financial difficulties while carrying out work under a fixed price contract for Roffey, the main contractor on a building contract. In the interests of avoiding the problems of engaging another carpenter, getting the work completed on time and thereby avoiding the consequences of a penalty clause in his own contract with the owner, Roffey agreed to pay Williams a sum in excess of the original contract price. He later contended that the 'extra' payment was not due for want of consideration. Williams had done no more than he was originally contracted to do.

The Court of Appeal held that Roffey was liable to make the 'extra' payment. The decision was explained in these terms by Glidewell LJ:

> 'Where B (a party to an existing contract) agrees to make an additional payment to A in order to ensure that obligations under the original contract with A are fulfilled, the new agreement will be binding, if by making it B gains in practice some benefit or obviates a disbenefit, providing that B's promise is not given as a result of economic duress or fraud on the part of A. The benefit to B is capable of being consideration for B's promise.'

The decision in *Williams v Roffey* does not overrule *Stylk v Myrick* (1809), it is merely modified in order to accommodate commercial realities. It was clearly in Roffey's interest to promise extra payment to Williams at the time that he made it. This way he avoided the trouble of finding a new carpenter and he was in a position to complete the main contract on time, thereby avoiding penalties for late completion. Since this decision the courts have limited its application. According to the decision in *Re Selectmove* (1994) a promise by a creditor to accept part payment of a debt in satisfaction of the whole amount was not binding despite the fact that the creditor may have gained a practical advantage from the arrangement. To decide otherwise would disturb other well-settled legal principles which were not even discussed in *Williams v Roffey*.

2.2.9 Existing contractual duty to third party

It was held by a group of cases in the 19th century that the law regards the performance of an existing contractual obligation to a third party as sufficient to support a new contract with the defendant (*Scotson v Pegg* (1861)) and of more doubtful authority (*Shadwell v Shadwell* (1860) and *Chichester v Cobb* (1866)).

The principle was affirmed by the Privy Council in *New Zealand Shipping Co v Satterthwaite & Co* (1974) where the plaintiff promised the defendant that if the defendant unloaded the plaintiff's goods from a ship (which the defendant was already contractually obliged to do for a third party) the plaintiff would not hold the defendant liable for any damage to the goods. The defendant's performance of the task of unloading was held to constitute consideration.

The doctrine of consideration gives rise to particular problems when applied to the situation where a debt is settled for an amount less than its full value. Such compromise agreements are not uncommon in business life yet, if challenged, the debtor can scarcely argue that his part payment of the debt is valuable consideration. To be binding a compromise agreement must, like any other contract, be supported by consideration. In return for the creditor's promise to forego his right to payment in full, the debtor's act of paying a lesser sum than that due cannot be regarded as consideration. There is, therefore, nothing at common law to stop the creditor going back on his promise and suing for the full amount.

2.2.10   Settlement of debts by part payment

The rule dates from *Pinnel's Case* (1602) where Pinnel sued Cole in debt for £8-10s due in November. Cole's defence was that he had paid £5-2s-6d in October at Pinnel's request, and this had been accepted by Pinnel in settlement of the full amount. Technical mistakes in the pleading of the defence resulted in Cole losing the case. Had it not been for these mistakes his defence would have succeeded on its merits.

The court laid down two branches to the rule, usually referred to as the *'dicta'* or the 'rule in Pinnel's case':

(a) payment of a lesser sum on the day in satisfaction of a greater cannot be any satisfaction for the whole; but

(b) the payment of the lesser sum, with the creditor's agreement, at an earlier time, different place, or the substitution of an article, is satisfaction, because it might be more beneficial to the creditor, otherwise he would not have accepted it.

Exchange the word 'consideration' for 'satisfaction' and the rule is brought up-to-date.

The court does not in (b) concern itself to see that the debtor's performance is of equal value to the full debt because of the rule: 'consideration need not be adequate'. It is left to the creditor to decide whether he would prefer payment of the debt in full or the debtor's substitute performance. What the courts are concerned with is whether the debtor has undertaken some new mode of performance, something he was not obliged to do under the original contract, and which can be regarded as real (sufficient) consideration.

Prior to *D & C Builders Ltd v Rees* (1965) there was authority for the view that part payment by a negotiable instrument was a new method of performance within (b) above. In that case the Court of Appeal stated that no distinction could be drawn between payment of a lesser sum by cheque and payment of it in cash.

The 'rule in *Pinnel's case*', inconvenient though it may be, was affirmed by the House of Lords in *Foakes v Beer* (1884) and is a settled part of contract law.

Apart from the defence of equitable or promissory estoppel (see 2.2.11 below) the following exceptions to the rule exist at common law.

(a) The terms of the settlement are contained in a deed. Because a deed is enforceable due to its form, the lack of consideration poses no problem to the debtor's release.

(b) The settlement is part of a 'composition arrangement'. This is where a group of creditors agree collectively to accept, say, 30p for each £1 owed to them by an insolvent debtor. The agreement is binding on all the parties. To permit one creditor to break the agreement and sue the debtor for the full amount would be a 'fraud' on the other creditors who had held back (*Wood v Robarts* (1818)).

(c) The debt is settled by a third party making part payment. Borrowing the reasoning used in (b) the courts have held that to allow the creditor to succeed in an action against the debtor would be a 'fraud' on the third party (*Welby v Drake* (1825)), where the creditor unsuccessfully sued the debtor for the total debt, and *Hirachand Punamchand v Temple* (1911), where the Court of Appeal refused the plaintiff's claim to be entitled to the balance of the debt.

2.2.11   Promissory estoppel

A partial exception to the doctrine of consideration is found in the equitable doctrine known as 'promissory estoppel'. Under the doctrine a promise may become binding in certain circumstances even though consideration has not been furnished by the promisee.

The doctrine stems from dicta in the judgment of Denning J in *Central London Property Trust Ltd v High Trees House Ltd* (1947), who in turn drew on the decision of the House of Lords in *Hughes v Metropolitan Railway* (1877). In the *High Trees case*, the landlord of a block of flats promised in 1940 to accept from the tenant half the rent stipulated in the lease, while wartime conditions lasted. In June 1945 the landlord claimed the full rent was payable for the future and was held to be entitled to it. The circumstances giving rise to the 1940 arrangement had ceased. However, it was said *obiter* that if the landlord company had sued for the arrears from 1940 it would, in equity, have been estopped.

The common law rule of estoppel, in *Jorden v Money* (1854), arises only in respect of a representation of an existing fact. 'In equity, a similar doctrine operates', said Denning J, 'where there is a promise of future conduct'.

The essential conditions necessary for the doctrine to operate

(a) one party (the promisor) makes a promise not to enforce his legal rights, intending the other (the promisee) to rely on it; and

(b) the promisee does rely, by acting to his detriment (*Emmanuel Ayodeji Ajayi v R T Briscoe (Nigeria) Ltd* (1964)), or altering his position in reliance on the promise (*W J Alan & Co Ltd v El Nasr Export and Import Co* (1972)); and

(c) in all the circumstances of the case it is inequitable (unfair) to allow the promisor to disregard his promise and enforce his legal rights (see *D and C Builders Ltd v Rees* (1965)).

It is important to note that the doctrine cannot be used to create a cause of action where none exists due to the absence of consideration. It may be used only as a defence, '... as a shield, not as a sword' (*Combe v Combe* (1951)).

There is still debate as to whether the doctrine is effective to extinguish liability permanently (Denning's view), or whether it merely suspends the promisor's legal rights, which may be resumed by him giving reasonable notice to the promisee (*Tool Metal Manufacturing v Tungsten Electric Co Ltd* (1955)).

As well as agreement being reached and consideration being present, the parties must intend to create a legally binding relationship.

2.3 The intention to be legally bound

The test of whether a contractual relationship has been entered into is objective, not subjective. What inference would a reasonable person draw from their conduct or words?

However, if the parties expressly declare their intention of not entering into a legally binding relationship the courts will accept this.

Cases in which, it is alleged, the intention to be bound is lacking fall into two broad categories. First, there is the category of the family or domestic arrangement where the law presumes there is no intention to contract. The inference may be reversed in circumstances which show evidence to the contrary, ie that the language of the parties and other contextual factors show there is an intention to be bound. Second, there are commercial agreements where the intention to contract is presumed but the presumption may be reversed by evidence to the contrary.

| 2.3.1 | Family and domestic agreements |

Agreements between husband and wife are not normally intended to create a contractual relationship (*Balfour v Balfour* (1919)).

On the other hand, the fact that they are husband and wife does not mean they cannot contract, but a clear indication of this is required (*Merritt v Merritt* (1970)), where the parties had separated and were bargaining about the future. Other relationships such as that of parent and child give rise to similar considerations (*Jones v Padavatton* (1969)), as do other domestic or social arrangements. For example in *Simpkins v Pays* (1955) an arrangement by three members of a household involving joint participation in a competition was held to show an intention that the arrangement should be contractually binding.

| 2.3.2 | Commercial agreements |

There is nothing to say that members of a family cannot make a commercial agreement merely because they are related (*Snelling v John G Snelling Ltd* (1972)).

Where an agreement falls into this category, the law presumes that the parties do intend to make a contract but will hold the presumption to be reversed (rebutted) if there is clear evidence to the contrary. Thus, in *Jones v Vernon's Pools* (1938) and *Rose and Frank Ltd v Crompton* (1925), 'honour clauses', by which the parties expressly denied any intention of contracting, indicating their agreements were binding in honour only, were held to be effective in rebutting the presumption.

In *Edwards v Skyways* (1964), a redundancy agreement involving an 'ex gratia' payment, the presumption was not rebutted. A contract had been made.

Two exceptions to the general rule require mention:

• Advertisements

  Advertisers commonly make exaggerated and often entertaining claims for their products. This is generally well known so that any argument that the claims form part of a contract is easily overturned by the advertiser. Such statements are merely 'puffing' and frequently so vague that in any event they could not be regarded as sufficiently definite to constitute offers capable of acceptance (see 2.1.3 above).

Thus, contrary to the general presumption in the case of commercial agreements, advertisements will not normally be considered as showing an intention to contract. In exceptional circumstances they may (*Carlill v Carbolic Smoke Ball Co* (1893)), where the plaintiff's case was helped by the fact that the defendant company stated in the advertisement that it had deposited £1,000 with its bank to show its sincerity.

• Industrial collective agreements

In industry, agreements may be made between an employer and a trade union covering the pay and conditions of employees. If such terms are incorporated into the employment contracts of individual employees they will, following the general rule, be presumed to be part of a binding contract (*National Coal Board v Galley* (1958)).

However, the question may arise as to whether the original collective agreement itself is binding. The position at common law is that it is not (*Ford Motor Co Ltd v AUEFW* (1969)). The situation is now governed by s 179 Trade Union and Labour Relations (Consolidation) Act 1992 under which a collective agreement is presumed not to be legally binding in the absence of an express, written declaration that it is.

The general rule is that a contract can be made in any form: word of mouth, writing, deed, or any combination of these.	**2.4 Formalities**

The widespread assumption among non-lawyers that a contract is valid only if in writing and bearing the signature of the parties is false and has never been the case in English law.

However, it is sensible and practical to record the terms of an agreement in writing if it involves substantial value or if its effects will last over a period of time. Human memory is notoriously fallible and the rules of evidence generally prefer written to oral evidence. There are, though, some exceptions to the general rule on formalities, each of which has been created by statute.

A deed is required in order to create a lease of land for three years or more (ss 52 and 54(2) Law of Property Act 1925). (An agreement that such a lease will be granted (created) need only be evidenced in writing, see below.)	2.4.1 Deeds

• A bill of exchange must be in writing (s 33 Bills of Exchange Act 1882).	2.4.2 Contracts in writing

- Under s 61 Consumer Credit Act 1974 a consumer credit agreement regulated by the Act must be in writing, in the form prescribed by the Secretary of State and signed by the consumer. If it is not it can be enforced against him only by order of the court (s 65).

- Contracts for the sale of land or any interest in land have, since 27 September 1989, been governed by the Law of Property (Miscellaneous Provisions) Act 1989. By s 2 the contract must be in writing, contain all the terms agreed, and be signed by both parties, or their agents. The terms may be:

  (a) in one document;

  (b) in each of two documents, if contracts are exchanged;

  (c) incorporated in a document by reference to some other document(s).

  If the contract is contained in two documents the signature of each party, or his agent, must appear but not necessarily on the same copy.

Excluded from s 2 are:

- agreements for a lease of three years or less. (Being governed by s 40 Law of Property Act 1925 they are required merely to be evidenced in writing);

- contracts made at a public auction;

- contracts regulated by the Financial Services Act 1986.

2.4.3	Contracts evidenced in writing

Contracts for the sale of land made before 27 September are governed by s 40 Law of Property Act 1925. This requires that written evidence of the material terms of the agreement, signed by the defendant or his agent, to be produced. Otherwise the agreement cannot be enforced. Section 40 still applies to an agreement to create a lease for less than three years.

The equitable doctrine of 'part performance' has sometimes alleviated unfairness caused by the technical requirements of s 40.

Where the doctrine is held to apply the court orders specific performance of the contract by the defendant.

It cannot apply to contracts made under s 2 Law of Property (Miscellaneous Provisions) Act 1989, which does not recognise the existence of the contract until the formalities are complied with.

By s 4 Statute of Frauds 1677 a 'promise to answer for the debt, default or miscarriage of another person' must be evidenced in writing and signed by the defendant or his authorised agent, if it is to be enforceable. These words have been interpreted as covering the promise of one party guaranteeing another's liability, the words 'debt' and 'default' referring to contractual liability, and 'miscarriage' to tortious liability (*Kirkham v Marter* (1819)).

For the statute to apply both of the following points must be satisfied:

- There must be three parties involved. Thus, in the case of a debt there must be a debtor, a creditor and a guarantor. The promise must be given to the creditor, not the debtor (*Eastwood v Kenyon* (1840)).

- The guarantor must have a secondary liability only. The essence of a guarantee is that the guarantor will discharge the liability only if the principal debtor fails to do so.

Thus, if the so-called 'guarantee' is a complete indemnity (*Goodman v Chase* (1818)), or there is no principal debtor (*Mountstephen v Lakeman* (1874)), the statute does not apply, and so written evidence is not required.

The Act does not apply where:

(a) the guarantee forms part of a larger transaction (*Sutton v Grey* (1894)); or

(b) the guarantee is given in order to secure the release of the guarantor's property from a liability due to a third party (*Fitzgerald v Dressler* (1859)).

This exception does not apply, that is the promise will be caught by the statutory requirement for written evidence, where the guarantor has only a personal, not a proprietary interest (*Harburg India Rubber Comb Co v Martin* (1902)), where a promise by a shareholder to guarantee the company's debt was held to fail within the provisions of s 4.

A person entering into a contract must have the legal capacity to do so if he is to be bound by it. All adults have contractual capacity but three special situations arise. These concern minors, corporations, and persons of unsound mind.

The age of majority was reduced from 21 years to 18 years by s 1 Family Law Reform Act 1969. Prior to this, a person under 21 years was known as an 'infant'. A person under 18 years is known as a 'minor'. Minors' contracts can be divided into three categories: valid contracts, voidable contracts, other contracts.

- Valid contracts

    A minor has capacity to make a binding contract for 'necessaries' (goods or services). These 'necessaries' are

2.5   Capacity

2.5.1   Minors

things which are 'suitable to the minor's station in life' and with which he is not already adequately supplied (*Nash v Inman* (1908)).

His liability extends only to paying a reasonable price (not necessarily the contract price), for goods delivered (s 3(2) Sale of Goods Act 1979).

The minor is likewise liable for a reasonable price for the supply of services, but in this case the contract is binding even though the consideration is only executory (*Roberts v Gray* (1913)).

A contract which would otherwise be enforceable against a minor as one for 'necessaries' will not be if it contains terms which are harsh or onerous on him (*Fawcett v Smethurst* (1914)).

A minor is also bound by a contract of employment, apprenticeship or an analogous contract which has in it some element of training or promotion of the minor in his chosen career (*Chaplin v Leslie Frewin (Publishers) Ltd* (1966)). However, the contract, looked at as a whole, must be substantially for the minor's benefit (*De Francesco v Barnum* (1890)).

A trading contract, however beneficial, will never be binding on a minor (*Cowern v Nield* (1912)).

- Voidable contracts

  Minors have the capacity to make certain contracts of a long-term or permanent nature. These are contracts relating to:

  (a) the purchase/sale/lease of land;

  (b) the purchase of shares;

  (c) marriage settlements;

  (d) partnership agreements.

  They are binding on the minor unless he expressly repudiates during his minority or within a reasonable time of attaining his majority.

  On repudiation, he cannot recover money paid unless there has been a total failure of consideration (*Steinberg v Scala (Leeds) Ltd* (1923)).

- Other contracts

  The situation here is governed by s 1 Minors Contracts Act 1987, which restored the position at common law and repealed the Infants Relief Act 1874.

  Other contracts, such as those for non-necessary goods, loans, and so on, are not binding on a minor unless he expressly ratifies them within a reasonable time of attaining the age of 18.

However, it should be noted that:

(a) the other party, if an adult, is bound by the contract;

(b) the minor cannot recover money or property transferred under the contract (that is, he is treated as having an immunity from liability which he may choose to waive).

- Other provisions of the Minors Contracts Act 1987

  (a) Section 2 renders valid and enforceable against an adult a guarantee given in respect of a loan to a minor.

  (b) By s 3 the court may, if it is just and equitable, order a minor to restore to the other party any property received by the minor under a contract which is not binding on him. The power extends to any property or money which represents the original property received, and is wider than the court's inherent equitable jurisdiction of order restitution.

- Minors' contracts and the law of tort

  A minor will not be held liable in tort if this would amount to an indirect way of enforcing a contract against him on which he is not liable. Thus, no action for deceit can be brought where a minor fraudulently misrepresents he is of full age.

A corporation may be created by royal charter, by statute or by registration under the Companies Acts:

2.5.2   Corporations

- Chartered corporations

  These possess full contractual capacity equivalent to that of an adult human being.

- Statutory corporations

  These are created by Act of Parliament, and have the contractual capacity given to them by the statute which created them. If a statutory corporation acts outside its given powers, ie it acts ultra vires, any contract made is void.

- Registered companies

  Every company on registration must file a memorandum of association. A clause in the memorandum states what the objects (purposes) of the company are. The company has the power (capacity) to make contracts which assist in attaining its declared objects.

The general rule is that a company which makes a contract outside its powers is acting *ultra vires* and the contract is void.

However, under s 35 Companies Act 1985, where the transaction has been decided upon by the directors, and the other contracting party deals in good faith without notice that the company is acting *ultra vires*, the contract is enforceable by the person dealing in good faith against the company.

2.5.3 Persons of unsound mind

A person of unsound mind has capacity to make a contract, subject to the following.

- The contract is voidable at the option of the person of unsound mind, provided he can show that the other party either knew or ought to have realised he was of unsound mind.

- Contracts for necessaries are an exception. A person of unsound mind to whom these have been supplied is liable to pay a reasonable price (s 3 Sale of Goods Act 1979).

- If the court is satisfied that a mental patient is incapable of managing himself and his affairs a judge can be appointed to make contracts on the patient's behalf (Mental Health Act 1983).

It is generally thought to be the case that the mental capacity of someone impaired by alcohol or drugs is similar to that in points one and two above.

Chapter 3

The Contents of Contracts

Even when it is clear that a contract has been made it is necessary to define the scope of the obligations the parties have created. As has been seen, the general rule is that no special formalities are necessary. A contract may be made orally or in writing or in any combination. However, not all statements made by the parties automatically become terms (obligations) of the contract. It depends on their intention.

A statement made during negotiations which is not intended to be a part of the contract is called a 'mere' representation, indicating it is only a pre-contractual representation and not an obligation in the contract itself.

This distinction between a term and a mere representation is important. If a term is broken the injured party may sue the other for damages; there has been a breach of contract. If a mere representation turns out to be false, the injured party may have a claim for misrepresentation (see 3.2 below) but cannot show that a breach of contract has occurred.

The intention of the parties here, as elsewhere in contract law, is ascertained by the application of objective rules. It does not matter what the parties actually (subjectively) intended, but rather what they must be taken to have intended if the situation was to be considered by a rational and disinterested observer. A number of guidelines assist the court when such decisions have to be made.

By this rule '... parole [extrinsic] evidence cannot be admitted to add to, vary or contradict a deed or other written instrument ...' (*Jacobs v Batavia and General Plantations Trust* (1924)). Thus, where a contract is put into writing and it appears on the face of it to be complete the court will not permit alteration based on conflicting oral evidence. In any event, where an oral statement made during negotiations is not included in the written contract the inference must be that the parties did not intend it to form part of that contract (*Routledge v McKay* (1954)).

The parole rule has proved difficult to operate strictly in practice and a number of exceptions exist so that:

- evidence of a trade custom has been permitted to be added to the terms of a written contract;

3.1   **Express terms**

3.1.1   Mere representation or term?

3.1.2   Parole evidence rule

- evidence has been allowed to show that the written contract was not intended by the parties to come into operation;

- it has been successfully argued that oral statements were intended to be read in conjunction with the written contract (*Walker Property Investments v Walker* (1947) and *Couchman v Hill* (1947));

- in equity the court has power to order rectification of a written contract if, due to a mistake, it does not actually reflect the agreement reached (see 3.1.3 below).

3.1.3	Time factor	Where a period of time elapses between the making of the statement and the making of the contract the statement is likely to be treated as a mere representation (*Routledge v McKay* (1954) – where seven days passed from the time the seller of a motorcycle said it was a 1942 model to the time the agreement was made). In *Bannerman v White* (1861) a statement that no sulphur had been used in the treatment of hops was made during the conversation which culminated in agreement being reached. The statement was held to be a term.
3.1.4	Manner of making statement	If one party suggests to the other that it would be wise to check his statement, the statement will probably be considered a mere representation (*Ecay v Godfrey* (1947)). Here the seller of a boat said it was sound but encouraged the buyer to have a survey done. If there is an active attempt to put off enquiry as in *Schawel v Reade* (1913) 'you need not look for anything; the horse is perfectly sound', it is likely the statement will be held to be a term.
3.1.5	Importance of statement	In *Bannerman v White* (1861) the buyer said that if sulphur had been used on the hops he was thinking of buying he would not even trouble to ask the price. The statement was a term.
3.1.6	Skill and knowledge	A further guide, sometimes used, is whether the party making the statement has superior skill or knowledge of the matter as compared to the recipient of the information (*Shawel v Reade* (1913)). In *Harling v Eddy* (1951) the plaintiff at an auction did not intend to bid for a heifer until the defendant owner 'absolutely guaranteed her in every respect'. The plaintiff bought the heifer which was infected with TB and which died. The Court of Appeal held the defendant's statement to be a contractual term.

Frequently, the test works to the advantage of a consumer, not expected to have special skill or knowledge, who is dealing with a trader. The trader will, of course, be expected to know his business. In *Oscar Chess Ltd v Williams* (1957) the defendant wished to buy a new car and to 'trade-in' his old car. He wrongly, but in good faith, said it was a 1948 model, taking the information from the log book. The plaintiff motor-dealer, who based the part-exchange allowance on the age of the vehicle, later discovered the car was a 1939 model. The Court of Appeal held the statement as to the car's age was only a representation, not a term. The defendant possessed no special skill or knowledge but the plaintiff did. On the other hand, where a *dealer* in good faith misrepresented the mileage done by the car he was selling, the statement was held by the Court of Appeal to be a contractual term (*Dick Bentley Productions Ltd v Harold Smith (Motors) Ltd* (1965)).

In order to avoid the difficulties inherent both in making the distinction between a mere representation and a term and also in the ensuing consequences, the courts have sometimes made use of the 'collateral contract' device. It operates in this way: A promises to enter into the main contract with B on the strength of a separate (collateral) promise by B concerning something of importance to A in the main contract. In *City and Westminster Properties v Mudd* (1958) the defendant was tenant of the plaintiffs' shop and, as they knew, accustomed to sleeping in an adjacent small room. He negotiated a new lease with them which contained a clause restricting use of the premises to 'showrooms, workshops and offices only'. The plaintiffs promised the defendant verbally that they would take no action if his sleeping arrangements continued as before. Later the plaintiffs claimed to be able to forfeit the lease for breach of the clause. It was held that the defendant had indeed broken the clause but he had a good defence. There was a valid contract under which the plaintiffs promised not to enforce the clause if the defendant would sign the lease.

> 3.1.7   Collateral contracts

There is a fine line between holding that a contract was made partly in writing and partly by word of mouth, and holding that there was a collateral contract. Sometimes the courts will choose one, sometimes the other. Both approaches were used by the Court of Appeal in *Evans & Son v Andrea Merzario Ltd* (1976). The court decided that an oral promise that goods would not be shipped on deck carried precedence over standard written conditions which allowed deck cargo. On the analysis of Denning MR there was a collateral contract but in the opinion of Roskill and Geoffrey Lane LJJ there was only one contract, partly written and partly oral.

In addition to terms expressly agreed by the parties, terms may be implied into the contract in three ways: by custom, by the court and by statute.

3.2   Implied terms

3.2.1	Terms implied by custom	Custom, or 'usage' as it is often referred to, can be a potent source of implied obligations. The custom may stem from what is normal commercial practice within a particular trade or it may be local, as in *Hutton v Warren* (1836) – where a tenant farmer was entitled on quitting to reasonable compensation for seed and labour expended on the land. Because the court acts upon the presumed intention of the parties in admitting the customary term, it follows that where the point is covered by an express term there can be no room for the custom to operate (*Les Affréteurs Réunis Société Anonyme v Walford* (1919)).
3.2.2	Terms implied by the court	Again, based on the presumed intention of the parties, the court may hold a term implied in order to make sense of the contract, to give it 'business efficacy'. The judges have indicated that a term will not be implied merely to make a contract more reasonable or fair, nor will it if one of the parties has no knowledge of the matter in question (*Spring v National Amalgamated Stevedores & Dockers Society* (1956)).

The implied term must be one which is so obvious and basic to the contract that it is only rational to assume the parties must have intended to include it. The 'officious bystander' test was suggested by the Court of Appeal in *Shirlaw v Southern Foundries Ltd* (1939): 'if, while the parties were making their bargain, an officious bystander were to suggest some express provision for it in the agreement, they would testily suppress him with a common 'Oh, of course!'.'

The rule whereby terms are imported into contracts in this manner is sometimes known as the 'doctrine in *The Moorcock* (1889)'. Here defendant wharf owners were held liable for damage to the plaintiff's ship when it grounded at low tide on a ridge in the mud. In the absence of an express term that the berth was safe to use the Court of Appeal held there was an implied term on the part of the defendant that, as far as reasonable care could provide, there was no danger to the ship. This term the defendant had broken.

The House of Lords has held implied in a contract of employment a term that a man engaged to drive a lorry should use reasonable care and skill (*Lister v Romford Ice & Cold Storage Co Ltd* (1957)).

In *Liverpool City Council v Irwin* (1976) tenants withheld rents because the landlord failed to repair vandalised lifts, stairs and rubbish shutes. The House of Lords held that there was an implied obligation on the part of the landlord to use reasonable care to maintain the common parts of the building are acceptable state of repair.

In cases such as these, the courts are, in effect, deciding what basic obligations should exist in contracts of this kind and imposing them on the parties. However, it is important to remember that the parties are free by express language in their contract to adopt contrary terms and thus forestall any opportunity for action by the courts.

Certain terms are implied into every contract for the sale of goods by the Sale of Goods Act (SOGA) 1979 as amended by the Sale and Supply of Goods Act (SSGA) 1994.

3.2.3   Terms implied by statute

Section 21(1) SOGA 1979 states: 'A contract for the sale of goods is a contract by which the seller transfers or agrees to transfer the property in goods to the buyer for a money consideration called the price.' Note that this definition excludes other forms of transaction including, eg contracts to sell land or securities and contracts for work and materials.

Section 12 implies a term that the seller has the right to sell the goods. Thus, if A buys stolen goods from B and the goods are recovered by the police and returned to their rightful owner, A can sue B for the price he paid – if B can be found (*Rowland v Divall* (1923)).

Section 13 implies a condition that where the goods are sold by description, the goods must comply with that description. Note that goods are not prevented from being sold by description because they are seen and selected by the buyer. In *Beale v Taylor* (1967) it was held that the sale of a car advertised as a '1961 Triumph Herald Convertible' was a sale by description, despite the fact that the buyer had taken a trial run as a passenger in the vehicle before purchasing it. It was later discovered that the car was a 'hybrid' consisting of a rear section, which was in fact from a 1961 Herald as advertised, but this was welded to a front portion from an earlier model.

The sellers were in breach of s 13.

Section 14(2) implies a term that where goods are sold in the course of a business the goods will be of satisfactory quality. Note, the word 'satisfactory' was introduced by the SSGA 1994 and it replaced the old and rather vague expression 'merchantable' quality. Furthermore s 2(A) SOGA 1979 now provides that goods are of a satisfactory quality if they meet the standard that a reasonable person would regard as satisfactory, taking account of any description of the goods, the price (if relevant) and all other relevant circumstances. Section 2(B) states that the following (among other things) are, in appropriate cases, aspects of the quality of the goods:

- fitness for all the purposes for which goods of the kind in question are commonly supplied;

- appearance and finish;

- freedom from minor defects;

- safety; and

- durability;

but s 2(C) provides that the above does not extend to any matter making the goods of unsatisfactory quality:

- which is specifically drawn to the buyer's attention before the contract is made;

- where the buyer examines the goods before the contract is made, which examination ought to reveal; or

- in the case of a contract for the sale by sample, which would have been apparent on a reasonable examination of the sample.

Note – for the purpose of determining whether or not goods are of a satisfactory quality an objective test is applied, ie whether a *reasonable* person would regard the defects as rendering the goods unsatisfactory.

Section 14(3) provides that where the seller sells in the course of a business and the buyer expressly or by implication makes it known to the seller any particular purpose for which the goods are being bought, there is an implied condition that the goods supplied are reasonably fit for that purpose ... unless the circumstances show that the buyer does not rely, or that it is unreasonable for him to rely on the skill or judgment of the seller ...

Section 15(1) provides that where goods are sold by sample, the bulk shall correspond with the sample and the buyer shall have a reasonable opportunity of comparing the bulk with the sample. Further, that the goods will be free from any defect which would make their quality unsatisfactory and which would not be apparent upon a reasonable examination of the sample.

| 3.2.4 | Remedies for breach of ss 13–15 SOGA 1979 | Liability for breach of ss 13–15 rests with the seller. As with any breach of condition, the wronged party can usually repudiate the contract. In practice this means that the buyer can return the goods to the seller and demand a refund. The buyer is not obliged to accept the offer of repairs, exchanges or credit notes. Under the SOGA 1979 the buyer is not obliged to produce a receipt for the goods, nevertheless this will always be good evidence of the price paid, the date of purchase and |

the identity of the supplier. A new provision of the 1994 amendments – s 15(A) – prevents buyers who do not deal as consumers from repudiating the contract for a minor breach which will now be treated as breach of warranty thus restricting their remedy to damages.

Liability for breach of s 12 can never be excluded. Section 6 Unfair Contract Terms Act 1977 provides that liability for breach of terms implied under ss 13–15 SOGA 1979 can never be excluded if the buyer is dealing as a consumer.

3.2.5   Exclusion of liability for breach of sections 12–15 SOGA 1979

If the buyer does not deal as a consumer, terms implied under ss 13–15 SOGA 1979 may be excluded providing that it is reasonable to do so in the circumstances.

This legislation deals with transactions that lie outside the scope of the SOGA 1979 including contracts for the transfer of property in goods other than by sale, contracts for the hire of goods and contracts for the supply of services.

3.2.6   SGSA 1982

Sections 2–5 SGSA provide that where goods are supplied, the supplier has the right to supply them, that the goods will correspond with description, be of satisfactory quality, reasonably fit for purpose and if supplied by sample, correspond with the sample.

In the case of contracts for the provision of services, the following terms are implied where the supplier is acting in the course of a business:

s 13 – the supplier will carry out the service with reasonable care and skill

s 14 – if the time for the service is not fixed by the contract, the supplier will carry out the service in a reasonable time

s 15 – where the parties have not previously agreed a price for the service, the supplier will make a reasonable charge.

If a party deals as a consumer or on the other's standard form contract, by s 3 Unfair Contract Terms Act 1977, terms implied by ss 13–15 can only be excluded if it is reasonable to do so in all the circumstances.

3.3   The relative importance of contractual terms

A term in a contract may be described as being:

- a 'condition' (a major obligation, going to the heart of the contract); or

- a 'warranty' (minor obligation, collateral to the main purpose of the contract); or

- an 'innominate term' (no technical name) and intermediate (part way between condition and warranty).

Note the word 'condition' may be used, depending on the context, in an entirely different sense. It may be used to mean not a term of the contract at all but an external event or contingency upon which the whole existence of the contract depends. Thus, a 'condition precedent' is one which must be fulfilled before the contract can take effect (*Pym v Campbell* (1856)) whereas a 'condition subsequent' is one which, if it occurs, will terminate the contract (*Head v Tattersall* (1871)).

<table>
<tr><td>3.3.1</td><td>Why classify terms?</td><td>The distinction is important because the remedies available on breach differ. In the case of breach of condition the injured party may treat the contract as at an end (ie treat himself as free from any further obligations on his part), and claim damages. In the case of a breach of warranty he may claim damages but is still bound to perform his own obligations under the contract.</td></tr>
</table>

The effect of the distinction can be seen in *Poussard v Spiers* (1876) (condition) and *Bettini v Gye* (1876) (warranty). Note how important it is for the injured party to make the correct judgment. If he repudiates the contract in circumstances which are later decided by the court to have amounted to breach of warranty only (as did the defendant in *Bettini v Gye*), the roles are reversed and he will be held to have broken (abandoned) the contract where he had no right to do so.

<table>
<tr><td>3.3.2</td><td>What about the innominate/ intermediate term?</td><td>The traditional approach, developed in the 19th century, was to consider the relative importance of the obligations which the terms created in the contract. The time to weigh their importance was when the contract was made. Furthermore, the definitions of condition and warranty in s 11(1)(b) SOGA 1893 (now SOGA 1979), was assumed by lawyers to be not only a guide for distinguishing between them but also a statement that all terms must be either conditions or warranties.</td></tr>
</table>

A new approach, taken by the Court of Appeal in *Hong Kong Fir Shipping Co Ltd v Kawasaki Kisen Kaisha Ltd* (1962), dispelled this assumption. The court indicated that, in its view, terms might be innominate or intermediate. Here the court chose to look at the effect of breach, and make its judgment in the light of events at that time.

The facts were: H chartered a ship to K for two years. When delivered the ship was unseaworthy, thus breaching the term to provide a ship 'in every way fitted for ordinary cargo service', since its engines were ancient and crew inadequate and incompetent. On the voyage to Osaka five weeks' sailing time was lost and once there, 15 weeks were spent on repairs. K repudiated the contract. The Court of Appeal held that K wrongfully repudiated. The court refused to consider whether the 'seaworthiness' clause was a condition or a warranty, saying it was a bundle of obligations some serious, some trivial. As the term was innominate the correct approach was to wait and see the effect the breach had. In the event, K had not been substantially deprived of what it had contracted for. The breach by H was not to be regarded as one enabling K to treat the contract as ended. K had, therefore, wrongfully repudiated.

The decision in *Hong Kong Fir Shipping*, although it may be regarded as 'fair', being related to the seriousness of the outcome of the breach, brings uncertainty not liked by the commercial world. The courts have, in later cases, been prepared to classify a term as a condition if it is customarily regarded as such (*The Mihalis Angelos* (1970), 'expected ready to load' clause in a charter party, and *Bunge Corpn v Tradax Export* (1981), a buyer's obligation to give a seller 15 days' notice of readiness to accept delivery of 5000 tons of soya bean meal).

    3.3.3   Where does this leave us?

The parties themselves may expressly declare what the consequences are to be in the event of breach of a particular term, or indicate the importance they attach to a specific obligation (eg time of performance) – the inference being that it should be treated as a condition. It will not be sufficient for the parties merely to label a term a 'condition' or a 'warranty', unless it is clear that they know and intend to use the word in its full technical meaning.

Under the SOGA 1979, some implied terms are designated conditions, others warranties. In respect of these certainty is provided by the statute. However, even where the contract is one of sale of goods the Court of Appeal has held in *The Hansa Nord* (1975) that it is wrong to assume that all terms in the contract have to be classified as either conditions or warranties merely because the SOGA 1979 has classified some this way. In this case the clause 'shipment to be made in good condition' was held to have been breached in only a minor respect. The buyers had been wrong to reject the goods.

Amendments to the 1979 Act made by the SSGA 1994 show a further move away from the traditional clarification by use of the neutral word *Term*. In non-consumer cases the Act has placed a restriction on the buyer's right to reject goods for breach of the statutory conditions which remain, where the breach is only slight. In these circumstances damages only are to be awarded.

3.4	**Exemption clauses**	An exemption clause is a term in a contract whereby one party seeks to excuse himself entirely, or limit his financial obligation to pay damages (strictly speaking a 'limitation' clause), for breach of contract, misrepresentation or negligence.

3.4.1   Background

The common law idea of 'freedom of contract' lies at the root of exclusion clauses. The law allows parties the freedom to create obligations between themselves having legal effect. Each is presumed to know his own interests best and is free to obtain maximum gain for himself.

This is a valid assumption where the parties are negotiating with each other on an equal footing, for example, in a commercial context. Here exclusion clauses may be no more than a sensible and business-like way of allocating the risk of some event, on which the contract depends, going wrong.

With the rise, in the industrial revolution, of mass-produced goods came the need for 'mass-produced' contracts for their sale. 'Standard form' contracts to sell similar products saved time and money. But because the contract was drawn up by the seller, rather than negotiated between buyer and seller, it naturally contained terms which favoured the seller's interests. Exclusion or limitation clauses were likely to be among them. The result was a 'take it or leave it' attitude on the part of sellers – have the goods on our terms or do not have them at all.

3.4.2   The contribution of the courts – case law

An imbalance in bargaining positions meant that real negotiation to reach an equilibrium of interest was not possible. The assumption, originally made by the common law, was no longer justified on the facts. Consumers, in particular, were disadvantaged and controls were seen as necessary to redress the imbalance in bargaining power. Initially, case law and later legislation contributed solutions to the problem. However, the social and economic pressures which gave rise to these issues in the first place have not yet spent their force. The law is still developing in this area.

3.4.3   Exclusion clauses as part of the contract

Control by the judges has proceeded on the basis that to be effective, exclusion clauses must:

• be part of the contract;

• when construed (interpreted) cover the event in question; and

• be limited in effect only to the immediate contracting parties.

It is important to note the distinction between signed and unsigned documents, such as tickets and notices.

With regard to signed documents the general rule is that a person is bound by a document to which he has put his signature, whether or not he has read or understands its contents (*L'Estrange v Graucob* (1934)).

An important qualification to the rule occurs where the signer is induced to sign as a consequence of the other party misrepresenting the effect of the exclusion clause. In *Curtis v Chemical Cleaning and Dyeing Co Ltd* (1951) the plaintiff took a dress embroidered with beads and sequins to the defendant's shop for cleaning. She signed a form after the assistant explained it exempted the cleaners for damage to beads and sequins. In fact it excluded liability for any damage. The dress was stained in the cleaning process. The Court of Appeal held the plaintiff was entitled to rely on what the assistant had told her and was not bound by the clause printed on the form.

With regard to unsigned documents the position is more complex. The person whose rights are being excluded must be given reasonable notice of the excluding term and given it in time, ie not after the contract has been made.

Thus the excluding term must be in a document which a reasonable person would take to be a contractual document and not, for example, a mere receipt (*Chapleton v Barry UDC* (1940)).

On the other hand, it may not be necessary for the plaintiff to be notified of the actual content of the clause. The question is: was the plaintiff given information that would alert a reasonable man to enquire further and discover the detail? However, the degree of effort the defendant must use to draw the plaintiff's attention to the clause will depend upon the severity and unusualness of the excluding term. It may be that an explicit warning is necessary in extreme cases.

It is probably now unsafe to rely on the decision in *Thompson v LMS Rly Co* (1930) where an illiterate passenger was held bound by a clause buried in the company's timetables (costing 6d) after having been notified on the back of her ticket that it was issued subject to those conditions. Indeed in *Spurling v Bradshaw* (1956) Denning LJ stated: 'Some clauses which I have seen would need to be printed in red ink on the face of the document with a red hand pointing to it before the notice could be held to be sufficient.'

Then in *Thornton v Shoe Lane Parking* (1971) both Denning MR and Megaw LJ emphasised the need to bring particularly onerous or unusual terms to the attention of the affected party.

The Court of Appeal in *Interfoto Picture v Stiletto Visual Programmes Ltd* (1988) extended the rule to harsh and unusual terms in general. It appears that it will not now be limited in scope to the exclusion clause context.

The requirement of notice merely restates the rule on the formation of agreements, namely, an agreement is made when an offer is accepted. Thus, in *Olley v Marlborough Court* (1949) the agreement was made when the plaintiff booked in at the reception desk of the defendant hotel. A notice containing excluding terms in the hotel bedroom was notified to the plaintiff too late to be part of the contract.

However, it is important to note that in these situations it is possible that a long established course of dealing between the parties may amount to sufficient notice of the defendant's intention to include excluding terms in the present contract (*J Spurling Ltd v Bradshaw* (1956)).

It is important that the course of dealing is regular and consistent: *McCutcheon v MacBrayne Ltd* (1964) and *Hollier v Rambler Motors Ltd* (1972) both of which lacked this element. The cases also involved consumer plaintiffs.

Where the contract is made in a commercial context it may be easier to establish incorporation of an excluding term by reference to a course of dealing (*Hardwick Game Farm v Suffolk Agricultural Producers Association* (1969)). Furthermore, the terms, including exclusion clauses, set out in a trade association document, customarily used as the basis of the contract by parties in the same line of business, were held to be incorporated in the present oral contract (*British Crane Hire Ltd v Ipswich Plant Hire Ltd* (1974)). Note that this case may be regarded as an example of terms implied as a consequence of trade custom or usage (see 3.2.1 above).

3.4.4	The construction of exclusion clauses

Even when an exclusion clause is judged to be part of the contract it requires interpretation to see if, properly construed, it covers the event in question. Clear language is needed to excuse liability for a serious breach of contract or negligence. Under the *contra proferentem* rule ambiguity of meaning will be construed against the interest of the party relying on it and in favour of the party whose rights are being diminished.

The result is that if there is more than one source of liability, the protection the clause gives to the defendant may well be cut down in scope. In *White v John Warrick & Co Ltd* (1953) the plaintiff hired a cycle from the defendants on terms whereby 'nothing in this agreement shall render the owners liable for any personal injury'. The saddle tilted forward and the plaintiff was injured. It was held that the clause excluded the defendants' liability in contract for hiring out a defective cycle but not their liability in tort for negligence.

The courts have sometimes gone out of their way to adopt an interpretation hostile to the defendant (*Hollier v Rambler Motors Ltd* (1972)) and have been warned against this by the House of Lords (*Ailsa Craig Fishing Co Ltd v Malvern Fishing Co Ltd* (1983)).

These are additional ideas used by the courts to limit the scope and application of exclusion clauses: 'If a man offers to buy peas of another, and he sends him beans, he does not perform his contract', Lord Abinger in *Chanter v Hopkins* (1838).

The courts have held that while an exclusion clause may relieve a defendant from breaching a term, it cannot relieve him from not performing it at all (*Nichol v Godts* (1854)). In *Karsales (Harrow) Ltd v Wallis* (1956) the Court of Appeal held that a 'car' which was incapable of self-propulsion was not a car. The plaintiffs, who were suing Wallis for non-payment of instalments on the 'car', were not able to shelter behind an exclusion clause relating to its roadworthiness, condition or fitness.

From this developed the doctrine of fundamental breach which stated that, as a rule of law, an exclusion clause could not be held to excuse a person from a fundamental breach of his obligations. Despite the House of Lords in *Suisse Atlantique Société d'Armement Maritime SA v NV Rotterdamsche Kolen Centrale* (1967) stating *obiter* that there was no such rule of law (that it was always a question of construction as to whether the wording of the clause covered the breach complained of), the Court of Appeal kept the doctrine alive in cases throughout the 1970s, such as *Harbutts Plasticine Ltd v Wayne Tank and Pump Co Ltd* (1970).

These cases were finally overruled by the House of Lords in *Photo Production Ltd v Securicor Transport Ltd* (1980). Here the plaintiffs engaged the defendants to protect their factory under a contract which contained the provision that the defendants would not be 'responsible for any injurious act or default by any employee'. An employee of the defendants started a fire which got out of control and destroyed the plaintiffs' factory. The House of Lords held the clause, as a matter of construction, clearly covered the event. There was no rule of law under which the widely expressed clause could be impeached. The 'fundamental breach' rule was merely a rule of interpretation which lent against exclusion of liability for a fundamental breach unless there was clear language to the contrary. The plaintiffs' action for damages failed.

3.4.5   **Non-performance and fundamental breach**

The court also considered it fair and reasonable that in these circumstances the parties, bargaining with each other at arms length, were able to decide which of them should bear the risk. It is normal for the owner of buildings to insure them. This the plaintiffs had done. If they had not agreed to the exclusion clause the defendants would have charged a higher fee and, in terms of overall costs, the plaintiffs would have been the losers.

3.4.6   Limited in effect to contracting parties

Under the doctrine of privity of contract (see Chapter 4), a person who is not a party to a contract cannot take any benefit from it. This includes the 'benefit' of an exclusion clause. In *Adler v Dickson* (1955) the plaintiff was a passenger on P & O's ship, *The Himalaya*. Her ticket contained a clause, 'passengers are carried at passengers' entire risk'. While she was embarking, the gangway moved and the plaintiff fell, sustaining serious injuries. She sued, not P & O, but the master and boatswain for negligence. The Court of Appeal held she was entitled to succeed. While the clause absolved P & O from liability, the defendants were unable to avail themselves of a clause in a contract to which they were not parties.

This decision was affirmed by the House of Lords in *Scruttons Ltd v Midland Silicons Ltd* (1962) where it was held that stevedores employed to unload a ship's cargo could not rely on a limitation clause in the contract made between the cargo owner and the carrier. However, in *NZ Shipping Co Ltd v AM Satterthwaite Co Ltd* (1975) the Judicial Committee of the Privy Council held that stevedores could benefit from an exclusion clause in a contract between the carrier and the owners of the goods which were damaged by the stevedores' negligence. This was the case because the carriers had acted as agents for the stevedores, bringing them into contractual relations with the owners. This contract was supported by consideration – the stevedores had unloaded the owners goods in return for payment. It did not matter that the stevedores had a pre-existing obligation to the carriers to unload the vessel. In the context of this contract between the stevedores and the owners of the goods, the carriers were a third party.

The performance of an existing obligation owed to a third party can be good consideration in a separate contract (*Shadwell v Shadwell* (1860)).

This newly found agency device to avoid the effects of the doctrine of privity on the protection afforded by exemption clauses will not work unless the 'agent' has specific authority to negotiate on behalf of the party who is seeking protection. For example, in building contracts it may be difficult for sub-contractors to benefit from exemption clauses in a contract between the owner of the project and the main contractor. This was the case in *Southern Water v Carey* (1985) because the contract containing the exemptions from liability was entered into before the appointment of the sub-contractors.

An alternative method of effectively excluding liability was employed by the defendants in *Norwich City Council v Harvey* (1989). In this case an employee of the sub-contractors negligently set fire to existing buildings and the new extension while using his blow torch. By a term of the contract the main building contractor had placed the risk of loss or damage by fire on the owner of the buildings thereby allocating the risk to him and affording protection to the main contractor and his sub-contractor.

The history of legislation in this field shows two main strands of policy. One aims at protecting the rights of fare-paying passengers on public transport, who suffer personal injury through the operator's negligence, eg Road Traffic Act 1960 and the Transport Act 1962. The other aims at protecting consumers, particularly in transactions involving goods, eg Supply of Goods (Implied Terms) Act 1973.

3.4.7   The contribution of statute law

The methods employed by legislators are either:

- to make certain exemption clauses void, ie totally ineffective; or

- to make the excluding term subject to the requirements of being fair and reasonable in the circumstances.

The most extensively applicable legislation to date has been the Unfair Contract Terms Act 1977. In this statute, both the above mentioned policy strands and the methods employed, can be detected, although their scope and application have been widened. (Unless stated otherwise, all references to 'the Act' and to sections and schedules in the Act, in the following passages are references to the Unfair Contract Terms Act 1977.)

3.4.8   Scope and purpose of the Unfair Contract Terms Act 1977

The Act does not apply to every contract which contains an exclusion or limitation clause. It governs contracts where a person is seeking to exclude or limit his 'business liability', that is, his liability arising from things done or to be done in the course of a business, or from the occupation of business premises (s 1(3)).

Exceptions to the above occur in the case of contracts of sale of goods and hire-purchase (s 6), supply of goods and services (s 7), and in respect of misrepresentation (s 8). All these are caught by the Act, whether or not 'business liability' arises.

Certain contracts are excluded from the effect of ss 2 to 4, of the Act. These are listed in Schedule 1 and include contracts concerned with insurance, land, patents, trade marks and copyright, company formation and dissolution, transfer of securities, marine salvage and carriage of goods by sea. Also outside the scope of the Act are international sale of goods contracts as defined by s 26.

Section 6 applies only to contracts of sale and hire-purchase of goods and s 7 applies similarly to other contracts involving goods – hire, exchange, work and materials. On the other hand, s 2 and s 3 apply generally to contracts governed by the Act, including those falling within the ambit of ss 6 and 7.

It is important to note that the Act does not give any 'rights' in substantive law to a person disadvantaged by an excluding term.

Whether or not a plaintiff has a *prima facie* right to compensation must first be determined by reference to the terms of the contract, express or implied, and the law of tort, eg negligence. What the Act does is to place limits on the situations in which and the extent to which the plaintiff's already existing rights may be diminished. It gives him no 'rights' directly. Therefore, it is never correct to write that a plaintiff 'may sue under the Unfair Contract Terms Act 1977'!

| 3.4.9 | Negligence |

Note the meaning of 'negligence' in s 1(1) and that the Act extends to notices, not only contracts, purporting to exclude liability.

The Act makes a distinction between terms or notices which attempt to exclude liability for death or personal injury resulting from negligence, and those which exclude liability for other kinds of loss, eg damage to property, caused by negligence. A term cannot exclude liability for death or personal injury (s 2(1)). A term will be effective to exclude liability for other kinds of loss, provided the term passes the reasonableness test (s 2(2)).

In *Smith v Eric S Bush* (1989) the House of Lords had to consider whether the defendant had successfully prevented liability for a negligent misstatement arising, rather than excluding it once it had arisen Smith, when applying for a building society mortgage loan, signed a form in which both the professional valuer of the property and the building society disclaimed responsibility for the accuracy of the valuation report. (See *Hedley Byrne v Heller & Partners* (1964) for the effect of a disclaimer on the duty of care.) The House of Lords held that the defendant could not evade s 2(2) by this device and pointed out that s 13(1) expressly states that any such attempts shall be of no effect.

There are special rules in s 6 and s 7 dealing with the statutory implied terms in contracts concerning goods. Apart from these, there are provisions in s 3 concerned with contractual liability generally.

First, note when s 3 applies. It applies when A and B contract, and:

(a) B 'deals as consumer' (see s 12 for the meaning of this phrase); or

(b) the contract is made on A's standard written terms of business.

These are not mutually exclusive so that in situation (b) B may again be dealing as consumer. However, in (b) it is certainly possible for both A and B to be in business.

Second, be aware of what happens when s 3 applies. When it applies, A cannot, by means of a contract term:

• when himself in breach, exclude or restrict his liability; or

• claim to be able to perform the contract in a way substantially different from that which was reasonably expected of him; or

• claim to be entitled to render no performance at all in respect of all or any of his contractual obligations,

unless the term passes the reasonableness test.

Sometimes a manufacturer of goods will give a 'guarantee' of them to the consumer. The guarantee is sent with the packaged goods and is passed on to the consumer by the retailer at the point of sale. The guarantee may be deceptive. The manufacturer may offer to put right certain defects in the goods in return for the consumer giving up his right to sue in negligence the manufacturer of a dangerous product which causes the consumer death or personal injury (see *Donoghue v Stevenson* (1932)). By s 5 such exclusion of liability terms in guarantees are ineffective. Note that s 5 applies only to the situation where no possession or ownership of goods passes under a contract between the parties. Therefore it cannot apply to the retailer/consumer relationship.

Note the terms which are implied in contracts of sale of goods and hire-purchase by statute (see 3.2.3 above). The Act deals with attempts to exclude or restrict these implied terms.

By s 6 implied terms as to title cannot be excluded. As against a person dealing as consumer the implied terms relating to goods corresponding with description and sample, being of satisfactory quality and fit for the buyer's/hirer's purpose cannot be excluded.

3.4.10   Contractual liability

3.4.11   Manufacturers' guarantees

3.4.12   Sale of goods and hire-purchase

Where a person does not deal as a consumer, these terms can be excluded, provided the excluding clause satisfies the reasonableness test.

There are similar provisions in s 7 relating to other contracts involving goods, such as contracts for the supply of goods and services, except that under s 7 the implied obligations as to title can be excluded, subject to the reasonableness test.

Note the reasonableness test as it applies to s 6 and s 7 includes not only the general guidelines (s 11) but also the specific guidelines set out in Schedule 2.

3.4.13   Misrepresentation

A term excluding or restricting liability for misrepresentation, or any remedy for misrepresentation, has no effect unless it passes the reasonableness test (s 8). This replaces s 3 Misrepresentation Act 1967.

Merely because an excluding term has been commonly used for many years in a particular trade or profession does not mean it is automatically to be considered fair and reasonable (*Walker v Boyle* (1982)).

3.4.14   The reasonableness test

The general guidelines provided in the Act are to be found in s 11. Note in particular that:

- the time for judging whether the term is fair and reasonable is when the contract is made (s 11(1));

- in the case of a limitation clause, consideration must be given to the extent to which the person relying on the clause:

  (i) has resources available to meet a claim, or

  (ii) could cover his liability by insurance;

- it is for a person claiming that a clause satisfies the requirement of reasonableness to show that it does (s 11(5)).

The final point is of the utmost importance. Note where the burden of proof lies. A plaintiff whose rights appear to be excluded by a clause subject to the reasonableness test does not himself have to show the clause is unreasonable. It is for the defendant to show the clause is reasonable. If he cannot, the clause will not stand.

The specific guidelines in Schedule 2 apply, in addition to the general guidelines, to situations governed by ss 6 and 7 (statutory implied terms). Of these, the most fundamental matter likely to be taken into account is whether the parties are of equal bargaining power.

In a case decided under similar provisions under the Supply of Goods (Implied Terms) Act 1973, *George Mitchell*

(Chesterhall) Ltd v Finney Lock Seeds Ltd (1983), the House of
Lords applied the reasonableness test to a limitation clause in a
contract under which the plaintiffs bought cabbage seed from
the defendants for £192. The seed did not produce cabbages,
only a few leaves. The commercial loss to the plaintiffs was
£63,000, but the clause limited the buyer's claim to the price of
the seed. In holding the clause unreasonable, the court
considered the fact that the sellers were seeking to excuse
themselves from gross negligence when they could have
insured against sending the wrong seed without significantly
increasing their costs and that they frequently made *ex gratia*
payments to disappointed customers when they felt the
complaint was justified.

For a further example of an application of the
reasonableness test see *Smith v Eric S Bush* (1989).

When applying the reasonableness test, each case must be
treated only as a specific application, on the facts, of the
principles contained in the guidelines.

By s 12 a person deals as consumer if: 3.4.15   'Deals as consumer'

- he does not make the contract in the course of a business,
  nor holds himself out as doing so; and

- the other party does make the contract in the course of a
  business; and

- where goods pass to him under the contract they are of a
  type ordinarily supplied for private use or consumption.

The burden of proof is upon the person who alleges that a
party does not deal as consumer to show this is so (s 12(3)).

The issue of when a party deals as consumer has not been
straightforward in practice (*R & B Customs Brokers Co Ltd v
United Dominions Trust Ltd* (1988)). Here the Court of Appeal
held that in the acquisition of a second-hand car on conditional
sale terms, partly for business use and partly for the private
use of the directors, the plaintiff company was dealing as
consumer.

The Act contains a number of provisions aimed at parties who,   3.4.16   Provisions preventing
with the clever drafting of conditions, hope to defeat the Act's   evasion
main purpose. Section 4 prevents unreasonable indemnity
clauses being imposed on someone dealing as consumer. An
indemnity clause occurs where one party to the contract, A,
agrees to pay any damages incurred by the other party, B,
towards a third party, C.

Note that s 4 does not apply to businesses contracting with
one another (*Thompson v T Lohan (Plant Hire) Ltd and JW
Hurdiss Ltd* (1987)).

Section 10 is intended to cover the situation where there are two related contracts, the second attempting to do indirectly what the first could not do without falling foul of the Act. It does not apply to a situation where the second contract has as its object the settlement of a dispute which had arisen under the first (*Tudor Grange Holidays Ltd v Citibank NA* (1991)).

Section 13 states that exclusion or limitation clauses appearing in other guises but which have as their purpose restricting, limiting or excluding a party's rights shall be treated as coming within the ambit of the Act (*Smith v Eric S Bush* (1989) and *Stewart Gill Ltd v Horatio Myer & Co Ltd* (1992)).

3.4.17   The European   The EU has taken an interest in the problem of 'unfair' terms in
           dimension   consumer contracts through the Directive 93/13/EEC. The Directive is in force from 1 January 1995 and the Unfair Terms in Consumer Contracts Regulations 1994 (the Regulations), which implement it, have been operational from 1 July 1995. These co-exist with and do not replace the Act. In some respects the scope of the Regulations is wider than the Act, in others it is more restrictive.

The Directive and the Regulations apply to the terms which have been individually negotiated in contracts made between a consumer and a seller/supplier acting in the course of business. Terms will not have been individually negotiated when they have been drafted in advance and the consumer has no real chance to influence their content. If a seller/supplier claims a term has been individually negotiated it is for him to show that this is the case. A 'consumer' is a natural person acting for purposes outside his trade, business or profession. It is therefore narrower in concept than the term 'consumer' in the Act. If a term, not individually negotiated, is 'unfair' it is not binding on the consumer, although the remaining terms will be valid provided that the contract can continue in the absence of the unfair term.

An unfair term is defined by Regulation 4(1) as being any term which is contrary to the requirement of *good faith* on the part of the seller/supplier and which causes a significant *imbalance* in the parties' contractual rights and obligations to the *consumer's detriment*. An assessment of whether or not a term is unfair must be made concerning the context at the time the contract is concluded. It must take into account all the circumstances including other contractual terms, or the terms of a linked contract.

Schedule 2 specifies things to be taken into account when an assessment is made as to whether or not the requirement of good faith is lacking. These include matters (some of which look familiar!) such as:

- the strength of the parties' bargaining positions;

- whether the consumer received an inducement to agree to the term;

- whether the goods or services were supplied to the special requirements of the consumer;

- the degree to which the seller/supplier has dealt fairly and equitably with the consumer.

Schedule 3 contains a list of terms which may be regarded as unfair. The list is 'indicative and non-exhaustive'. It includes such terms as those excluding liability for death or personal injury and those enabling a seller/supplier to change items unilaterally.

The application of the 'unfair term' concept is restricted. By Regulation 3(2) terms which define the main subject matter of the contract or concern the adequacy of the price or remuneration for the goods or services supplied cannot be subjected to assessment for fairness. However, even these must, like all other written terms in the contract, be expressed in plain, intelligible language. Any doubt or ambiguity in the meaning of a term is to resolved in favour of the consumer (Regulation 6). Compare the *contra proferentem* rule of interpretation in internal law.

The Directive provides that Member States ensure that the continued use of unfair terms in consumer contacts, drawn up for general use by individual traders or trade associations, is prevented (Article 7). The Regulations require the Director General of Fair Trading to consider complaints made to him about the fairness of any Contract term drawn up for general use (Regulation 8). The Director General may, if he considers it appropriate, take action against the trader of trade association seeking an injunction to restrain them from using the term. Alternatively, he may accept an undertaking to discontinue its use.

Chapter 4

Vitiating Elements in Contracts

Although it may appear a contract has been made by parties of full contractual capacity reaching agreement and exchanging mutually binding promises, there are factors known as vitiating factors, which, due to operation of law, may invalidate the apparent contract.

A contract may be void or voidable on various grounds, ranging from mistake through misrepresentation to duress and undue influence, in circumstances where the law regards it unfair, as between the parties, to hold the contract valid.

On grounds of public policy, as expressed in legislation and through case law, other contracts are regarded as reprehensible on account of their subject matter and effect. These are rendered illegal or void in whole or in part.

The word 'mistake' has a very restricted meaning in English law. Circumstances which, in normal parlance, would be regarded as sufficient to merit the use of the word, are ignored by the law. To be 'operative', ie to have some effect in law, a mistake must always be of fact (not law), and be fundamental in the context of the contract.	**4.1** **Mistake**
According to the classification used by Cheshire, Fifoot and Furmston (*Law of Contract*, 13th edn, Chapter 8), there are two types of problem.	4.1.1 Meaning and classification

- Agreement has been reached but on the basis of a common mistake. Both parties make the same fundamental assumption concerning an underlying fact, eg A and B make a contract the one to buy, the other to sell, certain goods only to find out afterwards that at the date of the contract the goods had been destroyed.

- It is alleged that agreement has not been reached due to a fundamental misunderstanding between the parties as to what the contract is about. This may be due to either a 'mutual' or 'unilateral' mistake.

  (i) A mutual mistake occurs where each party is mistaken as to the basis on which the other intends to contract, eg A thinks he is contracting to sell his Ford car to B, while B thinks he is contracting to buy A's Vauxhall car. The mistake will be operative only if, judged objectively by a reasonable third party, the contract cannot be inferred in relation to one car rather than the other. The parties are not permitted to bring evidence as to the state of their respective minds when the contract was made.

(ii) A unilateral mistake, as the name suggests, is where one party only is mistaken as to the terms on which he intends to contract. The other is aware, or must as a reasonable person be assumed to be aware, of the mistake, eg A writes to B offering to sell B his house for £20,000 and B, who has already received promotional material from A's agent with a price guide of £220,000, accepts at once. In contrast to the situation involving mutual mistake, the party mistaken in a unilateral mistake context, A in the example, is allowed to adduce evidence showing the state of his mind at the time.

Note that there is a sub-category of unilateral mistake involving the mistaken identity of one of the contracting parties. Special, additional rules apply here.

4.1.2	The consequences of mistake

Saying a mistake is 'operative' means the law will take notice of it. The precise consequences, ie the remedies available for an operative mistake, will depend on whether the court is exercising its common law or equitable jurisdiction.

At common law the result is drastic. The contract is void. The whole transaction fails. In essence, the court is saying that there is no contract and there has never been one. Goods and money must be returned, even by an innocent third party whose rights depend on the validity of the original contract (*Cundy v Lindsay* (1878)). Because of the dramatic consequences of declaring a contract void for mistake at common law, the courts have restricted the circumstances in which they are prepared to reach this conclusion.

When exercising their equitable jurisdiction the courts are prepared to be a little more lenient in deciding what amounts to an operative mistake and to be flexible in the remedies given. Remedies available include setting aside the contract on terms (*Cooper v Phibbs* (1867)), the granting or refusing of specific performance (*Grist v Bailey* (1967)), rescission (*Magee v Pennine Insurance Co Ltd* (1969)), and rectification of a document (*Joscelyne v Nissen* (1970)). These remedies, being equitable, cannot be demanded as of right and are always in the discretion of the court to grant or withhold. However, it is clear that the equitable remedy of rescission will never be given if it would prejudice the position of a third party who acquired rights, acting *bona fide* and giving value.

Circumstances in which the courts have had to consider whether a common mistake is sufficiently fundamental to be operative are as follows.

- *Res extincta*

  These are sometimes referred to as cases of 'initial impossibility'. The contract will be treated as void by both common law and equity where both parties believe the subject matter of the contract exists but it does not, having already perished by the time the contract is made (*Couturier v Hastie* (1856)), or possibly where the subject matter has never existed (*Galloway v Galloway* (1914) and *Associated Japanese Bank (International) Ltd v Credit du Nord* (1988)). The contract will not be void where one party impliedly warrants the existence of the subject matter (*McRae v Commonwealth Disposals Commission* (1951), an Australian case).

  Note, however, s 6 Sale of Goods Act 1979: Where there is a contract for the sale of specific goods, and the goods without the knowledge of the seller have perished at the time when the contract is made, the contract is void. Note also *Cooper v Phibbs* (1867) where the House of Lords held void a contract where A agreed to transfer to B property which B already owned; a case of impossibility through the subject matter being *res sua*. (See the use of the court's equitable jurisdiction in the order made.)

- Mistake as to quality

  At common law a mistake as to quality will not usually be regarded as sufficiently fundamental to render the contract void (*Bell v Lever Bros Ltd* (1932)). Here, Bell, employed by Lever Bros, entered into an agreement with them to cut short his contract of employment for compensation of £30,000. After this sum was paid it was discovered that Bell could have been dismissed without compensation for breaches of duty. (Bell did not have these in mind when negotiating the agreement.) The House of Lords held the common mistake made by the parties was not sufficiently fundamental to render the contract void.

  Other cases which support this line are *Leaf v International Galleries* (1950) and *Harrison & Jones Ltd v Bunten and Lancaster Ltd* (1953).

  Where, however, the courts exercise their equitable jurisdiction they are prepared to set aside contracts which at common law are regarded as valid (*Solle v Butcher* (1950)), sometimes on terms very specific to the circumstances of the case (*Grist v Bailey* (1966)). Note how equity is prepared to take into account price in deciding whether a mistake is fundamental. In *Magee v Pennine Insurance Co Ltd* (1969), a case comparable with *Bell v Lever Bros Ltd* (1932), the Court of Appeal held that an agreement to settle a claim made on a car insurance policy must be set aside in equity as the policy itself was voidable.

A further way in which the courts may offer equitable relief is through an order for rectification of a written document. The remedy is available where the parties are in agreement but in recording it in writing an error is made. The antecedent agreement does not necessarily have to be a fully binding contract. It is sufficient that there is a common prior intention shown (*Joscelyne v Nissen* (1970)). However, the remedy is not available where the written document does accurately record what the parties have agreed (*Frederick E Rose (London) Ltd v William H Pim Co Ltd* (1953)), where both parties, wrongly, believed 'feveroles' were horsebeans and entered into a contract for the sale of horsebeans. The Court of Appeal refused to order rectification of the contract substituting the word 'feveroles' for ' horsebeans'.

| 4.1.4 | Mutual mistake |

The essence of an operative mutual mistake is that there is no genuine consent as the offer was made in one sense and accepted in another (*Raffles v Wichelhaus* (1864) and *Scriven v Hindley* (1913), a more difficult case). If a reasonable man would infer from the actions of the parties a contract in a particular sense that contract will stand (*Wood v Scarth* (1858) and *Scott v Littledale* (1858)).

Common law and equity are at one here in deciding whether or not a mutual mistake renders the contract void. However, in exercise of its equitable jurisdiction the court, having decided a contract must stand, will refuse to grant specific performance of it if this would cause hardship (*Wood v Scarth* (1858)).

| 4.1.5 | Unilateral mistake |

An operative unilateral mistake occurs where one party only is mistaken as to the terms of the contract. The other knows of, or must be taken as a reasonable person to appreciate, the mistake made. In *Hartog v Colin and Shields* (1939) sellers of Argentine hare skins mistakenly offered to sell them at so much per pound, when they had intended to sell them at so much per piece. All preliminary negotiations had been undertaken on the basis of so much per piece. Held, the contract was void for mistake.

A mistake by one party as to some quality which he supposes the subject matter of the contract to possess will not be sufficient to render the contract void, even though the other party realises a mistake has been made and fails to correct it (*Smith v Hughes* (1871)).

As with mutual mistake equity 'follows the law' in deciding whether the contract stands or not (*Webster v Cecil* (1861) where the court refused to order a decree of specific performance). In *A Roberts & Co Ltd v Leicestershire County Council* (1961) the court ordered rectification of a written contract as a consequence of a unilateral mistake.

Most cases involving unilateral mistake have been instances of mistakes being made by a plaintiff with reference to the identity of the other contracting party. The classic scenario concerns a rogue who, fraudulently representing himself to be a person of high reputation, obtains goods (on credit or in return for a worthless cheque), from the plaintiff. He then sells the goods for cash to the second victim of his fraud, the defendant, and disappears. The resulting action between plaintiff and defendant hinges on whether the contract between the plaintiff and rogue is, or is not, void for mistake.

4.1.6   Mistaken identity

If it is void the rogue cannot obtain title to the goods in question and consequently cannot pass title to the defendant *nemo dat quod non habet* (no one gives that which he does not have). The defendant is ordered to return the goods to their true owner, the plaintiff, or pay their value.

If the contract between the plaintiff and the rogue is not void for mistake, title will have passed to the rogue, who is able to transfer ownership by contract to the defendant. Although in these circumstances the contract between plaintiff and rogue is voidable, ie one in respect of which rescission may be claimed by the plaintiff on grounds of the rogue's misrepresentation, the plaintiff is unable to avoid the contract once a *bona fide* third party has acquired rights for value and without notice of the misrepresentation. The defendant in these cases generally fits the description, so that, where the contract is not void for mistake, the defendant is entitled to keep the goods and the plaintiff is left without any remedy in practice, the rogue having vanished.

The issues raised by such cases have centred around the following questions. Did the party who was mistaken:

- intend to deal with some other company/person, who actually exists?

- regard the identity of the other as fundamental?

- take reasonable steps to check on the identity of the other party?

4.1.6.1	*The intention to deal with someone who actually exists*

In *Cundy v Lindsay* (1878) the plaintiffs believed they had received an order for goods from Blenkiron & Co, a reputable firm known to them, but with whom they had not previously traded. They had never heard of the rogue, Blenkarn, who had signed his name to appear 'Blenkiron & Co', and who had given an address only a few doors away from the reputable firm. The House of Lords held that the contract was void. The plaintiffs had never intended to make a contract with Blenkarn. They were unaware that he existed.

Contrast this situation with that found in *King's Norton Metal Co Ltd v Edridge Merrett Co Ltd* (1897) where the plaintiffs received an order on impressive-looking notepaper from a firm called 'Hallam & Co'. There was no business of this name in existence. It was a fictitious entity set up by a fraudster named Wallis. The Court of Appeal held that the plaintiffs must have intended to contract with the writer of the letter, whoever he was. The contract was not void for mistake.

The mistake made by the plaintiffs in this instance was of the 'attributes' of the other party, ie they believed the company to be creditworthy. It was not a mistake concerning 'identity'.

4.1.6.2	*Regarding the identity of the other as fundamental*

It is relatively easier where the contract has been made by correspondence, as in *Cundy v Lindsay*, to establish identity as being of importance. It is more difficult to establish this in face-to-face transactions (*Phillips v Brooks Ltd* (1919) and *Lewis v Averary* (1972)).

Ingram v Little (1961), where the Court of Appeal held the contract void, appears to conflict with these but may possibly be explained by drawing a fine distinction as to when the question of identity was raised – when the contract was made, or when it came to the method of payment?

The plaintiff in *Hardman v Booth* (1863), although confronted by a face-to-face situation, was well placed to show that the identity of the contracting party was of vital significance to him. Here the plaintiff mistakenly made a contract with an employee, wrongly but reasonably, supposing him to be an authorised representative of the company the plaintiff intended to do business with. It was held that no contract existed between plaintiff and employee.

4.1.6.3	*Taking reasonable steps to check on identity*

A person who wishes to persuade the court that the contract he apparently made is void must go further than establishing the fundamental significance of the identity of the other contracting party. In circumstances where the courts are being asked to choose between two innocent victims of a rogue's fraud they are anxious to see whether the plaintiff, the first victim, behaved reasonably or was careless. The plaintiff needs, therefore, to establish that he acted reasonably in verifying the identity of the other party. In contracts made by correspondence this may not be difficult. In *Cundy v Lindsay* (1878) the plaintiffs knew the respectable firm, Blenkiron & Co, had premises in Wood Street, Cheapside. They acted reasonably in dispatching goods to 37 Wood Street, Cheapside, where the rogue, Blenkarn, had set up business.

Where the contract is negotiated in a face-to-face situation the plaintiff's task is much more difficult (*Phillips v Brooks* (1919) and *Lewis v Avery* (1972)). The decision in *Ingram v Little* (1961) is of doubtful authority and reliance on it would seem unwise.

The general rule is that a person is bound by a document to which he has put his signature, whether or not he has read or understood it (*L'Estrange v Graucob* (1934)). As a consequence of the general rules relating to mistake or misrepresentation the signer may be able to escape the consequences of a contract contained in the document. However, even if these factors are absent, it is possible the signer may be able to use the plea *non est factum* (this is not my deed) in order to have the document declared a nullity. The drastic consequences of a successful plea, particularly on a third party who has acquired rights on the strength of the document, is such that its scope is severely restricted.

Originally, the plea was used for the protection of an illiterate person who had to rely on another's explanation of a deed before executing it. In time it became available in respect of any document, not just a deed, and was not limited to the illiterate. The courts, concerned that its wide application would lead to abuse, developed a number of rules to curtail the circumstances in which the plea might successfully be used.

The rules governing the present position are to be found in the judgment of the House of Lords in *Saunders v Anglia Building Society* (1970). The facts and decision are as follows: Mrs Gallie, a widow of 78 years, wanted to help her nephew raise money and agreed to transfer her leasehold house to him for this purpose, provided she could continue to live there. She understood her nephew's friend, Lee, would help in raising a loan. A document was prepared which, the nephew told her, was a transfer by way of a gift of the house to him. In fact it was drawn up as a sale to Lee. Mrs Gallie, who could not read it, because she had broken her glasses, executed the document. Lee mortgaged the property to the Anglia Building Society. He defaulted on the payments and the Society sought possession. Mrs Gallie resisted the action by seeking to have the document

4.1.7   Documents mistakenly signed

she had signed declared void. She died before the case reached the House of Lords. It was continued by her executor, Saunders. The House of Lords held the plea *non est factum* was not available to Mrs Gallie because:

- the document was not fundamentally different in effect from that which she believed she was signing; and

- she had been careless in not establishing the document conformed to her expectations before executing it.

Since this decision a successful plea of *non est factum* was made in *Lloyds Bank v Waterhouse* (1991). In this case an illiterate father signed a guarantee for his son's debts to the bank believing that the guarantee covered the purchase price of a farm when in fact it extended to all his son's liabilities to the bank. This mistake was held to render the document sufficiently different from that which he thought he was signing and there was no evidence of negligence on the part of the father.

| 4.2 | **Misrepresentation** | As we have seen above, a statement made by one party during negotiations may become a term of the contract or it may form part of a collateral contract. In each instance the remedy available to the injured party, should the statement turn out to be false, is an action for breach of contract. |

If a mere representation proves to be untrue the party misled may be entitled to a remedy or be able to set up the misrepresentation as a defence if sued for damages or specific performance. What remedy (if any) is available to the injured party will depend upon the type of misrepresentation made.

| 4.2.1 | Operative misrepresentation | For a misrepresentation to be operative (ie to have effect in law) two criteria must be met: |

- there must be a false statement of a material fact; and

- this must have induced the party to whom it was made to enter into the contract.

| 4.2.2 | False statement of a material fact | The following points should be noted. |

- A statement may be made by conduct as well as by words. In *Gordon v Sellico* (1986) the vendor's concealment of dry rot prior to the sale of a property to the plaintiffs was held to constitute misrepresentation, partly because of the 'sinister and menacing' nature of the defect which was being concealed.

- The statement must be of fact as opposed to law. It is occasionally difficult to distinguish between fact and law, as in *Solle v Butcher* (1950) where a statement that a flat was 'new' and hence outside Rent Act control was held to be a statement of fact not law.

- A promise of future action is not, on the face of it, a statement of fact because a 'fact' relates only to a present state of affairs. However, it is possible for a representation of intention to amount to a statement of an existing fact. This will happen if the person making the statement misrepresents the present state of his mind – he says he intends to do 'X', but all the time he intends, in fact, to do 'Y' (*Edgington v Fitzmaurice* (1885), 'The state of a man's mind is as much a fact as the state of his digestion').

- Similarly, a statement of opinion or belief is not, *prima facie*, a statement of fact (*Bisset v Wilkinson* (1927)). However, a statement in the guise of an opinion may amount to a misrepresentation if the person giving the 'opinion' could not, as a reasonable man, have held that opinion honestly in the light of facts known to him (*Smith v Land and House Property Corp* (1884)).

Remaining silent and not disclosing some fact likely to affect the decision of the other party does not, as a general rule, amount to a misrepresentation.

4.2.3   Non-disclosure

The following instances are exceptions to the general rule on silence.

A half-truth may amount to a misrepresentation. If a statement is made all relevant elements must be disclosed or the true picture will be distorted. If a vendor says all the farms he is selling are let, he must not omit to say that some tenants have given notice (*Dimmock v Hallett* (1866)). If a party makes a statement believing it to be true he must disclose the truth if he discovers his statement to be *incorrect*. Similarly, if a statement true when made subsequently becomes untrue there is an obligation on the maker of the statement to inform the other of the change (*With v O'Flanagan* (1936)).

4.2.3.1   Half-truths

In contracts *uberrimae fidei* (of the utmost good faith), where one party is likely to have exclusive access to the important facts, there is a duty upon that party to make a full disclosure of all material circumstances. The law recognises three types of contract as falling within this special group: contracts to take shares in a company on the basis of a prospectus issued by the promoters (s 56 Companies Act 1985), family arrangements (eg *Gordon v Gordon* (1821)) and contracts of insurance.

4.2.3.2   Contracts of the utmost good faith

This is the most important type of contract *uberrimae fidei*. The insured must disclose to the insurer every material circumstance, ie anything which would influence the judgment of a prudent insurer in deciding whether or not to accept the risk, and if to accept it, at what premium.

Note that the test of whether a circumstance is material is objective, not subjective. It is whether a 'prudent insurer' would be influenced, not whether the insured genuinely believes disclosure is relevant.

In the case of a policy of insurance which is renewable annually the duty of disclosure arises afresh, prior to renewal, in respect of any material change of circumstances. Each year's insurance is the subject of a separate contract.

In the event of non-disclosure the remedy available to the insurer is to avoid the policy, ie to treat the insurance contract as voidable and refuse to pay any claim made by the insured. It does not matter whether or not the loss resulted from a circumstance not disclosed.

4.2.3.3   *Fiduciary relationships*

Where parties, who are already in a relationship recognised by the law as fiduciary (trusting), make a contract, an obligation exists on the part of the dominant party in the relationship to disclose to the other all material circumstances known to him. Relationships which have been recognised as falling within this category have included: parent/child, solicitor/client, doctor/patient, trustee/beneficiary, tutor/tutee (*Tate v Williamson* (1866)). The dominant party, eg parent, solicitor, doctor, etc, is in a position where trust and confidence is naturally placed in him by the other. The dominant party thus has considerable influence. The other party is likely to be inhibited from asking probing questions and generally dealing with him at arms length.

4.2.4   Inducing the contract

To amount to an operative misrepresentation the false statement must have induced the person to whom it was made to enter into the contract (*Peek v Gurney* (1873)), where the House of Lords held the action failed as the defendant's misrepresentation had not been addressed to the plaintiff.

The misrepresentation does not have to be the sole cause of the plaintiff's decision to enter into the contract (*Edgington v Fitzmaurice* (1885)), neither is it a requirement that the plaintiff must show it would have induced a reasonable man to enter into the contract (*Museprime Properties Ltd v Adhill Properties Ltd* (1990)). It was held sufficient for the plaintiffs to show that their decision was affected by the defendants' misrepresentation.

Generally, if a plaintiff is shown to have sought independent advice this will establish his lack of reliance on the defendant's statement (*Attwood v Small* (1838)). However, the fact that the plaintiff was given the means of checking the accuracy of the defendant's statement, but failed to avail himself of the opportunity, will not harm his claim that he was induced by the defendant's misrepresentation (*Redgrave v Hurd* (1881)).

On the other hand, it will prove fatal to a plaintiff's claim to show the misrepresentation, although known to him, in fact had no effect on his mind (*Smith v Chadwick* (1884)), as also will the situation where it is established that the plaintiff's judgement was unaffected because he was unaware of the misrepresentation (*Horsfall v Thomas* (1862)).

In order to grasp the significance of the different types of misrepresentation it is essential to understand something of the history of the development of this area of law.

4.2.5   Types of misrepresentation and the remedy of damages

• Fraudulent misrepresentation

Prior to *Hedley Byrne v Heller* (1964) the law recognised only two types of misrepresentation – fraudulent and innocent. Fraudulent misrepresentation was defined by Lord Hershell in *Derry v Peek* (1889) as a false statement 'made knowingly, or without belief in its truth, or recklessly, careless whether it be true or false'. Any misrepresentation which was not shown to be fraudulent was termed 'innocent'. In this case the defendants were not guilty of fraud as they had honestly believed that what they said was true, although they may have been over optimistic.

Fraudulent misrepresentation constitutes the tort of deceit. Thus, a plaintiff who can prove fraud will succeed in an action for damages for deceit, even though the false statement is a mere representation and not a contract term. Furthermore, the defendant will be liable for all damage which flows as a direct consequence from the misrepresentation whether or not it was reasonably foreseeable at the time the statement was made (*Doyle v Olby (Ironmongers)* (1969)).

• Non-fraudulent misrepresentation

Since 1964 it has become necessary to distinguish between different types of non-fraudulent misrepresentation, remembering that in all previous cases these will have been referred to as instances of innocent misrepresentation:

(i) Negligent misrepresentation at common law – *Hedley Byrne v Heller* (1964) (frequently referred to as negligent mis-statement) established that where there is a 'special relationship' between plaintiff and defendant the defendant owes the plaintiff a duty to take care when making statements which he knows the plaintiff is likely to act on. Further, in *Esso Petroleum v Mardon* (1976) the Court of Appeal held a plaintiff entitled to damages under the *Hedley Byrne* principle where the defendant's misstatement had induced the plaintiff to enter into a contract with the defendant. The plaintiff was awarded damages for all losses reasonably foreseeable at the time the statement was made, the aim being to put him in the position he would have been in if the misrepresentation had not been made. (This follows the normal rules on remoteness and measure of damages in negligence. Contrast the position where damages are awarded for deceit/fraudulent misrepresentation.)

(ii) Negligent misrepresentation under the Misrepresentation Act 1967 – by s 2(1): '... where a person has entered into a contract after a misrepresentation has been made to him ... and as a result ... has suffered loss, then, if the person making the misrepresentation would be liable to damages ... had the misrepresentation been made fraudulently, that person shall be so liable ... [even though the misrepresentation is not fraudulent], unless he proves that he had reasonable grounds to believe and did believe up to the time the contract was made that the facts represented were true'.

Note that as a consequence the normal burden of proof is reversed. If the defendant is to escape liability he must prove, in effect, that he was not negligent by establishing reasonable grounds as the basis for making the statement and showing his belief in it up to the moment the contract was concluded (*Howard Marine v Ogden* (1978)). At common law the burden is upon the plaintiff to show the defendant was negligent.

Section 2(1) applies only where the misrepresentation has induced the plaintiff to enter into a contract with the defendant. The section is therefore narrower in scope than the common law duty (under negligent misstatement) which does not require a contract to have been entered into, merely reliance on the statement causing loss.

The wording of s 2(1) does not state how damages are to be assessed. However, look carefully at the language used to establish the liability of the person making the statement. A literal interpretation has been adopted. This renders the defendant liable for damages as if the misrepresentation had been made fraudulently. In *Royscot Trust Ltd v Rogerson* (1991), the Court of Appeal held that as a consequence of this 'fiction of fraud' the plaintiff was entitled to recover from the defendant all losses flowing directly from the defendant's misrepresentation ie the *Doyle v Olby (Ironmongers)* rule (above).

(iii) Wholly innocent misrepresentation – since 1964 'innocent' must be reserved only for a misrepresentation which is made entirely without fault, neither fraudulently or negligently.

No action for damages will lie in respect of an innocent rnisrepresentation. If, however, a plaintiff seeks rescission of a contract on the grounds that he was induced into it by the defendant's innocent misrepresentation it is possible that under s 2(2) Misrepresentation Act 1967 the court may exercise its discretion to declare the contract still subsisting and award damages instead of rescission (see 4.2.6 below).

Note, however, that s 2(2) never permits a plaintiff to seek damages directly in respect of a misrepresentation.

A party who has been induced into a contract by a misrepresentation, whether fraudulent, negligent or innocent, may wish to cancel (rescind) it and be restored to the position he was in prior to making the contract. This may involve a 'giving back and a taking back' on each side as property, goods and money are returned.

4.2.6   Rescission

The party misled (the misrepresentee) may elect to rescind by notifying the representor of his decision to do so, or by doing whatever he can in the circumstances to make clear his intention (*Car and Universal Finance v Caldwell* (1964)).

He can instead apply to the court for an order for rescission. In addition to cancelling the contract the court may order the defendant to pay an indemnity to the plaintiff in respect of any obligations created by the contract, ie things the plaintiff had to do (rather than chose to do) as a consequence of making the contract. An indemnity must be distinguished from an action for damages (*Whittington v Seale-Hayne* (1900)).

It is important to remember that rescission is an equitable remedy. It cannot be claimed as of right. Whether or not to award it is in the discretion of the court. However, there are very well defined guidelines as to how courts act. These are referred to as 'bars to rescission' and are as follows.

- Affirmation

  A plaintiff will not be granted rescission if he has expressly or impliedly affirmed the contract (*Long v Lloyd* (1958)). Lapse of time is evidence of affirmation but is not of itself conclusive. In the case of fraud time runs from the date when the fraud was discovered but in the case of non-fraudulent misrepresentation, probably the date of the contract (*Leaf v International Galleries* (1950)).

- Restitution impossible

  Because the object of rescission is to restore the parties to their pre-contract positions it follows that rescission will not be ordered if this cannot be achieved. Goods or property may have been consumed or substantially altered in character. In *Clarke v Dickson* (1858), shares in a mining company became worthless over a period of three years as the mine was worked to exhaustion. However, the courts will not refuse rescission where relatively minor changes have occurred or even where there has been a deterioration in the value of property due to market conditions (*Cheese v Thomas* (1994)).

- Injury to third party rights

  Rescission will not be ordered if an innocent third party has acquired rights on the assumption the contract is valid. See 4.1.6 above on mistaken identity for examples of circumstances where, despite a fraudulent misrepresentation made by a rogue to an innocent plaintiff, the court would not consider setting aside the contract. To do so would have harmed the defendant who had acquired the title to goods, bona fide and for value, without notice of the fraud.

  By s 2(2) Misrepresentation Act 1967 where a plaintiff seeks an order for rescission, and it is open to the court to award rescission, the court may award damages instead, if it believes this fairer in all the circumstances. But note the following:

- Section 2(2) does not apply to fraudulent misrepresentation.

- It must be open to the court to award rescission, ie no bars to rescission are present.

- In *William Sindall plc v Cambridgeshire County Council* (1994) it was stated *obiter* that the measure of damages awarded in lieu of rescission under s 2(2) would be:

  > 'the difference in value between what the plaintiff was misled into believing he was acquiring, and the value of what he in fact received' (Evans LJ).

- By s 2(3) the court must, if awarding damages under s 2(1), take into account any damages awarded under s 2(2).

- The decision to award damages is at the discretion of the court. A plaintiff cannot seek to claim damages under s 2(2). Interestingly, as a result of a recent decision it would appear that damages in lieu of rescission may still be available when the right to rescind has been lost. See *Thomas Witter Ltd v TBP Industries* (1996).

If the concept of contract is based on agreement it follows that no contract can be made in the absence of agreement. Agreement implies consent. If a person's will has been coerced how can he be said genuinely to have consented? The problem has been addressed by both common law, through the notion of duress, and equity through the more subtle idea of undue influence.

4.3   Duress and undue influence

Originally duress at common law meant illegal, unjustified violence or threats of violence to a person in order to induce him to contract. One of few modern examples can be seen in the Australian case of *Barton v Armstrong* (1975) which was heard on appeal by the Privy Council and involved one party's threat to kill the other unless he executed a deed. It was held that once unlawful pressure was established the burden was upon the person exerting it to show this had not negatived consent. Not an easy task, especially as the duress did not have to be the sole or even the main reason for the plaintiff entering into the contract. The defendant was unable to discharge the burden.

4.3.1   Duress

Historically, threats to property were not regarded as sufficient to constitute duress but *dicta* in *Occidental Worldwide Investment Corp v Skibs A/S Avanti, The Siboen and the Sibotre* (1976) indicate that today a more flexible approach will be taken. The real issue is whether there has been 'coercion of the will'.

In recent years a doctrine of 'economic' duress has begun to develop. Early reference to it can be found in statements by Lord Denning in *D & C Builders Ltd v Rees* (1965) in which he referred to the plaintiff having been held to ransom. 'The creditor was in need of money to meet his own commitments and she [Mrs Rees] knew it.' This idea of economic duress has been accepted in later cases but within narrower limits than that accorded duress in the form of threats of physical violence. It is clear that in essence economic duress shares with its earlier common law counterpart a coercion of the will, which negatives consent. There must be pressure which is unjustifiable. The courts decide on the facts of each case where to draw the line between commercial pressure which is acceptable and that which is illegitimate.

Clear guidelines for distinguishing between the two have not yet been produced, although some pointers have been given, for example by Lord Scarman in *Pao On v Lau Yiu Long* (1980) in a decision of the Privy Council.

- Did the person alleged to have been coerced protest?

- Did he have an alternative course open to him, eg some legal remedy?

- Was he independently advised?

- After entering into the contract did he take steps to avoid it?

In *North Ocean Shipping Co Ltd v Hyundai Construction Co Ltd, The Atlantic Baron* (1979) the threat by the defendants to breach the contract without lawful justification unless the plaintiffs would pay an additional 10% of the agreed price for a ship under construction was held to amount to economic duress. However, the delay in reclaiming the overpayment, some eight months, showed the plaintiffs to have affirmed the contract which was left to stand.

On the other hand, action was taken immediately by the defendants who were pressurised in *B & S Contracts and Design Ltd v Victor Green Publications Ltd* (1984). They deducted the sum they had been forced to pay over in advance from the contract price due to the plaintiffs after the contract had been carried out. The Court of Appeal decided that for this and other reasons the defendants had been subjected to economic duress.

There must be pressure and it must be illegitimate: *Universe Tankships Inc of Monrovia v International Transport Workers Federation, The Universe Sentinel* (1983). It is also clear that the causal link between economic duress and the contract being made by the party coerced should be very clear. The duress must be the only or, at least, the predominant reason. Compare the position in the case of physical duress where the rules are much more lax (*Barton v Armstrong* (1975)).

4.3.2   Undue influence

In response to the narrowness of common law duress equity developed the rule that a contract could be set aside for undue influence. This applies whenever one party exercises such a degree of influence over the other that the latter, being unable to exercise an independent judgment, is pressurised into a contract disadvantageous to him. Since *Allcard v Skinner* (1887), confirmed by the Court of Appeal in *Bank of Credit and*

Commerce International v Aboody (1990), two categories have been recognised: actual undue influence and presumed undue influence. If the transaction is to be avoided for presumed undue influence it is necessary to show that it was manifestly disadvantageous for the complainant but in the case of actual undue influence this is no longer necessary (*CIBC Mortgages v Pitt* (1993)).

Where no fiduciary or special relationship exists between the parties the burden is upon the party alleging undue influence to show it occurred and that it led to the transaction now complained of. In *Bank of Credit and Commerce International v Aboody* (1990) the Court of Appeal held that although undue influence had occurred by a husband over a wife the transactions between husband and wife and the bank would not be set aside at the request of the wife as none were shown to have been to her disadvantage.

In *Williams v Bayley* (1866) the House of Lords set aside a father's mortgage of his property to a bank after it had been procured by the bank exploiting the father's fears that his son would be prosecuted for forgery.

4.3.2.1   Actual undue influence

Where equity recognises a fiduciary or special relationship of trust between parties who then contract there is a presumption that the dominant party has exercised undue influence unless the opposite is proved to be the case. The best way to rebut the presumption is to show that the party supposedly influenced sought independent and informed advice from a third party before contracting.

The list of relationships which have been recognised by equity as giving rise to the presumption include: solicitor/client, doctor/patient, trustee/beneficiary, guardian/ward, parent/child, religious advisor/disciple, but not husband/wife (*Bank of Montreal v Stuart* (1911)).

The normal relationship of banker and customer does not give rise to the presumption. However, the particular facts of a case may show it to have become a relationship in which the elements of trust, confidentiality and reliance are such that the courts will apply the presumption. In *Lloyds Bank v Bundy* (1975), Bundy relied entirely on the advice given by the bank and the Court of Appeal set aside the transaction. In *National Westminster Bank v Morgan* (1985), where, on the facts, there was no undue influence, the House of Lords said that for the presumption to be made there must be a fiduciary relationship in which the one has a dominating influence over the other. However, in *Goldsworthy v Brickell* (1987) the Court of Appeal qualified this by holding undue influence could also be

4.3.2.2   Presumed undue influence

established by showing that in a fiduciary relationship trust and confidence had been abused.

The difficult position in which a bank or other creditor may find itself is illustrated by *Barclays Bank v O'Brien* (1993). A wife signed a guarantee of her husband's business overdraft, with their jointly owned house charged as security, for £130,000 having been told by her husband it was limited to £60,000 and would last three weeks. The Barclays employee, who presented the documents for the wife's signature failed to explain them or suggest she should seek independent advice. The House of Lords held that the bank was bound by the husband's misrepresentation and the legal charge was set aside. (Her claim of undue influence, rejected by the Court of Appeal, was not pursued.) Their lordships said that where the creditor (bank) was aware that a guarantor was a wife, or other cohabitee having an emotional relationship with the debtor, the creditor was 'put on enquiry' when:

- the arrangement was not on the face of it to the advantage of the wife, or other cohabitee; and

- there was a substantial risk that the debtor had committed a wrong which entitled the guarantor to set aside the transaction (as against the debtor).

According to Lord Browne-Wilkinson, the only way in which the creditor could avoid being fixed with constructive notice of the undue influence in such circumstances was for the creditor to see the wife/guarantor in the absence of her husband, to tell her of the risk that she is running and urge her to take independent advice. Furthermore, where the creditor has good reason to believe that undue influence is not just possible but probable he or she must insist on the wife having independent advice.

Following the decision in *Barclays Bank v O'Brien* there has been a series of cases relating to the circumstances under which a bank/creditor can be deemed to have discharged its liability to ensure that the wife/guarantor has received independent advice, following the possible/probable undue influence of a third party (the husband). It would now seem that providing that the bank has good reason to believe that the wife has been properly advised by a solicitor, this will suffice. The bank need not enquire into the quality of the advice given (*Massey v Midland Bank plc* (1995) and *Banco Exterior Internacional SA v Thomas* (1997)).

On the same day in *CIBC Mortgages plc v Pitt* (1993) the House of Lords made it clear that banks or other creditors were not automatically to assume undue influence or other wrong merely because the transaction involved husband and wife. In this case, although undue influence of the wife by the husband was established there was no notice of this, actual or constructive, to the lender. The borrowers had jointly signed a loan application for £150,000 ostensibly for the purchase of a holiday home, but which the husband intended to use for the purchase of shares on the stock market. The lender's solicitors had also acted for the borrowers. The wife had not read any of the documents she signed. *Barclays Bank v O'Brien* was distinguished as there the arrangement was manifestly not for the wife's financial benefit, which should have put the bank on enquiry, whereas here there was no indication that the transaction was anything other than a normal loan to husband and wife for their joint benefit.

In *Lloyds Bank v Bundy* (1975) Lord Denning suggested that an additional and independent reason for setting aside an 'unconscionable bargain' was the parties' inequality of bargaining power. The idea has received sympathy in some quarters but, perhaps due to the difficulty of setting limits to the scope of such a general doctrine, has elsewhere been rejected (Lord Scarman in *Pao On v Lau Yiu Long* (1980) and *National Westminster Bank v Morgan* (1985)).

Contracts induced by duress and undue influence are voidable and will be set aside at the option of the party affected. This may involve an order for rescission to which the normal 'bars' apply (see 4.2.6 above).

It is important to remember the equitable nature of the remedy and that the court is concerned to achieve practical justice for both parties. 'He who comes to equity must do equity.' In *Cheese v Thomas* (1994) an agreement between a great-uncle and a great-nephew to purchase and share a house was set aside on the grounds of the latter's undue influence. The house, bought in 1990, was sold in 1993 for a net loss of £27,500, due to general housing market conditions. The Court of Appeal held that the loss should be shared by the parties in the proportions in which they had contributed to the purchase price.

Contracts falling into this category do so as a consequence of their reprehensible nature. It is thought not to be in society's interests to allow them to stand as valid and enforceable agreements. Public policy in this area may be expressed through statute or at common law through precedents set by judges in successive cases.

4.3.3   A remedy for duress and undue influence

4.4   Illegal and void contracts

4.4.1	Contracts illegal by statute

Any contract which is expressly prohibited by statute is illegal (*Re Mahmoud v Ispahani* (1921)).

A contract may be impliedly prohibited by statute if on interpretation of the legislation it can be seen that the real object is to forbid that particular type of contract (*Cope v Rowlands* (1836)), where an unlicensed broker was unable to recover his fees for work done on behalf of the defendant. The statute which required him to obtain a licence was aimed at preventing unlicensed persons from acting as brokers, thus protecting the public. However, if the purpose of the statute is, for example, primarily administrative, non-compliance will not result in the contract being illegal. In *Archbolds (Freightage) Ltd v Spanglett Ltd* (1961) the Court of Appeal held a contract to carry goods on an unlicensed vehicle was not illegal, the object of the legislation being to achieve an orderly distribution of licence holders throughout the country.

A contract may be illegal as formed (ie from the outset), because contracts of this description have been expressly or impliedly banned by statute.

Alternatively, a contract may be illegal as performed. Such a contract is lawful at its inception but the method of performance adopted by one party contravenes a statute. Suppose, for example, on the sale of certain toxic substances specified information must, by legislation, be supplied by the seller to the buyer but the seller fails to do this. The contract is illegal only in the manner in which the seller performs it. He will be unable to sue the buyer successfully for the price, although the innocent buyer's rights will be unaffected.

4.4.2	Contracts illegal at common law

Contracts which are harmful to society as a whole are said to be 'contrary to public policy'. The more reprehensible category contains those which the common law has judged to be illegal. (The less damaging category of those considered merely void at common law are dealt with below.)

The principal reason for distinguishing between contracts which are illegal and those which are merely void at common law is that the rules preventing their enforcement are relaxed somewhat in the case of void contracts.

Contracts illegal at common law, like contracts rendered illegal by statute, may be illegal as formed or as performed. They include the following.

4.4.2.1	*Contracts to commit a crime, tort or fraud on a third party*

Clearly a contract is illegal if its purpose directly or indirectly is to do harm to another through the commission of a crime or tort, or to defraud or deceive a third party (*Everet v Williams* (1725), a contract of partnership between two highwaymen). A similar rule of public policy forbids someone to benefit as a consequence of his wrongdoing (*Gray v Barr* (1971)). Relatives of a deceased wrongdoer are in no better position (*Beresford v Royal Insurance Co Ltd* (1938)).

A prostitute cannot sue for his or her fees, and a landlord who lets a room to a prostitute, knowing the purpose of the letting is for the reception of clients, will not be able to sue for the rent. In the 19th century cases indicated that contracts which furthered cohabitation by unmarried couples were also caught by this rule. Today, it appears the courts have moved away from this position: in *Somma v Hazlehurst* (1979) a contract under which an unmarried couple occupied a room was not treated as being contrary to public policy.

4.4.2.2 *Contracts which are sexually reprehensible*

A contract made with an alien enemy in time of war is illegal. One already made becomes illegal at the outbreak of war (see Chapter 5, 5.3.2 below).

4.4.2.3 *Contracts detrimental to public safety*

The rule has also been extended to cover a contract which is likely to prejudice relations with a friendly foreign power in peacetime (*Foster v Driscoll* (1929) in which a contract to smuggle alcohol into the United States contrary to American prohibition laws was held to be illegal).

A private agreement to 'buy off' a prosecution is illegal. Other examples of contracts which affect the administration of justice include an agreement by a witness not to give evidence and an agreement not to oppose the discharge of a bankrupt.

4.4.2.4 *Contracts detrimental to the administration of justice*

Contracts 'tainted' with maintenance or champerty (at one time punishable as a crime, but no longer – Criminal Law Act 1967), nevertheless remain illegal in contract law in the sense that they are contrary to public policy.

Maintenance is 'improperly stirring up litigation and strife by giving aid to one party to bring or defend a claim without just cause or excuse', according to Lord Denning in *Re Trepca Mines Ltd (No 2)* (1962). Champerty occurs where the party giving the aid will, under the contract, receive a share of any fruits of the litigation.

A contract for buying, selling or procuring a public office is illegal, as is a contract to procure a title (*Parkinson v College of Ambulance Ltd and Harrison* (1925)).

4.4.2.5 *Contracts tending to promote corruption in public life*

A contract which is designed to defraud the revenue, whether national or local, is clearly contrary to public policy. In *Miller v Karlinski* (1945) it was held that a contract of employment, which allowed an employee to claim reimbursement from his employer as 'expenses' the income tax deducted from his salary, was illegal.

4.4.2.6 *Contracts to defraud the revenue*

4.4.3	Effects of illegality	It is important to recognise that the state of the parties' minds is relevant. If it is clear on the face of it that the contract is illegal either under common law or by statute the parties cannot be heard to say that they were ignorant of this.

However, the position is different where the contract appears to be a normal, lawful contract, eg the letting of a flat. Here the law will enquire as to whether the intention of one or both of the parties was to exploit the contract for an illegal purpose. For example, was it the parties' intention that the flat should be used for the purposes of prostitution? The law will not assist a guilty party to enforce an illegal contract but will look more kindly upon one who is innocent of any guilty intent. In *Pearce v Brooks* (1866) coachbuilders, who let out on hire-purchase to a prostitute a miniature carriage, intended to lure clients, were held unable to recover arrears of hire payments, as they were aware of her intended use of the vehicle.

4.4.4 Contracts which are illegal as formed

Where a contract is illegal at its inception the primary rule is *ex turpi causa non oritur actio* (no action arises from a base cause).

- the contract is void and neither party is able to sue on it; and

- if money has been paid or property has been transferred under the contract neither can be recovered.

Exceptions to the rule include the following.

- Where the party seeking to recover bases his claim on another cause of action, outside the illegal contract (*Bowmakers Ltd v Barnet Instruments Ltd* (1945)).

  The same principle was illustrated more recently in *Tinsley v Milligan* (1993) where the parties had performed an illegal act when jointly purchasing a property. The house was put into the name of Tinsley so that Milligan could still claim social security payments (unlawfully). After various disagreements Milligan sued for the return of her money. It was held that she could recover by basing her action upon the resulting trust created in her favour, rather than upon the illegal contract.

- Where the parties are not in pari delicto (not equally in the wrong). For example, the plaintiff may show he was a victim of the defendant's fraud or duress and the whole object of the statute which renders the contract void was to protect people like the plaintiff, eg a tenant who agrees and pays to a landlord an illegal premium (*Kiriri Cotton Co Ltd v Dewani* (1960)).

• Where the plaintiff repents of the illegal nature of the contract before it is substantially performed. A claim of repentance will not be regarded favourably by the court if it appears that the plaintiff's change of mind occurred only after the defendant had broken the illegal agreement (*Bigos v Bousted* (1951)).

Connected contacts will also be illegal. A purchaser of land to be used for the purposes of an illegal lottery later executed a deed in which he promised to pay the vendor the balance of the price still outstanding. The vendor was held to have no cause of action (*Fisher v Bridges* (1854)).

Case law would suggest that where a contract was legal at its inception but goes on to be performed in an illegal manner a party will not be unsuccessful in a claim unless:

    4.4.5   **Contracts which are illegal as performed**

(i) the illegal act was central (rather than merely peripheral) to the performance of the contract; and

(ii) the plaintiff knew of or participated in the illegal act.

In *Ashmore, Benson, Pease & Co v AV Dawson Ltd* (1973) the plaintiff's transport manager knew that the defendant's vehicle had been dangerously and unlawfully overloaded. This unlawful act was considered to be central to the performance of the contract and the plaintiffs had knowledge of the illegal act so they were unsuccessful in their claim when their goods were damaged as a result of the carriers' actions.

However in *St John's Shipping v Joseph Rank* (1957) where the plaintiff carriers had overloaded their vessel in breach of statute, this did not preclude them from bringing a successful action for damages claiming payment for their work. The purpose of the infringed statute was to penalise overloading, not to render the contract illegal.

For similar reasons, in *Shaw v Groom* (1970) a landlord's failure to supply his tenant with a rentbook was not fatal to his claim for arrears of rent.

Where one party relies on the other to see that the contract is performed lawfully he may be able to sue the other for damages for breach of his 'collateral warranty'. In *Stongman (1945) Ltd v Sincock* (1955) the defendant promised the plaintiff builders that he would obtain the necessary licences for the work he engaged them to do. He obtained licences for only part of the work and refused to pay them for the unlicensed work they had completed. It was held that, while not entitled to sue on the contract, the plaintiffs were able to recover damages for breach of the defendant's collateral promise.

A party who is innocent of the illegality has all the normal remedies open to him.

4.4.6	Contracts void by statute

A wagering contract is rendered void by s 18 Gaming Act 1845, so that 'no suit shall be brought ... in any court ... for recovering any sum of money or valuable thing alleged to be won upon any wager'.

Two provisions which seek to promote competition in manufacture and trade, and ban agreements that could lead to collusion and anti-competitive behaviour are the Restrictive Trade Practices Act 1976 and Article 85(1) of the Treaty of Rome.

Under the 1976 Act contracts which come within the statutory definition of restrictive trading agreements are void unless they can be shown not to be 'contrary to the public interest' and to pass at least one of a number of stringent tests laid down in the Act.

Article 85(1) prohibits all agreements which may affect trade between Member States of the European Union and which have as their object or effect the prevention, restriction or distortion of competition in the European market.

4.4.7	Contracts void at common law

Contracts which are void at common law are, like those illegal at common law, classified as such because they are regarded as not in the public interest and generally harmful to society. Note the way the rules which prevent their enforcement are less stringent than those applicable to illegal contracts.

4.4.8	Contracts in restraint of trade

For practical purposes the most important example of a contract which is void at common law is a contract in restraint of trade. '[T]he public have an interest in every person's carrying on his trade freely so has the individual. All interference with individual liberty of action in trading, and all restraints of trade themselves, if there is nothing more, are contrary to public policy, and therefore void' (Lord MacNaghten in *Nordenfelt v Maxim Nordenfelt Guns and Ammunition Co Ltd* (1894)).

Originally, all contracts in restraint of trade were void but the dictates of public policy have changed. Today, contracts which are subject to the doctrine are only *prima facie* void. They will be upheld if they are shown to be reasonable in the circumstances. To be classed as reasonable a restraint must be:

- not harmful to the public interest; and

- as between the parties drawn no wider than necessary to protect legitimate business interests. It cannot operate merely to stifle competition.

Although the categories of contract caught by the doctrine must remain fluid, the following have been held to fall within its sphere.

An agreement by an employee in his contract of employment that on leaving his job he will not take employment with another firm or set up on his own will be unreasonable and void unless there is some proprietary interest of the employer which requires protection, eg trade secrets (*Forster & Sons Ltd v Suggett* (1918), or the goodwill of customers: *Fitch v Dewes* (1921)).

4.4.9 Restraints by an employer on an employee

The courts will examine not only the subject matter of the restraint but also how long it is to last and the area of its operation (*Herbert Morris Ltd v Saxelby* (1916) and *Mason v Provident Clothing & Supply Co Ltd* (1913)).

Care has also been taken to prevent employers from acquiring by other means restraints which they could not have obtained directly. In *Bull v Pitney-Bowes Ltd* (1966), a rule in a pension scheme stated that a retired employee would lose his pension if he took up any occupation or activity in competition with his former employer. The restraint was held too wide and therefore void when the plaintiff took a job with another company in the same line of business. It was contrary to the public interest to deprive society of the expertise of a person skilled at his trade. In *Kores Manufacturing Co Ltd v Kolok Manufacturing Co Ltd* (1958) the Court of Appeal held unreasonable and void an agreement between two manufacturing rivals that they would not offer employment to anyone previously employed by the other company. The arrangement was far wider than necessary to protect the divulgence of confidential information or trade secrets.

The importance, in the public interest, of a person's right to work at his trade or profession can be seen in two cases involving professional sportsmen, although strictly speaking they fall outside the employer/employee relationship. The House of Lords held that the 'retain and transfer' system operated at the time by the Football League was an unreasonable restraint of trade (*Eastham v Newcastle United FC* (1964)). In *Greig v Insole* (1978) the rules adopted by the governing bodies of cricket, banning a professional cricketer who had joined a 'World Series', were also held to be unreasonable.

A person who buys a business pays not only for the tangible assets like the premises, fixtures and fittings, and the stock but also for an intangible asset – the goodwill of the business. Goodwill is the established custom or popularity of the

4.4.10 Restraints by a buyer on a seller of a business

business. If the seller were free to entice away the customers to a new business he set up nearby the buyer would lose the benefit of part of what he had paid for. It is, therefore, customary for the seller of a business to agree in the contract of sale not to compete in a way which will damage the goodwill of the business sold. For an example of a restraint of this nature which was held to be valid see *Nordenfelt v Maxim Nordenfelt Guns & Ammunition Co Ltd* (1894).

There must be a genuine proprietary interest which needs protection (*Vancouver Malt and Sake Brewing Co Ltd v Vancouver Breweries Ltd* (1934)). Only in respect of the business transferred can the buyer seek to have the restraint enforced (*British Reinforced Concrete Engineering Co Ltd v Schelff* (1921)).

4.4.11   Restraints agreed between manufacturers and suppliers to restrict output

The object of this kind of restraint is to prevent prices falling due to the over supply of goods.

At common law the courts upheld such agreements if they appeared to be reasonable to control the flow of products coming onto the market (*English Hop Growers v Dering* (1928)). However, views of what serves the public interest change over time. Collusive trading arrangements of this kind, which shelter businesses from the fierce winds of competition are now considered contrary to public policy. Under the Restrictive Trade Practices Act 1976 they are outlawed other than in the exceptional circumstances detailed in the Act.

4.4.12   Restraints imposed by suppliers on distributors

A manufacturer or supplier may agree to sell goods to a retailer or distributor only if the latter promises to abide by certain restrictions on his freedom to trade. For example, a garage may agree to buy all the petrol it sells from a particular oil company, a public house to buy all its beer from a particular brewery.

This arrangement, called a *'solus'* agreement, was held by the House of Lords to fall within the doctrine of restraint of trade and therefore to be *prima facie* void (*Esso Petroleum Co Ltd v Harper's Garage (Stourport) Ltd* (1967)).

Having decided that the two contracts between Esso and Harper's were caught by the doctrine, the House then had to decide whether, in the particular circumstances, the restraints could be upheld as being reasonable. Harper's had agreed to buy all its petrol and motor oils from Esso and to operate its two garages in accordance with the 'Esso Plan'. Under this they had to provide certain facilities and to stay open all reasonable hours. The garages were given a discount of 1.25 pence a gallon on petrol purchased. The agreement was to run four and a half years for one garage and 21 years for the other. The latter was subject to a mortgage in favour of Esso in respect of a £7,000 loan which could not be redeemed before the end of 21 years.

The House of Lords held that the *'solus'* arrangement was not unreasonable; both sides could benefit as could the public. However, the restraints became unreasonable if made to last for an excessive time. In the circumstances the four and a half year agreement was reasonable and valid, the 21 year agreement unreasonable and void.

Two further points regarding *solus* agreements and petrol companies should be noted. The law draws a distinction between someone who already has possession of the garage giving up his freedom to trade (*Esso v Harper's Garage*) and someone who acquires possession through the *solus* agreement, *Cleveland Petroleum Co Ltd v Dartstone Ltd* (1969), where the Court of Appeal held the restrictions *prima facie* binding. No freedom was surrendered. But even here if it is shown that the agreement is detrimental to the public interest the restraint will not be enforced (*Amoco Australia Pty Ltd v Rocca Bros Motor Engineering Co Pty Ltd* (1975)).

An observation by their lordships in *Esso v Harper's Garage*, that a restraint lasting more than five years is an indication of its unreasonableness, is not a hard and fast rule. In each case the particular circumstances of the parties need to be considered (*Alec Lobb (Garages) Ltd v Total Oil (GB) Ltd* (1985)). The garage company was in severe financial difficulty. The Court of Appeal upheld complex financial arrangements of sale and leaseback under which Alec Lobb (Garages) agreed to the exclusive purchase of Total petrol for the duration of a 21 year lease. The garage company was free to operate a 'break' clause to end the lease and the restrictions after seven years and 14 years. In the interests of the garage company the arrangements had to be relatively long term. Five years would have been insufficient to solve its financial problems.

Note that similar rules apply to contracts for exclusive services. In *Schroeder Music Publishing Co Ltd v Macaulay* (1974), the House of Lords held a contract between a songwriter and a music publishing company came within the doctrine of restraint of trade. The terms, being unreasonable and oppressive to the songwriter, were held void.

What is stated here applies to contracts void at common law. It applies also to contracts rendered void by statute except where the statute in question contains special provisions.

The position should be contrasted with contracts classified as illegal (see 4.4.3 above) and the following points noted.

4.4.13 Effects of the contract being void

- The contract is void only in so far as it contravenes public policy. Only the offending part of a contract, that which is contrary to public policy, is declared void. The remaining obligations in the contract are unaffected and therefore remain valid (*Wallis v Day* (1837)).

- Money paid or property transferred can be recovered

  In *Hermann v Charlesworth* (1905), H paid £52 to C to introduce gentlemen to her with a view to matrimony but C's efforts were to no avail, H was held entitled to the return of her £52.

- Severance and enforcement of lawful promises is possible

  The court may reject the void element in the contract by severing or cutting it away from the valid parts of the contact. The valid parts are then enforced. There are two ways in which this may operate.

  (i) The whole of the objectionable promise is severed. For this to occur the court must be satisfied that the offending promise is subsidiary to the main purpose of the contract. If it is a substantial part of the consideration the whole contract must fail;

  (ii) The scope of an objectionable promise may be cut down in extent by omitting the offending words. In *Nordenfelt v Maxim Nordenfelt Guns and Ammunition Co Ltd* (1894), the House of Lords permitted severance of a promise not to compete which was clearly divisible into two parts. The one relating to competition in the manufacture of guns and ammunition was valid and enforced, the other, relating to competition more generally, was declared void. See also *Goldsoll v Goldman* (1915).

  Note, however, that the courts will only strike out the offending words. They will not re-write a clause so that it becomes reasonable and thus acceptable (*Mason v Provident Clothing and Supply Co* (1913); see also *Attwood v Lamont* (1920)).

Chapter 5

The Doctrine of Privity of Contract

Under the doctrine of privity of contract a person who is not a party to a contract can take neither benefit from it nor have obligations imposed on him by it.

In *Tweddle v Atkinson* (1861) it was seen as part of the rule that consideration must move from the promisee and being a stranger to the consideration the plaintiff was unsuccessful in seeking to enforce an agreement in which he played no part. However, the House of Lords in *Dunlop Pneumatic Tyre Co v Selfridge Co Ltd* (1915) made it clear that privity was a separate requirement so that a plaintiff must show that he had both provided consideration and been a party to the contract.

The doctrine has proved very inconvenient in practice and attempts have been made to evade it, some more successful than others.	**5.1** **Attempts to evade the doctrine**
Often insurance is taken out specifically to benefit or safeguard a third party. As a consequence various statutes have given third parties in specified circumstances the right to sue on such policies. For example, when a husband or wife takes out life insurance for the benefit of each other or their children, the beneficiary may claim on the policy (Married Women's Property Act 1882). Similarly, a person injured in a road accident due to the negligence of the driver of a motor vehicle has the right to sue on the driver's policy (Road Traffic Act 1972).	5.1.1 Insurance
A well established exception to privity is to be found in the law of agency. A person (A) may make a contract on behalf of another (P) with a third party (T) so that a valid contract exists between P and T. Provided A has, at the time he makes the contract, authority to act on P's behalf he may, under the doctrine of the 'undisclosed principal', keep secret from T the fact of his agency, so that only later is the true contracting party P revealed to T.	5.1.2 Agency
The court may sometimes use the collateral contract device (see Chapter 2, 2.1.7 above) to construct a contract between the promisor and an apparent stranger to the contract (*Shanklin Pier Co v Detel Products Ltd* (1951) and *Wells (Merstham) Ltd v Buckland Sand & Silica Ltd* (1964)).	5.1.3 Collateral contract

5.1.4	Property law	• Leases

Leases

A lease of land creates obligations between the immediate parties, eg to pay rent, carry out repairs, etc. Both lessor and lessee are able to transfer these obligations to third parties.

• **Covenants**

A freehold owner who sells off part of his land may wish to retain some control over it. The 'restrictive covenant', now firmly established, by which he can impose an obligation on successive owners not to use the land sold for specific purposes can be traced back to the decision in *Tulk v Moxhay* (1848).

More doubtful is the ability of an owner to impose a positive covenant upon anyone other than the immediate contracting party, although in some circumstances this may be possible (*Smith and Snipes Hall Farm Ltd v River Douglas Catchment Board* (1949)).

5.1.5 Resale price maintenance

Dunlop v Selfridge (1915) was an attempt to enforce resale price maintenance which failed. The practice of allowing manufacturers to fix the minimum retail price of goods was permitted by the Restrictive Trade Practices Act 1956, provided certain conditions were observed. The Resale Prices Act 1964 (now Resale Prices Act 1976) effectively put a stop to such arrangements by making the practice invalid unless sanctioned by the Restrictive Practices Court.

5.1.6 Trusts

The beneficiary under a trust is entitled to take a benefit despite being a 'volunteer' to the setting up of the trust. Although a trust involves property (land, shares, money, etc), it seemed at one stage as if the courts might be prepared to hold that the benefit of a promise in a contract could form the subject matter of a trust. If A promises B that he (A) will pay money to C in return for goods/services from B, B could hold A's promise on trust for C and enforce it on C's behalf if A fails to pay. The device was approved by the House of Lords in *Les Afréteurs Réunis SA v Walford* (1919) but has since fallen into judicial disfavour (*Re Schebsman* (1943) and *Green v Russell* (1959)) with no signs of revival.

5.1.7 Section 56 Law of Property Act 1925

The wording of this section appears to allow someone, although not named as a party to a written contract or other instrument, to enforce rights which affect property. By s 206 'property' is expressed to cover personal property as well as land.

This liberal interpretation has been championed by Lord Denning in a number of cases culminating in the decision of the Court of Appeal in *Beswick v Beswick* (1966).

Peter Beswick contracted to sell his coal merchant business to his nephew John in consideration of John:

(1) paying Peter £6-10s per week for life; and

(2) after Peter's death paying his widow £5 a week for life.

After Peter's death John made one payment of £5 to the widow and refused to pay any more. The widow sued to enforce the agreement:

(a) as administratrix of Peter's estate; and

(b) in her personal capacity.

The Court of Appeal held unanimously that she was entitled to succeed under (a) and, (by a majority) under (b) on an application of s 56. On appeal the House of Lords (in 1968) agreed that as administratrix she was entitled to enforce the agreement. However, in her personal capacity she had no such right – the word 'property' in s 56 was to be construed restrictively and should not be extended to cover contracts.

The principle of the restrictive covenant, originally derived from *Tulk v Moxhay* (1848), that a person who had notice of a restriction in an agreement affecting the use to which land could be put was bound by it, has been applied to a case involving the chartering of a ship. In *Lord Strathcona Steamship Co v Dominion Coal Co* (1926) the owner of LS chartered the vessel to X for use during the summer months for a number of years. Each November she was returned to the owner. One winter, while in the owner's possession, she was sold to Y, who resold to Z. Although Z knew of the charter to X, Z refused to deliver the ship to X for the summer season. The Privy Council held X was entitled to an injunction against Z restraining Z from using the ship in breach of the charter.	**5.1.8** Restrictions on the use of chattels

The decision has been criticised on the ground that the charterer X had no equivalent proprietory interest to that of the enforcer of a restrictive covenant over land (*Port Line Ltd v Ben Line Steamers Ltd* (1958)). Some judicial support can be found for the Strathcona decision as being 'the counterpart' in equity of the tort of 'knowing interference with contractual rights'.

Where a person is, exceptionally, able to sue on a contract to which he is not a party the normal remedies are open to him. What is the position, though, where one of the contracting parties takes action in order to enforce it? As the contracting	**5.2 Remedies**

party will himself normally have suffered no actual loss the damages awarded should be purely nominal.

It seems that the courts are prepared to use various means to ensure that in such circumstances the benefit of the contract is passed on to the third party. In *Beswick v Beswick* an order for specific performance was made and in *Snelling v John G Snelling Ltd* (1972), where third parties relied on an agreement, the court ordered a stay of proceedings and dismissed an action brought in breach of the agreement.

The Court of Appeal in *Jackson v Horizon Holidays Ltd* (1975) permitted the plaintiff who had paid for a family holiday which had turned into a disaster to obtain damages by way of compensation not only for himself but his wife and children also. The decision was criticised by the House of Lords in *Woodar Investment Development Ltd v Wimpey Construction Ltd* (1980) who said that the decision in Jackson should be confined to that special category of contract where one person contracted on behalf of a group of people for the benefit of them all.

5.3	**Reform of the doctrine of privity**

Criticism of the doctrine of privity has come from many sources as it deprives third parties of the ability to enforce rights bestowed upon them by the contract of other parties. In 1966 the Law Commission produced a report and draft Bill (Law Com No 242, Cm 3329) suggesting the following reasons for reform:

- The present law prevents effect being given to the intention of the contracting parties.

- The privity rule is unfair to third parties who may rely upon a contract that they cannot enforce.

- Third party rights are accepted in the legal systems of most other Member States of the EU and in many Commonwealth countries.

The main provisions of the draft Bill include:

- A third party will have the right to enforce a contract where the contract expressly states that a third party is able to do so or if the contract purports to confer a benefit on a third party who is expressly named.

- A right created for the benefit of a third party cannot be varied or cancelled by the contracting parties without the third party's consent once he has informed the parties that he accepts the contract or if he has acted in reliance on it.

- A third party who sued as a result of these provisions would be subjected to any defences that the contracting parties have against each other.

If the draft Bill is adopted and becomes law it will do much to overcome the existing criticisms of the doctrine of privity. The restrictions contained in the first provision (above) should help to ensure that the courts will not be inundated with cases from any person who might be regarded as a third party.

Chapter 6

The Discharge of Contracts

There are four ways in which liability under a valid contract may come to an end: performance, agreement, frustration and breach.

If both parties fully and exactly perform their obligations under the contract they will both be discharged. Their liabilities have ended. If one party has agreed to perform a task in return for payment of a specified sum the task must be completed before the obligation to pay arises. This is often known as the rule in *Cutter v Powell* (1795). Cutter, who served as a second mate on a ship sailing from Jamaica to Liverpool, was to be paid 30 guineas for the voyage. When the ship was 19 days short of its destination Cutter died. His widow sued on his behalf for a proportion of the 30 guineas in respect of the work he had done prior to his death. It was held that she was entitled to nothing. The task had never been completed, therefore, nothing was payable.

6.1 Discharge by performance

The following are exceptions to this rule: contract promises severable, prevention of performance, acceptance of partial performance, substantial performance.

In *Cutter v Powell* the promises made by the parties were treated as interdependent. On the true construction of a contract it may be that promises are seen as separate or independent of each other. The courts tend to view, for example, contracts of repair in this light.

6.1.1 Contract promises severable

If one party, without just cause, prevents the other from completing performance of the contract the party so prevented may treat himself as discharged. In addition to treating himself as free he may either bring an action for damages or claim on a *quantum meruit* for the work he has done up to this point (*Planche v Colburn* (1831)).

6.1.2 Prevention of performance

In this context, a party who tenders or offers performance is in the same position as if he had actually performed. He is discharged from any further contractual liability (*Startup v Macdonald* (1843)).

Note, however, that in the case of an obligation to pay money a tender of payment, if refused, does not result in discharge. If sued the tenderer should pay the sum into court.

6.1.3	Acceptance of partial performance	It may be possible to infer a fresh agreement between the parties under which one voluntarily agrees to accept and pay for an incomplete performance by the other. The essential feature of this exception is that the inferred agreement is genuine and voluntary. Did the party upon whom the benefit was conferred have a real choice in deciding whether or not to accept the benefit? Buildings (*Sumpter v Hedges* (1898)) or repair work, or services performed (*Cutter v Powell*) cannot be given back. The circumstances in which it is possible to argue that this exception applies are therefore very narrow, eg where a seller delivers to a buyer the wrong quantities of goods (see s 30 Sale of Goods Act 1979).
6.1.4	Substantial performance	From *Boone v Eyre* (1779) developed a rule that where performance was substantially carried out by one party, although there were some minor discrepancies, the other was obliged to keep to his side of the bargain. He could not refuse to pay for work done. His remedy lay in claiming compensation for the extent to which he had been deprived of an exact or precise performance by the other. The rule uses a different conceptual approach but it results in the same outcome as if the deviation from exact or precise performance were termed a breach of warranty (see Chapter 3, 3.3.1 above). It is a question of fact whether the performance offered is 'substantial'. If the performance is so poor that it amounts to a serious breach of that party's obligations (breach of condition) he can recover nothing for the work he has done, ie the rule in *Cutter v Powell* applies (see *Bolton v Mahadeva* (1972)).
6.1.5	Time for performance	If a contract does not stipulate when it is to be performed then it must be performed within a 'reasonable' time. What is reasonable is a question of fact to be determined in each case. When a time is stipulated but not met, what is the position? At common law the other party could treat the breach as substantial and regard himself as discharged. However, the view of equity (which prevails) is that 'time is not of the essence of the contract'. It is only a minor term (warranty), breach of which does not operate to discharge the other party from liability. Exceptions to this rule, ie situations where time is 'of the essence' are:

- where the contract expressly indicates that the time for performance is of major significance;

- where the nature of the contract or the context shows by implication that the parties intend time to be of the essence;

- where, one party having delayed unreasonably, the other 'makes time of the essence' by giving the former reasonable notice to complete performance by a certain time.

What has been created by agreement may be ended by agreement. In the same way as liability is made so it can be discharged. The agreement which discharges liability must possess all the elements of a valid and enforceable contract: agreement, consideration (or deed) and intention to be legally binding. The question of formalities also needs to be looked at.

In the case of a contract which is wholly or partly executory on both sides it is clear where the consideration comes from for the discharging agreement. Each party gives up his legally enforceable rights in return for the other doing the same.

Where a contract has been completely executed by one party, (he is already discharged through performance), an agreement to release the other is unsupported by consideration. So, if A has, under a contract, delivered goods to B who has failed to pay, A's agreement to release B from liability for the price, either completely or in part, is a gratuitous and therefore unenforceable promise by A. It would be enforceable if A's release of B is in a deed, or if the agreement (accord) is supported by a fresh consideration (satisfaction) from B. When we discussed 'consideration' in the formation of contracts, this was what was referred to as the rule in *Pinnel's Case* (1602).

It was believed at one time that to be effective the fresh consideration must be executed before discharge took place. In *British Russian Gazette Ltd v Associated Newspapers Ltd* (1933) it was held that discharge is effective from the moment the deal is struck and the promise made. Thus, executory consideration is as valid in this context as it is when liability is first created.

The general rule is that no special formalities are necessary to discharge liability, whether the original contract was made orally, in writing or even by deed (*Berry v Berry* (1929)). Difficulties arise only when the first contract is one which is valid or enforceable only if certain formalities have been complied with, eg contracts caught by s 4 Statute of Frauds 1677 or s 2 Law of Property (Miscellaneous Provisions) Act 1989.

Formalities may be required in the discharging contract but this depends upon what the parties intend it to accomplish. They may intend:

- to extinguish their agreement entirely; or

- to modify or vary some term(s) without altering the substance of the agreement; or

- to extinguish the original agreement and to substitute an entirely new agreement in its place.

6.2   Discharge by agreement

6.2.1   Bilateral discharge

6.2.2   Unilateral discharge

6.2.3   Formalities

In the first situation no formalities are necessary. An oral agreement extinguishes liability. In the second situation an oral modification leaves the original agreement unaffected. Alteration of the terms takes effect only if the formalities required by the governing statute are complied with. In the third situation the original agreement is extinguished by a subsequent oral agreement but the new agreement, intended to be substituted for the old, will not take effect unless the appropriate formalities are observed.

6.2.4   Waiver

A waiver occurs where one party, A, agrees at the request of the other, B, not to enforce a right to which A is entitled under the contract. As A's promise is unsupported by consideration from B there should be no objection at common law to A withdrawing, at any, time his promise to waive his legal rights. Despite this such arrangements have been upheld, the issue of consideration being conveniently ignored.

As a waiver is effective when made orally a further objection can be raised in the second situation above, when the courts seem prepared to designate as a waiver what looks suspiciously like the variation of a contract term. In theory, a variation is an alteration of a contractual obligation agreed by both parties, whereas a waiver is an indulgence or forbearance given as a favour by one party to the other.

If the buyer of a consignment of goods due for delivery on 1 March asks the seller to hold up delivery until 1 April and the seller agrees, is this a variation or a waiver? It is likely to be treated as a waiver with the following results.

- The waiver is binding on the party for whose benefit it was granted. The buyer cannot reject the goods arguing the seller is in breach in not having delivered on 1 March.

- The seller is bound by the arrangement and cannot refuse to deliver on 1 April on the grounds that the buyer is in breach.

The waiver may be withdrawn by the party giving it provided he gives a clear indication to the other of his intention to resume his legal rights and allows a reasonable period for readjustment to take place (*Charles Rickards Ltd v Oppenheim* (1950)), where Denning, LJ referred to the principle as '... a kind of estoppel'. Although developed prior to the doctrine of promissory estoppel (see Chapter 1, 1.2.11 above) the nature and effect of a waiver is similar.

6.3   Discharge by frustration

After a contract is made but before the time for performance arrives circumstances may change. Through no fault of the parties the contract may become impossible or illegal to perform, or the purpose or object of the contract, which the parties had in mind when making it, is no longer attainable.

In these circumstances it is said that the contract is 'frustrated'. Where the doctrine of frustration applies both parties are discharged from their contractual liabilities as from the date of the frustrating event.

6.3.1   Theoretical basis of the doctrine

Originally, the common law position, called the rule in *Paradine v Jane* (1647), was that if a person bound himself to do a certain thing by an agreement freely entered into he could not escape liability merely because circumstances changed and performance became pointless or even impossible. From *Taylor v Caldwell* (1863) developed a line of cases which altered the position and gave rise to what is now called the doctrine of frustration. At first, termination of liability was said to be based on an implied term, ie what the parties presumably intended to happen but did not expressly mention in their contract. Later the test for intervention became objective. Was the change in circumstances so radical that the contract was essentially a different contract to that which the parties had originally undertaken? (*Davis Contractors Ltd v Fareham UDC* (1956)).

6.3.2   Frustrating events

- Physical impossibility

    In *Taylor v Caldwell* the plaintiff agreed to hire a concert hall from the defendant on specified dates. Before the first of these arrived the concert hall was destroyed by fire, neither party being to blame. It was held that the physical destruction of the subject matter of the contract discharged both parties from any further liability.

    The death and sometimes the illness of one of the parties may lead to the application of the doctrine if the contract calls for the performance of skilled services by that party on a particular date. In the case of a normal contract of employment a lengthy illness would have the same effect (*Notcutt v Universal Equipment Co Ltd* (1986)).

- Unavailability of the subject matter

    In *Bank Line Ltd v Arthur Capel & Co* (1919), for example, a ship was requisitioned for the remainder of a charter party. The position is more difficult to resolve when the unavailability is temporary and its duration uncertain (*Jackson v Union Marine Insurance Co Ltd* (1874)). The court will decide the question of frustration without taking into account what transpired after the frustrating event.

- Legal impossibility

  A contract may become impossible to perform lawfully due either to a change in the law or to a change in circumstances. An event such as the outbreak of war may have the effect of rendering a contract illegal at common law because it involves 'trading with the enemy'.

- Frustration of the common venture

  From the 'coronation cases' of 1903 the doctrine of frustration was applied to cases where, although literal performance was possible, it had become futile because the whole purpose of the contract, acknowledged by both parties, was no longer attainable. In *Krell v Henry* (1903) the defendant agreed to hire a room from the plaintiff in order to view the coronation procession of Edward VII. When the procession was cancelled due to the King's illness the Court of Appeal held that the contract was frustrated. In consequence, the defendant was not liable for the hiring fee. If, however, there are two objects as the foundation of the contract and only one is destroyed, the contract will not be frustrated (*Herne Bay Steamboat Co v Hutton* (1903)).

  Note that it is necessary to distinguish between the object which is the foundation of the contract and the motive one party had for entering into the contract. Merely because the contract has become more difficult or more costly to perform does not mean the doctrine will apply (*Davis Contractors Ltd v Fareham UDC* (1956)).

6.3.3   Points to note

The parties may expressly provide in the contract for the occurrence of a particular event and allocate the risk accordingly. The court will not then intervene. The event which the parties have provided for may turn out to be far more catastrophic in nature than they had contemplated. It is then a question of construction of the contract whether the provision covers the event or whether the doctrine intervenes to discharge the parties (*Jackson v Union Marine Insurance Co Ltd*).

The doctrine applies only where the event is beyond the control of the parties to bring it about. If 'self-induced' the contract will not be discharged (*Maritime National Fish Ltd v Ocean Trawlers Ltd* (1935)). The courts have been hesitant about applying the doctrine to leases of land on the ground that a lease is more than a contract. It creates a legal estate in land (*Cricklewood Property and Investments Trust Ltd v Leighton's Investment Trust Ltd* (1945)). More recently a majority of the House of Lords in *National Carriers Ltd v Panalpina (Northern)*

Ltd (1981) stated that frustration of leases could in theory occur, although the circumstances would, in practice be rare.

Frustration automatically brings the contract to an end so that both parties are discharged from any further obligations. At common law it leaves unpaid a party who has performed part of his obligations in circumstances when the contract is one where full performance is required before payment is due (*Appleby v Myers* (1867)). It also leaves unaffected obligations which should have been performed (but were not) prior to the frustrating event (*Chandler v Webster* (1904)).

6.3.4   The legal effect of frustration

However, in *Fibrosa SA v Fairbairn Lawson Combe Barbour Ltd* (1943) the House of Lords held that money paid in advance of the frustrating event could be recovered if there was a total failure of consideration. The case demonstrated the inadequacy of the common law to deal fairly with the problem and resulted in the Law Reform (Frustrated Contracts) Act 1943. The main features of the Act, which applies only to discharge through frustration, are as follows.

- Whether there is a total or a partial failure of consideration money paid in advance of the frustrating event is recoverable and money due to be paid before the frustrating event ceases to be payable (s 1(2)).

- Where the party to whom pre-payments are paid or payable incurred expenses in performing his side of the contract prior to the frustrating event the court may award him such a sum as it thinks just to cover those expenses. The maximum is limited to the amounts paid or payable in advance (s 1(2)).

- If one party prior to frustration performs the contract, wholly or in part, conferring a valuable benefit (other than money) on the other before the time of discharge the court may order that other to pay a sum which the court thinks just, not exceeding the value of the benefit (s 1(3)).

  In *BP Exploration Co (Libya) Ltd v Hunt (No 2)* (1979), affirmed by the House of Lords in 1983, Goff, J considered s 1(3), saying that the words 'valuable benefit' established a ceiling above which an award could not be made. The 'just sum' might be as it was in this case, a lower figure.

- the Act does not apply to certain contracts, namely,
  (i) carriage of goods by sea, including charter-parties, except a time charterparty or charterparty by demise;
  (ii) insurance contracts:

(iii) contracts for the sale of goods when the contract is caught by s 7 Sale of Goods Act 1979.

6.4   Discharge by breach

A breach of contract always entitles the injured party to damages (see Chapter 6). The question to be addressed here is when will it entitle the injured party to terminate the contract. The answer is that the injured party has this right in two situations only:

- when at some point between making the contract and fully performing it the party in default repudiates the contract;

- when the party in default commits a fundamental breach of the contract.

6.4.1   Repudiation

Repudiation occurs where a party abandons the contract either expressly or by implication. An example of an express repudiation can be seen in *Hochster v De La Tour* (1853) where the defendant engaged the plaintiff to act as a courier for a tour abroad, starting on 1 June. On 11 May the defendant contacted the plaintiff to say he no longer wanted to employ the plaintiff. A 'repudiation by implication' arises when a defendant acts in such a way as to make it impossible for him to carry out the contract with the plaintiff. Repudiation is often referred to as 'anticipatory breach'.

6.4.2   Fundamental breach

A breach is fundamental when either the term which is broken is a serious and important obligation in the contract or when the consequences resulting from a breach are serious (see Chapter 3, 3.3 *et seq* above).

6.4.3   Consequences of repudiation/ fundamental breach

In these situations the injured party has a choice.

- He has an immediate right to treat the contract as ended and to instigate an action for damages if desired. This was done successfully by the plaintiff in *Hochster v De La Tour* prior to 1 June.

- He may choose not to accept the breach as discharging him from the contract, instead holding the defaulting party bound in the hope that, in the case of anticipatory breach, he will change his mind. If this option is selected the innocent party must himself remain ready and willing to carry out his side of the bargain. The contract is kept alive as a consequence of his response and all his contractual rights with it (*White and Carter (Councils) Ltd v McGregor* (1962)).

This whole area is fraught with potential problems for the innocent party, following what may appear to them have been a repudiatory breach by the other party:

- first there is always a risk that the courts will view the wrongdoer's breach as something less than a repudiatory breach (*Hong Kong Fir Shipping* (1962) and *Hansa Nord* (1975)). If the 'innocent' party elects to treat themselves as 'discharged' in such circumstances, they lay themselves open to an action for wrongful repudiation;

- if the wrongdoer has actually committed a repudiatory breach, recent cases suggest that it is sometimes difficult to ascertain exactly what may constitute 'acceptance' of repudiation by the innocent party. In *Vitol v Norelf Ltd* (1966) the House of Lords reversed the Court of Appeal's decision that the defendant's failure to perform his own obligations did not constitute acceptance of the plaintiff's repudiation. It was held that in this case whether or not the innocent party had elected to terminate the contract was a question of fact within the exclusive jurisdiction of the arbitrator;

- what is clear is that once an innocent party has affirmed the contract, by refusing to accept the other's wrongful repudiation, he cannot afterwards change his mind if circumstances arise when he may wish to do so. If, for example, a subsequent event discharges the contract by frustration he will lose his right to damages for breach of contract (*Avery v Bowden* (1855)) the plaintiffs had failed to accept an anticipatory breach by the defendants then the outbreak of war frustrated the contract and their right to a remedy was lost.

Chapter 7

The Remedies for Breach of Contract

The principal remedy available at common law for breach of contract is damages. The law also permits a plaintiff, in appropriate circumstances, to sue for an agreed sum or to bring an action on a *quantum meruit*. Additionally, equity will in some circumstances offer relief through the remedies of specific performance and the injunction.

7.1 Damages

Damages are financial compensation for breach of contract. They are usually intended to put the parties into the position that they would have been in had the contract been performed properly.

Two ideas are of particular significance. The first is the concept of 'remoteness of damage' which seeks to address the question: for what kind of loss may a plaintiff claim? Some kinds of loss are considered to be too remote a consequence of the breach to be the proper subject matter of a claim. The second deals with the value to be placed on the plaintiff's loss and is referred to as the 'measure of damages'. It addresses the question: what is the amount of the plaintiff's loss? The answer is concerned with the approaches used when calculating the damages.

The question of remoteness of damage was first considered in *Hadley v Baxendale* (1854). The plaintiff owned a flour mill. It ceased to work because of a broken crankshaft. The broken shaft was given to a carrier to transport to a manufacturer to be used as the pattern for a new one. The carrier promised to deliver it the next day. Owing to the carrier's neglect, delivery was substantially delayed and the mill was closed down for longer than would otherwise have been the case. The mill owner sued the carrier for damages for loss of profit during the excess time the mill remained idle. The loss of profit was held not to be recoverable as it was too remote a consequence of the breach.

7.1.1 Remoteness of damage

From this case two rules emerged.

- Rule 1

  The plaintiff is entitled to compensation for a loss which arises naturally, in the usual course of things, as a result of the breach, ie one which is reasonably foreseeable as a consequence of a breach of this nature.

- Rule 2

The plaintiff is entitled to be compensated for a loss not foreseeable under Rule 1 (ie a 'special' or 'abnormal' loss) provided that the loss was reasonably foreseeable by the parties in the light of the special circumstances known to them at the time when the contract was made.

Note, that in *Hadley v Baxendale* the carrier was not told that the plaintiff had no spare shaft or that the mill had ceased work. Although the carrier's delay was undoubtedly the cause of the plaintiff's loss, it was not reasonably foreseeable by the defendant. This kind of loss (loss of profit) is not a loss which happens automatically when a carrier delays (Rule 1), neither was it within the carrier's contemplation when he entered into the contract as the plaintiff had not told him of the 'special circumstances', ie that the mill had stopped work (Rule 2).

The Court of Appeal reconsidered the Rules in *Hadley v Baxendale* in *Victoria Laundry (Windsor) Ltd v Newman Industries* (1949) and stated that knowledge possessed by the parties is of two varieties. The first is 'imputed', that is what everyone is taken to know (Rule 1). The second is 'actual', that is knowledge the parties have acquired concerning the particular circumstances of a case (Rule 2).

In *Kemp v Intasun Holidays Ltd* (1987) it was held that a casual mention by a wife of her husband's susceptibility to asthma attacks when booking the family holiday did not give 'actual' knowledge of this fact to the defendants. There was a place on the form for customers to record their 'Special Requests' which had been left blank.

In *Victoria Laundry* the Court of Appeal, in applying the test of 'reasonable foreseeability' indicated that the test of remoteness was the same in both contract and tort. However, the position was restated by the House of Lords in *Koufos v Czarnikow Ltd, The Heron II* (1969), where the terminology 'reasonably foreseeable' was judged appropriate to tort only, and 'within the reasonable contemplation of the parties' was to be applied for breach of contract cases. In essence, the difference is that a tortfeasor is liable for any loss which is reasonably foreseeable even if its occurrence is unlikely (ie the risk of it happening is low). In contract the defendant is liable only for loss caused by a breach which he, as a reasonable man, may be supposed to contemplate as the likely or probable consequence (ie the risk of it happening is a real danger or serious possibility).

If a particular kind of loss is within the reasonable contemplation of the parties it does not matter that the extent of the loss is greater than expected (*H Parsons (Livestock) Ltd v Uttley Ingham & Co Ltd* (1978)).

The object of awarding damages is to compensate the plaintiff not to punish the defendant. The plaintiff may be compensated in respect of his:

7.1.2   Measure of damages

- expectation loss, the purpose being to put the plaintiff financially where he would have been if the defendant had performed the contract properly;

- reliance loss, the object being to restore the plaintiff financially to the position he was in before he entered into the contract;

- (exceptionally) distress and disappointment, where the plaintiff is awarded damages to console him for what he has had to put up with as a consequence of breach.

One way of measuring this loss is to compare the difference between what the plaintiff actually received and what he should have received. The 'market rule' applies to the selling and buying of goods or services. Thus, if a buyer defaults by refusing to accept and pay for goods, so that the seller is forced to sell them elsewhere, the seller's *prima facie* measure of damages is the difference between the market price and the contract price at the time of the buyer's breach (s 50 Sale of Goods Act 1979). Similar rules apply in reverse where the seller is in breach (s 51).

7.1.2.1   Expectation loss

Note that the Sale of Goods Act measure of damages, presuming that the resale or repurchase takes place at the time of breach and at the market price, is only a *prima facie* rule, and will not be used where inappropriate, eg where there is no 'market'. See *WL Thompson Ltd v Robinson (Gunmakers) Ltd* (1955), *Charter v Sullivan* (1957) and *Lazenby Garages Ltd v Wright* (1976).

Sometimes, the court will award damages to enable a plaintiff to 'cure' the defect in the defendant's performance of his contractual obligations. In *Radford v De Froberville* (1978), the defendant had contracted to erect a boundary wall. Damages based on the cost of construction were awarded to the plaintiff. In contrast to this in *Watts v Morrow* (1991) the Court of Appeal refused to award the plaintiff the cost of repairs to a house (£34,000) which the plaintiff had purchased on the faith of a negligently prepared survey by the defendant. Instead, the plaintiff was given the difference between the true value of the house in its defective state at the date of purchase and the price paid by the plaintiff (£15,000). This placed the plaintiff financially where he would have been had the survey been properly carried out. To award him the cost of repairs would have amounted to holding that the defendant had warranted the house needed no repairs. In fact the defendants obligation had been to carry out the survey with reasonable skill and care.

The issue of whether damages should be calculated on a difference in value or cost of cure basis was disputed in *Ruxley Electronics & Construction Ltd v Forsyth* (1995). In this case contractors had built a swimming pool to a maximum depth which was nine inches shallower than the contractual specification. The House of Lords, reversing the decision of the Court of Appeal, held that this defect did not affect the value of the pool. Furthermore, as the pool was still fit for its intended purpose, which included diving into the pool from the side, it was unnecessary to award the £21,560 claimed for reconstruction. On this basis the only damages payable were £2,500 for 'loss of amenity'.

Although it may be very difficult in some situations for the court to calculate the amount of the damages, the plaintiff cannot be denied compensation for this reason and an award must be made (*Chaplin v Hicks* (1911)).

7.1.2.2	*Reliance loss*

If a plaintiff chooses to claim damages calculated on this basis he may include expenses incurred prior to the contract being made. In *Anglia Television v Reed* (1971) the Court of Appeal held the plaintiffs entitled to damages for all their expenditure in preparation for the making of a film in which the defendant was to play the leading role. He pulled out at the last moment and the plaintiffs had no option but to cancel the project.

In *Anglia Television* the award assumed that had the film been made it would have covered its costs. The onus is on the plaintiff to establish this (*CCC Films (London) Ltd v Impact Quadrant Films Ltd* (1984)). It is open to the defendant to show that on an 'expectation' basis there was no loss, because the plaintiff had made such a bad bargain. The expenditure would have been wasted whether or not the defendant broke the contract (*C & P Haulage v Middleton* (1983)).

7.1.2.3	*Distress and disappointment*

Historically no damages were payable for injured feelings resulting from a breach of contract (*Addis v Gramophone Company Ltd* (1909)). This rule has been relaxed in special types of contract where the object of the contract was 'to provide entertainment and enjoyment' (Denning MR in *Jarvis v Swan Tours* (1973)) or where the contract which has been broken was itself '*a contract to provide peace of mind or freedom from mental distress*' (Dillon LJ in *Bliss v South East Thames Regional Health Authority*).

Thus damages have been awarded for mental distress in breaches involving: holidays which have not lived up to tour operators' claims (*Jarvis v Swan Tours* (1973)), where a solicitor failed to obtain an injunction which would have spared the plaintiff from molestation by a former boyfriend (*Heywood v Wellers* (1976)), where discomfort was caused by living in a property which the surveyor had stated was in good order (*Watts v Morrow* (1991)) and where (as above) loss of 'amenity' arose as a consequence of failing to build a swimming pool to its full specification (*Ruxley Electronics* (1995)).

However injured feelings arising from the breach of an employment contract cannot be compensated by damages (*Addis* and *Bliss* above) and as a matter of policy, damages for mental distress are not available for breach of a purely commercial contract (*Hayes v James & Charles Dodd* (1990)). To decide otherwise would 'open the floodgates' to litigation and would introduce an unnecessary degree of uncertainty regarding potential liability for the breach of business contracts.

A plaintiff is under a duty to act as a reasonable person would to minimise his loss (*Brace v Calder* (1895)). He will not be awarded damages for any part of his loss which the defendant can show was a consequence of the plaintiff's failure to mitigate (*British Westinghouse Electric Co v Underground Electric Railway Co of London* (1912)). The duty extends only to behaving as a reasonable and prudent person would in the circumstances. The plaintiff is not obliged to protect the defendant from the results of his breach by undertaking a risky or hazardous course of action (*Pilkington v Wood* (1953)).

7.1.3   Mitigation

In the case of an anticipatory breach (see Chapter 5, 5.4.3 above) where the plaintiff chooses not to treat the breach as discharging him from the contract, opting instead to confirm it, he is under no duty to mitigate (*White & Carter (Councils) Ltd v McGregor* (1962)).

However Lord Reid observed: 'it may well be that, if it can be shown that a person has no legitimate interest, financial or otherwise, in performing the contract rather than claiming damages, he ought not to be allowed to saddle the other party with an additional burden with no benefit to himself.'

This opinion was subsequently applied in the case of *Clea Shipping Corp v Bulk Oil International: The Alaskan Trader* (1984). Here the owners of a vessel refused to accept the charterer's repudiation and kept it at anchor and fully crewed until the charter was due to expire and then the boat was scrapped. The court held that charter fees for the period following repudiation did not have to be paid. The owners had no legitimate interest in keeping the vessel at anchor, fully crewed, when they knew that the charterers would not require it.

7.1.4 Liquidated damages and penalties

Sometimes when a breach occurs it is difficult to calculate the amount of the plaintiff's loss. In such circumstances the parties, anticipating this difficulty, may agree in the contract itself that a specified sum will be payable on breach. If the sum is a genuine attempt to estimate the amount of the plaintiff's loss it is properly referred to as a 'liquidated damages' clause. In the event of breach the plaintiff is entitled to recover this sum and this sum alone. He cannot be heard to argue that the amount should be disregarded because his actual loss turned out to be greater than was originally estimated.

If the sum stipulated is out of all proportion to the likely amount of the plaintiff's loss, the object being to punish the defendant, to use it as a threat, forcing him to complete the contract, it is called a 'penalty'. The sum is not recoverable. The plaintiff is free to sue the defendant for damages in the normal way, which means he will need to establish the value of his loss.

The leading case which offers guidance on how to distinguish between liquidated damages and penalties is *Dunlop Pneumatic Tyre Co Ltd v New Garage & Motor Co Ltd* (1915). Here the defendant agreed, *inter alia*, not to tamper with marks on the plaintiff's products, not to supply persons on a 'suspended' list and not to sell the goods below a fixed minimum price. For contravention of any of these the defendant became liable to pay the plaintiff the sum of £5. The House of Lords held the amount of £5 was liquidated damages. Although it might appear large for a single item sold in breach of the agreement the effect on Dunlop's organisation, once the news became known among traders, was incalculable. The £5 was not, in the circumstances, an extravagant amount.

In his judgment Lord Dunedin summarised the position and set out rules for guidance.

- The sum is a penalty if it is unconscionable in amount and greater than the greatest loss which could result from the breach.

- If on failure to pay a sum under the contract a larger sum becomes payable, the larger sum must be a penalty.

- Subject to the above, if a single sum is payable in respect of one event only there is a presumption that it is liquidated damages. If it is payable in respect of several breaches, varying in gravity, the presumption is that the sum is a penalty.

- A sum is not prevented from being liquidated damages because an accurate estimate of the plaintiff's loss is impossible. If not unreasonable in amount, it is likely to be acceptable.

In *Ford Motor Co v Armstrong* (1915) under an agreement similar to that in *Dunlop* the Ford Motor Co sued the defendant, a retailer, for breach where the agreed sum for every contravention of the restrictions was £250. The Court of Appeal held this sum to be a penalty.

The rules against penalty clauses apply only where the sum is payable on breach. They will not operate when the amount is payable on the happening of some other event (*Exports Credits Guarantee Department v Universal Oil Products Co* (1983)).

In order that the plaintiff is not overcompensated the court sometimes needs to take into account the incidence of taxation. Damages awarded for loss of commercial profits are taxable as if they were the plaintiff's income.

7.1.5   Taxation

By s 1 Law Reform (Contributory Negligence) Act 1945 where a plaintiff suffers damage partly as a result of his own fault the court may reduce the damages payable to him according to the court's assessment of his share of responsibility for the damage. In *Forsikringsaktieselskapet Vesta v Butcher* (1988) the Court of Appeal confirmed that this section applies to a situation where the defendant's liability in contract is the same as his liability in the tort of negligence independently of the existence of any contract.

7.1.6   Contributory negligence

The Act does not apply to other situations where the defendant's liability arises from:

- some contractual provision which does not depend on negligence on the part of the defendant (*Barclays Bank v Fairclough Building Ltd* (1994));

- a contractual obligation expressed in terms of taking care (but this does not correspond to a common law duty of care existing independently of contract).

Note here that the Law Commission in 1993 recommended legislation to extend the court's discretion to apportion damages (Law Com No 219).

Where the plaintiff has performed his part of the bargain and the only liability outstanding is the defendant's obligation to pay a specified sum of money (eg the price of goods which the plaintiff has sold and delivered to the defendant) the plaintiff may sue for this sum instead of bringing an action for damages.

7.1.7   Action for an agreed sum

The action for a liquidated sum, although simple to bring, suffers from two defects. First, the rules relating to remoteness do not apply, so that the plaintiff is unable to recover in respect of loss consequent upon non-payment. Second, the debt does not at common law carry interest from the date it became due: affirmed by the House of Lords in *President of India v La Pintada Cia Navegacion SA* (1984). However, under s 35A Supreme Court Act 1981, as amended, the court has a discretion to award interest when giving judgment for an agreed sum. Also, the parties themselves may use their freedom of contract to stipulate for interest on late payment of the agreed sum.

7.2   *Quantum meruit*

The primary rule is that payment should be determined according to the terms of the contract. However, this quasi-contractual action (*quantum meruit* means 'as much as is deserved') is available to a plaintiff in the following circumstances.

- Under the contract the price has not been fixed but the parties have impliedly agreed a reasonable price is payable, eg s 8 Sale of Goods Act 1979.

- Partial performance has been voluntarily accepted (see Chapter 5, 5.1.3 above).

- The defendant prevents the plaintiff from completing performance (see Chapter 5, 5.1.2 above).

If the action is successful the court will award the plaintiff a reasonable sum for the goods supplied or the services performed.

7.3   Equitable remedies

The remedies of specific performance and injunction, being equitable, are awarded at the discretion of the court. They cannot be claimed as of right.

Specific performance is an order of the court addressed to the defendant compelling him to carry out the contract made with the plaintiff. An injunction is an order directing the plaintiff to refrain from a continuing breach of duty. In the contractual context it may be granted to restrain breach of a negative stipulation in a contract (ie a promise not to do something by one party).

7.3.1   Specific performance

In deciding whether to grant or withhold the remedy the court will take the following into account:

- Damages inadequate

  Damages are normally an adequate remedy for breach of a contract of sale of goods, so that specific performance will not be awarded unless the goods in question are unavailable elsewhere.

Specific performance is usually awarded in respect of breach of a contract to sell land. No two pieces of land are exactly the same. In *Beswick v Beswick* the House of Lords ordered specific performance of an obligation to pay money, because in the special circumstances of the case damages would be inadequate (see Chapter 4, 4.2 above).

- Hardship

  Even in the case of a contract for the sale of land the remedy may be refused if to order it would cause exceptional hardship to the defendant (*Patel v Ali* (1984)).

- Constant supervision

  If it would be impractical for the court to oversee the proper performance of the contract no order will be made (*Ryan v Mutual Tontine Westminster Chambers Association* (1893)), where the contract contained an obligation to provide a resident porter to service a block of flats.

- Contracts for personal service

  The court will not enforce a contract of this nature, eg employment, by compelling one person to work with another.

- Mutuality

  Specific performance will not be ordered unless there is 'mutuality' or balance between the parties; that is unless the court could also force the plaintiff to carry out his side of the bargain. Thus, an order will not be granted:

  (i) in respect of a gratuitous promise under seal;

  (ii) in favour of a minor who is not liable on the contract;

  (iii) where the plaintiff's part of the bargain is the performance of personal services.

7.3.2   Injunction

An injunction will not be ordered when to do so would amount to specific performance of the contract by a different name, eg to compel the performance of a contract for personal service. In *Page One Records Ltd v Britton* (1968) the court refused to order an injunction restraining the pop group 'The Troggs' from appointing a new manager in place of the current manager, the plaintiff company. It would not have been right to make the defendants continue to employ a manager in whom they no longer had trust and confidence.

Where the injunction to prevent breach of a negative stipulation would encourage rather than force the defendant to perform the contract with the plaintiff it may be granted. In *Warner Bros v Nelson* (1937) the actress Bette Davis agreed with Warner Bros that she would not work as an actress for anyone except them for a period of one year. In breach of this she agreed to work for another film company. Warner Bros were successful in obtaining an injunction to prevent this happening.

The Law of Contract

The essentials of a legally binding contract include:

- agreement formed by offer and acceptance;

- consideration or form;

- intention to be legally bound.

Formation of contracts

Further requirements for the enforcement of contracts:

- capacity;

- legality;

- genuine consent of the parties – destroyed by – misrepresentation, duress, undue influence or, in limited circumstances, mistake.

Note: while most contracts can be made informally, by word of mouth, in writing or by conduct, a few require a special format.

Traditionally agreement has been analysed in terms of offer and acceptance, thus an agreement is formed when an offer made by the offeror is unequivocally accepted by the offeree. Today a more flexible approach is sometimes adopted (*Gibson v Manchester City Council* (1978); *Trentham Ltd v Archital Luxfer Ltd* (1993)).

Agreement

Essential features:

- must be certain (*White v Bluett* (1853));

- can be made by word of mouth, in writing or by conduct (see auction sales);

- must be communicated to the offeree before acceptance (*R v Clarke* (1927));

- can be made to an individual, a specified group of individuals or to the world at large;

- may lead to a unilateral or bilateral contract:

    unilateral – obligations imposed on offeror only if accepted by compliance with specified act of offeree);

    bilateral – obligations on both parties from outset.

Offer

Invitation to treat

Offer must be distinguished from invitations to treat as they simply invite offers:

> eg displays (*Pharmaceutical Society v Boots* (1953); *Fisher v Bell* (1961));
>
> advertisements – but depends upon wording (*Partridge v Crittenden* (1968));
>
> mere supply of information (*Harvey v Facey* (1893); *Gibson v Manchester City* (1979));
>
> statement of intention (*Harris v Nickerson* (1873)).

Tenders

May be:

> definite offers – leads to contract if accepted; or
>
> standing offers – separate contract formed each time an order is placed (*GNR v Witham* (1873)).

Referential bids are invalid if inconsistent with a request for fixed bids (*Harvela Ltd v Royal Bank of Canada* (1985)).

An offer comes to an end when accepted, when rejected, when a counter-offer is made, through lapse of time, by death of offeror or offeree before acceptance or on the failure of a condition.

Revocation

In the absence of an option, an offer may be revoked any time before acceptance (*Payne v Cave* (1789)) but revocation must be communicated to the offeree (*Byrne v Van Tienhoven* (1880)); this can be through a reliable third party (*Dickinson v Dodds* (1876)).

The revocation of an offer in a unilateral contract made to the world at large may be effective by a similar display (*Shuey v USA* (1875)) and revocation may be ineffective once the offeree has started to perform (*Errington v Errington & Woods* (1952)).

Acceptance

The offeree must accept the offer unequivocally as it stands otherwise a counter-offer is made and this will destroy the original offer (*Hyde v Wrench* (1840)). However a request for information is not a counter-offer (*Stevenson v McClean* (1880)).

Acceptance may be by conduct (*Brogden v Metropolitan Railway Co* (1877)) and note the effect in 'battle of the forms' situations (*Butler Machine Tool Co Ltd v Ex-Cell-O Corporation* (1979)).

Manner of acceptance stipulated in the offer must be complied with if mandatory but if it is only directory, another method of acceptance, which does not disadvantage the offeror – will suffice (*Manchester Diocesan Council for Education v Commercial & General Investments Ltd* (1970)).

Acceptance must be communicated to the offeror by some positive act. Silence will not normally constitute acceptance (*Felthouse v Bindley* (1862)).

Exceptions:

- unilateral contracts where acceptance is by performance of specified act (*Carlill's Case);*

- when postal rule applies – acceptance communicated when letter properly posted (*Adams v Lindsell* (1818), *Household Fire Insurance v Grant* (1879)), unless an express intention to the contrary by the offeror overrides the postal rule (*Holwell Securities v Hughes* (1974)).

When instantaneous/electronic communications are used the contract is formed where the acceptance is received (*Entores v Miles Far Eastern Corporation* (1955) (re a telex)).

Instantaneous communications

Also see *The Brimnes* (1975) and note – in *Brinkibon v Stahag Stahl* (1983) Lord Wilberforce stated: 'there is no universal rule' regarding the moment when messages transmitted by these means will be deemed to have been 'communicated' to the other party – much depends upon the circumstances of individual cases, eg if a message is left on an answer machine or electronic mailbox, or if it is delivered by fax or telex.

In order to be recognised as a contract, an agreement must either take the form of a bargain to which each party contributes (be supported by consideration) or contained in a deed. Rules re consideration include:

Consideration

- consideration must be real (sufficient) – over and above existing legal duties (*Collins v Godefroy* (1831)) or contractual obligations (*Stilk v Myrick* (1809)) unless:

  (i) the exception in *Williams v Roffey* (1990) applies, when the promise of extra payment for the performance of existing contractual obligations will be enforceable in the absence of economic duress, providing that the promissor gains some benefit or obviates some disbenefit by offering the extra payment;

  (ii) the existing duty is owed to a third party (*Shadwell v Shadwell* (1860); *Pao On v Lau Yiu On* (1980));

- consideration need not be adequate (*Chappell v Nestle Co Ltd* (1960));

- consideration may be executed (present), executory (future) but may not be past (*Re MrArdle* (1951));

- consideration must 'move from the promisee' – related to the doctrine of privity (*Tweddle v Atkinson* (1861));

- the payment of a smaller sum will not discharge the liability for a larger debt (*Pinnel's Case* (1602), *Foakes v Beer* (1884)), unless payment is in a different form/time/place from that agreed – providing that the creditor consents (*Pinnel's Case* (1602));

- a waiver of contractual rights (eg a promise to take less than is owed) must be supported by consideration unless the defendant can raise the defence of promissory (equitable) estoppel (*High Trees Case* (1947)):

   where a person makes a promise waiving their full contractual rights in return for no consideration, the promissor will be estopped (prevented) from going back on the promise where the promisee has relied upon it and it would be inequitable to go back on the promise. This doctrine can be used as a defence but not as a cause of action (*Combe v Combe* (1951)).

Capacity

Certain groups – minors (infants), those of unsound mind or drunk at the time of making a contract, may avoid contracts in certain eventualities to prevent others from exploiting their predicament.

Minors' contracts

Minors' (under 18 – otherwise known as 'infants') contracts may be:

- Valid – contracts for the purchase of 'necessaries' (*Nash v Inman* (1908)), beneficial contracts of education, training and employment (*Doyle v White City Stadium* (1935); *De Francesco v Barnum* (1890)).

   Effect – valid contracts are fully enforceable by and against the minor – as if he or she were an adult.

- Voidable – contracts where the infant has an obligation of an ongoing nature eg leases, partnership agreements.

   Effect – the infant can repudiate these contracts at any time before he or she is 18 or within a reasonable time thereafter. He or she cannot recover any money paid over before repudiation unless there has been a 'total failure of consideration'; he must pay for any benefit received before repudiation but he is not liable for any debts incurred following repudiation.

- Unenforceable – all other infants' contracts fall into this category including contracts for the purchase of 'non-necessaries' and loans.

Effect – contract may be enforced by the infant but not against him, thus, eg if a minor buys 'non-necessary' goods which turn out to be defective, he or she can enforce statutory rights against a trader but if he or she buys 'non-necessaries' on credit and fails to pay for them, the seller cannot enforce payment – Minors' Contracts Act (MCA) 1987 – trader may, at the discretion of the court, obtain an order of restitution to recover the goods or the direct proceeds of their sale.

An adult's guarantee of a minor's unenforceable contract is binding on the adult (MCA). An unenforceable contract cannot be enforced indirectly by bringing an action in tort (*Leslie v Shiell* (1914)).

A corporation has capacity to make contracts. The extent of a corporation's capacity depends on whether the corporation was created by royal charter, statute or under the Companies Act. A corporation which acts beyond its powers is said to be acting *ultra vires* and any purported contracts are *prima facie* void.

A person of unsound mind has capacity to make a contract for necessaries but other contracts are voidable at his option if he can show the other party must have recognised his condition. It is likely that someone whose mental capacity is impaired by drugs or alcohol is in a similar position.

We need to distinguish between a pre-contractual statement made by one of the parties (mere representation) and a contractual obligation (term). A number of guidelines exist:

The contents of contracts

- the parole evidence rule;

- the time which elapses between the making of the statement and the making of the contract;

- whether one party encourages or dissuades the other from further enquiry;

- the importance attached to the statement;

- the relative skill and knowledge of the parties. We can see how this works to the advantage of the consumer and imposes higher standards on a business (*Oscar Chess Ltd v Williams* and *Dick Bentley Productions Ltd v Harold Smith (Motors) Ltd*).

In order to avoid the difficulties inherent in distinguishing between a mere representation and a term the courts sometimes use the 'collateral contract' device.

In addition to terms expressly agreed by the parties terms may be implied:

- by custom – commercial or local;

- by the court – to give the contract 'business efficacy';

- by statute – note terms implied under the Sale of Goods Act 1979 as amended by the Sale and Supply of Goods Act 1994:

  s 12 – the seller has the right to sell the goods (*Rowland v Divall* (1923))

  s 13 – where goods are sold by description, the goods must comply with the description (*Beale v Taylor* (1967))

  s 14 – where goods are sold in the course of a business the goods must be:

  s 14(2) of satisfactory quality – note objective test for determining satisfactory quality.

  s 14(3) reasonably fit for their purpose if the buyer has expressly or impliedly made this known to the seller.

  s 15 – where goods are sold by sample the bulk shall correspond with the sample and the buyer will have a reasonable opportunity of comparing the bulk with the sample.

  Remedy for breach of implied terms – repudiation of contract – buyer entitled to cash refund from seller.

  Exclusion of implied terms – s 12 can never be excluded; ss 13–15 cannot be excluded where a party deals as a consumer but may be excluded, *if reasonable*, in a business to business transaction.

  Supply of Goods and Services Act 1982 – where a *service* is supplied in the course of a business the supplier will:

  s 13 carry out the service with reasonable care and skill;

  s 14 carry out the service in a reasonable time (where time not fixed by contract);

  s 15 make a reasonable charge (where the price has not been agreed).

A term in a contract may be either a condition (major obligation) or a warranty (minor obligation) or an innominate term (a term which may be treated as either condition or warranty by the courts depending on the circumstances). The distinction is important because the remedies available on breach differ. In the case of breach of condition the injured party may treat the contract as ended and claim damages; for breach of warranty he may claim damages only.

In answer to the question: 'how is the distinction to be made?', the traditional approach was to consider the relative importance of the obligation in the contract when it is made. It also assumed that all terms had to be classified as either conditions or warranties. This view was dispelled by the Court of Appeal in *Hong Kong Fir Shipping Co Ltd v Kawasaki Kisen Kaisha Ltd*, which held that some terms might be innominate. In these circumstances the court looks to the effect of the breach after it has occurred to determine whether the breach should be treated as one of condition or one of warranty.

The parties may themselves declare terms to be conditions or warranties or this may be determined by long established commercial practice or statute, eg Sale of Goods Act 1979.

An exclusion clause is a term inserted into a contract to benefit one party by excusing him entirely from liability, or limiting his liability, to pay damages for breach of contract, misrepresentation or negligence. The imbalance in the bargaining power of the parties, resulting in the exploitation of the weaker party has led to an attempt, through case law and statute law, to control the use and effect of such clauses.

Case law has proceeded on the basis that an exclusion clause must:

- be part of the contract;

- when construed (interpreted) cover the event in question;

- be limited in effect only to the immediate contracting parties.

A person who has signed a document containing an exclusion clause is bound by it (*L'Estrange v Graucob*) unless induced to sign through misrepresentation of the clause by the other party (*Curtis v Chemical Cleaning & Dyeing Co*). In the case of an unsigned document, such as a ticket, the person whose rights are being excluded must be given reasonable notice of the term (*Chapleton v Barry UDC*) before the contract is made (*Olley v Marlborough Court*).

It is possible that an excluding term may be incorporated in a contract as a consequence of a regular, long-established course of dealing.

When the courts construe the words of an exclusion clause to see if it covers the event in question they interpret any ambiguity of meaning against the interest of the party who stands to gain from it and in favour of the party whose rights are being diminished (*contra proferentem* rule). From the idea that a party who offered no performance at all could not shelter behind an exclusion clause developed the rule that a party who had committed a fundamental breach of the contract was in no better position. However, in *Photo Production Ltd v Securicor Transport Ltd* the House of Lords said that the fundamental breach rule was not a matter of law. It was a rule of interpretation which assumed there was no exclusion of liability for a fundamental breach unless there was clear language to the contrary.

Only a person who is a party to a contract can take any benefit from it, including the benefit of an exclusion clause (*Adler v Dickson*). By careful drafting it is sometimes possible to make an exclusion clause constitute an offer to a third party who is able to accept it and do business on this basis (*NZ Shipping Co Ltd v Satterthwaite*).

Various statutes have attempted to control the use of exclusion clauses in particular situations. The most comprehensive of these is the Unfair Contract Terms Act 1977 which governs contracts principally where a person seeks to exclude or limit his 'business liability'. (Note the exceptions to this.)

The policy of the Act has been to make some exclusion clauses totally ineffective while permitting others, if they can be shown to be fair and reasonable in the circumstances. Singled out for protection by the first method are persons who suffer personal injury as the result of negligence (s 2) and consumers who enter into contracts to buy, hire, etc, goods (s 6 and s 7).

While the Act contains specific provisions dealing with particular types of exclusion clause, s 2 and s 3 apply to all contracts caught by the Act. They control clauses attempting to exclude liability for negligence and breach of contract respectively.

General guidelines on the application of the reasonableness test are to be found in s 11. Most importantly it is for a person claiming that a clause passes the test to show that it does. More specific guidelines appear in Schedule 2, particularly for use with s 6 and s 7 (statutory implied term exclusion clauses).

We have seen how the definition in s 12 of 'deals as a consumer' has been liberally interpreted (*R & B Customs Brokers Co Ltd v United Dominions Trust Ltd*) and that there are a number of provisions in the Act aimed at preventing the clever drafting of contracts destroying the Act's purpose and effect which have proved fruitful (*Smith v Eric S Bush*).

Adler v Dickson (1954)

Bentley (Dick) Productions Ltd v Harold Smith (Motors) Ltd (1965)

Chapleton v Barry UDC (1940)

Curtis v Chemical Cleaning & Dyeing Co (1951)

Hong Kong Fir Shipping Co Ltd v Kawasaki Kisen Kaisha Ltd (1962)

L'Estrange v Graucob (1934)

Olley v Marlborough Court (1949)

Oscar Chess Ltd v Williams (1957)

NZ Shipping Co Ltd v Satterthwaite (1974)

Photoproduction Ltd v Securicor Transport Ltd (1980)

R & B Customs Brokers Co Ltd v United Dominions Trust Ltd (1988)

Smith v Eric S Bush (1989)

A contract may be rendered void or voidable on a number of grounds where either it is unfair as between the parties to hold the contract valid or the contract cannot be permitted to stand on grounds of public policy.

Vitiating elements in contracts

Generally, a plea of 'mistake' made by one of the contracting parties will not be accepted by the courts as sufficient to invalidate the contract. Occasionally it will be.

Mistake may be classified as common, mutual or unilateral. To be operative it must be of fact and of fundamental significance to the contract. If the mistake is operative the contract will be void at common law but in the exercise of their jurisdiction in equity the courts have been more flexible in some situations.

A common mistake, where both parties incorrectly assume the subject matter exists will render the contract void both at common law and in equity. The parties are attempting to do the impossible (*Couturier v Hastie*). A common mistake as to quality will not have this effect at common law (*Bell v Lever Bros Ltd*) but it may be otherwise in equity (*Magee v Pennine Insurance Co Ltd*). The equitable remedy of rectification may be granted where the parties are in agreement but an error is made in recording it.

For a mutual mistake to be operative both at common law and in equity there must exist no apparent consent by either party to the other's terms (*Raffles v Wichelhaus*).

A unilateral mistake occurs where one party only is mistaken and the other is aware, or must be taken as a reasonable person to be aware, of the mistake made (*Hartog v Colin and Shields*).

Most unilateral cases have involved mistaken identity, scenarios where a rogue, representing himself as a person of substance, tricks the plaintiff into contracting with him and handing over goods. Having sold the goods on to his second victim, the defendant, the rogue, disappears. Issues raised by these cases focus on the question of whether the plaintiff:

- intended to deal with someone who really exists (contrast *Cundy v Lindsay* with *King's Norton Metal Co Ltd v Edridge Merrett Co Ltd*);

- regarded the identity of the other party (the rogue) as fundamental;

- took reasonable steps to check the identity of the other party.

The second and third issues present easier tasks when the contract is formed by correspondence (*Cundy v Lindsay*), than in face-to-face transactions (*Phillips v Brooks*).

Generally, a person is bound by a document to which he has put his signature whether or not he has read it. The signer may be able to invoke the plea non est factum, originally used to protect illiterate persons, in order to have the document cancelled (*Saunders v Anglia Building Society*). The plea will be successful only when:

- the document turns out to be fundamentally different in effect from that which the signer thought he was signing; and

- the signer has not been careless.

An operative misrepresentation occurs where one party makes a false statement of a material fact which induces the other to enter into the contract. Note that the false statement:

- may be made by words or conduct;

- must be of fact not law;

- cannot be the promise of future action, but that a person may misrepresent the present state of his mind – an existing fact (*Edgington v Fitzmaurice*);

- cannot be an honest opinion (*Bissett v Wilkinson*) but that an opinion which could not genuinely be held in the light of facts known to the representor may be held to be a misrepresentation (*Smith v Land and House Property Corporation*).

Generally, silence does not amount to a misrepresentation but there are three exceptions.

- A half-truth may constitute a misrepresentation in view of the distortion engendered by what is left unsaid. Similarly, a failure to update information true when given but which subsequently becomes false due to a change in circumstances can also constitute a misrepresentation (*With v O'Flanagan*).

- Three types of contract are designated by the law as being of the utmost good faith and where in consequence there is a duty to make a full disclosure of all material facts. The most important of these is a contract of insurance where non-disclosure by the insured entitles the insurance company to avoid liability on the policy.

- Where the contracting parties are already in a fiduciary (trusting) relationship recognised by the law there is an obligation on the person in the dominant position to disclose all material circumstances known to him.

To amount to an operative misrepresentation the false statement must have acted upon the mind of the representee to induce him into entering into the contract. Consequently, there will be no inducement if the representee was unaware of the misrepresentation; it had no effect upon his mind; or he sought independent advice from a third party.

Prior to *Hedley Byrne v Heller* the law recognised only two types of misrepresentation – fraudulent and innocent. Note the House of Lords' definition of fraudulent misrepresentation in *Derry v Peek*, that it also constitutes the tort of deceit and that the rules for calculating damages are especially advantageous to the plaintiff. Since 1964 it has become necessary to distinguish between different types of non-fraudulent misrepresentation: those made purely innocently, those made negligently at common law (*Esso v Mardon*) and those caught by s 2(1) Misrepresentation Act 1967.

We have seen how advantageous it is for a representee to sue under s 2(1), the burden of proof shifting to the defendant representor to show that he had reasonable grounds for making the statement and believed it to be true right up to the moment the contract was made. Thanks to the fiction-of-fraud wording in s 2(1) the defendant, if liable, will have to pay damages as if the statement had been made fraudulently.

A further remedy may be available to the victim of a misrepresentation – rescission. This aims to restore the parties to their original pre-contract positions. It is the only remedy available for a purely innocent misrepresentation. However, being an equitable remedy it is available at the discretion of the court. It is well established what 'bars' to its award exist. Note these. Under s 2(2) Misrepresentation Act 1967 the court has a discretion to award damages in lieu of rescission in some circumstances.

Consent to contract may be lacking due to duress or undue influence exerted by one party over the other. Originally duress, at common law, involved illegal violence or threats of violence to the person but we have seen how a new concept of economic duress is developing. There are as yet no definitive criteria for distinguishing between legitimate commercial pressure and that which is illegitimate, but consider the guidance offered by Lord Scarman in *Pao On v Lau Yiu Long* and note that unlike physical duress, economic duress must constitute possibly the only or, at the very least, the predominant reason for the party allegedly coerced to have entered into the contract.

Undue influence, an equitable idea, exists whenever one party has such an influence over the other that the latter cannot be said to exercise an independent judgment. There are two categories: one where undue influence must be proved if the contract is to be set aside; the other where it is presumed until the contrary is shown. In the second category note the relationships recognised by the law which give rise to the presumption and that the relationship of banker and customer per se is not included. However, we have seen that the facts of a particular case may well give rise to the presumption (*Lloyds Bank v Bundy*) and the difficult position in which a bank or other creditor may find itself in dealing with a husband and wife (*Barclays Bank v O'Brien*). See the advice which should be given to a bank faced with this situation but note also the limits within which the bank is put on guard (*CIBC Mortgages plc v Pitt*).

Contracts induced by duress or undue influence are voidable at the option of the party affected.

Contracts may be illegal because they are have been prohibited either expressly or impliedly by statute, or because they are, at common law, highly reprehensible and contrary to public policy. They may be illegal when made or become illegal due to the way in which performance takes place. We have considered the wide variety of contracts which have been held to be illegal by the courts as the judges seek to ban contracts thought to be harmful to society as a whole and seen the old concept of 'maintenance' tested in a very modern setting (*Giles v Thompson and Devlin v Baslington*).

Where a contract is illegal as formed it is void and neither party may sue on it. Money or property handed over pursuant to the contract cannot be reclaimed. Note the limited range of exceptions. If the contract is only illegal as performed (ie lawful when made but exploited or carried out in an illegal manner) the general rule is that the party responsible for the illegality cannot sue upon the contract or recover money or property transferred. The innocent party has all the normal remedies open to him.

Contracts which are less reprehensible but still not regarded as being in society's interest are classed as void either because declared so by statute or because they have been so designated at common law by the judges. Apart from wagering contracts most contracts rendered void by statute involve those leading to collusion and anti-competitive practices by businesses in manufacture and trade with the UK and in the European Union.

Among contracts declared void at common law on grounds of public policy the most important are contracts in restraint of trade. These are treated, however, as being only *prima facie* void and will be upheld as valid if they can be shown to be reasonable in the circumstances. To be reasonable the restraint must be (a) not harmful to the public interest and (b) drawn no wider than is necessary to protect legitimate business interests.

Although the categories of contract within the doctrine of restraint of trade must remain fluid, typically they include:

- an employer on an employee;
- a buyer on a seller of a business;
- a manufacturer and supplier to restrict output;
- a supplier on a distributor.

In recent years the courts have had, on a number of occasions, to consider the reasonableness or a solus agreement under which a garage contracts to buy all its supplies of petrol from a particular oil company. Note the leading case of *Esso Petroleum Co Ltd v Harper's Garage Ltd* and that a distinction is drawn between the situation where the garage owner, already in possession, gives up his freedom and that where a person acquires possession of the garage by means of the *solus* agreement.

One of the significant differences between contracts which are illegal and those which are void lies in the way the courts deal with them. While the illegal contract fails in entirety this is not necessarily so with the void contract. It is void only to the extent to which it contravenes public policy. The offending part may be severed (cut out) leaving the remainder valid and enforceable. Money or property transferred can be recovered.

Barclays Bank v O'Brien (1993)

Bell v Lever Bros Ltd (1931)

Bissett v Wilkinson (1926)

CIBC Mortgages plc v Pitt (1993)

Couturier v Hastie (1856)

Cundy v Lindsay (1878)

Derry v Peek (1889)

Edgington v Fitzmaurice (1885)

Esso v Mardon (1976)

Esso v Harper's Garage (1967)

Giles v Thompson and Devlin v Baslington (1993)

Hartog v Colin and Shields (1939)

Hedley Byrne v Heller (1963)

King's Norton Metal Co Ltd v Edridge Merrett Co Ltd (1897)

Lloyds Bank v Bundy (1974)

Magee v Pennine Insurance Co Ltd (1969)

Pao On v Lau Yiu Long (1979)

Phillips v Brooks (1919)

Raffles v Wichelhaus (1864)

Saunders v Anglia Building Society (1970)

Smith v Land and House Property Corporation (1884)

With v O'Flanagan (1936)

The doctrine of privity of contract

Under the doctrine of privity of contract a person who is not party (privy) to a contract can neither lay claim to benefit from it nor have obligation imposed on him by it (*Dunlop Pneumatic Tyre Co v Selfridge Co Ltd*). Because the doctrine has proved inconvenient in practice, attempts have been made to evade it. These include the following.

- Insurance – where statute often gives third parties the right in specified circumstances to sue on a policy.

- Agency – a well established exception at common law.

- Collateral contract – a device used to construct a contract between the promisor and an apparent stranger to the contract.

- Property law – through leases and covenants. Note the different treatment of restrictive and positive covenants.

- Resale price maintenance – now generally not permitted (Resale Prices Act 1976).

- Trusts – the device of holding a promise on trust for another, approved by the House of Lords in *Les Afrèteurs Réunis SA v Walford* (1915), has since fallen into disfavour and should not be relied on.

- Section 56 Law of Property Act 1925 – despite the liberal interpretation favoured by Lord Denning the House of Lords in *Beswick v Beswick* held it should be construed restrictively and not extended to cover contracts.

- Restrictions on the use of chattels – there has been some judicial support for the proposition that the purchaser of a ship which he knows is subject to a charterparty in favour of a third party is bound by that charterparty (*Lord Strathcona Steamship Co v Dominion Coal Co*).

Where the exceptions occur and a person is able to sue despite not being a party to the contract the normal remedies are available to him. The position is more complex where one of the contracting parties seeks to enforce the contract on behalf of the third party it was intended to benefit. We have seen the courts prepared to use various devices (*Beswick v Beswick* and *Jackson v Horizon Holidays Ltd*) but not so as to undermine the fundamental concept of privity (*Woodar Investment Development Ltd v Wimpey Construction Ltd*).

Note the Law Commission's proposals for reform – report and draft bill (1996) which would permit enforcement of contracts by third parties in specified circumstances.

Beswick v Beswick (1967)

Dunlop Pneumatic Tyre Co v Selfridge Co Ltd (1915)

Jackson v Horizon Holidays Ltd (1975)

Les Afrèteurs Réunis SA v Walford (1919)

Lord Strathcona Steamship Co v Dominion Coal Co (1925)

Woodar Investment Development Ltd v Wimpey Construction Ltd (1980)

There are four ways in which contractual liability may end: The discharge of performance, agreement, frustration and breach.

A party who has fully discharged his obligations has no further liability under the contract, until then as a general rule he cannot claim to be entitled to payment (*Cutter v Powell*), but note the exceptions:

The discharge of contracts

- contract promises severable;

- prevention of performance by the other party;

- acceptance of partial performance by the other party;

- substantial performance.

If a contract does not stipulate the time for its performance the general rule is that it must be performed within a reasonable time. Breach of an obligation relating to time is generally only regarded as a minor breach. 'Time is not of the essence of the contract'. Be aware of the three exceptions.

In the same way that liability is created so it may be terminated – by agreement. The discharging agreement must contain all the elements of a valid and enforceable contract. These are not difficult to discover in a situation of bilateral discharge but as we saw in the rule in *Pinnel's Case* the issue of what is sufficient consideration may pose problems in the case of unilateral discharge. Note that executory consideration (a promise) is as valid in this context as when a contract is formed (*British Russian Gazette Ltd v Associated Newspapers Ltd*).

The question of formalities arises only when the original contract is one which itself is caught by statutory requirements such as s 2 Law of Property (Miscellaneous Provisions) Act 1989. Such an agreement may be extinguished entirely without attendant formalities. Variation of terms will be effective only if the formalities are complied with. If the intention is to extinguish the original agreement and substitute a new one the termination will be effective. However, the new agreement will come into being only if the appropriate formalities are observed.

See the distinction the law makes between a variation and a waiver ('a kind of estoppel') and note how difficult it may be in practice to distinguish between them.

The original position at common law was that a person who had freely entered into a contract continued to be bound by it even though subsequent events made the contract impossible to perform.

After *Taylor v Caldwell* a line of cases developed what is now known as the doctrine of frustration. Under this a variety of events, beyond the control of the parties, have been held to frustrate the contract and bring it to an end:

- physical impossibility;

- unavailability of the subject matter;

- legal impossibility;

- frustration of the common venture where literal performance becomes futile (*Krell v Henry*). Here it is important to distinguish between object and motive.

The doctrine of frustration does not apply merely because a contract has become more burdensome (*Davis Contractors Ltd v Fareham UDC*).

Note what happens under the doctrine when:

- the parties expressly provide for the frustrating event;

- the frustration is 'self-induced';

- the contract is a lease of land.

The legal effect of frustration is to bring the contract to an end so that both parties are discharged from any further obligations. Obligations which should have been performed before frustration (but were not) are unaffected (*Chandler v Webster*). In *Fibrosa SA v Fairbairn Lawson Combe Barbour Ltd* the House of Lords decided that money paid in advance was recoverable by the payer if there had been a total failure of consideration. The Law Reform (Frustrated Contracts) Act 1943, which followed, attempts to alleviate the unfairness demonstrated in *Fibrosa* and in the earlier decision of *Appleby v Myers* so that the burden of the contract becoming frustrated is more evenly shared between the parties.

A breach of contract entitles the injured party to terminate the contract where the defaulter

- repudiates;

- commits a fundamental breach.

Repudiation occurs where before (fully) performing the contract the defaulter abandons the contract expressly or by implication (*Hochster v De La Tour*). Such repudiation is often referred to as 'anticipatory breach'. A fundamental breach occurs when either the obligation broken is an important one or the effect of the breach is serious.

Note the consequences of repudiation or a fundamental breach for the injured party and that non-acceptance of an anticipatory breach will keep the contract alive (*White and Carter (Councils) Ltd v McGregor* and *Avery v Bowden*).

Appleby v Myers (1867)

Avery v Bowden (1855)

British Russian Gazette Ltd v Associated Newspapers Ltd (1933)

Chandler v Webster (1904)

Cutter v Powell (1795)

Davis Contractors Ltd v Fareham UDC (1955)

Fibrosa SA v Fairbairn Lawson Combe Barbour Ltd (1942)

Hochster v De La Tour (1853)

Pinnel's Case (1602)

Taylor v Caldwell (1863)

White and Carter (Councils) Ltd v McGregor (1961)

The remedies for breach of contract

The main remedy available for breach of contract is damages. Others include the right to sue for an agreed sum, an action on a *quantum meruit* and the equitable remedies of specific performance and injunction.

In connection with the award of damages two significant issues arise: remoteness of damage and measure of damages.

The first, concerned with the question, 'for what kind of loss may a plaintiff claim?' was considered in *Hadley v Baxendale*. The answer given in that case was that a loss caused by a breach of contract may be the proper subject matter of a claim provided it was reasonably foreseeable, at the time the contract was made, as a likely consequence of breach. Note the approaches taken in the two rules which emerged from the case and the way in which they were subsequently developed, particularly in *Victoria Laundry v Newman Industries* and *Koufos v Czarnikow Ltd, The Heron II.*

The second issue is concerned with measuring the loss caused through the breach, the object being compensation for the plaintiff. This may take the form of the plaintiff being compensated for:

- expectation loss, where the purpose is to put him financially where he would have been if the defendant had performed the contract properly. Expectation losses may be calculated on the basis of (i) the cost of cure or (ii) the difference in value caused by the breach. The latter approach is used in contracts for the sale of goods and was recently adopted re a building contract in *Ruxley Electronics & Construction Ltd v Forsyth* (1995);

- reliance loss, where the idea is to restore the plaintiff financially to the position he was in before making the contract (*Anglia TV v Reed*);

- distress and disappointment as a consequence of the breach, but only in exceptional circumstances, eg where the contract was supposed to provide peace of mind or freedom from distress (*Jarvis v Swan Tours* (1973)).

A plaintiff is under a duty to act as a reasonable person would in the circumstances and mitigate (minimise) his loss.

Sometimes the parties may agree in the contract itself that in the event of breach by one of them a specified sum will be paid to the other. If this appears to be a genuine attempt by the parties to estimate the amount of compensation needed in the circumstances the term is properly called a 'liquidated damages' clause and may be claimed by the injured party if breach occurs.

If the sum is out of all proportion to the loss likely to be suffered it is termed a 'penalty' and is not recoverable. See the guidance given by the House of Lords-in *Dunlop Pneumatic Tyre Co Ltd v New Garage and Motor Co Ltd* for distinguishing between liquidated damages and penalty clauses.

There is very limited scope for a defendant to plead that the damages for which he is liable should be reduced under s 1 Law Reform (Contributory Negligence) Act 1945 as a consequence of the plaintiff's contributory negligence. The Act will apply only where the defendant's liability in contract is co-extensive with his liability in negligence, the tortious liability arising independently of the contract.

Where a plaintiff has performed his part of the contract completely and the only outstanding liability is that of the defendant to pay a specified sum, eg the price of goods sold to him, the plaintiff may sue for that sum instead of bringing an action for damages.

Note the circumstances in which a plaintiff may have available to him the quasi-contractual action of *quantum meruit*. Here the plaintiff is asking the court to award him a reasonable sum in respect of goods supplied or services performed.

The equitable remedies of specific performance and injunction cannot be claimed as of right. They are awarded only at the discretion of the court and in circumstances where the common law remedies are inadequate. It is fairly well established how the courts exercise their discretion in practice. Note the things the court will be likely to take into account when asked to award either of these remedies.

Specific performance, if granted, is an order addressed by the court to the defendant directing him to carry out the contract he has made with the plaintiff. The injunction is an order similarly addressed directing the defendant to refrain from doing something which is a breach of the contract.

Anglia TV v Reed (1971)

Dunlop Pneumatic Tyre Co Ltd v New Garage and Motor Co Ltd (1915)

Hadley v Baxendale (1854)

Koufos v Czarnikow Ltd, The Heron II (1967)

Victoria Laundry v Newman Industries Ltd (1949)

Ruxley Electronics & Construction Ltd v Forsyth (1995)

PART II

THE LAW OF TORT

Chapter 8

Introduction to Tort

Put simply, a tort is a civil wrong. The 'wrong' can take many forms. It might be punching someone, knocking him down with your car, causing him nervous shock, telling lies about him or his business, keeping a book he lent you or shooting his dog, flooding, polluting or setting fire to his land and so on. In most cases the victim (as plaintiff) will be suing for compensation for the harm he has suffered (the compensation will be in money form, that is, damages), or occasionally to prevent harm occurring to him (by means of an injunction).

But in all cases the court will be balancing both the plaintiff's and the defendant's competing interests. The defendant may have punched the plaintiff, but was it in self-defence, or was the defendant making an unlawful arrest? In short, the defendant may have a defence to his actions.

Beyond the label 'civil wrong', definition is difficult. *Winfield and Jolowicz on Tort* put it thus:

'Tortious liability arises from the breach of a duty primarily fixed by law; this duty is towards persons generally and its breach is redressible by an action for unliquidated damages.'

Salmond and Heuston's version is:

'... a civil wrong for which the remedy is a common law action for unliquidated damages, and which is not exclusively the breach of a contract or the breach of a trust or other merely equitable obligation.'

These establish that the action is civil and for damages (*cf* criminal law), which are unliquidated (*cf* contract), and for a breach of a common law duty fixed by the general law and towards people generally (*cf* contract).

Clearly, tort differs in several respects from criminal law and contract, so it would be useful, before trying to determine what tort is, to distinguish it from:

- criminal wrongs; and

- other forms of civil liability, especially breach of contract; and

- briefly, breach of an equitable obligation.

8.1   Definitions

8.1.1	Tort and criminal law

In certain cases, a single act may in fact be both a tort and a crime, eg an intentional punch on someone else's nose. The state could prosecute the defendant in the criminal courts, and the victim could sue in the civil courts. What makes it a crime as opposed to a tort is not so much the act, but what the defendant is being taken to court for. In other words, the distinction depends on the nature of the remedy. Thus, criminal sanctions punish the wrongdoer; whereas the civil remedy of damages (the usual remedy for a tort) compensates the victim.

Some acts are both crimes and torts, eg trespass to the person, or libel. But apart from these, the breach of a criminal rule will not automatically give rise to civil liability. Thus, in *Lonrho v Shell* (1981) a plaintiff company which had obeyed a prohibition on selling oil to rebellious Rhodesia could not sue another company which had ignored the prohibition and picked up all the oil trade.

The two exceptions to this rule are the torts of public nuisance and breach of statutory duty, where a crime is committed and if certain conditions are met a victim of the crime can sue.

8.1.2	Tort and contract

Both of these are part of the civil law. But, in contract, as a result of the doctrine of privity, the duties are only owed to the other contracting party (though the Law Commission are looking at this); whereas in tort the duties are potentially owed to the 'world at large'.

In contract, the content of the duties is primarily fixed by the parties; whereas in tort the content is normally fixed by law (since in many instances, eg road accidents, the parties may have never met each other prior to their legal collision).

In contract the duties are generally imposed by the parties' consent (most offerees are free to reject the offer); whereas in tort the duties are generally imposed irrespective of consent.

And whereas in contract the claim is often liquidated, ie it can be quantified by the plaintiff, such as the cost of a ruined holiday, or the cost of a pair of underpants, in tort the claim is primarily unliquidated, or not fixed by the plaintiff: only the judge can put a figure on pain and suffering, or a jury on the loss of a reputation.

But recent developments in the tort of negligence have re-emphasised the different primary purposes of these two areas of law. Contract is concerned to ensure performance of a contractual duty, thus, mere non-performance, even without damage, is a breach of contract; tort is solely concerned with compensation for damage.

In *Murphy v Brentwood District Council* (1990), for example, the House of Lords held that a builder who built badly, necessitating repair costs, had not caused damage if the building, cracks and all, was still standing. Someone might have a claim in contract for the defects, ie for failure to build a good building according to the contract, but no-one would have a claim in tort unless he or his property was physically damaged, ie by the building falling onto them.

This disparity can also be shown in a purchase of goods. If underpants are purchased with an excess of sulphite in them and liable therefore to burn the skin on contact, the purchaser has a right to sue in contract for the mere fact that they are defective (under ss 14(2) and (3) Sale of Goods Act 1979: not of satisfactory quality and not fit for their required purpose). But only if they are worn and cause damage can there be an action in tort (as indeed there was on these facts in *Grant v Australian Knitting Mills* (1936)).

Either area of civil law might be the better course of action, depending on:

- whether the defendant is a minor (they are generally liable in tort as an adult would be);

- on the limitation of action rules (in contract, time to sue runs from the breach; in tort, from when a complete cause of action accrues, in most torts, when the damage occurs);

- on the remoteness of damage rules (these may be different: certainly there is no attempt to harmonise them); and

- on the matter of privity of contract (irrelevant in tort).

Opinions differ as to whether concurrent liability in both contract and in tort is possible. Our view is that liability in negligence is not permissible if the parties have made a contract between themselves, or with a third party, which does or should cover liability and loss distribution or both.

There is no equity in tort; tort is mainly common law, with some statute law (but hardly any European Community influence).

8.1.3   Tort and equity

However, once a tort is proved, equitable remedies may be available, and be more useful than common law damages. These include injunctions; restitution (eg to the plaintiff of a chattel which he has a right to) and an account of profits unlawfully made, which the plaintiff can lay claim to.

You may notice that different books adopt 'tort' or 'torts' in their titles. This is not a minor point; there are differing views on whether 'the law of torts consist(s) of a fundamental

8.2   Tort or torts?

general principle (not to cause harm) ... or ... consist(s) of a number of specific rules' (Salmond).

Whatever the case, these four general principles certainly do exist, which perhaps indicate that, for all the differences between the various torts, there is unity of purpose between them; in short, there is possibly a general principle of tortious liability.

| 8.2.1 | The four general principles of tortious liability |

Generally speaking, the tortfeasor (ie wrongdoer) is liable for unliquidated damages in tort when he is at fault in doing (or not doing) something wrong which damages a protected interest of the plaintiff.

Looking at this statement:

- The plaintiff's damaged interest – the law must deem worthy of protection

  For example, the victim's person, goods, land, reputation, the goodwill and other assets of his business, the financial interests of himself and his business (sometimes) will be deemed worthy of protection. However, his pride or dignity, or grief or sorrow will not. The Courts have consistently denied a right to privacy, but note should be made of the new statutory tort of harassment, alarm or distress created by the Protection from Harassment Act 1997. In the tort of negligence in particular the courts have been aware of the need to keep liability in check. We shall see later that the courts are very cautious of claims for pure economic loss, independent of physical damage (as instanced by *Murphy v Brentwood District Council* and *Grant v Australian Knitting Mills*, above).

- Wrongful act or omission – what the defendant does, or fails to do, must be wrong in itself

  This is essential. There is no liability for damage-without-a-tort (sometimes stated in Latin, *damnum sine injuria*). In *Bradford Corporation v Pickles* (1895), when the Corporation announced its intention to fill a reservoir the plaintiff diverted the underground flow of water away from the site, hoping to force the Corporation to buy his land at an inflated price. The House of Lords agreed that he was only doing what he was lawfully entitled to do.

  Consider also fair competition: supermarkets are forever putting comer shops out of business, but without liability.

- Defendant at fault – the defendant must be proved to have been at fault, ie have caused the harm intentionally or negligently

In *Fowler v Lanning* (1959) a claim that 'the defendant shot the plaintiff' disclosed no cause of action since it did not allege any fault.

Why should he have to pay damages if he has acted completely innocently? Why indeed! But remember that the purpose of tort is to get the plaintiff his compensation. In some torts, therefore, the defendant will be strictly liable, irrespective of fault.

These torts are:

(i)   under the rule in *Rylands v Fletcher*

(ii)   under the Animals Act 1971

(iii)   defamation

(iv)   conversion

(v)   some statutory torts

(vi)   breach of statutory duty

(vii)   public nuisance (sometimes)

(viii)   under the Consumer Protection Act 1987 Part I

(ix)   where one person is liable for the tort of another, especially a master for the tort of his servant (called 'vicarious liability').

The fault principle (which is also very strong in criminal law) has come under criticism, or at least review, over the last 20 years.

Why should one baby injured at birth recover damages, while in similar circumstances another is unable to solely because the first doctor is proved to have been negligent, but the second not? Is this fair? Both have to go through life with the same handicap. Remember, tort is concerned with compensation. (Both doctors are either indemnified or insured.)

The principle accordingly came under review in the 1970s, in Britain by the Royal Commission on Civil Liability and Compensation for Personal Injury, Cmnd 7054 (1978) (producing the 'Pearson Report'), at the Council of Europe, and in the European Economic Community (now the European Union).

The recommendations of the Pearson Report fell on deaf ears, but the (then) EC did produce a Directive on strict liability for defective products which cause injury, obliging the British government to enact the Consumer Protection Act 1987. But liability for road accidents and in the increasingly prominent area of medical negligence (ie for negligent diagnosis, advice and treatment) is still fault-based.

'Malice', meaning improper motive or spite, must be distinguished from fault. 'The law asks what the defendant has done, not why he did it' (Salmond).

Thus, malice is generally irrelevant; though relevant in private nuisance and some defences to defamation (ie fair comment on a matter of public interest, qualified privilege, and under s 4 Defamation Act 1952). Equally, good motive (eg to protect a person from himself 'for his own good') is no excuse.

Accordingly, an improper motive will not make a lawful act unlawful (see *Bradford Corpn v Pickles* (1895), above); and an innocent motive will not make an unlawful act lawful. In *Wilkinson v Downton* (1897) having unlawfully shocked the plaintiff by a false tale that the latter's husband had been injured in an accident, the defendant could not plead that she had meant it 'as a joke'.

- The plaintiff must have suffered damage

  In general, proof of damage is required; after all, a person who has suffered no injury needs no compensation.

  So if your car nearly hits me, and I am left merely annoyed (but not having suffered nervous shock, which would be actionable), I cannot sue you. I cannot justify my action on the ground that your driving needs to be better regulated in the interests of the public: that is the role of the criminal law. (Look back too at the section above on contract and tort, in particular at the cases of *Murphy v Brentwood DC* (1990) and *Grant v Australian Knitting Mills* (1936).)

  Note that 'damage', 'injury', and 'harm' are strictly interchangeable. But 'injury' is generally used in personal injury; 'damage' in other cases; 'harm' covers both; and 'loss' is usually reserved for economic loss, or where a chattel is actually lost. (But no harm is done by using the wrong word.)

  Some torts are said to be 'actionable *per se'*. That is, actionable without proof of damage (sometimes in Latin, *injuria sine damno*).

  These include all forms of trespass, libel, and the four exceptional forms of slander (see below).

  So if I commit trespass against you, eg by stroking your hair against your will, but causing you no real harm, you can sue me; but if I act negligently towards you, you can only sue me if I thereby caused you injury.

Before embarking on a study of the tort system, it is important to consider that there are other means of compensation for harm. There are, for example:

- Private insurance and private pensions

  But distinguish between the two types of insurance:

  (i) loss insurance – where a potential victim insures himself against damage which others might cause him, eg house contents against burglary; and

  (ii) liability insurance – where a potential tortfeasor insures himself against his liability towards others, eg third-party road traffic insurance.

- Social security

  That is, public insurance and pensions.

  New Zealand has had a no-fault compensation scheme for all accidents since 1974. But the UK has left the fault-based tort system to take the vast bulk of claims, while introducing piece-meal schemes to cope with isolated groups of victims.

  Notable are:

  (i) the scheme under the Vaccine Damage Act 1969, and the scheme for payments to haemophiliac sufferers of AIDS, infected through NHS transfusions; and

  (ii) the Motor Insurers Bureau, whereby the state and insurers agree to pay compensation where a vehicle driver who has injured another person or (within defined limits) property turns out to have been uninsured or unidentified.

- alteration of the existing fault-based tort system, by changing to a no-fault (ie strict liability) tort system.

  The defendant's fault would be ignored, and the sole question becomes, 'Did the defendant cause (ie simply, 'bring about') the plaintiff's injuries?'

  But a 'no-fault' approach does not remove the problems of causation of damage. Thus, the baby plaintiff in *Wilsher v Essex Area Health Authority* (1988) who failed to prove that the defendant's negligence, one of five possible causes, had caused his blindness, would still have failed under this new system.

- Charters

  The nature of the charters' 'standards of service' is uncertain. 'Respect for privacy' is assured by The Patient's Charter, though the courts have consistently denied its existence as a legal right.

Are charters ambivalent? What will making contractors 'incur a financial penalty if they cone off more of the motorway than is strictly needed' (The Citizen's Charter) do for the safety of those working on the motorway?

| 8.3.1 | The present proportional breakdown of sources of compensation |

The Pearson Commission in 1978 found that just over one half of compensation monies for accidents came from social security, one quarter from the tort system, and one quarter from private sources, especially insurance and occupational sick pay.

The Commission found, however, that the tort system is expensive. For every £1 paid as tort damages, 86p is paid in operating the system (ie someone pays a solicitor, barrister, judge, expert etc); but for every £1 paid as social security, only 11p is spent in operating the system. In *Whitehouse v Jordan* (1981) a boy who had been brain-damaged at birth was 11 years old when the House of Lords decided that the surgeon who used forceps on his head was not at fault. The boy got nothing: the lawyers shared £250,000 in legal-aid fees.

8.4 The cause of action

The rules of civil litigation are complex and beyond the scope of this book. But it is worth understanding this phrase. The plaintiff in his pleadings does not plead law or evidence. He pleads material facts only, ie those facts which he must prove at trial in order to succeed (as does a defendant).

These facts constitute the cause of action, and once they exist, the plaintiff can issue his writ. He might have, say, a cause of action in negligence, meaning he can prove sufficient facts to enable him to sue in that particular tort.

Those same facts might also cover, without addition, trespass. Or, in another situation, a set of facts might be common between two torts eg 'the defendant shot the plaintiff' (*Fowler v Lanning* (1959)), but be insufficient by themselves to succeed in either. He must, in that case, prove not only those common facts, but also the additional facts, if he wishes to succeed in one or both torts.

It is the plaintiff's choice as to which tort he sues in. In *Joyce v Sengupta* (1992) the facts allowed the plaintiff to sue both in defamation, for which legal aid was not available, and in injurious falsehood, for which legal aid was available. The Court of Appeal rejected the defendant's complaint that the plaintiff should be restricted to defamation. It was the plaintiff's good fortune to have a second tort which allowed him legal aid; that was how the system worked.

It is also the defendant's choice as to which defences he relies on, if any at all. When reading some cases, it is important to understand that the defendant may have chosen the wrong defence. In *Dann v Hamilton* (1939) the judge was later asked why, when denying the defence of consent or assumption of the risk, he did not allow the defence of contributory negligence. He replied, they did not plead it! Nor, as he read in the notes of the case, would counsel amend his defence when invited to do so at the trial.

Chapter 9

Trespass to the Person, Goods and Land, Intentional Physical Harm and Conversion

Maitland, writing at the end of the 19th century, called trespass 'the fertile mother of actions', as all other common law torts had developed from it.

There are in fact three separate forms of trespass, each a separate tort: trespass to the person (itself divided into three torts, as we shall see), trespass to goods, and trespass to land. An important distinction of all forms of trespass is that the harm caused is *intentional and direct* (see below).

Also intentional, but causing indirect harm, is the tort called 'intentional physical harm'. This tort is much neglected, but is a useful comparison with trespass, as is private nuisance with trespass to land, both dealt with later.

Another tort usefully compared with trespass to goods is conversion. An interference with goods might easily concern both torts.

We have already seen that trespass is actionable *per se*, though only nominal damages would be awarded unless real damage were caused; the other two torts here both require proof of damage.

In trespass the cause of action accrues on the interference, eg the touch in battery, whether or not there is 'real' damage (see Introduction, Chapter 1, above).

As these torts are well established many of the cases are old. But these are the torts we are looking at in arrest and detention, entry of premises and search and seizure of goods, in detention of immigrants, and detention and treatment of patients of all states of mind and consciousness.

These are clearly important matters where the state has to balance competing interests: the right of the individual to the freedom of his person and property, and the right, and indeed duty, of the state to regulate individuals in the best interests of all.

Understandably, therefore, these torts are the starting point to a study of police powers (dealt with in Part IV on Civil Liberties).

There are three forms of trespass to the person: battery, assault, and false imprisonment (each a separate tort, and, incidentally, all crimes too). Each consists of an *intentional*, and

9.1 Trespass to the person

direct interference with the plaintiff by the defendant, without the plaintiff's consent or other excuse. There is argument that trespass to the person can be committed negligently, as well as intentionally. It is, however, clearer to assume that it must always be intentional.

Certainly, fault is required (see *Fowler v Lanning* (1959), above), and negligent conduct is well covered by the tort of negligence (below).

9.1.1   Battery

- Force

  Physical contact is necessary. 'The least touching of another in anger is battery' (*Cole v Turner* (1704)). But in *F v West Berkshire HA* (1989), where the House of Lords agreed to the sterilisation of a woman who on account of her mental disorder could not consent to it but might well become pregnant otherwise, the court rejected both anger and hostility as requirements of battery. An unwanted kiss, or a gentle restraint by a policewoman, could both be battery.

  Further, in *F v West Berkshire HA* (1989) the House stated that there was no battery, as Lord Goff put it, in 'all physical contact which is generally acceptable in the ordinary conduct of everyday life'.

  So a policeman's tap on someone's shoulder to attract his attention is acceptable as something to be expected as part of life (*Donnelly v Jackman* (1970)), but restraint by a policewoman who takes someone's arm, where no arrest has been made, is not acceptable (*Collins v Wilcock* (1984)).

  Further, in cases where the plaintiff consents there is no trespass.

- The absence of consent

  The definition of trespass to the person puts the burden on the plaintiff to show that he did not consent. (The view that consent is a defence is not strictly true, therefore, as it implies that the defendant must prove consent to counter the *prima facie* case of trespass established by the plaintiff.) In *Ford v Ford* (1887) it was said that 'the absence of lawful consent is part of the definition of assault'.

  There are two forms of consent: consent to a specific invasion of the plaintiff's interest which will definitely occur, eg an operation; and assumption of risk, ie the willingness to run the legal risk of a possible injury from a specific source, eg the risk of falling on rotten stairs. (The latter will be dealt with after the tort of negligence, to which it particularly applies, although consent is a general defence applicable to most torts.)

- Express and implied consent

  Consent can be either expressly or impliedly given, but the consent must be to the act complained of. Thus, in *Nash v Sheen* (1953), where the plaintiff agreed to a permanent wave at the hairdresser's but the hairdresser gave her a tone rinse, which caused a rash, the court held that only the wave was consented to, and that the rinse had been a battery.

- Vitiation of consent

  The consent will be vitiated by fraud, duress, non-disclosure going to the real nature of the act, not the consequences.

  Thus, in the Irish case of *Hegarty v Shine* (1878) where the plaintiff consented to sexual intercourse and got venereal disease from the other person, the plaintiff had no action as she knew what act she was letting herself in for. Similarly, in *Sidaway v Bethlem Royal Hospital* (1985), where the plaintiff was paralysed in an operation which involved a '1% or 2%' risk of it happening even where there was no negligence (as was so here), she claimed that her consent was void as she had not been able to make an informed decision. Again, there was no doubt as to the nature of the act she had agreed to; ignorance of a consequence did not vitiate the consent.

- Withdrawal of consent

  The plaintiff can of course withdraw his consent, on giving reasonable notice.

- Consent to a crime

  In criminal law, consent is not a defence to a crime. But it is a defence to torts which are also crimes.

  Thus, in *Murphy v Culhane* (1976) a man who started a fight consented to the other side's battery which in fact killed him.

- Unconscious or mentally disordered plaintiffs and medical treatment

  Before *F v West Berkshire HA* (1989) the justification for treating, say, road accident victims who were unconscious, or mentally disordered persons, was 'implied consent'. But this was a fiction: how could they be said to have consented? The House of Lords in this case justified such interference on grounds of necessity (see defences, later).

  However, in a Canadian case, even this did not prevent a surgeon being held liable who gave a blood transfusion to an unconscious patient he knew to be a Jehovah's Witness (*Mallette v Shulman* (1988)).

- The method of the interference

  The interference must be direct; ie by the defendant's person, or by an object held, or by an object thrown at the plaintiff.

  In *Reynolds v Clarke* (1725) the court stated: 'if a man throws a log into the highway, and in that act it hits me, I may maintain trespass, because it is an immediate [sc direct] wrong; but if as it lies there I tumble over it, and receive an injury, I must bring an action upon the case [ie for indirect harm], because it is only prejudicial in consequence.'

  Thus, spitting on the plaintiff (*R v Cotesworth* (1704)), or interfering physically with an article in contact with him, or throwing a firework at X, who instinctively throws it on to the plaintiff (*Scott v Shepherd* (1773)), all commit battery.

  Moreover, the plaintiff can be battered without knowing it; this will be the case in many medical treatment cases, for example, *Mallette v Shulman*, above. But an omission to act will not suffice except where there is already physical contact and the defendant ignores a request to desist, say, by refusing to let go of a girl he is hugging.

  So, in the criminal case of *Fagan v Metropolitan Police Commissioner* (1968), a man who accidentally drove onto a policeman's foot (committing no tort), but who intentionally delayed moving off it, as the policeman requested, committed battery once a reasonable time had elapsed after the request was made.

- No transferred intent

  Where the defendant intends to hit T, but instead hits P, his intent to batter T is transferred to P in criminal law, but not in battery. P would have to sue in negligence.

9.1.2 Assault

Assault is a misleading term since in criminal law it is used to denote both battery and assault. In tort, however, it denotes the defendant putting the plaintiff in reasonable apprehension of an immediate battery, by means of an attempt at battery, or a threat to commit battery.

It follows from this definition that the plaintiff must be aware of the assault.

Further, there must be the means of carrying the threat into immediate effect. Thus, in *Thomas v NUM (South Wales)* (1985), there was no assault by striking miners who shouted threats at miners entering the place of work as the striking miners were being held back by police. But provided the plaintiff reasonably apprehends the immediate battery, it is probably immaterial that there is in fact no danger at all; thus pointing a gun at the plaintiff which he is unaware is unloaded is probably an assault.

Similarly, there has been dispute as to whether words alone can amount to assault. Old cases tend to deny a right of action, but modern cases such as *Thomas v NUM (South Wales)*, above, support it. But the issue is rather that of immediacy of the ensuing battery than one of the form of the threat.

This is committed when the defendant *intentionally and directly* confines the plaintiff, without the plaintiff's consent or other lawful excuse. The confinement must be total. In *Bird v Jones* (1845) a closing of one side of Hammersmith Bridge was not a tort, as the other side of the bridge could still be used.

As in battery the plaintiff can be falsely imprisoned in his ignorance. In *Meering v Graham-White Aviation* (1919), the plaintiff was answering questions in a room about thefts from an aircraft factory. Unknown to him (but on view to everyone else) were two policemen outside the room to stop him leaving if he were to try. The court held that he was falsely imprisoned, and the House of Lords has recently confirmed that this was correct (*Murray v MOD* (1988)).

The case of *Meering v Graham-White Aviation* shows that a man's reputation is not to be meddled with by falsely imprisoning him: even if the plaintiff is incapable of escaping, say, through disability (*Grainger v Hill* (1838)), he still has a right not to be imprisoned.

Before leaving trespass to the person, it is interesting to note the tort of intentional physical harm, committed, it should be noted, *indirectly*.

In the leading case, *Wilkinson v Downton* (1897), the defendant had informed the plaintiff, falsely and for a joke, that the latter's husband had been injured in an accident. Not surprisingly, the plaintiff suffered nervous shock. This was held to be actionable on proof of damage.

This tort has not proved popular, probably because foreseeable nervous shock is well catered for in the tort of negligence. But it covers actions such as lacing a drink which causes harm when a person drinks it, or putting a bucket of water on a partly open door to fall on the person who next walks through, and putting a log on the highway (see *Reynolds v Clarke* (1725), above). It is also interesting that a *quia timet* interlocutory injunction was awarded under this tort to stop harassment by a former boyfriend in *Khorasandjian v Bush* (1993).

9.1.3   **False imprisonment**

9.1.4   **Intentional physical harm**

It may be that this is the first step towards civil judicial protection not merely from harassment but on a wider scale from infringement of privacy. (As to the criminal law's recent developments in this area see Part IV on Civil Liberties.)

9.1.5	Protection from Harassment Act 1997

Perhaps these common law developments prompted Parliament to enact the Protection from Harassment Act 1997. Section 3 creates a tort of, on at least two occasions, committing an 'actual or apprehended' ... 'course of conduct' which causes harassment, alarm and distress to the plaintiff, and which the defendant knows, or should reasonably know, will harass, alarm or distress the plaintiff. It should be noted that the burden of proving reasonableness of the conduct lies with the defendant. (Distinguish assault, where the plaintiff must prove reasonable apprehension.)

9.1.6	Trespass to goods

Trespass to goods can be defined as intentional and direct interference with goods in the possession of the plaintiff, without lawful excuse.

Dispossession is irrelevant; mere touching will suffice, or even frightening animals: in *Kirk v Gregory* (1876) it was simply moving some rings from one room to another.

Thus, wrongful interference with personal documents by the police will amount to trespass (*Reynolds v Metropolitan Police Commissioner* (1984)) (dealt with in Part IV on Civil Liberties).

9.1.7	Conversion

This can be defined as intentional interference, direct or indirect, with goods in the possession of the plaintiff amounting to a denial of the plaintiff's title.

This is a particularly harsh tort since so long as the interference is intentional it does not matter that the conversion is not, nor that the defendant was mistaken as to ownership of the goods or that he acted in good faith.

Thus, in *Hollins v Fowler* (1875) an auctioneer who sold the plaintiff's cotton believing that it was the property of the third party who asked him to sell it was liable. The interference can be of many kinds, from keeping to disposing of or destroying, and is, with trespass to goods, often brought against the police or government departments such as Customs and Excise and the Inland Revenue to challenge the legality of a seizure of the plaintiff's goods. In cases such as these the plaintiff will often seek re-delivery of the goods instead of mere damages.

9.1.8	Trespass to land

This tort can be defined as an intentional, direct and physical interference with land in the possession of the plaintiff without lawful excuse.

Land includes, not only the sub-soil, but also a reasonable air-space, and the interference can be not only entry but also remaining on land after the right to remain has ceased, for example, refusing to vacate your theatre seat at the end of the performance, or abusing your right of entry. It can also be committed by animals under the defendant's control, for example the hounds in *League against Cruel Sports v Scott* (1985).

An amusing example of the last is *Harrison v Duke of Rutland* (1893) where Harrison, clearly an early conservationist, stood on the Duke's road opening and shutting his umbrella thereby frightening off the grouse on the Duke's moor, and as a result depriving the Duke of the pleasure of blowing the birds' brains out with his gun. When Harrison complained of being man-handled by the Duke's servants it was held that 'the easement acquired by the public is a right to pass and repass ... for the purpose of legitimate travel' and that by abusing this right he had become a trespasser, and could be forcibly evicted.

The remedies to this tort, apart from damages, centre around the recovery of possession of the land, whether by self-help ejection of a trespasser or by court action, and include the ability to enlist the aid of the police where sizeable 'hippy convoys' squat on the plaintiff's land (s 61 Criminal Justice and Public Order Act 1994: see Part IV on Civil Liberties). This alleviates the plaintiff of the need to obtain, at his own expense, an injunction.

It must not be thought that once the plaintiff had made out his case on the rules set out above that he had won his case. It is open to the defendant to prove, on a balance of probabilities, that he is protected by a defence.

We have already seen that consent, which is a general defence to most torts, and therefore to be proved by the defendant, is a part of the plaintiff's burden in trespass.

A defendant may plead that he acted under a mistake. This is normally no defence, either to trespass (if I unlawfully punch X, thinking he was Y, could I reasonably excuse myself?), or to other torts (see *Hollins v Fowler*, above), but under s 24 Police and Criminal Evidence Act 1984, an arrest can generally be founded on reasonable, if mistaken, grounds for suspicion.

It is sometimes said that a defendant can plead inevitable accident, but this will usually mean that the plaintiff has usually failed to prove the defendant's fault and has therefore failed to prove the commission of the tort.

9.2   Defences to the intentional torts

9.2.1   Consent

9.2.2   Mistake

9.2.3   Inevitable accident

9.2.4	Defence of the person or property	This defence may be available, but the defendant has the burden of proof.

Section 3 Criminal Law Act 1967 says that reasonable force can be used to prevent a crime. As all trespasses to the person and, where criminal damage is caused, to goods will also be crimes, the section is available in a civil action.

However, the common law also allows a person to use such force in the defence of himself, his relatives and friends, and probably anyone, and in defence of the property of those same people. The common law will apply where there is no 'crime', eg where the assault is by a nine year old, who is incapable of crime in law.

The defendant must prove:

- that it was reasonable to use force, which will cover a preemptive strike, though not mere retaliation; and

- the force used was reasonable and proportionate.

Thus, in *Lane v Holloway* (1967) a 64 year old man, offended by the 27 year old defendant's saying to the former's wife, 'shut up, you monkey-faced tart', gave the younger man a pathetic tap on the shoulder. The old man was able to prove that the crushing blow he received in reply, which put him in hospital for a month, was out of proportion to the older man's battery, and was outside the defence and therefore a battery.

Further, the closeness of relationship and whether the protection is that of a person or property will also influence whether the force is correct or not.

In cases of trespass to land it is not reasonable to use force which does not remove the trespasser. Thus in *Collins v Renison* (1754) when the trespasser, who was up a ladder, would not quit the land, and the defendant 'gently shook the ladder .... and gently overturned it, and gently threw the plaintiff from it upon the ground', the Chief Justice found this to be a battery: 'The overturning of the ladder could not answer the purpose of removing the plaintiff out of the garden; since it only left him upon the ground at the bottom of the ladder, instead of being upon it.'

9.2.5	Necessity	The courts have always been wary of this defence. One judge was reminded that Milton called it, 'the tyrant's plea'. It differs from the last defence in that there the original threat came from the plaintiff himself, whereas here it comes from elsewhere, for example, nature or circumstances. The defendant here will be harming an innocent plaintiff.

It is a defence to all forms of trespass where there is 'an urgent situation of imminent peril' (*Southwark London Borough*

Council v Williams (1971), where homelessness did not justify squatting) and the defendant takes reasonable steps to avert the threat.

There is necessity to act in the plaintiff's best interests (whether or not there is also emergency) and the defendant cannot communicate with the plaintiff.

For example, in cases of medical care of a plaintiff who is mentally incapable of making the relevant decision (as in *F v Berkshire Health Authority* (1989), where a mentally disordered woman who would not have made a good mother was sterilised to prevent her from becoming pregnant).

Cases have justified acting to save life. For example, jettisoning oil (which damaged the plaintiff's beaches) to lighten a ship which otherwise would have broken up, putting the crew's lives in danger (in *Southport Corporation v ESSO* (1952)); or to save property, as in *Cope v Sharpe (No 2)* (1912), where the defendant's servant destroyed some heather on the plaintiff's land to stop a fire coming onto his master's land; or for the public well-being, as in *Rigby v Chief Constable of Northamptonshire* (1985), where firing gas-canisters into the plaintiff's shop, causing it to catch fire, would have been justified if the police had not been negligent in allowing the fire-engines to go away.

In most cases of necessity the defendant is seeking to excuse himself after the event, but in *F v Berkshire Health Authority* (1989) (above) the court gave consent to a future sterilisation 'in the best interests' of the patient.

This principle was applied in *Airedale NHS Trust v Bland* (1993) to allow the withdrawal of antibiotics from Tony Bland, who had been crushed in the Hillsborough football disaster and who had remained ever since in a persistent vegetative state. But this was novel: it was not a tortfeasor pleading best interests for past damage to the victim; indeed the original tortfeasor, Chief Constable of South Yorkshire, was not a party to this application. This was another party claiming it would be in the victim's best interest to be allowed to die, as it was futile to prolong his life and would not confer any benefit on him.

This may well have been in his 'best interests', but can it be said to have been 'necessary'? Have we two distinct defences? One, necessity, a defence for a past tort, and best interests, presumably for past and future torts?

At common law, a parent or person *in loco parentis* can impose reasonable corporal punishment and authorise medical care. Prison authorities also have this power.

9.2.6 The 'best interests'/inability-to-communicate cases

9.2.7 Discipline and lawful authority

Thus, in *Leigh v Gladstone* (1909) a suffragette was lawfully force-fed, who would otherwise have died of hunger.

We have discussed above the position of health authorities in matters of sterilisation and allowing patients to die. The case law is scanty on this subject as yet, and it may be in the future that the defence lies here rather than in necessity, particularly in the death cases as considered above.

| 9.2.8 | *Ex turpi causa non oritur actio* |

This means that a legal action will not arise from a wrongful act. It is a doctrine borrowed from the law of contract ('contracts void as illegal') with the result that it may be a defence that the plaintiff is himself a wrongdoer.

Thus, in *Murphy v Culhane* (1976) a widow suing for the death of her husband at the hands of the defendant lost her claim as her husband and his pals had started the fight. And in *Pitts v Hunt* (1990) a pillion-passenger on a motorbike was injured when the motorbike crashed, killing the rider. Both had been drinking and the rider had been driving very fast, encouraged by the plaintiff pillion-passenger. The pillion passenger lost his action. (See further Chapter 11, 11.1.3 below.)

But not every illegality will support the defence; my action in respect of your damaging my car when you reversed your car into it could not be defeated by your proving that I parked on double yellow lines at the time. And a burglar does not become an outlaw unable to sue (*Revill v Newbery* (1996); see Chapter 11, 11.1.5 below.

| 9.2.9 | Statutory or judicial authority |

As can be expected, any order or sentence of a judge or any action sanctioned by statute or common law cannot be made the subject of an action in tort. (See especially the powers of arrest, search, entry and seizure contained in the Police and Criminal Evidence Act 1984, examined in Part IV on Civil Liberties.)

Chapter 10

The Tort of Negligence

A quick consideration of how most people are injured will reveal that little harm is, in fact, caused intentionally: rather, most harm is caused carelessly, or negligently. Virtually all actionable industrial accidents (which for these purposes can include the occurrence of an industrial disease) and road traffic accidents are caused by negligence.

10.1   Introduction

We should be careful with the word 'accident'. Legally, it means 'with no fault'; in common speech it means 'with negligence' or other breach of duty. Furthermore, actions in respect of careless services by professional or skilled people are usually brought in the tort of negligence, whether or not also in contract.

The word 'negligence' has two meanings: firstly, a type of fault in several torts, for example, I could commit nuisance negligently; and secondly, the tort of negligence, which we shall consider in this chapter.

As to the nature of the tort of negligence we could usefully heed the warning in *Moorgate Mercantile v Twitchings* (1976) that 'in most situations it is better to be careful than careless, but it is quite another thing to elevate all carelessness into a tort'.

This warning was earlier given in the leading case, *Donoghue v Stevenson* (1932), thus:

> 'The law takes no cognisance of carelessness in the abstract. It concerns itself with carelessness only where there is a duty to take care and where failure in that duty has caused damage.'

Thus to succeed the plaintiff must not simply claim some vague lack of care but must prove:

- that the defendant owed him a *duty of care*; and

- that the defendant was in breach of that duty; and

- that the plaintiff has suffered reasonably foreseeable *damage*, caused by that breach.

Duties of care were recognised before 1932, but a single concept of a duty of care was only recognised in that year, in the following case.

10.2   Duty of care

10.2.1   The general theory

In *Donoghue v Stevenson* (1932) the plaintiff, Mrs Donoghue, had been served with a drink of ginger beer from an opaque bottle. She drank some of the ginger beer, but when the rest was poured out a partly decomposed snail floated out with it. The plaintiff claimed to have then suffered from a stomach illness and claimed damages from the defendant, the manufacturer. The drink had been bought by her friend, so the plaintiff had no claim in contract. She therefore claimed that the manufacturer, in producing a drink in a sealed bottle, thus preventing inspection of the drink, owed her as the ultimate consumer a duty of care to see that the drink was safe, and that he had broken that duty, causing her damage.

A duty of care could indeed exist at that time, but only in specific, independent relationships, for example, a landlord to a tenant, or a salesman to a customer. But one Lord of Appeal, Lord Atkin was interested in finding, as he put it, 'some general conception of relations giving rise to a duty of care'.

This 'general conception' Lord Atkin restated in his neighbour principle, as follows:

> 'The rule that you are to love your neighbour becomes in law: You must not injure your neighbour, and the lawyer's question: Who is my neighbour? receives a restricted reply. You must take reasonable care to avoid acts or omissions which you can reasonably foresee would be likely to injure your neighbour. Who then, in law, is my neighbour? The answer seems to be persons who are so closely and directly affected by my act that I ought reasonably to have them in contemplation as being so affected when I am directing my mind to the acts or omissions which are called in question.'

Thus Mrs Donoghue's claim succeeded, but only by three Lords of Appeal to two.

By the late 1970s the emphasis on taking care against what 'I should have contemplated', or as is now more commonly said, 'what is reasonably foreseeable', had meant that a duty was established in a factual situation simply on the basis of foreseeability of harm. The duty of care was then seen to need some control.

In a series of cases, culminating in *Caparo Industries v Dickman* (1990) the required relationship was summarised as involving three concepts:

- 'foreseeability of harm': and

- 'proximity or neighbourhood', meaning the closeness of relationship between the parties; and

- that it be 'just and reasonable' for the plaintiff to be owed a duty of care by the defendant.

So to establish whether the defendant owes a duty of care to avoid a certain type of harm to the plaintiff, the plaintiff must establish all three points. A suggestion in *Caparo Industries v Dickman* that in cases of foreseeability of direct physical harm, only 'foreseeability of harm' need be proved, was quashed by the House of Lords in *Marc Rich v Bishop Rock Marine (The Nicholas H)* (1995).

And to decide whether a duty of care exists in a new situation the House of Lords in *Caparo Industries v Dickman* (1990) approved the approach of an Australian case (*Sutherland Shire Council v Heyman* (1985)) 'that the law should develop novel categories of negligence incrementally and by analogy with established categories'.

Thus, in contrast with the position in the late 1970s and early 1980s, it is no longer possible to establish a duty of care merely by showing foreseeability of harm; the court must be convinced of the closeness of the parties and the fairness of its being owed. Furthermore, the court will move the duty of care forward step-by-step through the cases, rather than creating a duty whenever foreseeability of harm alone existed.

We have seen that foreseeability of harm is an essential ingredient of the duty of care. If this is lacking there can be no proximity even if the parties are physically close.	**10.2.2** **Proximity and foreseeability of harm**

Hence the 'unforeseeable plaintiff' cases, for example, *Bourhill v Young* (1942) where the defendant motor-cyclist killed himself by careless riding out of sight of Mrs Euphemia Bourhill, a pregnant Leith fishwife, who was standing on the other side of a tram which blocked her view. Her claim of nervous shock was dismissed as he could not, when causing the accident in which he died, have reasonably foreseen harm to her.

Similarly, in *Roe v Ministry of Health* (1954) a glass ampoule containing anaesthetic was contaminated such that it paralysed the plaintiff when injected into him. The cause of the contamination was a hairline crack, unknown to science at that time, which allowed another liquid, in which the supposedly intact ampoule was correctly immersed, to seep into it.

The defendant must take account of any disability of the plaintiff of which he is aware or ought reasonably to be aware. Thus, in *Haley v London Electricity Board* (1964) the Board should reasonably have foreseen that a blind person might come along the pavement where they had insufficiently	**10.2.3** **Abnormal plaintiffs**

guarded a hole they had dug, even though the hole posed no danger to a sighted person.

10.2.4 Nervous shock

Judges have always been sceptical about nervous shock, or psychiatric damage, as the courts now prefer: it cannot be seen as can, say, a broken leg. Nevertheless, over the course of this century liability has gradually widened on the basis that a defendant ought to foresee that his actions might cause the plaintiff nervous shock.

But note that we are talking here about something that goes beyond mental suffering and grief. It was described in *McLoughlin v O'Brian* (1982) as 'recognisable and severe physical damage to the human body and system ... caused by the impact, through the senses, of external events on the mind' and constituted 'what is as identifiable an illness as any that may be caused by direct physical impact'.

Where it accompanied actual physical harm to the plaintiff it caused no problem, but in *Dulieu v White* (1901) a barmaid who feared immediate physical injury to herself when a horsevan crashed through the wall of a public house towards her won her claim even though she suffered no physical injury.

Liability then continued to widen – through cases where the plaintiff saw the infliction of physical injury to a relative, friend or colleague, for example, in *Hinz v Berry* (1970), a wife and mother watched as a jaguar car ploughed into her family in a lay-by (in *Attia v British Gas* (1987) a claim succeeded where she watched fire destroy her home and possessions) – to cases where she saw or heard something which caused her to assume physical injury to a relative, friend or colleague.

For example in *Hambrook v Stokes* (1925) a mother, having watched her children pass out of sight round a corner, immediately saw a driverless lorry come quickly round the same corner, causing her to assume (correctly) that her children had been injured by it.

By 1967, the general position was that the plaintiff had to be concerned for herself, or a relative, friend or colleague, and she had to be there at the scene. (The more recent *Attia v British Gas*, which raises problems – do we equate pet animals with relatives and homes? – has not yet stood the test of time.) Liability then took a plaintiff who was a rescuer at an horrible railway accident in which strangers alone were victims (*Chadwick v BRB* (1967)), but he was there at the scene.

Then came *McLoughlin v O'Brian* (1982). Here a wife and mother was called to hospital an hour after her family had been the victims of a road traffic accident. One child was dead and her husband and two other children were covered in grime and blood and in various states of consciousness and hysteria.

Not surprisingly, she suffered nervous shock and claimed against the owner of the lorry and others. The Court of Appeal, afraid to 'open the floodgates' to this kind of claim, rejected her claim on grounds of public policy (as being against the public interest: see later). But the House of Lords allowed her claim, Lord Wilberforce specifying that three requirements had to be satisfied in these 'aftermath' cases. These were:

- the plaintiff had to be within the protected: class of persons this includes close family (spouses, parents, children, siblings), although the House of Lords in *Alcock v Chief Constable of South Yorkshire Police* (1991) allowed a fiancee to succeed on the basis of 'love and affection';

- there was *proximity to the accident*, ie that the plaintiff was close in both time and space;

- the *means of communication* were sight, hearing or immediate aftermath.

Thus in *Alcock v Chief Constable of South Yorkshire Police* (1991), where relatives of victims of the Hillsborough football disaster made claims, most failed on the second and third requirements since the claimants had first heard of the accident over the radio or television, and had first seen the deceased relatives in the mortuaries the following day.

Further, some Lords of Appeal in *Bourhill v Young* (1942) and *McLoughlin v O'Brian* (1982) have said that no duty of care is owed to the 'ordinary frequenter of the streets' not to cause him nervous shock.

A problematic case from the House of Lords is *Page v Smith* (1995) where a 'primary' victim (ie one fearful for his own safety) suffered a relapse into 'ME' (chronic fatigue syndrome) after a road accident. The majority of three Lords of Appeal held that a primary victim must prove reasonable foreseeability merely of physical harm (not of shock as favoured by the other two judges), but that a witness or bystander must prove reasonable foreseeability of nervous shock. Further, the majority held that a defendant must take his victim as he finds him (the 'egg-shell skull' rule; see Chapter 10, 10.4.2 below). It is suggested that this is wrong: only if an abnormality (which is what an 'egg-shell skull' is) is reasonably foreseeable should the defendant have to care about it (see the reasonably foreseeable blindness of the plaintiff in *Haley v London Electricity Board* (1964), above).

10.2.5 Duty to 'rescuers'?	In *Chadwick v BRB* (1967) it was held that British Railways, held negligent in causing the Lewisham train crash, could reasonably have foreseen that rescuers would come to help to extricate victims, and that those rescuers would suffer nervous shock from the terrible injuries they would see.

In *Haynes v Harwood* (1935) a policeman was injured stopping a runaway horse negligently left unattended, and in *Ogwo v Taylor* (1987) a fireman sued for burns incurred in fighting a fire negligently started by the defendant.

Both policeman and fireman were rescuers and accordingly owed duties of care not to be caused injury by the respective defendants. It is after all foreseeable that these people will perform these heroic deeds, and it is surely just and reasonable to impose a duty of care in these circumstances. If it were otherwise, who would be a rescuer, or a fireman? Further, as Cardozo J said (in *Wagner v International Rly Co* (1921), an American case): 'danger invites rescue. The cry of distress is the summons to relief ... the emergency begets the man.'

10.2.6   Personal liability for the acts of third parties

It is sometimes claimed that a defendant owes a duty of care not to cause harm to the plaintiff, not by any personal act of the defendant's, but by some act of a third party. Thus, here, the defendant is personally liable in negligence.

Do not confuse this with a master's vicarious liability for the act of his negligent servant, which we shall consider later, in 'parties'.

Liability for the act of a third party is liability for an omission, ie a failure to control, which, as in trespass, does not impose liability. 'The general rule is that one man is under no duty of controlling another man to prevent his doing damage to a third. There are, however, "special relations" which are the source of a duty of this nature': *Smith v Leurs* (1945), an Australian case, approved in *Home Office v Dorset Yacht Co Ltd* (1970), below.

An example of the 'special relations' which will raise a duty of care is where the defendant has a right of control over the third party. Thus in *Home Office v Dorset Yacht Co Ltd* (1970) the Home Office were negligent in allowing borstal boys to escape from Brownsea Island, upon which the latter damaged the plaintiff's yachts moored nearby.

But it is more difficult where the third party is an independent person over whom the defendant has no control, for example vandals. In *Smith v Littlewoods Organisation* (1987), where vandals entered the defendant's derelict cinema and started a fire which damaged the plaintiff's nearby premises, the House of Lords said that it was not enough that intervention by the third party was foreseeable; it had to be likely to impose a duty of care on the defendant. This was not the case here, so the defendant owed the plaintiff no duty of care.

Similarly, in *Topp v London Country Bus (South West) Ltd* (1993), no duty was owed for leaving an unattended bus for nine hours parked outside a public house with its doors unlocked and key in the ignition. It was only foreseeable, not likely or probable, that yobs would drive the bus away, killing the plaintiff's wife five minutes later.

So far, in considering the rules for establishing that the defendant owed a duty of care not to cause damage to the plaintiff we have looked at the three *Atkinian-Caparo* elements of foreseeability of harm, proximity or neighbourhood, and the just and reasonable test. But it is clear that another element is at work: this is public policy, representing the interests of the public as a whole, as seen by the judges.

10.2.7   Public policy

In *Anns v Merton London Borough Council* (1977), a case now overruled, public policy in so far as it affects negligence was described as:

> 'considerations which ought to negative, or to reduce or limit the scope of the duty or the class of person to whom it is owed or the damages (sic) to which a breach of it may give rise'

and in *Sutherland Shire Council v Heyman* (1985), the Australian case mentioned above, as:

> 'those further elements ... which confine the duty of care within narrower limits.'

At the end of the 1970s this was the only restriction on the imposition of a duty of care once foreseeability was established, but it has been said since by one Lord of Appeal that this restrictive test is 'one which will rarely have to be applied'.

Public policy is now less common in this context, but it still prevents a barrister (or solicitor) from being sued for his advocacy (*Rondel v Worsley* (1967)). In this case it was said that he owes a greater duty to the court than to his client, that he should be free to act without fear of being sued by his client and, on a practical basis, it would cast doubt on the correctness of a previous case if it were later held that the barrister had been negligent in conducting it. It would open the floodgates to many criminal appeals. (Similarly, a claim that the police were negligent in failing to arrest the 'Yorkshire Ripper', who eventually killed the plaintiff's daughter, a notorious murderer of several women, was dismissed on the ground of opening up the floodgate to every burgled citizen, thereby diverting police attention and time from their real work (*Hill v Chief Constable of West Yorkshire* (1988)). But the main area of influence of public policy in this tort is in the area which now follows.

| 10.2.8 | Economic loss |

Economic loss, also known as financial or pecuniary loss, is actionable in contract and in other, intentional, torts. In this tort, however, the use of public policy is to prevent 'liability in an indeterminate amount, for an indeterminate time, to an indeterminate class' as Cardozo J put it in *Ultramares Corpn v Touche* (1931), an American case.

To use an example, in *Weller v Foot & Mouth Research Institute* (1965), the defendant's negligently allowing germs to escape forced the cancellation of an auction of livestock. The plaintiff, an auctioneer, lost money, but so did the shops, public houses, transport companies, petrol stations etc, all who would have taken in money had the auction been held. Needless to say, the plaintiff lost.

Economic loss is not to be confused with monetary compensation. Most damage can only be compensated in damages: how else could a broken leg or smashed car be compensated? But in the case of a broken leg or smashed car there is physical damage; here, in cases of pure economic loss, there is none.

| 10.2.9 | Careless acts |

Economic loss arising from a careless act is only actionable if connected to or dependant on physical damage to property of which the plaintiff is owner or possessor.

In *Spartan Steel Alloys Ltd v Martin & Co Ltd* (1972) the defendant's servant carelessly broke an electricity cable causing the plaintiff's furnace to stop in the middle of a job. The metal in the furnace was damaged and useless. The power was off for 14 and a half hours, during which the plaintiff claimed it could have done four further melts. Three claims were made:

- for the damaged metal in the furnace (physical damage);

- for the lost profit on that metal (economic loss);

- for the lost profit on the four further melts (pure economic loss).

The first claim was clearly admissible; most tort claims are for physical damage to person or property. The second claim also succeeded as the loss was connected to the plaintiff's physical damage. But the third claim failed as it was not so connected.

Recently, there has been a blurring of the boundaries between physical damage and economic loss, but the traditional analysis as explained above was affirmed in *Murphy v Brentwood DC* (1990), which affirmed that the costs of repair of a defect in property (in this case, a dwelling-house) is pure economic loss, and that the defect is evidence of breach of duty of care, but not physical damage.

Finally, in *Leigh & Sullivan v Aliakmon; The Aliakmon* (1986) where the defendants negligently damaged goods while loading it on ship, the seller and the buyer (the plaintiff) of the goods had agreed that the seller still had title to them, in which case the buyer, being neither owner nor possessor of the damaged goods, could not sue for the damage.

Thus a decorator whom I contract to paint my house cannot sue my negligent neighbour who burns my house down for the loss of his contractual fee. (As to whether he can sue me, see frustration in contract, in Chapter 6.)

A careless statement causing physical damage ('the brakes on your care are quite safe, sir') is actionable in negligence, as is a fraudulent (ie intentionally false) statement causing economic loss in the tort of deceit. But it was only in *Hedley Byrne v Heller* (1963), where the defendant bank falsely and negligently gave its opinion that a company was financially sound that a careless statement causing pure economic loss was held actionable by the House of Lords.

But here was a classic area of potential 'indeterminate liability', as the most ill-thought-out statement could be relied on by the most unexpected listener. Lord Morris therefore confined the duty of care as arising only in a special relationship where the defendant has an expertise or skill which he knows the plaintiff is relying on or the defendant expert knows that the plaintiff is relying on him to make careful enquiry.

The essence of all five Lords of Appeal was that an expert who assumes or accepts responsibility should owe a duty of care. The House of Lords was reluctant to impose liability where the 'advice' was made on a social occasion and subsequent dicta have taken a similar view on off-the-cuff statements. But a layman having no expertise was admitted by counsel to have owed a duty of care when advising on the state of a car which the plaintiff intended to buy (*Chaudhry v Prabhakar* (1988)). As the 'just and reasonable' test applies here too, it might be that this liability is too wide.

In a recent case a solicitor has been held liable to a beneficiary who would have benefited under a will had the

10.2.10   Assumption of responsibility and careless statements

solicitor not delayed so long (the client died before the will was ready for execution). The solicitor had assumed the responsibility of putting the client's instructions into effect (*White v Jones* (1995)).

10.2.11 Proximity and *Hedley Byrne*

Problems have arisen with *Hedley Byrne* duties of care as statements, whether oral or written, are often passed on and can easily reach an 'indeterminate class'. The question arises as to how far proximity can extend.

Under *Caparo Industries v Dickman* (1990) the defendant must be aware that his statement will be communicated to the plaintiff either as an individual or as a member of an identifiable class and in connection with a specific transaction or type of transaction. Thus, in that case, careless auditors of a company's annual accounts (a task required by the Companies Act) were held to owe no duty of care to a company which, on the strength of the accounts, bought shares in that company. The auditors' statutory duty was owed to the audited company's shareholders as a group, but no duty was owed to the shareholders either as prospective investors or as individual existing shareholders, still less as members of the ordinary public.

On the other hand, in *Smith v Eric Bush*; *Harris v Wyre Forest District Council* (1989), the plaintiffs, each intending to buy houses, each applied for a mortgage to, respectively, a building society and the district council. The prospective lenders had the properties in question valued, in the first case by an independent firm of valuers, and in the second case by an employee of the council. As is usual, the cost of the valuations fell on the applicants, but no privity of contract existed between applicant and valuer. It was always intended that the valuation in the first case would be shown to the applicants, which it was, and they went ahead with their purchase on the strength of it. The valuation in the second case, however, was not shown to the applicant, but he assumed that if the council were prepared to grant the loan then the house must surely be all right; he accordingly went ahead with his purchase also. Both valuations were wrong. Again the question arose: did the valuers owe a duty of care to the respective applicant: was there proximity between them? The House of Lords held that there was as the valuer in each case must have known that the applicant would rely on his valuation: most did; and in any case he would know that the applicant was footing his bill! But that was as far as liability went: it was pointed out by the House of Lords that no duty of care would be owed if a subsequent purchaser were to rely on that same valuation. No 'indeterminate class' here!

Liability for a mis-statement can also lie in contract for misrepresentation.

10.2.12   *Hedley Byrne* proximity pre-contract

But liability in tort is wider than in contract:

- tort covers statements of law, and opinion: not just fact;

- a duty of care can arise in pre-contractual negotiations, whether a contract is concluded or not;

- the negligence limitation period starts on the occurrence of damage; in contract, on the breach.

On the other hand, liability in contract is wider than in tort:

- contractual liability applies irrespective of the existence of a duty of care;

- the burden of proof in negligence is on the plaintiff, but in contract, under s 2(1) Misrepresentation Act 1967, it lies on the defendant.

Having established that the defendant owed him a duty of care to avoid foreseeable harm, the plaintiff must also prove that the defendant was in breach of his duty of care.

10.3   Breach of duty

The standard of care required of the defendant is that of the reasonable man.

10.3.1   The standard of care

'Negligence is the omission to do something which a reasonable man, guided upon those considerations which ordinarily regulate the conduct of human affairs, would do, or doing something which a prudent and reasonable man would not do' (*Blyth v Birmingham Waterworks* (1856)).

And in *Glasgow Corporation v Muir* (1943) Lord MacMillan said that: 'The reasonable man is presumed to be free both from over-apprehension and from over-confidence.' And the reasonable man is not incompetent through, say, inexperience. Thus, in *Nettleship v Weston* (1971) a learner driver who failed to straighten the wheels after turning a corner thereby injuring the supervisor's knee, could not plead her inexperience. And in *Wilsher v Essex Area Health Authority* (1986) a junior doctor inserted a catheter into a baby's vein, which showed a lower oxygen reading than if it had been correctly put into his artery; the oxygen flow to the baby was therefore increased, ultimately causing blindness. Again, his plea of inexperience was dismissed although the baby lost his action on damage grounds (see below).

But a failure to use higher-than-reasonable skill is not negligent. In *Argyll v Beuselinck* (1972) the plaintiff instructed a solicitor-author with a reputation in the literary world to advise her generally in her intention to publish her memoirs. His primary role was to advise on libel; he included advice on copyright, but although he thought of income tax he did not raise it with her. Although the plaintiff failed on other grounds, the Vice-Chancellor made it clear that if a consumer requires a higher skill it has to be paid for under a contract, and that the only required standard in tort is a reasonable one.

| 10.3.2 | Professional or skilled persons |

In many cases the issue arises as to the standard of a professional or skilled person. We would expect, surely, that a reasonable surgeon would show a higher standard of care at surgery than would a reasonable man on the Clapham omnibus.

This is not to contradict the last paragraph, we are concerned here with whether the surgeon owes a greater duty at surgery than the ordinary man would, not whether a highly skilled surgeon owes a greater duty than an ordinary surgeon. In *Bolam v Friern HMC* (1957) the judge said that 'the test is the standard of the ordinary skilled man exercising and professing to have that special skill'. Thus, the standard is in effect that of a reasonable surgeon or whatever he professes to be, but it is obviously important to establish what skill the defendant does profess to have.

| 10.3.3 | How is the 'reasonable' standard of care determined? |

So, in *Philips v William Whiteley* (1938) a jeweller who pierced the plaintiff's ears, causing injury, did not claim to be a surgeon; he merely owed the standard of care of a reasonable jeweller who pierced ears. On the other hand, in *The Lady Gwendolen* (1965), when Guinness, the brewers, operated ships to carry their brew to England, the court would not accept their claim to be judged merely as brewers: 'having become owners of ships, they must behave as reasonable ship-owners'.

| 10.3.4 | The likelihood of injury |

In considering the standard of care which the defendant was expected to meet the court will consider:

- the *likelihood* of injury;

- the *gravity* of the injury;

- the *social importance* of the defendant's actions;

- the burden of *adequate precautions*.

The defendant is not bound to guard against all reasonably foreseeable harm, but only that which is likely or probable. 'One must guard against reasonable probabilities, not fantastic possibilities' (*Fardon v Harcourt-Rivington* (1932)).

In *Bolton v Stone* (1951) a batsman at a cricket pitch in Manchester hit the ball out of the ground, hitting Miss Stone who was stood nearly 100 yards away from the crease on the road outside her house. The ball cleared a fence 17 feet above the pitch, some 78 yards from the crease. Such cricketing prowess had only been shown about six times in the past 30 years. The House of Lords held that though this was foreseeable and would certainly happen again at some time, it was not likely. Thus, there had been no negligence in allowing cricket there.

Likelihood of harm is of course dependent on current general knowledge. Thus, in *Roe v Ministry of Health* (1954), above, because hairline cracks were not known to be possible, no harm was likely.

Sometimes it may not be likely that the harm would be caused, but the gravity or severity of the harm which would be caused if it did would make the reasonable take steps to reduce the risk.

10.3.5   The gravity of the injury

It may not have been likely that a ferry-boat sailing with its bow doors open would capsize: it transpired after the Zeebrugge disaster that many had been doing so, but just imagine the harm that would be caused if it did. In *Paris v Stepney Borough Council* (1951) a worker used a hammer without being provided with goggles. A splinter flew into his eye, blinding him. Perhaps not likely, but this man was already blind in one eye, and now, of course, was completely so. The defendants should have taken particular care here; they had not, and were therefore liable.

The social usefulness of the item or practice might justify the risk. In *Daborn v Bath Tramways* (1946) it was said that 'if all the trains in this country were restricted to a speed of five miles an hour, there would be fewer accidents, but our national life would be intolerably slowed down'.

10.3.6   The social usefulness of the defendant's actions

Many items and practices of modern life cause harm, from trains, cars and aeroplanes to the use of gas, kitchen knives or petrol. The judge will be looking for a reasonable compromise. Thus, in *Watt v Herts County Council* (1954) a firearm was injured when a crane which was urgently needed to lift a vehicle under which a woman was trapped and which, to save time, had been loaded onto the fire brigade's lorry without being fixed in position, shifted as the lorry sped to the scene. The court held that the emergency justified the taking of the risk. However, in the same case Denning LJ said:

'If this accident had occurred in a commercial enterprise without any emergency there could be no doubt that the (plaintiff) would succeed ... The commercial end to make profit is very different from the human end to save life or limb.'

| 10.3.7 | The burden of adequate precautions |

In *Latimer v AEC Ltd* (1952) Denning LJ said, 'In every case of foreseeable risk, it is a matter of balancing the risk against the measures necessary to eliminate it.' Thus, driving trains, or cars, at five miles an hour would remove the risk of accident, but is too burdensome, as is covering all cricket pitches with huge roofs to stop cricket balls from leaving.

In *Latimer v AEC Ltd* (1952) a factory floor had flooded. Sawdust was thrown down but it ran out leaving an area untreated. The plaintiff was loading a barrel on a trolley when he slipped on the untreated floor, but the only alternative to carrying on working in this area was to have closed the whole factory until the floor had dried out. The House of Lords held that this was too burdensome given the risk involved, so the plaintiff lost in his claim.

| 10.3.8 | The burden of proving the breach |

The burden of proof of the breach is on the plaintiff (as it is in all three parts of this tort).

But this burden may weigh heavily on a plaintiff who does not know how the damage occurred. It is all the more galling if the damage so obviously reeks of negligence. In these circumstances the doctrine of *res ipsa loquitur* will apply.

The burden of disproving negligence is thrown onto the defendant if:

- the plaintiff cannot establish exactly what caused the thing;

- the thing was under the control of the defendant;

- the thing is not something that normally happens if those in control show reasonable care.

The rule was stated in the leading case, *Scott v London & St Katherine's Dock* (1865) in which bags of sugar fell from a warehouse window onto the plaintiff, a customs officer!

Other cases have involved swabs left in a patient after an operation (*Mahon v Osborne* (1939)) and yoghurt falling on a supermarket floor, or at least remaining there for some time (*Ward v Tesco* (1976)).

As to what the effect is where the doctrine applies, certainly, if the defendant offers no explanation then judgment can be entered for the plaintiff. If the defendant can show that he took reasonable care then whether he can explain how it happened or not, the burden of proving breach shifts back to the plaintiff.

So far, the plaintiff must have proved that the defendant owed him a duty to take reasonable care to avoid harm to the plaintiff, and secondly, that the defendant was in breach of that duty of care. Now the plaintiff must prove that he has suffered reasonably foreseeable damage as a result of the defendant's breach of duty. He must prove both:

- *causation* of damage; and

- *reasonable foreseeability* of damage.

Both of these will curb the defendant's liability, thus relieving him of liability for damage which is too remote. They are therefore called the rules of *remoteness of damage*.

10.4   Damage

The plaintiff must prove that the defendant caused the damage. There must be a *chain of causation* leading from the breach to the damage. This is sometimes called the 'but for' test, in other words, if he can prove that 'but for' the breach there would have been no damage, then he has proved causation of damage.

In *Barnett v Chelsea & Kensington Hospital Management Committee* (1968) the plaintiff's husband, a nightwatchman, turned up at hospital one night complaining of stomach pains, asking to see a doctor. The doctor, in breach of duty, refused to see him, telling him to see his own doctor in the morning. The husband died the following day of arsenical poisoning and it would have been no use had the hospital doctor in fact seen him. It could not be said that 'but for' the doctor's breach he would have died; he would have died anyway, thus the hospital doctor did not cause the damage.

In some cases, the plaintiff may not be able to prove that a particular source of harm was the sole cause; in these cases, the plaintiff must prove that the defendant's fault caused, or *materially contributed* to, his injury. In *Wilsher v Essex Area Health Authority* (1988) there were six possible causes of a premature baby becoming blind: one was a junior doctor's breach of duty (see 'breach' and 'reasonable standard of care', above), but the other five were purely accidental causes all found in premature babies. The plaintiff argued on the basis of a 1972 case, that the defendant's breach had caused a material risk of the damage occurring, but this was not enough; the plaintiff had to prove not simply that the breach could have caused the damage but that it did do or materially contributed to it. The baby's claim failed.

10.4.1   Causation of damage

The plaintiff must also prove that his damage was reasonably foreseeable, ie that the reasonable man would have seen the damage as a result of the breach. In *The Wagon Mound (No 1)*

10.4.2   Reasonable foreseeability of damage

(1961), a ship (*The Wagon Mound*) carelessly spilt some oil in Sydney Harbour, which floated towards another ship 200 yards away which was tied up to a wharf and having some welding done to it. The welders stopped welding when they saw the oil while enquiries were made as to whether a spark could ignite the oil. The answer was, no, it could not, so the welders continued. Sixty hours later a spark fell on some cotton waste floating on the water, ignited that, which in turn ignited the oil, damaging both ship and wharf. The owners of the wharf sued. Granted, there was a chain of causation leading from the oil spill to the damage by fire of the wharf, but the Privy Council held that the damage was not a reasonably foreseeable result of the spillage of the oil.

But what damage must be foreseeable? The precise damage? The damage need only be within the foreseeable kind of damage.

Thus, in *Hughes v Lord Advocate* (1963) post office workers left a hole they were digging marked by lit oil lamps. This was negligent; children could foreseeably meddle with the lamps setting their clothes alight and causing themselves burns. The plaintiff, a little boy, did meddle with one of the lamps, but dropped it in the hole. An explosion followed, causing him burns. The attitude of the House of Lords was that burns were foreseeable, and burns were caused; the difference in method of causation was irrelevant.

Similarly, where it was reasonably foreseeable that a fireman might suffer flame burns when fighting a fire caused by the defendant's negligence, it did not matter that the burns were caused by scalding caused by the water hosed in by the firemen being turned to steam by the heat of the fire (*Ogwo v Taylor* (1987)).

Contrast *Crossley v Rawlinson* (1981) where an AA man, running to a burning lorry along a trodden path, and still some distance from the lorry, trod in a hole causing him to fall and injure his back. While it was foreseeable that he might have suffered, say, burns from the petrol exploding or the cargo falling off the lorry, it was not foreseeable that he would hurt his back after treading in a hole.

Once the plaintiff proves that his injury is within the reasonably foreseeable kind, it can be of any degree. Thus, in *Bradford v Robinson Rentals* (1967) it was reasonably foreseeable that a man driving his master's unheated van in a cold winter would suffer some cold injury. He did – frostbite! But this was merely an extreme degree of the reasonably foreseeable kind of injury, rather than a different kind of injury, such as the AA man suffered above.

It might be assumed that reasonable foreseeability presupposes causation, but *Performance Cars v Abraham* (1962) shows that this is not the case. The defendant drove his car into a Rolls-Royce already damaged in a previous accident. While it was foreseeable that the defendant in the later accident would be liable for the cost of repair and re-spray, this damage was already caused by the earlier defendant. The defendant Abrahams in this action did not cause the damage!

Occasionally, the damage is of the foreseeable kind, but a sensitivity of the plaintiff causes further damage of an unforeseeable kind. For example, I carelessly drop a book on the plaintiff's head. It is foreseeable that he will suffer a bruise, but he has an abnormally thin skull which cracks, causing him brain damage. The attitude of the common law is that the tortfeasor takes his victim as he finds him. These are called 'egg-shell skull' conditions (only a 1963 South African case involved this precise condition). The leading egg-shell skull case in negligence is *Smith v Leech Brain Ltd* (1961), where the plaintiff, who worked in a factory, suffered some flying zinc on his lip. This caused a burn which was reasonably foreseeable, but because of a pre-malignant condition, cancer developed from which he died. The defendant owner of the factory was held liable for this extra injury. In another case, *Robinson v Post Office* (1974) the plaintiff's leg was cut at work due to the defendant's fault. He then underwent foreseeable and reasonable medical treatment which involved a tetanus injection. The plaintiff's allergy to this caused encephalitis, for which the defendant was held liable.

The rule applies throughout tort, so if I intentionally stab someone, who turns out to be a haemophiliac, and who bleeds to death, I am liable in trespass to the person for the death as well as the wounding. In negligence the cases apply the rule to both known and unknown conditions, to psychological conditions, and in a Canadian battery case, *Malette v Shulman* (1988), to religious beliefs. Here, a surgeon performed an emergency operation involving blood transfusion on a person not known to be a Jehovah's Witness. The Witness' action in battery succeeded.

This phrase means 'a new, intervening act' and brings together the two aspects of causation and reasonable foreseeability.	10.4.3 *Novus actus interveniens*

It may happen that a chain of causation follows from a breach, but that a new act intervenes. Does this break the chain of causation leading from the defendant's breach? The 'but for' test is deficient here. For example, can a plaintiff who has been knocked down by a car say that 'but for' the manufacturer making that car it would not have existed to have knocked the plaintiff down? Strictly, the answer is 'yes', but a judge would say that many intervening events had broken the chain of causation, not least the driving of the person behind the wheel at the time the plaintiff was knocked down.

So the character of the new act can affect its effect on the chain of causation. If it is not a *novus actus interveniens*, the defendant's chain of causation is unbroken, and he is liable for the original and any further damage. But if it is a *novus actus interveniens* the defendant's chain of causation will be broken. This will result in his breach not causing any damage to the plaintiff (as in *Wright v Lodge* (1993) and *Smith v Littlewoods* (1987), below), or not causing further damage to the plaintiff (as in *McKew v Holland & Hannen & Cubitts* (1969), below).

Intervening natural forces are not a *novus actus interveniens* they are foreseeable.

Thus, if my negligent neighbour causes a hole in my roof and it rains immediately afterwards, causing damage, he will not be able to say that the rain breaks my chain of causation.

An intervening act of the plaintiff is a *novus actus interveniens* only if the plaintiff acts reasonably. In *Wieland v Cyril Lord Carpets* (1969) and *McKew v Holland & Hannen & Cubitts* (1969) the respective plaintiffs, who were already in incapacitated states as a result of the defendants' actions, both descended staircases but fell in the process, suffering further injuries.

In *Wieland*, the plaintiff, who wore bi-focal spectacles, was fitted with a collar round her neck two days after being negligently injured by the defendant. She was in a nervous state as a result of the events of the two days and finding that the collar impeded her use of the bi-focals she went to her son's office for him to take her home. There, although accompanied by her son, she fell on some stairs suffering further injuries. In *McKew*, the plaintiff's first injury had resulted in his occasionally losing control of his left leg. Soon afterwards, he was descending a staircase after inspecting a flat, without a stick, ahead of two adult members of his family, and accompanying his child down the stairs when his leg gave way, and he fell injuring himself. It was held that the plaintiff in *Wieland* had acted reasonably in the purpose of using the staircase and in how she went about it, the same could not be said of the plaintiff in *McKew*. The behaviour in *McKew* was therefore a *novus actus interveniens*, whereas that in *Wieland* was not, for which the defendant was liable.

More problematic is the new act of a third party. In one case a useful example was given: if the defendant's act causes the plaintiff to have to leave his car to go to telephone for a mechanic to come to repair it, is the defendant liable if thieves steal the wheels of the car in the plaintiff's absence?

A series of cases in the 1980s concerned the liability of a derelict property from which third party vandals either themselves obtained access into the plaintiff's adjoining property or allowed, say, fire to spread to that property. You will no doubt be thinking back to the issue of duty of care for acts of third parties, and indeed the two are related.

There we saw that there is generally no liability for what a third party does. The conclusion was that no duty of care was owed unless there was a right of control of the third party. Here, we are concerned with whether the third parties act breaks the defendant's chain of causation. In *Home Office v Dorset Yacht* (1970) Lord Reid said in the House of Lords that to be part of the chain of causation (and not, therefore, a *novus actus interveniens*) the third party's act 'must at least have been something very likely to happen'.

Thus, in the stolen wheels example above, while the theft of the wheels might have been foreseeable, something that could be expected to happen some day, it was nevertheless not likely, still less very likely. Similarly, in most of the vandal cases, for example *Smith v Littlewoods* (1987), where Lord MacKay LJ preferred the word 'probable' rather than 'likely' (though in tort they usually mean the same thing), it was not likely or probable that vandals would get into a derelict cinema and set fire to adjoining property, though it may well have been foreseeable.

You may recall that when we were dealing with breach and the reasonable standard of care, above, it was stated that the defendant need only take care against what is likely or probable, not against what is foreseeable.

On the other hand, in *Home Office v Dorset Yacht* (1970), given that the borstal boys were imprisoned on an island where boats were moored but were unskilled in sailing, it was likely that they would take a boat and damage it.

As a final point, it is useful to apply these principles to 'motorway pile-ups', where the issues of causation and intervention arise. A motorist causes an accident and also thereby an obstruction, but is he liable for all the damage that ensues? In *Rouse v Squires* (1973) a lorry negligently jack-knifed and a car crashed into it. Minutes later another lorry, also negligently driven, piled into the other two, killing someone who was helping at the scene. In *Wright v Lodge* (1993), a broken-down 'mini' car was negligently left by the owner, unlit, in a dangerous position on a foggy night. Shortly afterwards, a recklessly driven lorry hurtled into the car and glanced off it. The lorry crossed the central reservation and crashed into a oncoming car, killing the driver. In *Rouse v Squires* the second lorry driver's negligence did not break the first's chain of causation; the first lorry driver's negligence was the cause of the death. But in *Wright v Lodge* the reckless driving of the lorry did break the mini driver's chain of causation; the lorry driver's negligence, not that of the driver of the mini, was the cause of the death. A fine distinction, but perhaps negligent driving is 'likely to happen', whereas 'reckless' driving is not.

Chapter 11

Defences to Negligence and to Other Torts

The following two defences are 'general defences', that is to say they apply also to some other torts. But they are the main defences to negligence, and the negligence-related torts looked at in the next chapter.

Furthermore, most of the cases are negligence cases (or from related torts), so it is appropriate to follow on from negligence into these defences. Note that sometimes certain facts might lead into either defence (for example, there are cases on joining a pub-crawl as consent to injuries and as contributory negligence).

One important difference between the two defences is that consent, wherever it is found, is a complete defence to the plaintiff's claim, whereas contributory negligence is a partial defence, ie the plaintiff wins, but loses some of his damages in proportion to his own negligent contribution to his injuries.

This translates as 'an injury cannot be done to a willing person'.

11.1 Volenti non fit injuria

There are two forms of *volenti* in tort:

- the first is consent to an intentional interference which will definitely happen and would otherwise be a battery, for example a medical operation;

- the second type is *assumption of risk*, where there is no certainty that a tort may happen, but the plaintiff agrees to run the legal risk of it doing so. The principle of this defence is that 'one who has invited or assented to an act being done towards him cannot, when he suffers from it, complain of it as a wrong' (*Smith v Baker* (1891)).

The consent can be given expressly, but generally it cannot be implied from the plaintiff's conduct. In *Slater v Clay Cross Co Ltd* (1956) the plaintiff was hit by a train while lawfully walking along the defendant's railway track in a tunnel. The defendant argued that she had impliedly consented. Denning LJ said, 'It seems to me that when this lady walked in the tunnel, although it may be said that she voluntarily took the risk of danger from the running of the railway in the ordinary and accustomed way, nevertheless she did not take the risk of negligence by the driver.' Thus, in *Dann v Hamilton* (1939), where the plaintiff accepted a lift from a driver who 'while far from being dead drunk, was under the influence of drink to such an extent as substantially to increase the chances of a collision', there was no consent and her claim succeeded.

However, there can be implied consent to run a particular, identified and obvious, risk. In *ICI v Shatwell* (1964), two brothers, both experienced shot-firers working in a quarry, knew very well the risk they ran when they intentionally caused an explosion in negligent circumstances. Further, in *Morris v Murray* (1990), the defendant, with whom the plaintiff went for a flight in the defendant's light aircraft, had drunk the equivalent of 17 whiskies. In both cases the plaintiffs lost. The risk in each case was not an unknown, vague risk of something which might happen, as was the case in *Dann v Hamilton*; in both cases the risk was obvious and clearly identifiable and therefore capable of being consented to by the plaintiffs in the other two cases.

11.1.1	Reality of consent

The use in the Latin maxim of *volenti* and not merely *scienti* makes it clear that knowledge alone is not consent; there has to be a voluntariness about it.

In *Smith v Baker* (1891) a man who worked in a quarry had known that rocks were being carried over his head, before one fell and injured him; his claim nevertheless succeeded.

By the same token rescuers, who in many cases are aware of the risk of danger but are nevertheless driven on by some altruistic force are not volunteers. In *Haynes v Harwood* (1934) a policeman was injured while stopping a runaway horse in a busy street.

Similarly, in *Chadwick v BRB* (1967), the rescuer at the Lewisham railway crash, and in *Ogwo v Taylor* (1987), the fireman were held not to have volunteered: in all three cases human life and safety were at stake.

Compare *Cutler v United Dairies* (1933) where the plaintiff was injured stopping a runaway horse in an empty field; not surprisingly he was held to be a volunteer and not a rescuer.

11.1.2	Defendant's exclusion of liability

At common law the defendant can in general exclude his liability (either orally or in writing, in words such as, 'all liability in negligence is hereby excluded').

This amounts to the plaintiff's consent when having dealings with the defendant. But statute law has restricted the defendant's power to exclude liability in some areas: firstly in purely business dealings, and secondly, generally.

The business restriction applies where the defendant is conducting a business activity (for example, a surgeon doing an operation or a plumber mending pipes at the plaintiff's house), and on business land or premises, s 2(1) Unfair Contract Terms Act 1977 (which deals also with notices in tort, as here) says that an attempt to exclude such business liability for personal injuries, including always death, is void. Section 2(2) says that an attempt to exclude such liability for other loss or damage (ie economic loss or property damage) is only valid if 'fair and reasonable ... having regard to all the circumstances' at the time when the alleged tort was committed.

In *Hedley Byrne v Heller* (1963) the plaintiff bank who relied on the careless mis-statement in fact lost the action, because, although the defendant owed a duty of care to the plaintiff to avoid economic loss, the defendant had excluded his liability in negligence. Since 1977 such a disclaimer would have to survive the 'fair and reasonable' test.

Finally, s 1(3) Law Reform (Personal Injuries) Act 1948, makes void an attempt at excluding liability for personal injuries suffered by an employee which is contained in an employment contract.

Although, as we have seen, anyone can exclude his private liability (for example, a man trying to pick the lock of his neighbour's house which the neighbour has closed without taking a key, can say, 'I'll try to open the door, but if I break the lock completely I'm not paying for another'). However, all persons, in all situations are bound by s 149 Road Traffic Act 1988, which says that liability owed by an insured vehicle owner to passengers cannot be excluded. (In *Pitts v Hunt* (1990) two drunken youths rode recklessly on a motorbike which eventually crashed, killing the rider and injuring the plaintiff pillion-passenger. The rider's estate, when sued, knowing that consent could not be used because of s 149, instead pleaded *ex turpi causa non oritur actio*, which the Court of Appeal accepted (see also Chapter 9, 9.2.8 above)).

11.1.3   Exclusion of liability generally

At common law, the plaintiff's contribution to his own damage barred his action. The Law Reform (Contributory Negligence) Act 1945 now allows the claim, and allows the judge, after fixing the total damages, to reduce the award to reflect the various contributions towards the damage. Thus, the Act alters only the legal consequences of contributory negligence, but not the rules for determining whether contributory negligence exists in the first place.

Remember that this is a defence, which must of course be pleaded by the defendant; the court cannot apportion damages of its own volition. This is a partial defence; the plaintiff's damages are reduced in proportion to his 'fault'.

11.2   Contributory negligence

11.2.1	The plaintiff's 'fault', or negligence	The defendant need only prove a contribution to the damage, not necessarily to the 'accident'. (Though that would probably increase the likelihood of a finding of contributory negligence.)

11.2.2   The defendant's
burden of proof

The defendant must prove 'fault', ie 'that the injured party did not in his own interest take reasonable care of himself and contributed, by this want of care, to his own injury' (*Nance v British Columbia Electric Rly* (1951)). In *Froom v Butcher* (1975), long before it became a criminal offence not to wear a seat-belt, the plaintiff lost 20% of his damages, for not wearing his. The plaintiff's claim that he was free not to wear it (free from criminal prosecution – then) was met by Lord Denning MR: 'Free in the sense that everyone is free to run his head against a brick wall ... But it is not a sensible thing to do.'

The defendant must also prove causation and reasonable foreseeability, ie that the plaintiff's negligence contributed to his damage, and the damage was of the kind which the plaintiff should reasonably have foreseen.

In *Jones v Livox Quarries Ltd* (1952), the plaintiff hitched a lift on the back of his employer's slow-moving track-laying vehicle, against orders. The driver had had to almost stop in order to change gear, when a dumper, following, ran into the back of the track-layer, injuring the plaintiff. At the trial his damages were reduced by one fifth. On appeal, Denning LJ said, 'if the plaintiff, whilst he was riding on the towbar, had been hit in the eye by a shot from a negligent sportsman, I should have thought that the plaintiff's negligence would in no way be a cause of his injury ... His dangerous position on the vehicle was one of the causes of his damage'. Thus, he had been contributorily negligent.

11.2.3   Behaviour not
amounting to
contributory
negligence

If the plaintiff reasonably apprehends danger and acts reasonably, he or she cannot be faulted, even if, in hindsight, it was the wrong decision.

Thus, in *Sayers v Harlow UDC* (1958) a woman found herself locked in a public toilet because of the rusty state of the lock. After shouting for help for some time, she was faced with the alternatives of staying put, or attempting to climb out of the toilet. She was held to have acted reasonably in attempting to escape even though she found it too high and had to back down, on which she fell, injuring herself (but see below).

Similarly, a rescue attempt is not contributory negligence; but the rescuer might be contributorily negligent in the way he conducts the attempt. In *Harrison v BRB* (1981) a train guard who tried to pull a passenger aboard and who was injured when they both fell out of the train, was contributorily negligent when he gave the signal for the train to stop instead of that to cause it to stop. And the plaintiff in *Sayers v Harlow UDC* (1958) was held to be so in that in climbing back down after her unsuccessful self-rescue, she put her weight on the toilet-roll holder, which, as the Master of the Rolls said, 'true to its mechanical requirement revolved', throwing her to the ground.

Finally, when considering the contributory negligence of an employee who is suing his employer it is accepted that not every slip will amount to contributory negligence. If the job involves noise, fatigue, monotony etc, the likelihood of a finding of contributory negligence decreases (*Caswell v Powell Duffryn Collieries* (1939)).

Chapter 12

Applied Common Law Negligence and Statutory Duties

This section looks at liability for injury caused by the state or condition of premises (eg a badly fitted carpet, a wall that collapses), or things done during the defendant's occupation (eg cricket allowed in the corridors).

Until 1957 liability throughout lay in negligence. This is still the case where the defendant is other than an occupier of the land, for example he is a builder or a local authority inspector with power to inspect the building as it is built. (The case which restated that a defect in a building is evidence of a breach of duty of care and not damage itself, and which therefore ruled out most claims in negligence against builders and local authority inspectors, is *Murphy v Brentwood District Council* (1990), discussed above at Chapter 10, 10.2.9 above).

However, where the defendant is the occupier of the land and premises, he may owe a duty to a person coming onto the land. His liability will depend on whether the plaintiff is a lawful visitor, in which case a duty is owed under the Occupiers' Liability Act 1957, or whether he is a trespasser, in which case a duty is owed under the Occupiers' Liability Act 1984.

Curiously, while persons using a private right of way, or within a National Park are within the 1984 Act, those on a public right of way, which includes roads and footpaths, are outside both Acts.

A lawful visitor (in fact called 'visitor' in the Act) will sue under the Occupiers' Liability Act 1957.

Section 2(1) imposes the 'common duty of care' on an occupier of premises, which s 2(2) defines as a duty 'to take such care as in all the circumstances of the case is reasonable to see that the visitor will be reasonably safe in using the premises for the purposes for which he is invited or permitted by the occupier to be there'.

Note than the duty is 'to see that the visitor is reasonably safe', not that the premises are reasonably safe. The duty is on the 'occupier' of premises, whether or not also the owner, but 'occupier' is not defined in the Act. Accordingly, the courts take a wide view and do not restrict it to physical control.

Further, there can be several occupiers. In *Wheat v Lacon* (1966), where the plaintiff, a paying guest in a public house fell

12.1   Dangerous land and premises

12.1.1   Occupiers' liability

12.1.2   Lawful visitors

down an unlit staircase with a banister which was too short, and was killed, both the brewery and the managers who lived there were held to be occupiers and to be in breach of their duties.

'Visitor' is also not defined but it includes all invitees and licensees; thus, so long as the visitor is lawful, it makes no difference whether he is:

- invited to come on the premises (eg the milkman); or

- allowed (or 'licensed') to come on, such as the postman; or

- he entered as of right conferred by law, for example, the police when exercising power of entry.

But a lawful visitor who abuses his right or privilege of entry is not within s 2(2); as Scrutton LJ said in *The Carlgarth* (1927), 'when you invite a person into your house to use the staircase, you do not invite him to slide down the banisters'.

12.1.3	The characteristics of the plaintiff	The duty is owed to the 'visitor', so the duty will take account of whatever reasonably foreseeable characteristics the visitor has (see *Haley v LEB* (1964) above).

But it is necessary to consider the care, or lack of it, that might reasonably be expected of the visitor. For example, with children, s 2(3)(a) says that extra care must be taken, but this supposes that the child is a lawful visitor and not a trespasser.

A line of cases indicate that a child has an implied licence to come onto the premises, by virtue of the occupier not preventing the child from coming on. The child accordingly assumes that it is allowed to come on, and this is more justifiable if the child is allured onto the land, for example, by berries in a park in *Glasgow Corp v Taylor* (1922).

On the contrary, where the visitor is a skilled person who could reasonably be expected to take care of himself, the standard of care demanded of the occupier takes account of this (s 2(3)(b)).

Thus, in *Roles v Nathan* (1963), where two chimney sweeps killed themselves by going up a chimney in Manchester with a fire still burning in the grate below, the occupier was not in breach of his duty.

The plaintiff has to prove both breach and damage, on principles similar to those in common law negligence. He can claim for injury to the person and to goods, even those of a non-visitor's which have been carried there by the visitor.

12.1.4	Defences	• Exclusion or restriction (s 2(1))

It is possible at common law to exclude liability by an appropriate notice, oral or written. Thus at a party in my home a notice such as 'all liability in negligence or under statute to persons using these stairs is excluded' would be effective, but the same notice on business premises would be subject to s 2 Unfair Contract Terms Act 1977 (see above at Chapter 11, 11.1.2 above).

- Visitor's knowledge by a warning (s 2(4)(a))

  A warning, whether written or oral, amounts to a performance and discharge of the common duty of care, and therefore, provided the warning makes the visitor reasonably safe, there is no breach. Thus, 'Keep Out' or 'Danger, Keep Out' would probably not be sufficient, but 'Danger, Keep Out: Mineshafts' or 'Danger of falling down Mineshafts: Keep Out' probably would be.

  But it is important to distinguish between a warning which performs a duty under s 2(4)(a) and a warning which excludes liability under s 2(1) (which may be caught by s 2 Unfair Contract Terms Act 1977). In *Roles v Nathan* (1963) 'they were repeatedly warned about it', ie the danger from the smoke.

  Finally, a warning under s 2(4)(a) does not always have to be verbal. In *Titchener v BRB* (1983) an embankment and a fence were held to be warnings of the dangers of a railway line.

- Visitor's knowledge by assumption of risk (s 2(5)) (*volenti non fit injuria*)

  The normal common law principles of *volenti* apply. Again a notice must make the visitor reasonably safe.

- Contributory negligence

  Normal principles apply including the Law Reform (Contributory Negligence) Act 1945.

- Acts of an independent contractor

  Under s 2(4)(b) the occupier can plead that it was reasonable to entrust work to an independent contractor and that he used reasonable care in choosing a competent contractor and in checking that the job had been properly done. Thus, whereas in *Haseldine v Daw & Sons* (1941), it was reasonable to instruct a contractor to mend a lift, thus shifting liability from the occupier, this was not the case in *Woodward v Mayor of Hastings* (1944) where the job of sweeping snow off a school step need not have been contracted out.

These are protected by the Occupiers' Liability Act 1984, which offers reasonable protection from dangers arising from the

12.1.5   Trespassers

state or condition of the land and premises rather than the reasonable safety of the visitor of the 1957 Act.

The duty on an occupier arises under s 1(3) if:

- '[the occupier] is aware of the danger or has reasonable grounds to believe that it exists; and

- he knows or has reasonable grounds to believe that the [trespasser] is in the vicinity of the danger concerned or that he may come into the vicinity of the danger; and

- the risk is one against which ... he may reasonably be expected to offer the other some protection.'

The duty is 'to take such care as is reasonable in all the circumstances of the case to see that he does not suffer injury on the premises by reason of the danger concerned' (s 1(4)). Here only personal injury is protected.

Where the danger arises from the defendant's activities (rather than from the state and condition of the land) the defendant will owe a common law duty which follows the provisions of the Act (*Revill v Newbery* (1996)). In this case an 82 year old man shot a burglar who returned to break into his shed. The old man was sleeping there to protect a television and washing-machine, and was frightened, especially when (as his counsel put it) the burglar banged on the shed shouting, 'If the old bastard's in there, we will do him'. The old man was liable in damages, however, to the burglar.

The defences are *volenti non fit injuria* and contributory negligence.

The reader may be glad to learn that the aforesaid burglar was held to have been two-thirds contributorily negligent, but burglary is not so illegal as to raise the defence of *ex turpi causa* (see Chapter 9, 9.2.8 above), as a burglar would otherwise become an outlaw (*Revill v Newbery* (1996)).

Further, a notice to exclude liability is not caught by the Unfair Contract Terms Act 1977, as it is not specifically mentioned in that Act, but it is arguable that at least the duty of 'common sense and common humanity' of *Herrington v BRB* (1972), the former leading authority where a boy was injured while trespassing on a railway line, ought to apply.

12.1.6   The duty to employees

An employee injured at work has the benefit of three more actions, in addition to an action under the Occupiers' Liability Act 1957 which are:

- an action for employers' liability at common law (negligence); and

- an action for breach of a statutory duty; and

- an action for the negligence of another employee where the employer, or master, is vicariously liable (dealt with later).

This action is one under *Donoghue v Stevenson* (1932) as applied to the employment relationship.

It is owed to employees (sometimes called servants), but not to independent contractors. In *Wilsons and Clyde Coal Co Ltd v English* (1937) it was defined as:

> 'a duty which rests on the employer and which is personal to the employer, to take reasonable care for the safety of his workmen, whether the employer be an individual, a firm, or a company, and whether or not the employer takes any share in the conduct of the operations ... The obligation is threefold – the provision of a competent staff of men, adequate material, and a proper system and effective supervision.'

Case law has added the provision of safe premises, although we have already seen that judicial latitude is shown where the premises or access are only temporarily unsafe (*Latimer v AEC Ltd* (1953), above).

As well as the duty of care in negligence and the common duty of care under the Occupiers' Liability Act 1957, there are many statutory duties imposed by statute, delegated legislation and European Communities legislation.

Many are the detailed rules that protect workers against the dangers from chemicals, machinery and the industrial process generally. Recent regulations cover visual display units on computers. Each duty is different: it relates to a particular industrial process, whereas the common law duty of care is a general rule. This section concentrates on the statutory duties imposed on an employer, but statutory duties cover many other things, eg a duty to allow someone to vote; a duty not to wrongfully ban turkey imports.

Some statutes specifically provide for a civil remedy; some statutory codes are treated as part of mainstream tort as they clearly state rules of tort, for example, the Occupiers' Liability Acts 1957 and 1984. Some statutes prohibit civil remedies. But in most cases, it is a matter of construction of the statute by the court to work out whether Parliament intended a statute that would benefit workers in general and also allow an injured individual to sue for damages.

The plaintiff must prove, firstly, that the statute must impose a duty: a power, prohibition, or discretion is not enough. Secondly, if the duty is intended to benefit a class of persons, the plaintiff can sue if within that class. So in *Groves v Lord Wimborne* (1898), where a boy worker lost an arm in

12.1.7   Employers' liability at common law (negligence)

12.1.8   Breach of statutory duty

machinery, a statute on factory machinery was held to benefit a class of workers in that industry; in *Reffell v Surrey County Council* (1964), where a girl put a hand out to restrain a school door, which broke, cutting her, the statute was held to be for the benefit of a class, this time school children, staff etc. But the plaintiff cannot sue if the statute is passed for the benefit of the general public.

Thirdly, if the statute imposes a duty but provides no remedy or sanction, then it is presumed that a civil action is available. This was presumed in both *Groves v Lord Wimborne* (1898) and *Reffell v Surrey CC* (1964).

The final point, whether, if the performance of the duty is to be enforced in a specific manner, it is presumed that no other mode of enforcement is permitted, is unclear as cases support both views.

The standard of care required depends on the statute. Where the duty is absolute (eg 'all machinery shall be fenced') it is no defence that if absolute care had been taken a machine would have been unusable (*John Summers & Sons Ltd v Frost* (1955)). Qualified duties, eg 'possible'; 'practicable'; 'reasonably practicable' (in descending standard of care) impose different standards. These standards fall either side of the common law standard of negligence; some cases succeed in one tort but not in the other.

Whether damage is required, or whether it is actionable *per se*, depends on the statute. If personal safety, or prevention of damage to property, is the purpose of the duty, then damage is required. It must be caused by the breach of duty, and it must be within the kind of damage which the statute was intended to guard against.

Thus, in *Gorris v Scott* (1874) the duty was that sheep had to be penned on board ship to avoid spread of disease; the sheep were washed overboard. The plaintiff's claim failed as that was not the danger which Parliament had taken steps to cure. However, once proved that it is within the envisaged kind of damage, *Hughes v Lord Advocate* (1963) applies, ie the precise method of harm is irrelevant.

Thus, in *Donaghey v Boulton and Paul* (1967) the duty was to prevent falls through fragile roofing material; in fact the plaintiff fell through a hole in the roof. The court held that prevention of falling was the point of the statute, and that the method was irrelevant; thus the claim succeeded.

12.1.9   Defences

- *Volenti non fit injuria*

  If the duty is on the employer, this defence is not available to the employer when sued by the employee (on grounds of public policy).

- Contributory negligence

  This is available to apportion the damages under Law Reform (Contributory Negligence) Act 1945. But the Health and Safety legislation is aimed at protecting the workman, so that 'Regard must be had to the dulling of the sense of danger through familiarity, repetition, noise, confusion, fatigue and preoccupation of work' (Winfield). The standard is the ordinary prudent workman, but 'it is not for every risky thing which a workman in a factory may do in his familiarity with the machinery that a plaintiff ought to be held guilty of contributory negligence' (*Flower v Ebbw Vale Steel Co* (1934)).

Chapter 13

The Tort of Defamation

This tort is different from the others we have been studying. In the play *Othello*, when Cassio complains that his reputation is gone he bemoans that he has 'lost the immortal part of myself, and what remains is bestial' (Act 2, Scene 3). If nervous shock is a nebulous thing, how more so is damage to a person's 'immortal part', his reputation?

It perhaps comes as no surprise that this tort is exceptional in several respects. There is no survival of the action after either party's death (all other torts allow the deceased's estate to sue or be sued). There is a right to a High Court trial, unless both parties agree to the county court. This is one of the four civil causes of action (all concerning reputation) where there is a right to a jury trial, unless s 69 Supreme Court Act 1981 applies (ie there are many documents involved, or other cumbersome evidence). Corporations can sue; trades unions and local authorities cannot.

Legal aid is not available. In *Joyce v Sengupta* (1992) the plaintiff got around this last restriction by suing in another tort called injurious falsehood where it was available. She had been accused of stealing Princess Anne's letters when a maid to her, damaging both her reputation and her professional fitness, the latter constituting a cause of action in injurious falsehood. The court dismissed the defendant's complaint, saying that if the plaintiff's facts fit more than one tort that is his good fortune; it is always the plaintiff's choice as to which tort to sue in.

This is a good tort to use in an essay on the balance of competing interests, namely the right to protect your reputation, and the right of free expression.

A libel is in permanent form, usually visible, actionable *per se* and also a crime whereas slander is in transient form, usually audible, it requires proof of damage (save in four cases) and is not a crime.	**13.1 Two forms: libel and slander**

Examples of libel are words in print, pictures and effigies, both what they depict and their juxtaposition, as in *Monson v Tussauds* (1894), where placing a wax effigy of a man who had been found not proven of murder in Scotland in the entrance to the Chamber of Horrors was a permanent defamation, therefore libel. Examples of slander are spoken words, gestures, or the playing of music (say, 'The Stripper' when a woman is introduced). Permanent items which are not defamatory on sight, such as records, tapes and films, and broadcasting and plays have all been declared to be libel, usually by statute. The only practical difference arises in whether damage is required to be proved (see below).

13.2   Proving defamation

In all defamation actions the plaintiff must prove:

- that the statement was *defamatory*; and

- that it *refers* to the plaintiff; and

- that there was *publication* by the defendant to a third party; and, in actions for ordinary slander;

- damage.

13.2.1   Proving that the statement was defamatory

Several complementary tests have been stated. 'Would the words tend to lower the plaintiff in the estimation of right-thinking members of society generally?' (Lord Atkin in *Sim v Stretch* (1936)). A statement 'which is calculated to injure the reputation of another, by exposing him to hatred, contempt, ridicule' (*Parmiter v Coupland* (1840)), or which makes 'the plaintiff be shunned and avoided' (*Youssoupoff v MGM* (1934)).

Whichever test is used, the standard is objective, the standard of the ordinary, 'reasonable man'. It is not what the defendant intended but what he is reasonably understood to mean. Thus, in *Youssoupoff v MGM* (1934), where a film showed a princess (played by an actress) being raped by Rasputin, although 'right-thinking members of society' would not think any less of her, the ordinary man might still 'shun and avoid' her. (This might be even more so if she were insane instead.)

It follows, too, that it is not defamatory if it lowers the plaintiff in the eyes of a section of society only. In *Byrne v Deane* (1937), after someone had tipped off the police about illegal gambling machines at a golf club, a verse went up on the notice-board which ended, 'But he who gave the game away/May he byrnne in hell and rue the day'. The plaintiff's complaint that he was now shunned and avoided at the club was rejected since 'right-thinking' people would applaud his actions and think more highly of him.

Insults and jokes might be defamatory, or might not; it depends on the circumstances. In *Berkoff v Burchill* (1996) an article described an actor as 'hideous-looking'. On a preliminary point, the Court of Appeal rejected the defendant's claim that this could only amount to injury to feelings and not to reputation. The plaintiff's action was left to proceed. But all statements must be considered in context – in

Charleston v News Group Newspapers (1995) the *News of the World* showed headlines: 'Strewth! What's Harold up to with our Madge?' and 'Porn Shocker for *Neighbours* Stars' above a photograph of a man and woman nearly naked and engaged in sexual activity, but with the heads superimposed of the plaintiffs, an actress and actor in an Australian television 'soap' series. Having made the most of the headlines and the photographs, the newspaper then sided with the actors by complaining about a 'sordid computer game' made without the actors' consent and showing similar photographs to those which the newspaper had shown! The issue was whether the headlines and photographs alone were libellous, given, as Lord Bridge put it: 'a significant number of readers will not trouble to read any further', or would 'right-thinking members of society' not form a judgment before reading the article? The House of Lords agreed with the latter argument, quoting from an 1835 case that 'the bane and antidote must be taken together'. It can be defamatory even though no-one believed it to be true. The judge decides whether the statement was capable of a defamatory meaning; and the jury decides whether it had that meaning on that occasion. If there are two meanings, the judge decides which of them is capable of being understood; and the jury decides which of them the statement did have on that occasion.

It can easily happen that a *prima facie* innocent statement may have a second, defamatory meaning; this second meaning is called an innuendo. There are two types of *innuendo*: first, by there being further facts, known to a third party to whom the statement is published, which put the statement in a defamatory light: a true innuendo and second, by the third party reasonably reading in some other meaning inherent or implied in the statement: a false innuendo.

13.2.2   The innuendo

- The true innuendo

    In *Tolley v Fry* (1931), a chocolate advertisement depicting a golfer teeing off, innocent enough even if he were being paid for it, would appear in a different light to those who knew that he was an amateur, who as such should not gain money from his sport. At least Fry, the chocolate company, must have known the status of the man whose photograph they used.

    In *Cassidy v Daily Mirror* (1929), Mr Cassidy was photographed at the races with a lady-friend. The photograph appeared in the newspaper with the caption, 'Mr Cassidy and Miss X, whose engagement has been announced'. Mr Cassidy himself had supplied this information. But it was Mrs Cassidy who sued, claiming that the innocent caption would take on an innuendo to those aware that she had been living with him all these years, and who had now been told that they were unmarried (as he was impliedly free to marry Miss X). Both Tolley and Mrs Cassidy won.

- The false innuendo

Even the right-thinking member of society knows a thing or two, and will read between the lines. Even without any further knowledge he may well derive a second meaning from the statement. 'Logic is not the test', as Lord Devlin said in *Lewis v Daily Telegraph* (1963).

But the courts will not let him go too far. In this case, several newspapers commented on the fact that the fraud squad were enquiring into the affairs of a firm: a defamatory statement. The House of Lords agreed that stating this may give the impression that there were grounds for suspicion (an innuendo). But the trial judge had allowed the jury to go one further stage (and to award damages on the strength of that further stage) by inferring, not only suspicion, but also guilt. The House of Lords disallowed the damages awarded on this second innuendo.

It should be understood that an innuendo is in effect a second statement, on which the plaintiff can build a second action, and which the defendant has to defend.

The harshness of the strict liability of the common law here should also be noted. So long as there is an intention to publish, there need not be an intention to defame.

13.2.3	Proving that defamation refers to the plaintiff

'The only relevant rule is that ... the words must be understood to be published of and concerning the plaintiff' (Lord Atkin in *Knupffer v London Express* (1944)).

The name of the plaintiff is not essential, so long as she can be reasonably identified.

Thus, in *Cassidy v Daily Mirror* (1929), although there was no mention of Mrs Cassidy in the caption, those with knowledge of her relationship with Mr Cassidy would naturally think of her.

13.2.4	Innocent reference

At common law, the standard is objective. Again, it is not what the defendant intended but what he is reasonably understood to mean. Thus, if the defendant creates a fictional character which happens to be similar to the plaintiff, a third party could reasonably assume him to intend reference to the latter. Thus, in *Hulton v Jones* (1910), a fictional character called 'Artemus Jones, church-warden at Peckham', who nipped over to Dieppe to cavort with women, was understood to refer to

Artemus Jones, an English barrister by some of the latter's friends.

Even a reference to a real person can create liability if he is similar to the plaintiff and causes some people to assume reference to the other person of that description. In *Newstead v London Express* (1939), a true newspaper account of a bigamy trial of one Harold Newstead, a 30 year old Camberwell barman, was taken to refer to Harold Newstead, about 30, living in Camberwell, a barber. Thus, as in defamatory meaning, liability is strict at common law, the clear message being publish at your peril. But s 4 Defamation Act 1952 again provides a possible defence in these circumstances.

It is sometimes said, wrongly, that a class of persons cannot be defamed. The problem is, more correctly, 'the difficulty of establishing that the plaintiff was, in fact, included', according to Lord Atkin in *Knupffer v London Express* (1944), where an allegation of 'pure Fascist ideology' was made of the Young Russian Party, which had 24 British members and 2,000 worldwide. The House of Lords held that the words were a 'vulgar generalisation' which did not refer to any person, and cited 'All lawyers were thieves' as another example.

13.2.5   Defamation of a class

It is, of course, different if there is a reference by innuendo. Thus, a slur on Irish factory owners that the conditions in their factories were bad, which also contained clues which could be interpreted by those who understood them as referring to the plaintiff, was held to refer to him by true innuendo (*Le Fanu v Malcolmson* (1848)).

The defendant must have published the statement, ie made it known to any third party who understands it. Generally, the defendant has published it if he intended publication, or ought to have foreseen it.

Each repetition is a fresh publication, and a person who authorises, or can or should foresee a repetition is *prima facie* liable for it. This would be hard on a so-called 'mechanical distributor, 'a person who is not the printer or the first or main publisher of a work ... but has only taken ... a subordinate part in disseminating it' has a defence of claiming that he did not publish it (*Vizetelly v Mudie's Select Library* (1900)).

Libel is actionable *per se*; damage will be assumed, although the plaintiff can produce evidence of real damage, to boost his award. As mentioned above, slander normally requires proof of damage, but is actionable *per se* in four cases:

13.2.6   Special damage in ordinary slander

- an imputation of an imprisonable offence, carrying five years on first conviction; it is not necessary to specify the crime, for example 'I know enough to put you in gaol' sufficed in *Webb v Beavan* (1883);

- an imputation of an existing contagious or infectious disease;

- an imputation of unchastity, adultery or lesbianism in a woman;

- an imputation of incompetence or corruption of the plaintiff in his business or office.

Otherwise, the plaintiff must prove special damage as the natural and probable result of the publication, that is, actual loss of some material advantage, for example loss of employment, loss of a contract, loss of hospitality of friends (but not mere loss of society of friends), marital breakdown.

The usual rules of remoteness of damage apply, namely causation and reasonable foreseeability. In *Slipper v BBC* (1990), a senior policeman claimed that a programme made by the BBC on his failure to bring back a bank robber from Brazil was defamatory of him, and that it was foreseeable that the programme would be reviewed after transmission in the national press. On a preliminary point the Court of Appeal agreed that the jury should be allowed to decide on this foreseeability, which, if found, would make the BBC liable for any foreseeable repetition in the press.

13.3	**Defences to defamation**

The harshness of the strict liability of the common law in this tort made it inevitable, if free speech were not to be extinguished, that counter-balancing defences would be available. Only the first of these is a general defence, and even then is used rarely. The full list is.

- consent;

- justification;

- fair comment on a matter of public interest (which the plaintiff can defeat on proof of malice);

- absolute privilege;

- qualified privilege (which the plaintiff can defeat on proof of malice);

- no responsibility for publication (s 1 Defamation Act 1996);

- offer to make amends (s 2 Defamation Act 1996).

13.3.1	Consent

The usual rules applicable to this defence apply. In *Chapman v Ellesmere* (1932), a man who objected to a report accusing him of breaches of the rules was held to have consented as racing licences were granted subject to a condition that breaches of rules could be published in the racing calendar.

The plaintiff need not prove that the statement is false to succeed. But the defendant can defend himself by proving it to be true, even if he was not aware it was true when he said it, or he said it maliciously.

It need only be substantially true (so long as the false parts do not aggravate the defamation), and the justification need only meet the common sting of the statement (s 5 Defamation Act 1952 and *Alexander v NE Rly* (1865), where it was immaterial that a report that a man convicted of travelling without a ticket on a train stated that he had been sentenced to three weeks' imprisonment in default of payment of a fine, instead of two weeks).

If there are two meanings (say, an innuendo also), the defendant must justify both. As we have seen, in *Lewis v Daily Telegraph* (1963), having reported a police enquiry afoot, raising the innuendo of suspicion, the defendant had to defend both statements, the express one (that there was an inquiry) and the implied (that there was suspicion), which it could not do. Finally, a rumour must be proved to be true, not just that it existed.

The courts are keen not to stifle comment on public matters. The defendant must prove:

• the matter is of public interest; and

• the statement is comment on a matter of fact; and

• the statement is fair.

Matters of public interest include not only government, industry, unions, churches, the courts etc, but also matters put forward for public criticism, such as artistic works, performances etc. But public interest should not be confused with national interest. In *South Hetton Coal Ltd v North-Eastern News Ltd* (1894), a case later cited with approval by Lord Denning MR, it was held that the insanitary conditions of cottages owned by the colliery company of a Durham village was a matter of public interest. The words must be comment, based on true fact. Thus in *Merivale v Carson* (1887), a defendant who called a play immoral for the amount of adultery in it failed in his defence as there was none in it at all!

Lord Esher MR, in *Merivale v Carson* (1887), said that the test of fairness was, 'Would any honest man, however prejudiced he may be, however exaggerated or obstinate his views, have said that?' In a modern case the test was 'could any fair-minded man honestly express that opinion on the proved facts?' (*Telnikoff v Matusevitch* (1990)). Proof of malice will defeat this defence.

| 13.3.4 | Absolute privilege |

If the statement is published on an occasion of absolute privilege, the defendant is not liable, even if it is untrue or malicious.

This defence covers anything published in judicial proceedings, Parliament (Bill of Rights 1688), or reports of either of these (eg *Hansard*, by the Parliamentary Papers Act 1840, and contemporaneous Law Reports, by the Defamation Act 1996). It also covers matters published between ministers of the crown, and between husband and wife.

| 13.3.5 | Qualified privilege |

Whereas the last defence was protecting free speech in public matters, this defence is mainly concerned with private matters.

This is only a defence in the absence of malice, for example, that the defendant was motivated by ill-will or has improperly used the occasion or knows what he says to be untrue. In *Horrocks v Lowe* (1974) a Labour councillor at Bolton, Lancashire, said that a Conservative councillor had 'misled the town' and should be removed from a committee. In finding for the defendant Labour man, Lord Diplock said that councillors 'may be swayed by strong political prejudice, they may be obstinate and pig-headed, stupid and obtuse; but they were chosen by the electors to speak their minds on matters of local concern'. This the Labour councillor had done.

There are many situations, especially:

- Statements in performance of a duty (legal, moral or social) or in protection of an interest, to someone under such a duty or with such an interest. For example, in *Watt v Longsdon* (1930), a company's employee found out that another employee, the plaintiff, was defrauding the company and messing about with women on his company trips abroad. He told a chairman and the plaintiff's wife about the appropriate parts of the story. It was held that his communication to the director was privileged, but that he was under no duty to inform the man's wife, so that this communication was not privileged.

- Communications between solicitor and client.

- Reports and registers made in the public interest under s 15 Defamation Act 1996.

| 13.3.6 | No responsibility for publication – s 1 Defamation Act 1996 |

A printer or distributor (ie not an 'author, editor or publisher') who took reasonable care in relation to the content of the publication has a defence if he neither knew nor ought to have known of its defamatory content.

Any defendant (whether knowingly or strictly at fault) can make the plaintiff an 'offer to make amends', ie to correct the statement, apologise and pay agreed or determined damages. The plaintiff can accept or reject the offer, but the offer is a complete defence under s 4 if made by a defendant who has innocently defamed (as in *Cassidy v Daily Mirror* (1929)) or innocently but without negligence referred to the plaintiff (as in *Newstead v London Express* (1939)).

13.3.7   Offer to make amends
– s 2 Defamation Act
1996

Damages are awarded by the jury. They used to amount to very large sums, eg £1,500,000 for libel (later reduced by consent) in *Lord Aldington v Tolstoy and Watts* (1989) and £150,000 for slander in *Smith v Houston* (1991). Section 8 Courts and Legal Services Act 1990 now gives the Court of Appeal power to decrease a ridiculous jury award.

13.4   Damages

Many cases may now go through the summary procedure created by the Defamation Act 1996. On either side's application (or of the court's own motion) a judge sitting alone can dispose of the case if 'it appears to the court that [either side's pleading] has no realistic prospect of success'. The judge then can declare the statement to be false and defamatory and make an order for correction, apology, damages of up to £10,000 and an injunction, or any of them or dismiss the application.

If the plaintiff still insists on a jury trial, and is allowed one, he runs one further risk: the award in *Newstead v London Express* (1939) was one farthing for contemptuous damages, as the jury, while agreeing that the law was on the plaintiff's side, nevertheless thought that the plaintiff was in it to make some money rather than to clear his name.

Chapter 14

The Tort of Nuisance

It is perhaps unfortunate that two torts share the same name. Granted, they overlap and a set of facts will constitute a cause of action in each; but they are quite different torts with different histories, and many examples of public nuisance, for example, a loose dog in a public street (in *Pitcher v Martin* (1937)), will have nothing to do with private nuisance, which is more concerned with interference with land or the use of land.

Public nuisance is one of the two torts founded upon a breach of a criminal rule (the other being breach of a statutory duty) and the problem again arises as to whether the plaintiff can show himself to have suffered more than others have.

A public nuisance can be defined as 'an act or omission which materially affects the reasonable comfort and convenience of life of a class of Her Majesty's subjects' (*AG v PYA Quarries* (1957)). It is a crime but any member of that class who can show special damage over and above that suffered by the rest of the class can sue in it as a tort. (If nobody can do so, the defendant can still be prosecuted for the crime, eg in *R v Johnson* (1996) for making hundreds of obscene telephone calls to different women in a particular area.) The plaintiff need not be interfered with in his use of the land.

Generally, it will cover things which generate large scale noise, pollution, traffic, and interference with passers-by using the highway. In *Benjamin v Storr* (1874), it was urinating cab-horses and parked cabs which caused inconvenience to other residents of Covent Garden and loss of trade to the plaintiff's cafe, as the cabs parked outside the windows made the cafe dark, and the smell and sound of the horses' urination put off would-be customers.

In *Halsey v Esso* (1961), the defendant's oil refinery, operating in an industrial planning zone in Fulham, caused much inconvenience to the plaintiff, living opposite in a residential zone. Acid smuts floating out of the refinery caused damage to his car parked in the road; and the noise of tankers entering and leaving the refinery right through the night and sometimes in convoys of four caused him loss of sleep. Both of these amounted to public nuisance, even though the defendant had lawful authority to operate the refinery. We can presume that the class constituted the residents of that road, but that the plaintiff suffered more than they did.

14.1 Public nuisance

Many public nuisances involve obstructing the highway (eg the River Thames by building a pier which caused siltation, in *Tate & Lyle v GLC* (1983)), or using the highway itself or adjoining land for purposes dangerous to users of the highway. In *Castle v St Augustine's Links* (1922), it was a public nuisance to place a golf tee so close to the highway that poor golfers were forever slicing the balls into the highway, thus affecting the class of lawful users of the highway. The plaintiff's special damage was his being blinded by one of these balls.

On the fault required for public nuisance, Denning LJ suggested in *Southport Corpn v Esso* (1954) that 'in an action for public nuisance, once the nuisance is proved and the defendant is shown to have caused it, then the legal burden is shifted on the defendant to justify or excuse himself'. If this is so, then the advantage over Negligence is apparent.

Further, this tort does not require a duty of care, and while damage to the person (*Castle v St Augustine's Links* (1922)) and to goods (*Halsey v Esso* (1961)) is also covered by negligence, economic loss (loss of custom (*Benjamin v Storr*)) causes no problem here.

14.2   Private nuisance

Private nuisance can be defined as 'indirectly and unreasonably causing either physical damage to land in the possession of the plaintiff, or substantial interference with his use and enjoyment of that land (or an interest in it)'.

In whichever case the defendant will be the creator of the nuisance or a person responsible for it as occupier or landlord of the land where the nuisance is.

This is a very old action, covering indirect harm, as opposed to the direct harm covered by trespass. Thus, if I myself enter your garden, or I throw rubbish onto it, I am causing direct harm as I apply my personal force to either action. If on the other hand my land slides onto yours, or my noises or smells affect you, I have no physical influence in the movement of my land, nor in how my sound-waves or smells will be carried from my land. I cannot will my land to slide in your direction, nor my smells to waft there. This is indirect harm, and is the subject of nuisance as opposed to trespass to land.

The cause of the nuisance will normally be a *state of affairs* from which there is usually an escape of a noxious substance onto the plaintiff's land.

The state of affairs is the nuisance, not the escape or invasion, and it will be a continuing one; the fact that there is only one escape and invasion will not preclude an action.

Thus in *British Celanese Ltd v AH Hunt Ltd* (1969), although only a single escape of zinc foil occurred, causing a stoppage of power to the plaintiff's factory, this was held to merely be evidence of a state of affairs on the defendant's land which constituted a nuisance in that loose foil was left to be blown about by the wind.

- Physical injury to the plaintiff's land

    This type of harm requires a *material* (ie not trivial) physical injury, reducing the value of the property. In *St Helens Smelting v Tipping* (1865), fumes from a factory destroyed foliage and shrubs on the plaintiff's land; and in *Leakey v National Trust* (1980), a conical hill in Somerset, called Burrow Mump, slid causing damage to the plaintiff's cottage after heavy rain followed drought conditions in 1976. The sole test here is whether this a material and sensible physical injury; the character of the locality is not relevant.

- 'Sensible' (appreciable) interference with use and enjoyment

    We have already seen that acid smuts and tanker noise were held to be public nuisances in *Halsey v Esso* (1961). But this very useful case goes further. The acid smuts also damaged clothing hung out to dry in the plaintiff's back garden; the smell of the refinery was overpowering; and the noise from the boilers and the road tankers inside the refinery, and the noise of the tankers while on the road outside interfered with the plaintiff's sleep at night. All these were held to be evidence of a private nuisance as they amounted to sensible interferences with the plaintiff's use and enjoyment of his land. But note that the damage to the car could not amount to private nuisance as the car was not on his land. Further, although the smell and noise nuisances both affect the person, the criterion is interference with use and enjoyment; injury to health is not necessary.

    Perhaps the fringe of this tort can be seen in *Laws v Florinplance Ltd* (1981), where a sex-shop was held to be a private nuisance as it interfered with the plaintiff's use and enjoyment of his land, say, his front garden, by attracting 'dirty' men to the neighbourhood, making sitting in a deckchair on the front lawn a hazardous past-time.

    This case was in fact an application for an interlocutory injunction (which was granted) and therefore not as thoroughly explored as it might have been at a full hearing, and how far this can go is uncertain: what about loud,

14.2.1   The harm

aggressive behaviour in next door's garden, which keeps me out of my garden for fear of becoming involved?

In the use and enjoyment cases only, the *character of the locality* is relevant in determining whether the interference is appreciable and substantial. 'What would be a nuisance in Belgrave Square would not necessarily be so in Bermondsey' (*Sturges v Bridgman* (1879)).

• On both heads of harm

The interference can come from the *highway*. This was the case with the tankers outside the refinery in *Halsey v Esso* (1961).

Where the complaint concerns the plaintiff's sensitive use of land it will not be a nuisance if the plaintiff only suffers sensible damage because of his own sensitive use of it.

In *Robinson v Kilvert* (1889), the plaintiff had upstairs premises where he made brown paper, a sensitive process. The paper was spoilt by heat rising from the defendant's pipes below. There was no nuisance affecting normal use of the upstairs premises; the sensitivity of the plaintiff's paper-making was the sole cause of his damage.

But once a nuisance is proved, then damages for injury to a sensitive use can be claimed. In other words, sensitivity cannot establish a nuisance, but once it is established on normal principles sensitive injury is not too remote.

So in *McKinnon Industries v Walker* (1951), a Privy Council case from Canada, the fact that sulphur fumes were interfering with the growing of orchids, a sensitive flower, was not fatal to the plaintiff's claim since the fumes were a nuisance to ordinary plants too.

14.2.2   The unreasonableness

In establishing the presence or absence of reasonableness the following are relevant:

• The ordinary and reasonable user of the land by the defendant – there is, firstly, 'a rule of give and take, and live and let live' (*Bamford v Turnley* (1862)). But the use of the word 'reasonableness' is bound to provoke comparison with the use of it in negligence.

In negligence, the question is whether the care is reasonable; if it is, the behaviour can harm your neighbour with impunity. In nuisance, if, after considering give and take, it causes harm, it is a nuisance, and the state of affairs is unreasonable, even if the defendant has taken all reasonable care. (Or, harm in negligence might still be lawful; harm in nuisance cannot be unless within the give and take.)

Under *Bamford v Turnley* (1862), reasonableness of user is established if the state of affairs is 'necessary for the common and ordinary use and occupation' (operation of oil refineries in *Fulham: Halsey v Esso* (1961), or having natural conical hills in Somerset: *Leakey v National Trust* (1980)), and the state of affairs is 'conveniently done', that is, if the state of affairs is an activity, it is done reasonably and not excessively (not having lorry convoys throughout the night), or if the state of affairs is a condition of the land, it is reasonable to take no steps to prevent its causing harm (the National Trust had the means to take steps to stop the Mump's slide).

If the defendant complies with these rules, his user is reasonable, and the plaintiff must accept any harm still occurring as give and take.

With regard to the burden of proof of the reasonableness, in private nuisance also the burden is probably on the defendant to rid himself of fault (Denning LJ, in *Morton v Wheeler* (1956)).

• The defendant's malice

It was said in *Allen v Flood* (1898), following *Bradford Corporation v Pickles* (1895) (a case we have already considered) that 'an act *prima facie* lawful is not unlawful and actionable on account of the motive which dictated it'.

In tort we are concerned with what the defendant has done, not why. But two cases suggest that malice can be relevant. In *Christie v Davey* (1893) the plaintiff gave music lessons at home. Her neighbour, the defendant, who was annoyed by the music, banged trays, shouted, blew whistles etc to annoy her and in *Hollywood Silver Fox Farm v Emmett* (1936), the defendant got his son to fire shots at the edge of his land near the plaintiff's farm where silver fox cubs were bred to make expensive fur coats. He knew that the vixens were sensitive at whelping time and would, if frightened, abort or destroy their cubs. In both cases the plaintiff won, but why?

Will malice always indicate a nuisance? If, having discovered that my neighbour is sick at the sight of anything yellow, I buy a yellow suit and car and paint my house yellow, am I liable in nuisance?

The better explanation of these cases is probably that it is not reasonable behaviour to shout and bang trays, or to fire shots gratuitously, where there is no competition in progress or no pests to be cleared. In other words, purely malicious use of property prevents the claim of 'ordinary and reasonable user'. The reasonable man does not go about doing these things. Thus, malice is still irrelevant (the yellow fixation) where the behaviour is reasonable (yellow clothes and cars are common), but it helps to tip the balance where the behaviour is *prima facie* unreasonable.

But was not the plaintiff's user in Christie (the music teacher's) 'sensitive'? The answer is no. The defendant's behaviour was a nuisance in any case, and interference with her music lessons would come within *McKinnon Industries v Walker* (1951). Was not the user in Hollywood (the touchy vixens) 'sensitive'? Probably it should have been, as in other circumstances (eg clearing rabbits) the shots would have been reasonable but causing the same damage. This would have invoked *Robinson v Kilvert*; it should have been invoked on the actual facts of Hollywood.

- Duration, frequency and transience

  Short duration or infrequency of damage does not rule out nuisance, as the question is whether the state of affairs on the land constitutes a nuisance. We have already seen that a single occurrence sufficed in *British Celanese v Hunt* (1969), where the state of affairs which enabled the escape was the significant factor. In *Matania v National Provincial Bank* (1936), temporary works to a building causing dust and noise still amounted to a nuisance.

14.2.3	Fault in private nuisance

Must the defendant be at fault, or is there strict liability? It is sometimes said that private nuisance is a tort of strict liability; this is not true. Lord Reid, speaking for the whole Board of the Privy Council in *The Wagon Mound (No 2)* (1966) (brought by the owner of the damaged ship, on different pleadings, as a result of which this action succeeded):

> 'It is quite true that negligence is not an essential element in nuisance. Nuisance is a term used to cover a wide variety of tortious acts or omissions, and in many negligence in the narrow sense is not essential. And although negligence may not be necessary, fault of some kind is almost always necessary, and fault generally involves foreseeability.'

For example, in cases like *Sedleigh-Denfield v O'Callaghan* (1940), below, the fault is in failing to abate a nuisance of the existence of which the defender is or ought to be aware as likely to cause damage to his neighbour.

Thus, in private nuisance fault is required in the sense of knowledge, whether actual or reasonable, of the nuisance coupled with unreasonable failure to abate it. (There is a small element of strict liability in the rule in *Wringe v Cohen* (1939), on which Lord Reid declined to pass comment.)

The definition above indicates that the plaintiff must be in possession of the land affected: the rule in *Malone v Laskey* (1907), in which the wife of the tenant was unable to sue when the lavatory cistern fell onto her, as it was not she who was in possession but her husband. This is why the damage to the car parked in the street in *Halsey v Esso* (1961) could only be actionable in public nuisance: the plaintiff did not possess the public highway. The rule has now been confirmed as correct by the House of Lords, in *Hunter v London Docklands Development Corpn* (1997), where a wife with no proprietary interest could not sue for dust damage caused by roadworks.

The defendant could be any of: the creator of the nuisance, the occupier of the offending land or the landlord of the offending land. A creator may of course also be liable as occupier, but he will only be liable as creator if the nuisance arises from acts done on the highway, eg in *Halsey v Esso* (1961). An occupier of the offending land is, as mentioned above, liable if he knows or should know of the nuisance arising out of his land, and fails to abate it. Thus where the cause is an act of a trespasser, the issue hinges on whether the defendant knew or should have known of that act.

In *Sedleigh-Denfield v O'Callaghan* (1940), the defendants (trustees of a religious mission) owned a building alongside of which was a ditch. Trespassers laid a culvert in the ditch, but failed to put a grill at the upper end to stop rubbish getting into the culvert and blocking it. After a heavy rainstorm it did overflow and flooded the plaintiff's land. Unfortunately, Brother Dekker, of the mission, who was responsible for cleaning the ditch, saw the trespassers carrying out the work. The defendant trustees of the mission were accordingly at fault, and held liable.

An occupier is also liable where the nuisance is a natural thing of which the defendant has knowledge and which might foreseeably cause damage to or interference with the plaintiff's land. This was the case in *Leakey v National Trust* (1980), above, where the National Trust were well aware of the Mump, the sliding, and the nearby cottages.

As we have just seen, the fault lies in knowledge plus failure to abate. It logically follows that if the nuisance is latent, or hidden, the occupier should not be liable. This is the case if the defect is due to operation of nature: thus the defendant was not liable when he had only realised that a branch was rotten

14.2.4   The parties

14.2.5   The occupier and latent defences

once it had fallen onto a motor-coach (*Noble v Harrison* (1926)). But if the latent defect is man-made, due to want of repair, then under the rule in *Wringe v Cohen* (1939), where a gable-end, unknowingly defective for three years, fell onto the plaintiff's shop, the defendant occupier is strictly liable.

14.2.6   Damage

The plaintiff must prove both causation and reasonably foreseeability of damage (*The Wagon Mound (No 2)* (1966)).

14.3   Defences to both forms of nuisance

As can be expected, the rights of the plaintiff are tempered with various defences; but before considering these, it is useful to consider some claims that do not constitute defences.

The first is that the plaintiff came to the nuisance. This rule arose in *Sturges v Bridgeman* (1879), where a doctor, in an area in which doctors' surgeries were common, complained that the machinery of the adjoining toffee factory interfered with his work in a consulting room he built against the factory wall. The court held that the factory was a private nuisance, and that the fact it had been there for over 20 years did not excuse its interference.

This was followed in *Miller v Jackson* (1977) and in *Kennaway v Thompson* (1980). In both, the plaintiffs came to live next to, in the first case a cricket pitch, and in the second a lake on which speedboat racing took place. Again, in both cases, it was no defence that the defendant was there first.

Neither is it a defence that the defendant's act is for the public benefit, as it was sought to justify the fried-fish shop in *Adams v Ursell* (1913); nor that the defendant had taken reasonable care and skill; nor that the nuisance was caused by the acts of others combined with those of the defendant, eg in pollution cases.

The following are defences.

14.3.1   Prescription

It is a defence to prove that an actionable nuisance (not just the activity) must have been carried on openly and to the knowledge of the *servient tenement* (ie the owner or possessor of the affected land), for at least 20 years. In *Sturges v Bridgeman* (1879), the toffee factory had operated for over 20 years, and in *Miller v Jackson* (1977), there had been village-green cricket for over 70 years, but in neither case was there any nuisance until the plaintiff moved there. In both cases the defence failed.

But this is no defence in public nuisance. I cannot claim a right to commit a crime, just because I have been committing crimes for over 20 years! Nor is it a defence if the activity is prohibited by statute, nor if the interference is secretive.

It must be decided, on a matter of construction, whether the statute gives the defendant absolute authority, or conditional authority.

- Absolute authority

  An imperative authority such as where the statute orders someone to operate, say, a refinery, will always fall into this category. The defendant is authorised to commit his act without liability for any inevitable damage. Thus, the defendant can cause inevitable damage. But it is for the defendant to prove that the damage was inevitable, despite his having taken reasonable care. In *Allen v Gulf Oil* (1981), the defendant oil company successfully pleaded this defence when sued for nuisance by smell, noise and vibration caused by their constructing and operating a refinery near Milford Haven.

- Conditional authority

  Mere permissive authority, for example, where the statute merely allows someone to operate the installation, will *prima facie* be of this type. Authority is given on condition that the defendant exercises the power so as not to interfere with private rights. Thus, the defendant must not cause damage. In *Metropolitan District Asylum Board v Hill* (1881), the Board were empowered to operate a smallpox hospital. They chose to site it in a built-up area, causing risk of infection to residents. The defence was held not to apply.

  As we have seen, reasonable and ordinary use by the defendant, and, as can be expected, consent and contributory negligence are also defences.

  Finally, distinguish this defence from the grant of a planning consent, the only effect of which is possibly to alter the character of the locality (see Chapter 14, 14.2.1 above).

A plaintiff in this tort will claim either damages or an injunction, or both. A self-help remedy is also available.

14.4   Remedies

Nuisance is one of those torts where the plaintiff may not be satisfied with damages alone. He may well seek an *injunction*, either 'mandatory', to abate the nuisance, or 'prohibitory', to desist from carrying on the nuisance. In urgent cases he may seek an *interlocutory* injunction, which the court will grant if damages are inadequate as a remedy.

Thus, one was granted in *Laws v Florinplance Ltd* (1981) to remove the nuisance caused by the sex-shop.

To apply for an interlocutory injunction the plaintiff need not make out a *prima facie* case; the rule is that the court must decide:

- whether there is a serious question to be tried; and

- on the balance of convenience (*American Cyanamid v Ethicon* (1975)).

Even where no damage has yet occurred a plaintiff who fears that it will do so can apply for a *quia timet* injunction. It must be sufficiently probable that:

- the defendant will commit the nuisance; and

- injury will be substantial and be caused in the not-too-remote future, for which damages will not be sufficient.

In accordance with general principles damages in lieu of injunction might be awarded under s 50 Supreme Court Act 1981. They may be awarded if the defendant shows that the injury is small, and can be reduced to money, and it would be oppressive to grant injunction (*Shelfer v City of London Electric Lighting* (1895)). The court will consider the gravity of the injury, the conduct of the parties, and the effect on the interests of the defendant and of the public. In *Miller v Jackson* (1977) a majority of the Court of Appeal held that the public interest of watching village cricket always outweighed the private interest, but this was overruled in *Kennaway v Thompson* (1980) where the Court of Appeal held that there was no such general rule.

Finally, damages can be granted in lieu of a *quia timet* injunction.

Kennaway v Thompson (1980) is an interesting example of how the court can use the remedy of injunction in order to do equity. We have seen that a newcomer house-holder had succeeded in a claim of nuisance against speedboat racers on a lake. Rather than stop the activity completely by injunction, the court did issue an injunction but which contained a compromise, limiting the racing to certain times of the year, to certain weekends and events, to certain times, and the noise level to certain decibels.

| 14.4.2 | Abatement (self-help) |

Instead of pursuing a claim for damages an injured party can abate the nuisance himself. This must be done in the way least harmful to the defendant, unless that way is harmful to a third party or to the public. Notice need only be given to the occupier of the land where the nuisance is if entry is necessary. Thus, no notice need be given of intended chopping off of tree branches or roots at the boundary (though detention of the cut branches would be conversion).

It is important to compare private nuisance both with public nuisance and with negligence.

- Public nuisance is primarily a *crime*.

- In public nuisance, a *class* must be affected. In private nuisance, only the plaintiff need be.

- In public nuisance, the plaintiff must show damage over and above that suffered by others. In private nuisance the plaintiff need only suffer to some extent.

- Personal injury is only actionable in public nuisance.

- In private nuisance, there must be interference with *land*.

- Prescription is only a defence to private nuisance.

- Duty of care is not required in nuisance.

- Title to land is not required in negligence.

- Reasonable care might not be a defence to nuisance, if the user, despite the reasonable care, is still unreasonable.

- In nuisance burden of proof is probably on the defendant to rid himself of blame. In negligence the burden is on the plaintiff to prove defendant was at fault.

14.5 Comparison of nuisance with other torts

14.5.1 Public and private nuisance

14.5.2 Nuisance and negligence

Chapter 15

Strict Liability and the Law of Tort

Strict liability is liability without fault. It should not be confused with 'absolute' liability, which denies the availability of defences; all the torts discussed here have available defences.

The torts discussed in this part relieve the plaintiff of part of the burden normally placed on a plaintiff, in that here the plaintiff need not prove that the defendant acted intentionally or negligently in causing the damage. The list of strict liability torts has grown haphazardly. The predecessor to s 4 Animals Act 1971 (liability for straying livestock) was medieval in origin; others are very recent, for example liability for dangerous products under the Consumer Protection Act 1987. Similarly, many consumer protection and factory protection provisions are strict.

Further, while these and many other examples are statutory, the common law has been active also: the original liability for cattle trespass and the rule in *Rylands v Fletcher* (1866), being examples. This part will briefly outline some torts, before discussing whether there is in fact some common thread, and whether the pressure towards strict liability in some areas is ill-founded.

As we have seen, the rationale in English liability in tort (and in criminal law) is that a person should only be liable where he is at fault, that is, where he is blameworthy. Torts like trespass, negligence and private nuisance rely fundamentally on proof of fault (consider *Fowler v Lannin* (1959); *Bolton v Stone* (1951) and *The Wagon Mound (No 2)* (1967)), while some introduce elements of strict liability: conversion, for example, requires an intention to interfere, but not an intention to convert (*Hollins v Fowler* (1875)), and defamation requires an intention to publish, but not an intention to defame (*Cassidy v Daily Mirror* (1929); *Hulton v Jones* (1910); *Newstead v London Express* (1939)).

The rule in *Rylands v Fletcher* (1866) is a prominent common law tort of strict liability. The defendant mill owner employed independent contractors to construct a reservoir on the defendant's land, between Bury and Bolton in Lancashire. The contractors negligently failed to realise that some mine shafts connected with the plaintiff's mines. In consequence, the shafts

15.1   *Rylands v Fletcher*

were not filled in. When the reservoir was filled with water, it flooded the plaintiff's mines.

The modern mind would think in terms of the contractors' negligence, but this was before *Donoghue v Stevenson* (1932), and of course the contractors might have been wound up. The Court of Exchequer Chamber and the House of Lords agreed that irrespective of any liability of the contractors, the defendant was strictly liable for the damage to the plaintiff's mines. Blackburn J expounded the rule for the whole court:

> 'We think that the true rule of law is, that the person who for his own purposes brings on his lands and collects and keeps there anything likely to do mischief if it escapes, must keep it in at his peril, and, if he does not do so, is *prima facie* answerable for all the damage which is the natural consequence of its escape.'

In the House of Lords, Lord Cairns LC (speaking for himself, Lord Cranworth and a still unidentified third Lord) introduced the requirement that the defendant must have done his bringing-on and collecting in furtherance of some 'non-natural use'. This has been held to include a reservoir, poisonous trees (*Crowhurst v Amersham Burial Board* (1878)), acid smuts (*Halsey v Esso* (1961)), a flagpole, fairground chair-o-planes and slag heaps; and in *Cambridge Water Co v Eastern Counties Leather* (1993) the storage of substantial quantities of chemicals on industrial premises was said by Lord Goff to be 'an almost classic case of non-natural use'. The reader may wonder where chemicals can therefore be properly kept! Probably the correct interpretation of Lord Cairns' LC's phrase 'non-natural use' is 'brought on' (such as cattle or planted trees), which adds nothing to Blackburn J's rule, rather than 'unusual' or 'unreasonable'.

There is a tendency to look for some common thread, say, that these are all naturally, hazardous things, but Blackburn J is clear that it is not the thing itself which must be mischievous; the requirement is that it must be 'anything likely to do mischief if it escapes'. Thus, it might be quite harmless while kept in; perhaps cotton wool stored in bulk might be within the rule. Further, this is not a form of activity liability: 'our law of torts is concerned not with activities but with acts' (Scott LJ in *Read v Lyons* (1945) in the Court of Appeal). This is emphasised by the failure of the plaintiff in *Read v Lyons* (1946), who was a wartime munitions inspector. She was injured by an explosion inside the factory. Because the rule requires an escape her claim failed. But in *Crowhurst v Amersham Burial Board* (1978) the planted poisonous yew branches overhung the boundary fence, where they were eaten by the plaintiff's horse, which died. Here, the overhang was the escape. But no amount of collection of dangerous things will incur liability in this tort if there is no escape.

Further, there is no liability for things not 'brought on', ie for things naturally on the land. No matter how hazardous the state of the land is, if this is as a result of nature there is no liability (as there might be in private nuisance: *Leakey v National Trust* (1980)). And while liability for the escape is strict, the damage must be foreseeable, as held in *Cambridge Water Co v Eastern Counties Leather* (1993), where the storage and use of a toxic chemical could not be foreseen as getting into the plaintiff's underground water supply. But note that it is a defence that 'the escape was caused by an unforeseeable act of a stranger', for example the boy who in *Perry v Kendricks* (1956) threw a lighted match into the drained petrol tank of a parked coach thus causing an explosion which injured the plaintiff, another boy.

Perhaps because of the uncertainty in this tort, Parliament has clarified the liability in some areas by statute. Thus, the Nuclear Installations Act 1965 replaces the common law for liability for personal injury or property damage caused by radioactive material and channels all such liability onto the person licensed to operate the nuclear plant, who is strictly liable.

As we have seen the Animals Act 1971 replaced a mixture of common law and statutory torts with four strict liability torts: one for injury or damage done by an animal of a dangerous species (defined roughly as foreign species); the second for an animal of a species not usually known for dangerous behaviour but where the keeper knows his individual to be uncharacteristically dangerous; a third for damage by a dog to livestock (only); and the last for property damage (only) caused by straying livestock.

It is noticeable that damage to livestock by a dog or other livestock fares better than personal injury caused by either. If your dog bites me or your bull gores me, I only have the protection of the second of these torts, and only then if the dangerous tendency is unusual for that species and the keeper is aware of that tendency. Otherwise I have to sue in trespass, negligence or public nuisance, all involving fault of some nature.

Until 1 March 1988, liability in tort for damage caused by products lay entirely in common law negligence, under *Donoghue v Stevenson* (1932). (The ginger beer in that case and the underpants in *Grant v Australian Knitting Mills* (1936) (see

15.2 Dangerous products

Chapter 8, 8.1.2 above) were classic examples of products defective at common law.) However, the thalidomide tragedy (a medical product taken by pregnant women to treat morning sickness caused limb deformities in their babies), caused a re-assessment of the principles of product liability, not only in Great Britain, but across Europe. In particular the principle of 'no liability without fault' came under scrutiny.

The Council of Europe (in 1976), the European Commission (in 1976) and in this country, the Law Commission and Scottish Law Commission (in 1977) and the Royal Commission on Civil Liability and Compensation for Personal Injury, Cmnd 7054, the 'Pearson Commission' (in 1978) all recommended a form of strict liability for products, which incidentally already existed in England in contract (*cf* ss 12–15 Sale of Goods Act 1979).

From the late 1970s until 25 July 1985, no implementation was made of any strict liability system which affected Great Britain. However, on that date the Council of Ministers of the European Economic Community made Directive 85/374/EEC on Strict Product Liability, leaving Member States to implement it within three years. In England it was implemented by the Consumer Protection Act 1987, which came into force almost on the last minute, on 1 March 1988.

The basic rule under the Act is that the producer shall be strictly liable for damage caused by a defect in his product. Thus, duty of care and reasonable foreseeability of damage are immaterial; and liability is strict, not fault-based. The plaintiff victim will have the burden of proving the damage, the defect and the causation between the defect and the damage.

'Product' means all goods, even if incorporated into other goods or into some other form of property eg land. It includes electricity, but excludes primary agricultural products (the products of the soil, stock farming and of fisheries except where these have undergone initial processing). A 'producer' is any of the following: the manufacturer of a finished product or of a component part, a producer of raw material (ie he who gains or wins it from the earth, etc), any person who presents himself as producer by putting his own name or distinguishing feature on the product (eg supermarket chains who sell, but do not make, 'own brands'), and any person who imports into the European Union a product for sale, hire, lease or any form of distribution in the course of his business (thus there is always a defendant within the EU). The Act binds the Crown, thus the National Health Service drug-making service is within the Act.

A product will be defective when it does not provide the safety which might reasonably be expected of it taking into account all the circumstances, including the get-up and presentation of the product, the reasonably expected use of the product, and the time when the product was put into circulation. A good example is the oral contraceptives which, in 1997, women were claiming to be the cause of their blood clots. Damage actionable under the new provisions is personal injury or death, and damage (valued at over £275) to private property other than the defective product itself (thus the rule in negligence of *Murphy v Brentwood* (1990) is incorporated). Finally, there can be no exclusion of the consumer's rights, by anyone, and whether in a contract, notice or otherwise.

We would expect to find some defences, and it is here that the true value of the Act is revealed. Firstly, the Directive allows the Member State to restrict the producer's total liability for death or personal injury caused by identical items to 70 million ECUs (European Community Units), approximately £38,500,000. This ceiling could apply to drug-damage cases (such as the original thalidomide cases, or the recent Opren or Benzo-drug cases). The British government has not implemented this provision in the Act, but it is still available as the Directive still applies.

Secondly, the notorious development risks ('the state of the art') defence is available.

The producer will be able to show that the state of scientific and technical knowledge at the time when he put the product into circulation was not such as to enable the existence of the defect to be discovered. Thus, the consumer runs the risk of bad side-effects occurring in the future. (It was optional for each Member State to remove this defence; the British government did not exercise this option, thus leaving the defence available to a producer. But if this defence did not exist, would drug companies continue to produce new drugs? The defence has not been allowed at all in France, Belgium or Luxembourg, nor for drugs in Germany.)

So what does this leave the consumer to prove when he is met by this defence: that by the state of scientific knowledge the defendant could or should have foreseen harm and knowingly took the risk? But is this not back to having to prove 'negligence'? In 1997 the manufacturer of the oral contraceptive referred to the above stated that it had 'total confidence' in its product and would 'strenuously defend' any claims made by the women suffering from blood clots.

A final provision which could work harshly against the consumer is the limitation period. Briefly (this subject is outlined below), this is the period within which the plaintiff must issue his writ, in order to sue the defendant. The plaintiff shall have until the earlier of the following times in which to sue the producer: either three years from the date on which he became aware, or ought reasonably to have become aware, of the damage, the defect and the identity of the producer (this is similar to the personal injury provision in negligence), and 10 years from the date on which the producer put into circulation the actual product which caused the damage.

This last point is unusual, especially in personal injury cases. We were considering above a drug which caused bad side-effects after a period of years. If this period exceeds this 10 years, then the plaintiff cannot sue under the Act, and must resort once more to the common law.

15.3 Strict liability in tort: conclusion

We have seen that the torts of strict liability cover a wide range. If a common thread is to be found, it can only be in the extra-hazardous nature of the things which cause the damage. This is not satisfactory; judges have, for instance, denied the 'hazardous activity' liability of *Rylands v Fletcher* (1866) (see Scott LJ in *Read v Lyons* (1945), above). But it is the only rationalisation that can be made to link such diverse torts.

More important than this, however, is the question of whether strict liability should be extended in tort. Firstly, if much factory protection legislation is strict, why is road traffic liability also? Strict liability does not deny the operation of the contributory negligence defence (both the Animals Act 1971 and the Consumer Protection Act 1987 allow the defence), so could not a system of strict liability with contributory negligence work? Or is this just shifting the burden of proof of fault from plaintiff to defendant, and is that fair?

Another area in which there is some pressure to install strict liability is medical negligence. See again the discussion on this in the introduction to this chapter. Bear in mind also that strict liability would not affect causation of damage; thus cases would still exist such as *Wilsher v Essex Health Authority* (1987), where the plaintiff, a blind premature baby could not prove which of six possible causes was the one which actually caused his blindness.

A further suggested contender for strict liability is major disasters, such as train crashes, ferry-boat capsizes or football crowd disasters. But why should plaintiffs be under different burdens according to the scale or type or emotional impact of the negligence?

Chapter 16

Parties

It often happens that more than one person is liable for damage.

It may be that each is separately negligent, but that the two lots of negligence together cause the plaintiff one lot of damage. For example, I am the passenger in a car being driven negligently, which collides with another car being driven negligently, and I am injured in the collision. These tortfeasors are called separate tortfeasors.

In addition, it might happen that two defendants are jointly and severally liable for the damage. This would happen where all the partners in a firm are liable for the tort of one, and where a master, or employer, is liable for the tort of his servant, or employee.

In both situations, both tortfeasors are each liable for the whole damage. Moreover, in both situations, judgment against one is not a bar to action against another. Further, the later action may obtain judgment for a sum exceeding that awarded in the first or earlier action. In circumstances such as these, the Civil Liability (Contribution) Act 1978 allows any person (including the estate of a deceased defendant) who has been held liable, to claim contribution 'from any other person liable in respect of the same damage', 'whether jointly' (ie joint tortfeasors) 'or otherwise' (ie separate tortfeasors).

In addition, a party might be able to claim from another person under a contract of indemnity existing between the parties, or where an indemnity is implied, for example a tortfeasor servant must indemnify his master who is found vicariously liable for the tort of the servant (as the servant is in breach of his contractual obligation to his master to take care). In *Lister v Romford Ice & Cold Storage* (1957), both father and son were employed by the same master. The son negligently backed a lorry into the father. The father sued the master for the tort of the son, and the master, having paid out damages to the father claimed an indemnity from the son as the son had been negligent in the conduct of his work, thus constituting a breach of the terms of his contract of employment.

Whenever a tort in committed, someone is personally liable. However, another person might also be liable vicariously for the other's tort.

16.2.1	Master and servant	A master (or employer) is vicariously liable for the tort of his servant (or employee) acting in the course of his employment.

Thus, as well as proving that the tortfeasor committed the tort he must prove, if he wishes to sue the master, that the tortfeasor was his servant and that the tort was committed in the course of the servant's employment. It is important to realise than this is not a tort. It is a way of being liable for a tort. Thus, the servant's liability in a tort must first be proved by the plaintiff in the usual way. And a statement: 'the master is vicariously liable', is as meaningless as, the servant is 'personally liable'. Both beg the question: liable in what tort? Prove the tort first!

16.2.2	Master and servant relationship	A distinction must be drawn between servants, operating under a contract of service, for whom the master is liable and independent contractors, operating under a contract of services, for whom the 'master' is not liable (and is in truth no 'master', but the label is a convenient one to denote the man who engages the contractor).

Various tests have emerged to determine which the tortfeasor is. An old test was whether the master controlled the work of the tortfeasor, indicating a contract of service; but whereas perhaps even 50 years ago the boss would understand the whole of the tortfeasor's work, and could therefore control its many aspects, that is not always the case today, where many servants are highly specialised beyond the understanding of the master. Denning LJ introduced an integration test in *Stevenson Jordan & Harrison v MacDonald Evans* (1952), whether the tortfeasor's work was an 'integral part of the business', or as he put it in another case 'part and parcel of the organisation', and drew the distinction between a chauffeur, for whose negligent driving, I am liable, and a taxi-driver, for which I am not.

Probably more significant nowadays are the economic tests. McKenna J in *Ready Mixed Concrete v Ministry of Pensions* (1968) listed as relevant the method of provision, if any, of tools etc, whether payment was by wages or lump sum, and whether tax and national insurance were deducted therefrom, whether the tortfeasor had any discretion, and so on. What is clear, however, is that no single test is decisive; the court will balance the tests and the weight from each test. Finally, note that superior servants can never be masters.

16.2.3	A tort committed in the course of the servant's employment	Firstly, it is not necessary that the plaintiff identifies the particular servant. Indeed, this will be impossible, say, where the plaintiff is unconscious during a medical operation.

The action is in the course of employment:

- Where the act is authorised, expressly or impliedly

In an emergency, it is implied that the servant has wider powers. Thus, in *Poland v Parr* (1926) a servant pushed away a boy stealing goods from the master's lorry. The boy fell under a wheel and was injured. The battery was authorised (impliedly, to save the goods) and within the scope of the servant's employment.

- Where the act is wrong mode of doing an authorised act

In the farcical case of *Century Insurance Co v Northern Ireland Road Transport Board* (1942), a petrol deliverer stopped his tanker in a filling station forecourt, put the hose into the underground tank, switched it on, took a cigarette from his pocket, lit it, and threw the match down. The match ignited the petrol, but our hero was equal to the moment. Ignoring the petrol stopcock, he jumped into the cab, and drove the tanker down the street. Imagine the tanker, in true cartoon fashion, trailing a hose behind it, still gushing out petrol, and with a flame carefully following the trail of petrol catching up on the tanker all the time. There followed the inevitable explosion, and the petrol company was sued by the owners of damaged property. The issue was whether such a daft thing as smoking and throwing a match down was within the scope of his employment. The answer was that it was, it may have been an unwise way of delivering petrol, but delivering petrol was what he was authorised to do, and was doing.

Even if the master has specifically forbidden the servant to do something, the issue is still whether he was doing his authorised job. Thus, the coach driver who raced other coaches to pick up the passengers first, in *Limpus v London General Omnibus* (1862), and the milkman who allowed children to ride on the milk-float to help him deliver milk, in *Rose v Plenty* (1976), who were each acting against orders, were nevertheless acting within the scope of their employment, as they were after all simply doing the task they were authorised to do.

The act is not in the course of employment:

- Where the employee is 'on a frolic of his own'

Parke B in *Joel v Morrison* (1834) put it thus:

> '... if he was going out of his way, against his master's implied commands when driving on his master's business, he will make his master liable; but if he was

16.2.4   A tort committed outside the course of the servant's employment

going on a frolic of his own, without being at all on his master's business, the master will not be liable.'

Thus, whereas in *Whatman v Pearson* (1868) a servant who deviated a quarter of a mile out of his authorised route was still acting within the scope of his employment, the workmen in *Hilton v Thomas Burton (Rhodes)* (1961) who, although authorised to use the company's van to travel to a demolition site in the country, were on a frolic of their own when they used it to go to a cafe seven miles away, when there was an accident in which one was killed.

- Where the act is so unconnected and independent of the employment as to be completely outside it

  Thus, in *Keppel Bus Co v Ahmad* (1974) a bus-guard who poked a passenger in the eye with the ticket machine, was acting outside the scope of his employment.

16.2.5   Liability for independent contractors

We have just discussed that it is a crucial matter as to whether a workman is a servant or an independent contractor, as a master is only vicariously for the torts of the former. A defendant cannot be vicariously liable for the torts of his independent contractor, as they are not 'master' and 'servant'.

But a defendant may owe a personal duty to the plaintiff in relation to the contractor's conduct which is not delegable, and the defendant might accordingly be personally liable for a breach of that duty.

The duty may be:

- A personal duty to take reasonable care in his act, including the choice of a competent contractor, and his equipment etc

  Thus, a person who engages a contractor would owe a duty of care to the plaintiff under *Donoghue v Stevenson* (1932), or an occupier of land would owe the common duty of care under s 2 Occupiers' Liability Act 1957 (unless the liability under the Act can be discharged under s 2(4)(b) by a reasonable delegation of work to a reasonably selected contractor).

  But the duty is of course only one of reasonable care, and if the defendant complies with that standard there is no breach. Thus, in *Rivers v Cutting* (1982), where the police called out a local garage to attend to the plaintiff's care which had broken down on the motorway, the police were able to defend the action by showing that they took reasonable care in the choice of garage. *Salmond & Heuston on the Law of Torts* quote Baty on *Vicarious Liability*:

'The late Mr Southmayd, of New York, though he possessed a fine carriage and horses, used always to drive in a hired conveyance for this reason.'

The consumer should always enquire, when he hands in something to a shop to be repaired or altered, whether the work will be done by the shop's servant, or contracted out to an independent contractor. There will, however, be a breach if the person who owes the duty does not reasonably ensure that the contractor is competent, or that he has proper equipment or proper instructions.

- A duty to ensure that care is taken

The defendant is under a personal duty to act and if he fails to do so it is at his own peril. He cannot shift the responsibility onto an independent contractor. His taking reasonable care will be of no avail here. This is the case in the strict liability torts, for example, *Rylands v Fletcher*. Here, the defendant landowner was personally liable, as the person who had brought on and kept the water there. He could not shift his liability in that capacity.

Similarly, a 'keeper' under the Animals Act 1971, or an employer on whom lies a strict statutory duty, say to fence machinery, cannot in law delegate his duty or liability, even if, for practical purposes, he employs others to perform the statutory tasks.

Chapter 17

Remedies

In tort remedies are mainly damages, but injunctions are common in some torts, eg nuisance (where the remedy is considered, above) and the land or strict liability torts. Certain self-help remedies also exist, dealt with above under the relevant torts: self-defence (in trespass), recaption of chattels (where they have been converted), ejection of a trespasser, and abatement of a nuisance. Distress damage feasant, and its version under the Animals Act 1971, is a remedy of keeping a chattel which has entered the plaintiff's land, causing damage (eg a cricket-ball through a glass window), until the damage is paid for. The Animals Act now gives a right of sale of such an animal.

17.1 General issues

The purpose of an award of damages in tort is to put the plaintiff in the position he would have been in if the tort had not been committed.

There are various classifications and types of damages representing:

- the exact extent of the damage; or

- a token sum; or

- more than the extent of the damage.

17.2 Damages

Real or compensatory damages are intended to compensate for the material damage or loss suffered by the plaintiff. Thus, in torts which require proof of damage, for the action to succeed there must be actual or real damage: in which case 'real' damages, as opposed to a token sum, will be awarded as compensatory damages.

Compensatory damages can never be 'nominal' or 'contemptuous'.

Compensatory damages can be either general or special damages, awarded respectively for general or special damage.

General damage is the damage which the plaintiff proves to have been caused by the defendant's tortious act, and which only the judge or jury, but not the plaintiff, can assess (though the court will have heard argument on quantum, or the amount of damages).

An example is damages for nervous shock. The judge is acting, though, as jury, and cannot be bound by precedent; but

17.2.1 The exact extent of the damage

in the interests of consistency and justice he follows the conventional figures.

Special damage is the damage which the plaintiff can quantify, eg past (but not future) loss of earnings and expenses, repair costs etc. Damages for this damage or loss is therefore called special damages, or liquidated damages.

| 17.2.2 | A token sum |

Awards of nominal, and contemptuous damages are token sums. They can never be awarded in torts requiring proof of damage, as that would imply that there was no real damage, and that the plaintiff had not discharged his full burden of proof.

Nominal damages are awarded where an action is brought to prove a valid point, for example, in torts actionable *per se*, for example, trespass to prove the legality of a detention. Damages were awarded in *Kirk v Gregory* (1876) (in trespass to goods). The legal result of the action is the true gain to the plaintiff.

Contemptuous damages are awarded where the court thinks the action, although good in law, is vexatious or gold-digging, in any tort. One farthing was awarded in *Newstead v London Express* (1939) (in defamation).

| 17.2.3 | More than the extent of the damage |

In nominal damages, costs will normally be awarded; in contemptuous, they will not.

Extra damages might be awarded as:

- aggravated damages, where the tortious act was committed in a manner calculated to aggravate the plaintiff;

- exemplary, or punitive, damages, to make an example of the defendant, or to punish him;

- parasitic damages, which cannot be claimed alone but can sometimes be awarded as an adjunct to a claim for other damage. For example, damages in defamation for loss of reputation can only be awarded if damages are also awarded for loss of a material benefit.

17.3 Extinction of remedies

There are various ways that a right to sue in tort might be extinguished. The main way is that the claim becomes statute-barred under the Limitation Act 1980, which consolidated previous statutes. This is in effect a normal defence which the defendant must plead; the court cannot take notice of it of its own initiative. The Act provides limitation periods of six years in the case of all torts save those now mentioned, or three years in the cases of claims for personal injuries, including death, and one year in the cases of defamation and injurious falsehood from the accrual of the action. When the period expires, the plaintiff can still issue his writ but the defendant can raise limitation as a defence.

Time begins to run when the action could first have been brought. This means there must be a plaintiff and a defendant; in torts actionable *per se*, time runs from the tortious act, even though damage may not occur until years later; and in torts not actionable *per se*, time runs from when damage first results or the plaintiff is first aware of the fact of the injury.

But in personal injury cases, a plaintiff who is ignorant of the fact that he has suffered an injury has three years from when he first became aware of the facts of his injury, if later (s 11), and even if aware of it can still apply under s 33 for an extension if out of time. In cases of latent negligently caused damage to property, time also runs from the later of the time of the damage or the plaintiff's awareness of it, under the Latent Damage Act 1986.

A novelty in two recent statutes is the absolute long-stop limitation period. The Latent Damage Act 1986 (which only applies to cases of latent negligently caused damage to property, say, to buildings), quite apart from the provisions above, also has a absolute limitation of 15 years from the breach of duty of care. Similarly, the Consumer Protection Act 1987 has a absolute limitation of 10 years from the product first being put into circulation by anyone (nor can this be extended by s 33 Limitation Act 1980, above).

Case law, supplemented by statute law, has built up the principles on which compensation is paid for personal injury (including death).

17.4   Compensation in personal injury actions

> 'A man is not compensated for the physical injury; he is compensated for the loss which he suffers as a result of that injury. His loss is not in having a stiff leg; it is in his inability to lead a full life, his inability to enjoy those amenities which depend on freedom of movement and his inability to earn as much as he used to earn or could have earned if there had been no accident' (Lord Reid in *Baker v Willoughby* (1969)).

17.4.1   To living plaintiffs

The award of damages will cover pecuniary loss (that is, special damages for the pre-trial loss of earnings and pre-trial expenses, and general damages for anticipated lost earnings and expenses in the unknown future, based on an expected annual sum multiplied by a figure of years); and non-pecuniary loss (ie for the past and future pain and suffering, and the past and future loss of amenity (loss of ability to do something, for example, play the piano)).

17.4.2   The gamble

To some extent personal injury litigation is a gamble. If the plaintiff is deteriorating, his lawyers will want to delay the trial, since the worse he gets, the more damages he might be awarded. A plaintiff can in any type of High Court case apply for an interim payment under court rules, and since the mid-1980s he can apply to the judge at the trial for an award of Provisional and Further Damages. These can be awarded where the plaintiff pleads, and the court accepts, that there is a 'chance' that as a result of the defendant's tort there may be either serious disease, or serious deterioration in the plaintiff's physical or mental condition. If satisfied, the court can award damages assessed on the assumption that such disease or deterioration will not occur, and can order that one application may be made for further damages for each specified disease or deterioration within the time limit specified by the court. In this way, a plaintiff's lawyers need not be fearful about a (foreseeable) deterioration.

But in 1991, a new way of settling damages in personal injuries appeared. In a few cases, the parties settled (ie agreed out of court) on the basis of a structured settlement.

In *Field v Herefordshire Health Authority* (1991) a settlement of lump sum and annuity income was agreed to provide the plaintiff, a young girl, with financial provision until she reaches the age of 76. Structured settlements are still only the subject of settlements, as opposed to court awards, but they raise interesting points. If a plaintiff expects to live for a long time, then he would prefer a structured settlement, but if he expects only to live for a short time, he would prefer a lump sum. The tactics of both sides in the litigation and negotiation can be expected to differ accordingly.

17.4.3   The effect of death

Two types of action can be brought on a person's death. The first is for a cause of action vested in the deceased (in other words, the deceased's own action, had he lived); the second is an action by the dependants of the deceased.

The first action, in respect of the cause of action vested in the deceased is brought on behalf of the deceased's estate by the personal representatives (executors or administrators), under the Law Reform (Miscellaneous Provisions) Act 1934.

Where the deceased died immediately on the tortious act, for example, in a car crash, only a claim for funeral expenses may be made. But where the plaintiff survives, the action is regarded as the plaintiff's action and the normal rules for pecuniary loss and non-pecuniary loss apply. Thus, claims for loss of earnings, expenses, pain and suffering, and loss of amenity may be made (also the funeral expenses). The damages are treated as part of the deceased's estate for all purposes.

The dependant's action is brought by the personal representatives under the Fatal Accidents Act 1976, but this time for the benefit of the deceased's dependants against the person whose 'wrongful act, neglect or default' 'caused' the death. 'Dependants' is defined to include closest relatives, including a reputed spouse, or former spouse (even by void or annulled marriage), and persons treated as in the lineage. The damages are recovered for the dependants and do not form part of the deceased's estate.

The Law of Tort

We have seen that the law of tort consists of several torts covering between them various types of damage. These torts all follow four general principles of liability. These principles are:

- the plaintiff's protected interest;

- the defendant's wrongful act;

- the defendant's fault; and

- the existence of damage.

The first principle divides torts by protecting, firstly, the plaintiff's person (trespass to the person; intentional physical harm; negligence and similar torts such as breach of statutory duty, especially the Occupiers' Liability Acts 1957–84, and the strict liability of the Animals Act 1971). Secondly, property is protected, either goods (trespass to goods and conversion; negligence; public nuisance and the Animals Act 1971), or land (either physically, as in trespass to land, negligence, public nuisance, private nuisance, *Rylands v Fletcher*, or by interference with use and enjoyment of land, as in the two forms of nuisance). Reputation is protected (defamation), and in many torts other than negligence so is pure economic loss, but at that the list ends. Other forms of harm are not protected by the law of tort (though they may be so by other areas of law).

The second of the four main principles is that the defendant must have committed a wrongful act. This rule is universal. The law balances the respective values of the parties behaviour or injury to ascertain whether, given all the circumstances, which are wrong and which are right and allowable in a civilised society. To take some extreme examples, squeezing gently through a queue of people, or acting in self-defence or giving urgent medical treatment are clearly not wrong (see *F v West Berks HA*), nor is reasonable behaviour within the give and take principle (see *Bamford v Turnley*, in private nuisance, and *Bolton v Stone*, in negligence). The law of tort did not evolve to protect people from the knocks of fortune, or the perils of being alive on the planet. A plaintiff must always show a wrongful act on the part of the defendant.

The third principle, that the plaintiff must prove the defendant's fault, also separates the various torts by the different forms of fault. From the early torts intentional harm has been accountable in damages. All forms of trespass require the defendant's intentional behaviour, as do torts which also contain an element of strict liability, such as conversion and defamation. In the last two torts there must at least be an intention to interfere with goods, or an intention to publish. But experience has shown that man is careless rather more than he is mischievous, and a defence of 'I did not mean to do it' might not always be successful since the emergence of the tort of negligence in *Donoghue v Stevenson*. In that tort, as under the Occupiers' Liability Acts and to some extent in breach of statutory duty, negligence will amount to fault. But apart from these torts, either the defendant s knowledge is required (to a nuisance: see *The Wagon Mound (No 2)*, or to an animal's harmful propensity: see the Animals Act 1971), or the tort is one of strict liability. This principle is under constant review as a result of the recognition of the need to compensate the plaintiff, but reforms in favour of strict liability are infrequent (see Consumer Protection Act 1987), and fault remains a crucial element of tortious liability.

The final element recognises that compensation implies harm or damage. A man who has not been harmed does not need compensation. This principle is almost universal. Only trespass and libel (and the four exceptional cases of slander) are actionable *per se*. But as we have seen not all damage is actionable. Again, the principle of reasonableness is important to prevent a defendant being held liable for all the damage he has caused irrespective of its being unforeseeable.

While the facts of the various causes of action in tort are very varied, the main principles of liability are, with exceptions, consistent. The interests of the two parties must be balanced against each other to decide liability and therefore a right to compensation.

PART III

CRIMINAL LAW

Chapter 18

Introduction to Criminal Law

A crime (equally called an 'offence') is as difficult to define as is a tort. It might be equated with a public wrong, a wrong against society. But this is problematic; some crimes are solely directed against the perpetrator, eg illegal drug use, suicide before 1961. And if we talk about a 'threat to society', the problem is that the conduct might cease to be a threat, while remaining a crime. Furthermore, not all threats to society, nor causes of public approbation, are crimes; nor should they be.

Is it a *moral wrong*? Not all crimes have a 'moral' content. Not all immoral acts are criminal; nor should they be. But Viscount Simonds, discussing conspiracy to corrupt public morals in *Shaw v DPP* (1961) claimed that there remained in the judiciary a residual power to protect the moral welfare of the state (see Chapter 31, 31.1 below in Part IV on Civil Liberties); this trend was restricted in *Knuller Ltd v DPP* (1972), but the defendants who claimed that they consented to their acts of sado-masochism in *R v Brown* (1993) (see Chapter 21, 21.3.1 below) were denied their defence of consent on grounds of 'policy and public interest'. While, therefore, it is accepted that many criminal wrongs are also moral wrongs, it is also generally accepted that morality is essentially a matter for the individual, as was argued by JS Mill in *On Liberty*.

But where does this leave the definition of a crime? A better test is simply whether criminal proceedings can follow the conduct. If so, it is a crime; if not, it is not a crime. As we have just seen, to attempt to link it with morality is a hazardous exercise.

The English criminal justice system, unlike many others, has evolved, rather than been created. There has, therefore, not been as much thought given here as to what we expect or want our criminal law to do. It has simply evolved along with the legal system, itself a part of government. It is surprising, therefore, given that it is generally accepted that a criminal law is a necessary part of a civilised society, but given also that the criminal law has power to deprive its citizens of life, liberty and property, that we must look elsewhere to study a rationale of a criminal law.

The US, which also has a common law jurisdiction, is a country where such thought has been given. The American

18.1 Definitions

18.2 The purpose of the criminal law

Law Institute's Model Penal Code states that the law's purpose is to:

- *forbid and prevent* conduct which inflicts or threatens unjustifiable and inexcusable substantial harm to an individual or the public interest;

- subject would-be criminals to *public control;*

- *safeguard faultless conduct;*

- give *fair warning* of what is criminal;

- differentiate on *reasonable* grounds between *serious* and *minor* crimes.

18.3 Aims of sentencing

Thought has been given in England to the aims of sentencing. In *R v Sargeant* (1974) Lawton LJ said:

> 'Those classical principles are summed up in four words: retribution, deterrence, prevention and rehabilitation. Any judge who comes to sentence ought always to have these four classical principles in mind and apply them to the facts of the case to see which of them has the greatest importance in the case with which he is dealing.'

18.3.1 To seek retribution or revenge

A criminal system should be clear as to whether this is for the moral blameworthiness or for the harm that is caused. For example, a simple common assault might produce anything from a bruise to death. The moral blameworthiness is slight in common assault; but the harm could be severe. The law recognises the grading both of blameworthiness (murder is more seriously treated than manslaughter on account of its greater fault, even though both cause death), and of harm (grievous bodily harm is covered by more serious offences than is actual bodily harm); each of these systems of grading will qualify crimes for different grades of punishment.

An important requirement of retribution is proportion, that the sentence should fit the crime, if a sense of grievance is to be averted. Accordingly, the prescribed maximum sentences of different offences take account, with opposite effects (ie increasing or decreasing the sentence), for example of not using violence, and of using it. And to achieve some consistency of effect on those convicted, the Magistrates' Association, with the backing of Lord Bingham CJ, issued sentencing guidelines in April 1997 which will impose a sliding scale of fines according to the income of the offender, on the principle of 'equality of hardship' and not 'equality of monetary penalty'. The Criminal Justice Act 1993 already requires the court to take into account the financial circumstances of the offender.

AV Dicey, a 19th century academic lawyer, talked of 'equality before the law'. In the criminal process this should not only apply to the trial itself, but should do so also at the time of the decision whether to prosecute and at the sentencing stage, where the police and the court respectively have a certain amount of discretion, which it is essential they do not abuse. The law cannot but be brought into disrepute if rapists are simply put on probation or civil servants are prosecuted for official secrets leaks but ministers are not.

At its crudest, protecting the public and providing a deterrent can take place simply by the offender being put in prison, where he cannot be harmful, until, obviously, he comes out. But a sensible system will seek to deter by discouragement, not only the particular offender who is sentenced, but also the rest of society, in particular those who might otherwise be tempted.

18.3.2 To protect the public, to deter the offender and to deter others

The principle of proportion applies equally here. If a lesser crime is punished as a more serious one, the offender may as well be hung as a sheep than a lamb. Thus, the maximum sentence for theft (s 1 Theft Act (TA) 1968) is seven years and for robbery (s 8 TA 1968) is life imprisonment; for burglary (s 9 TA 1968), 14 years, and aggravated burglary (s 10 TA 1968), life imprisonment.

If the criminal stood to be punished whether he committed the simple offence or the aggravated version then he might as well commit the more serious one; he could not be punished any more severely for it. This may be in the mind of a future criminal who commits his second attempt, conspiracy or incitement to commit murder, or second offence of rape, manslaughter, wounding or grievous bodily harm with intent (s 18 Offences against the Person Act 1861), robbery with a firearm (s 8 TA 1968) or solicitation to murder (s 4 TA 1861). The Crime (Sentences) Act 1997 imposes a mandatory life sentence on him for his second or third such offence. But as this is the penalty for murder, what is to stop him committing murder during the crime, eg of the woman he rapes? Incidentally, it was also enacted that a third burglary of a dwelling (s 9 TA 1968) would receive an extended sentence, but the plan was dropped in midsummer 1997 – in fear of overcrowding the prisons!

However, it seems that sentences, both maximum and actual, are of little deterrent value. There is some evidence that the perceived chance of being caught is the main deterrent, not the possible sentence.

18.3.3	To rehabilitate and reform the offender	

The final aim, to rehabilitate and reform the offender, is still controversial. It is close to, though distinct from, the 'nurture' argument, that environment is a powerful influence in making people commit crimes. Remove that influence and the problem is solved.

But attitudes differ widely. The 'hard-liners' see the sentences imposed with this aim as a soft option; whereas the 'reformists', taking into account the fact that even a term of imprisonment will in most cases end, with the result that the offender is again at large, seek to reform his character such that he leads a more useful, and reformed, life.

This aim is sought to be met by the use of such sentences as probation or community service, by the parole system, discharge, suspended sentences, and the power of binding over to keep the peace. All these adopt a conciliatory approach, holding back the full force of the punishments also available, such as gaol and fines. Clearly, to make no attempt at reform is to simply allow back into society a person who is just as likely to commit the crime again.

Linked to this approach is the Rehabilitation of Offenders Act 1974, whereby certain convictions become spent after a while, and the 'victim support system' and the reparation schemes whereby the defendant must physically help his victim, say by repairing the damage caused by his burgling and damaging the victim's house.

18.4   The rule of law

But while the divide between law and morality is somewhat vague, it is crucial to distinguish between law and the arbitrary, or whimsical, exercise of power.

AV Dicey, the 19th century academic lawyer, was clear that 'a man may be punished for a breach of law, but he can be punished for nothing else'. And in *R v Charles* (1976), a case on dishonest use of cheque-cards, the Court of Appeal gave a similar warning to those judges who would follow Viscount Simonds:

> 'Again it is right, we think, to shun the temptation which sometimes presses on the mind of the judiciary to suppose that because a particular course of conduct, as was this course of conduct, was anti-social and undesirable, it can necessarily be fitted into some convenient criminal pigeonhole.'

18.5   The presumption of innocence

That a man is presumed innocent until the prosecution proves him guilty is 'the one golden thread always to be seen throughout the web of the English criminal law' (Lord Sankey in *Woolmington v DPP* (1935)). In this case the defendant shot his wife, who had left him and whom he was trying to persuade to return home. He claimed that it was an accident, and that he carried it only to threaten to kill himself if she did not return. The trial judge summed up to the jury, that once the Crown (as prosecutor) had shown that he caused the death 'he has to show that there are circumstances ... which excuse the homicide altogether by showing that it was a pure accident'. Thus, the judge put the burden on the defendant to prove he had not intended to kill her. The House of Lords stated clearly on appeal that the burden is on the prosecution to prove guilt.

Thus, the burden of proof is on the prosecution, at least at common law; there are some statutes which reverse the burden. An example is s 1 Official Secrets Act 1911, where it is an offence to communicate information to an enemy for a purpose 'prejudicial to the safety or interests of the state' and 'it shall be deemed to have been ... communicated for a purpose prejudicial to the safety or interests of the state unless the contrary is proved'.

The prosecution must prove its case, whether guilt, or the absence of any defence, as the case may be, beyond *reasonable doubt*. Thus, if the jury is left with any reasonable (or real) doubt whether the defendant is guilty, then they must acquit him, as the case against him has not been proved. He then continues to be presumed innocent, as he has in law been all along.	**18.6 The standard (or degree) of proof**

Where the defendant raises a *defence*, however, the defendant has the *evidential burden*, ie must introduce evidence to show on balance of probabilities that the defence applies in that case, and the prosecution then has the *probative burden*, to prove beyond reasonable doubt that the defence does not apply.

Many crimes are statutory. Two important rules of statutory interpretation are, firstly, a rebuttable presumption against the imposition of criminal liability (ie *penal provisions are to be construed narrowly*). But some judges seem to forget this; thus in *R v Oakes* (1959), where the defendant is guilty who 'aids or abets and does any act preparatory', the court interpreted this as 'aids or abets or does any act preparatory', making the prosecution burden easier.	**18.7 Special rules in statutory interpretation**

Secondly, there is a rebuttable presumption against the imposition of liability without fault. In *Sweet v Parsley* (1969) a landlord, who was usually absent from her property, was charged with being concerned in the management of premises used for illegal drug-taking. The statute was silent as to whether proof of fault had to be proved, ie whether it had to be proved that she knew that drugs were being taken there, which in fact she did not. Lord Reid, in the House of Lords said that some statutes clearly state a requirement of *mens rea* while others indicate otherwise:

> 'But in a very large number of cases there is no clear indication either way. In such cases there has for centuries been a presumption that Parliament did not intend to make criminals of persons who were in no way blameworthy in what they did. That means that, whenever a section is silent as to *mens rea*, there is a presumption that, in order to give effect to the will of Parliament, we must read in words appropriate to require *mens rea*.'

18.8 Codification of the criminal law

Whereas, the law of tort has remained a largely common law subject, there has, over the last 100 years or so, been much argument in favour of the codification of the criminal law. In 1861, several statutes were enacted, covering many of the more basic offences. The Offences against the Person Act 1861 and the Accessories and Abettors Act 1861, which we shall consider below, are still in force, in part. And in 1989 the Law Commission produced a Criminal Code Bill, of 219 clauses. However, this has not as yet been enacted; nor have the recent Law Commission recommendations, eg on *Offences against the Person* (Law Com No 218) or on *Involuntary Manslaughter* (Law Com No 237). Thus the law remains a mixture of statute law, enacted or amended as the need is seen to arise, and some common law. Most case law is interpretation or application of the statutory rules.

18.9 Classification of crimes

Crimes can be classified in several ways. Firstly, the Criminal Law Act 1967, having abolished the distinction between felonies and misdemeanours, which had become out-of-date, divided crimes into arrestable and non-arrestable offences, and treason (which had existed before 1967). The significance of 'arrestable offences', now defined by s 24 Police and Criminal Evidence Act 1984, and of non-arrestable offences, is more pertinent to powers of arrest, and further discussion is dealt with in Part IV on Civil Liberties, below.

A second classification, now contained in the Magistrates' Courts Act 1980, was made in 1977 relating to how crimes were tried. This division is between summary offences, indictable offences, and either way offences.

Summary offences are triable summarily only, in the Magistrates' Courts, and consist of the majority of offences, mainly of a regulatory nature. Indictable offences are triable on indictment, before a judge and jury in the Crown Court. The third class are either way offences. Here, the examining justices first decide whether trial should be summary or on indictment. If they decide on trial on indictment, that is final. But if the justices decide on summary trial, they must inform the accused of his right to elect trial on indictment at the Crown Court, before a jury, and that even after summary trial, he might be committed to the Crown Court for sentencing. The accused then decides his mode of trial.

Controversy surrounds the constant conversion of either way offences to summary offences. Some of these are offences which can be acutely sensitive, involving a confrontation between policeman and defendant (for example, s 51(1) Police Act 1964: assaulting a policeman in the execution of his duty, converted in 1977), and in July 1993 controversy has arisen over the recommendation of the Royal Commission on Criminal Justice 1993, to allow the magistrates alone to decide where theft, an either way offence involving an allegation of dishonesty, should be tried.

Appeals are mentioned here only because they explain why criminal cases are styled in different ways. Most appeals from *summary trial* in the magistrates' court which are reported are to the Divisional Court of the Queen's Bench Division, or from there to the House of Lords. (These cases are styled, eg *Anderton v Ryan*, the prosecutor's name appearing, as here, Anderton, the former Chief Constable of Greater Manchester Police, although sometimes it is the individual police constable whose name appears.)

18.10   Appeals and case names

Appeals from trial on *indictment* (in Crown Court: a judge and jury) are to the Court of Appeal or from there to the House of Lords. (These cases are styled, eg *R v Shivpuri*, or sometimes *DPP v Lawrence* (DPP connoting the Director of Public Prosecutions), or *Metropolitan Police Commissioner v Charles*). The defendant can appeal against conviction or sentence, or on a point of law, in all cases if leave to appeal is given.

The prosecution cannot appeal from the Crown Court (as trial court) against an *acquittal.* It can only refer a point of law to the Court of Appeal for consideration. The Court of Appeal's opinion is styled, eg *AG's Reference (No 1 of 1993)*. It is binding precedent, but does not upset the jury's acquittal. The prosecution can appeal against an unduly lenient sentence.

Chapter 19

The Elements of a Crime:
Actus Reus and *Mens Rea*

The general rule is that the prosecution must prove that the defendant has brought about a *prohibited act*, or a *prohibited omission*, or a prohibited state of affairs (the *actus reus* of the crime), while having at the same time a *specified state of mind* (the *mens rea* of the crime). It is sometimes difficult to distinguish between the *actus reus* and the *mens rea*; for example, does 'permits' describe what the defendant does, or does it also connote a willingness to allow, therefore a state of mind?

There must always be an *actus reus*. It normally consists of conduct, plus consequences, plus circumstances.

19.1   *Actus reus*

Some crimes are conduct crimes, ie the conduct, whether or not it brings about a certain result, is criminal, eg assault, or dangerous driving; others are result, or consequence, crimes, ie the conduct is required to bring about a certain result, eg murder, or causing death by dangerous driving. And either might require a condition, or circumstance, to be proved as existing as part of the actus reus, eg handling 'stolen' goods requires the goods to be stolen. Some crimes concern all three parts, an example being s 1 Infanticide Act 1938:

> 'Where a woman by any wilful act or omission causes [conduct] the death of her child [result] being a child under the age of twelve months [circumstance] ...'

The state of mind of the victim is a circumstance which sometimes part of the *actus reus*, for example in rape, is the fact that the victim did not consent.

A complete *actus reus* must be proved. In *R v Deller* (1952) the defendant made a statement about a car he was selling, that the car was unencumbered. In fact, a loan agreement existed, as he knew, but was void as it was unregistered. The defendant was ignorant of the fact that the agreement was void, so unintentionally had told the truth, and had not obtained property by deception.

19.1.1   A complete actus reus must be proved

In contrast, the defendant in *R v Dadson* (1850), a policeman, shot a man who was stealing wood. It was a defence to the shooting that the man was a felon, ie had two previous convictions. These the man had, but the defendant was ignorant that he had. Thus, the defendant's ignorance prevented him from relying on that defence, resulting in his conviction of assault, as the *actus reus* of assault had been committed. (Deller would now be charged with an attempt, and the rule in *R v Dadson* has now been reversed by s 24 Police and Criminal Evidence Act 1984, considered below in Part IV on Civil Liberties.)

| 19.1.2 | The *actus reus* must be voluntary |

The *actus reus* must be voluntary, ie willed by the defendant. Thus, if the actus is involuntary, caused by a third force which physically controls the defendant's act, for example, if X pushes Y into the victim, the act is X's, not Y's. In *R v Mitchell* (1983) the defendant pushed into a post office queue, causing Y, an old man, to fall into an old lady, who later died. The defendant caused the death; Y was an involuntary participant.

It might also be involuntary if caused by a third force which otherwise interferes with the defendant's act, eg a sudden noise, or a swarm of bees which enters the car (an *obiter dictum* in *Hill v Baxter* (1958)). An involuntary *actus reus* caused by unconscious effort, called *non-insane automatism*, has also been regarded as involuntary, for example, during sleep (*R v Cogdon* (1951) where a mother killed her daughter, thinking in her sleep that they were being attacked by Korean guerrillas). But some regard the involuntariness as part of the *mens rea*, the mental element of the crime. If this is correct, and it is caused by a 'disease of the mind', then certainly we are discussing the defence of insanity, a matter of *mens rea* (which will be considered later).

| 19.1.3 | Causation |

This must be proved if a result, or consequence, is part of the *actus reus*. In *R v White* (1910) the defendant gave the first intended instalment of poison to his mother, intending that the course of poison should kill her; she had a heart attack quite independently of her having been given the poison. Thus, the defendant had not caused the death.

Problems of causation arise particularly in homicide, in deciding whether the defendant's action caused the death, for example, where a life-support machine is switched off, or where a wound is followed by negligent medical or other treatment, or where the victim refuses treatment, or where a person in a persistent vegetative state is allowed to die. These problems are considered under the *actus reus* of murder and manslaughter, below.

| 19.1.4 | *Actus reus* as a state of affairs |

In some crimes, the *actus reus* consists of a state of affairs, a circumstance. Common examples are the offences where the defendant must be proved to 'have with him' a knife (Prevention of Crime Act 1953) or 'an article for use in the course of or in connection with any burglary, theft or cheat' (s 25 Theft Act 1968), or anything with which he might cause criminal damage (s 3 Criminal Damage Act 1971). 'Possession' of controlled drugs is also an offence under s 5 Misuse of Drugs Act 1971.

The courts recognise the need for caution here. The general rule, as in tort, is that there is no liability for an omission. But it might constitute an *actus reus*, provided there is a duty to act, of which the omission is a non-performance. Thus, a failure to administer food or get treatment might be a cause of death, as in *R v Stone & Dobinson* (1977) for not getting care for a bedridden sister, or in *R v Gibbins & Proctor* (1918) for not feeding a child. In both cases, a duty existed to care for the sister and the child, as the common law will impose a duty on close relatives in these circumstances.

Until recently, it was unclear to what extent a doctor was under a duty to sustain the life of a patient. The answer is, only so far as it is in the patient's 'best interests' to do so. Thus, in *Airedale NHS Trust v Bland* (1993), the House of Lords relieved a doctor of his duty to sustain the life of his patient (by feeding and administering antibiotics, to ward off illness), a Hillsborough football disaster victim who had remained in a persistent vegetative state, since his recovery to full consciousness was not likely and it was therefore in his best interests to allow him to die naturally.

Other cases of *actus reus* by omission, well known to the conscientious car-driver, are failures to comply with the obligations under the Road Traffic Act 1988, ie to stop after an accident and to exchange details of car-ownership and insurance.

A different situation arises where the defendant unwittingly causes a likelihood of harm, but subsequently fails to remove he threat on realising it. In *R v Miller* (1983) a squatter fell asleep on a mattress, smoking a cigarette. He woke to find the mattress smouldering, but did nothing to extinguish it. The House of Lords held that the subsequent failure to perform his duty (or 'responsibility' as Lord Diplock preferred), after realising the danger, constituted an *actus reus*. The House of Lords preferred the 'failure to perform a duty' theory to a theory based on a continuous act, as the former would be easier to explain to a jury. But in cases like *Fagan v MPC* (1968), the continuous act theory might seem more appropriate. In this case a motorist innocently drove onto a policeman's foot. The policeman told him to 'get off my foot', but the motorist was rather slow in doing so. The problem was the requirement that *actus reus* and *mens rea* coincide; that at the time of committing the act (driving on) he had no *mens rea*, whereas

19.1.5   *Actus reus* as an omission

19.1.6   Omission and subsequent fault

when he formed the *mens rea*, he committed no positive act, or so it seemed. The Divisional Court held that the continuous contact constituted the *actus reus* and that *mens rea* at any time during that contact would satisfy the coincidence requirement. In *R v Ahmad* (1986), on the other hand, a requirement in the Protection from Eviction Act 1977 that the defendant 'does acts' likely to interfere with a tenant's peace or comfort was held to require a positive act.

19.2   *Mens rea*

The prosecution must prove that the defendant had a defined state of mind in relation to the causing of the event or the existence of the state of affairs. This defined state of mind is the mens rea, and constitutes the fault element of a crime.

All crimes have some *mens rea*, though in crimes of strict liability, considered at the end of this chapter, the prosecution is relieved of the duty to prove mens rea as to some, but not every, part of the *actus reus*. Thus, in *R v Prince* (1875), the leading case on strict liability, the defendant was convicted of 'without lawful authority or excuse [taking] an unmarried girl under the age of sixteen out of the possession of her parent or guardian against his will' (the forerunner of the present s 20 Sexual Offences Act 1956). The defendant thought she was at least 16, and did not therefore have any intention (*mens rea*) as to that part of the *actus reus*, ie the circumstance of her being under 16.

Mens rea does not mean *evil* or *bad motive*, or even good motive, for that matter. In *R v Gray* (1965), a father killed his 11 year old son out of mercy, who was dying of cancer and in pain; the father was convicted of manslaughter. In *Hills v Ellis* (1983), a man who had watched a football crowd incident and knew that the policeman was arresting the wrong man was convicted of 'wilfully obstructing' a policeman in the execution of his duty, after interfering in the arrest, though with good intention. In both cases the court was not concerned with why the defendant committed his *actus reus*, simply whether it was committed intentionally.

19.2.1   The type of *mens rea*

The types of *mens rea* are intention, recklessness, or negligence. Each type might relate to a different form of *actus reus*. For example, s 1(2) Criminal Damage Act 1971 states that

'A person who without lawful excuse destroys or damages any property, whether belonging to himself or another.

(a) intending to destroy or damage any property or being reckless as to whether any property would be destroyed or damaged; and

(b) intending by the destruction or damage to endanger the life of another or being reckless as to whether the life of another would be thereby endangered; shall be guilty of an offence.'

The *actus reus*, in the first clause, consists of conduct (destroying or damaging), and result (again, the destroying or damaging; simply touching would not do). The phrase 'whether belonging to himself or another' sounds like a circumstance part of the *actus reus*, but on examination it relieves the prosecution of the burden of proving any ownership at all, rather than imposes an additional burden on him. (The phrase 'belonging to another' used in s 1(1) is a true circumstance which the prosecution must prove.)

The *mens rea* is clearly set out; a defendant can be convicted on the basis of his intention to commit the *actus reus* of destruction or damage, or on the basis of his recklessness as to that *actus reus*; either will suffice. Had, also, the 'belonging to another' phrase applied to s 1(2), then intention (ie knowledge or belief) or recklessness would have been required as to that circumstance. Similarly, either form of *mens rea* will suffice in s 1(2)(b). Section 1(2)(b) is entirely *mens rea*, consisting of an intention or recklessness as to a result or consequence which does not form part of the *actus reus*; no endangering of life need be proved to have actually taken place.

In summary, then, the offence of s 1(2) can be committed with an intention in both clauses (a) and (b), recklessness in both, intention in (a) and recklessness in (b), or *vice versa*.

Before examining the forms of *mens rea*, two points are worth noting: Firstly, s 1(2) only concerns intention and recklessness, not negligence. Some crimes, for example, murder, only concern intention; some only negligence. In other words the *mens rea* required is that specified by the crime itself, which might be restrictive as to what form is required. Secondly, on an evidence point, it used to be said that in establishing whether a man intended a result, or was reckless in that he should have foreseen it (for example, the endangering of life in s 1(2), above) he was presumed to have intended or foreseen the natural and probable consequence of his act, whether or not he actually intended or foresaw it. This presumption was abolished by s 8 Criminal Justice Act 1967; the court must now decide whether he actually intended or foresaw a consequence on all the evidence, which includes any inferences it may make.

In many crimes the defendant will only be liable if he has committed the *actus reus* intentionally. Murder is an example, where the *mens rea*, called 'malice aforethought', is the

19.2.2   Intention

intention to kill or cause grievous bodily harm, though the killing need be neither malicious nor pre-meditated.

There are two forms of intention: firstly, if it is the defendant's *purpose* to bring a result about (in colloquial speech, he did it on purpose, or deliberately), he intends that result. Lord Bridge, in *R v Moloney* (1985), said:

> 'A man who, at London Airport, boards a plane which he knows to be bound for Manchester, clearly intends to travel to Manchester, even though Manchester is the last place he wants to be and his motive for boarding the plane is simply to escape pursuit.'

(Do not confuse purpose and desire. You can intend, while not desiring or wanting.)

Lord Bridge in the same case said that the presence of intention would be obvious 'if the offence consisted of a direct attack on the victim with a weapon'. In such a case the jury need not be exposed to the second form of intention, which now follows.

The second form of intention arises where it is not the defendant's purpose to bring about that result (or so he says), but the result is something that *could have been expected* in the circumstances. In the 1980s this problem arose in connection with malice aforethought, described above.

In *R v Moloney* (1985) a soldier at a family party shot his step-father's head off when the latter, in friendly rivalry, dared the soldier to fire a rifle which the soldier had just loaded. And in *R v Hancock & Shankland* (1986), during the Miners' Strike some striking miners dropped a concrete block from a bridge onto a taxi passing underneath, to frighten working miners who were travelling to work. The concrete block fell on and killed the taxi driver. The problem in both cases was that it was not the purpose to kill or cause grievous bodily harm. Could they, in that case, be said to have nevertheless intended to kill or cause grievous bodily harm, on the basis that the results were foreseeable or likely?

The combined statements of the House of Lords in *R v Moloney* (1985) and *R v Hancock & Shankland* (1986) make it clear that while the jury might properly infer that the greater the probability of a consequence the more likely it was foreseen, and if foreseen the greater the probability it was intended, nevertheless, the jury must in the end decide beyond reasonable doubt, not merely that he must have foreseen the result (prohibited under s 8, above), but that he actually intended it.

But these were difficult niceties for jurors to understand, who might in any case put too much reliance on the foresight element. In *R v Nedrick* (1986), therefore, Lord Lane CJ refined the definition of 'intention' of causing an *actus reus* where there was no purpose in causing it. He explained it as the defendant's 'appreciation' that causing the *actus reus* was a 'virtual certainty' of his act or omission. (The 'virtual certainty' is objective, what ordinary people as represented by the jury would regard as so; the 'appreciation' is subjective, that the defendant realised that in the opinion of ordinary people it was virtually certain. Thus, s 8 Criminal Justice Act 1967 is complied with.)

This argument will now resolve the question: where a defendant intends to carry out an act, the inevitable result of which would be the carrying out of a second act, does he intend to carry out that second act? The facts of *R v Steane* (1947) are typical. Here, the defendant was forced by the Gestapo to broadcast for the Nazi regime, on pain of his family being sent to concentration camps. He was acquitted, but, surprisingly, not on the ground of his being under duress, but on the ground of his not intending to broadcast. But in the light of *R v Moloney*, *R v Hancock & Shankland* and *R v Nedrick* this is wrong; granted that he may have been acting under duress, he must surely have appreciated that his broadcasting would certainly assist the enemy (the *actus reus*), and a jury could properly infer that he did appreciate it.

A correct decision is *Arrowsmith v Jenkins* (1963), where the defendant, making a speech in the street, did not have the purpose of obstructing the highway, but was nevertheless guilty of 'wilfully obstructing it', as she appreciated the virtual certainty of a crowd gathering to hear her, thereby blocking the highway.

19.2.3   The doctrine of transferred intent

If the defendant has *mens rea* for a specific crime against a specific person or thing, but misses, and commits the same crime against another person or thing, the malice (in other words, the *mens rea*) is transferred to the actual victim. The defendant is guilty, as both *actus reus* and *mens rea* exist. In *R v Latimer* (1886) a defendant who aimed a blow with his belt at one person, but which bounded off and hit a woman, causing her injury, was nevertheless guilty of wounding her. And in *R v Mitchell* (1983), a defendant who pushed an old man in a post office queue, who fell into an old lady, who later died from her fall, was guilty of the manslaughter of the old lady. But the doctrine does not apply where a different kind of harm results from that which was intended. Thus in *R v Pembliton* (1874), a defendant who threw a stone intending to hit some people he was quarrelling with, was not guilty of damaging the window which the stone actually hit and smashed. (This case must be treated with caution, however, since the interpretation in *R v Caldwell* (1981) of 'recklessness' in s 1 Criminal Damage Act 1971. The defendant in *R v Pembliton* might now be convicted of s 1, based on reasonable foresight of damage, if that is held to exist.)

19.2.4	Recklessness

But let us now consider the situation where intention is not present but the crime allows recklessness to suffice as the *mens rea*, for example s 1(2) Criminal Damage Act 1971 (19.2.1 above).

> 'A person who does not intend to cause a harmful result may take an unjustifiable risk of causing it. If he does so he may be held to be reckless' (Smith and Hogan, *Criminal Law*).

But as the social acceptability increases, so does the justification also, of him taking that risk, for instance, acting in self-defence, in *Sears v Broome* (1986), or 'evasive action in an emergency' in *R v Reid* (1992), a case on the now repealed causing death by reckless driving. If, on the other hand, the act is objectively unjustifiable, the defendant must have had 'one of three minds', two of which will make him liable. (However, the test of liability will depend on whether the crime is statutory or common law, and whether, if the former, the statute which defines the crime requires that he acts 'maliciously' or 'recklessly'.)

19.2.5	The three states of mind

The three states of mind are:

- that the defendant considered whether there was an unjustifiable risk, and decided that there was but carried on (thus, there was actual foresight of the risk);

- he did not consider whether there was an unjustifiable risk, but the risk was 'obvious' and he carried on (thus, there was reasonable foresight of the risk);

- he considered whether there was an unjustifiable risk, and decided that was none, or that there was only a negligible risk, and carried on (thus, there was neither actual nor reasonable foresight): this is sometimes called the *lacuna*, or the *loophole*.

Only the first two states of mind amount to recklessness; in some cases only the first is reckless, as we shall now consider.

19.2.6	Actual foresight of the risk

This will always amount to recklessness. In *R v Cunningham* (1957) it was held that where a statute requires a defendant to have acted 'maliciously', actual foresight of the risk is required for a conviction.

'Maliciously' is used in the offences of wounding or grievous bodily harm contrary to s 18 and s 20 Offences of the Person Act 1861, dealt with later, in Chapter 21 below, but actual foresight is, by extension, required in any assault and in gross or criminal negligence manslaughter.

In *DPP v K (a minor)* (1990) a school-boy who took some acid from the laboratory and, in panic when he heard footsteps, put it in the hot-air dryer in the toilets, was convicted of assault occasioning actual bodily harm, contrary to s 47 Offences of the Person Act 1861, after he had foreseen what in fact happened, namely that the acid flew into another boy's face who used the dryer.

Where the statute requires that the actus reus is committed 'recklessly', actual foresight of any risk will come within Lord Diplock's test of recklessness in *R v Caldwell* (1981). Thus, in *Chief Constable of Avon & Somerset v Shimmen* (1986), the defendant, a kung fu expert, showed off by kicking at a window intending to miss it by two inches; in fact, he broke it. He was convicted of criminal damage as he had recognised that there was a risk. His argument that he thought he had eliminated the risk was irrelevant; it mattered only whether he had he had recognised that there was a risk.

Until *R v Caldwell* (1981) it was assumed that recklessness was based on actual foresight in all crimes. In that case the House of Lords held that where a statute requires the defendant to have acted 'recklessly', there is liability if, in Lord Diplock's words, there is '(1) [an] obvious risk ... and (2) [the defendant has] either not given thought or has recognised ... some risk and has nevertheless gone on to do it'.

On the same day, in *R v Lawrence* (1981), a case on the now repealed causing death by reckless driving, a differently constituted House of Lords agreed with *R v Caldwell*, though Lord Diplock altered the test from 'obvious risk' to 'obvious and serious risk'. But the House in *R v Reid* (1992) used both phrases.

There has also been discussion as to which risk must be obvious. Lord Goff in *R v Reid* (1992) clarifies that the defendant will be reckless if either:

- he has actually foreseen *some* risk of injury or substantial damage (though it need not be an obvious one); or

- the risk is in fact an *obvious* one, and he has not foreseen any (or some) risk of either of those thing, ie of personal injury or of criminal damage. (Thus the obviousness relates only to what the risk is, not what he failed to recognise:

19.2.7   Reasonable foresight of the risk

what he failed to recognise was simply some, or any, risk. Moreover, the obviousness only applies to the reasonable foresight leg.)

Further initial doubt surrounded the question: obvious to whom? *R v Caldwell* leans towards the subjective ('he'), but *R v Lawrence* is objective: 'the ordinary prudent motorist'.

In *Elliott v C* (1983), a mentally-subnormal 14 year old girl, who had stayed out all night, unintentionally committed arson (criminal damage by fire) to a shed. Was she reckless? She did not actually foresee the risk of arson, and while the risk might have been obvious to the reasonable man, this girl, young, mentally-subnormal and tired, could not have perceived the risk. The Divisional Court held that she was reckless.

| 19.2.8 | The *Caldwell/Lawrence* loophole or *lacuna* |

If a person has considered the risk properly, he cannot be reckless, though he may still be negligent. In *R v Reid* (1992) Lord Goff, with whom three Lords of Appeal agreed, confirmed *obiter* that the defendant might, through mistake, shock, illness or emergency, not recognise the risk of harm.

Thus, in *W (a minor) v Dolbey* (1983) a defendant who shot someone between the eyes with a slug-pellet gun, thinking that the gun was empty, was acquitted of s 20 of the 1861 Act as there was no actual foresight of personal injury.

The case of *R v Lamb* (1967) emphasises, however, that a defendant who is not reckless might still be guilty on the basis of another type of fault. In this case, one lad shot and killed his friend with a revolver. He could see a bullet in the revolving part, but thought it safe as the bullet was not opposite the barrel. He was unaware that the revolver would revolve and then fire. Clearly, he fell into the loophole, but Sachs LJ observed that if he had considered it 'in a criminally negligent way', he might have been caught by gross or criminal negligence manslaughter, as opposed to reckless manslaughter.

Finally, it can be noted that recognition, and on that account disregard of a 'negligible' risk can be equated with 'no risk', falling into the loophole (Lord Diplock in *R v Caldwell* and Lord Ackner in *R v Reid*).

| 19.2.9 | Negligence |

Even in the cases where one considers the risk and decides that there is no risk, ie the loophole, if the failure to recognise the risk was 'criminally negligent', then the defendant might be liable where the crime's *mens rea* requires it, but, as we have seen, this will not be where either 'maliciousness' or 'recklessness' must be proved.

We have seen that *mens rea* can be intention, recklessness or knowledge (of possession of something), or negligence. And we have seen that the *mens rea* relates to the *actus reus*. If it relates to the *actus reus* but nothing more, or if the *mens rea* is wholly or partly recklessness or negligence, the crime is a crime of basic intent. If, however, it relates to some other consequence beyond the *actus reus*, or the *mens rea* expresses a particular intent, the crime is a crime of specific, or ulterior, intent.

Thus, a final definition of *mens rea*, according to Smith & Hogan, *Criminal Law*, is:

> '... intention, knowledge or recklessness with respect to all the elements of the offence together with ulterior [or specific] intent which the definition of the crime requires.'

19.2.10   A definition of mens rea

The *actus reus* and *mens rea* must coincide. If the *actus reus* is a continuing act (for example the contact with the policeman's foot in *Fagan v MPC* (1968)) the defendant will be guilty if he had *mens rea* at some time during the continuing act, even though not at the moment the *actus reus* is first accomplished.

If the *actus reus* is a series of acts, for example a defendant thinks he is killing someone (*mens rea*, but no *actus reus* of killing), but in fact does not succeed, and then disposes of what he thinks is the dead body, now killing the victim (*actus reus*, but no *mens rea*), the defendant will be guilty if the killing was the execution of a plan. Thus in *R v Thabo Meli* (1954), where the defendant got his victim drunk, then hit him over the head, and thinking him dead threw him over a cliff, where he died of exposure, the Privy Council held that it was 'impossible to divide up what was really one series of acts'. The defendant had had *mens rea* at the time of hitting him over the head, thus the two elements coincided.

Even where there is no plan, if the act which coincides with the *mens rea* is contributory to the death, or even if it is not, it is part of 'the same sequence of events, the same transaction' (Lord Lane CJ in *R v Le Brun* (1991)), there will be liability. Thus in *R v Le Brun* (1991), the defendant was convicted of manslaughter after he punched his wife in a quarrel, and then, trying to pick her up, dropped her, fracturing her skull and killing her. The whole sequence of events was seen as the same transaction, and the *mens rea* was coincidental with part of that transaction.

19.2.11   Coincidence of actus reus and mens rea

As is commonly said, ignorance of the law is no excuse; we are all presumed to know the law. This is true about the criminal law, thus we cannot say that the defendant had never heard of the Theft Act, but a defendant can plead ignorance, or honest

19.2.12   The effect of ignorance and mistake on mens rea

mistake, of matters of civil law in his defence. Thus in *R v Smith* (1974) a defendant's honest but wrong belief that wiring he had put in his rented flat was still his (it had thereby become the property of the landlord) was a defence to a charge of criminal damage. His honest mistake as to the ownership of the wiring meant that he had no *mens rea* as to the circumstance part of the *actus reus* of s 1(1) Criminal Damage Act 1971, namely that the wiring was property 'belonging to another'.

In *R v Smith* the defendant's mistake was to think that the property was his. This amounts to a 'claim of right', also available in s 2 Theft Act 1968, if I 'steal' property I honestly think is mine, and also available under s 5 Criminal Damage Act 1971 on a charge of criminal damage where I damage your property honestly believing it to be necessary in order to protect my own (say, by shooting your dog, which is worrying my sheep).

All these mistakes affect the defendant's belief as to law, and negate the defendant's *mens rea*. Further, an honest mistake of fact, even if unreasonable, which is inconsistent with that *mens rea*, must result in acquittal. In *DPP v Morgan* (1975), a husband persuaded three airmen to come to have sexual intercourse with his wife, because she liked that sort of thing; and the more she said 'no', the more she meant 'yes'. These were all lies. The three men did so, despite the woman's protestations, and they were charged with rape. The *actus reus* of rape is non-consensual sexual intercourse, and the *mens rea* was accordingly the intention to commit it. But this intention is not simply to commit sexual intercourse, but to commit non-consensual sexual intercourse, and forms part of the prosecution's burden of proof. Thus the honest mistake of the airmen would result in their not intending it to be non-consensual, a failing in the proof of *mens rea*.

In cases like this, therefore, where an honest belief in fact (here: her consent) or law negates *mens rea*, then really the prosecution have not established *mens rea*, and the case will fail because the prosecution has failed to prove a *prima facie* case.

So, since *DPP v Morgan*, the first question (whether there has been a mistake or not) is, 'what is the *mens rea*'?; and the second is, has the prosecution established that *mens rea*?

19.2.13 Strict liability

The general principle that proof of *mens rea* is required is subject to this exception. Here, *mens rea* as to some, but not every, aspect of the *actus reus* is dispensed with. Thus, as we have seen in *R v Prince* (1875), the prosecution did not have to prove knowledge that she was under 16. (There is, unfortunately, much confusion between 'strict liability' and 'absolute liability' among judges and writers.

The better meanings are that strict liability is as defined above, but that defences are still available; absolute liability (which might be fault-based or strict) means, no defences.

Very few common law, or formerly common law, crimes have strict liability. We saw in the introduction to this chapter, in *Sweet v Parsley* (1969), that generally, in important crimes there is a presumption that *mens rea* is required. Thus it is only in the criminal forms of libel, eg criminal libel, blasphemous libel (*Whitehouse v Lemon* (1979)), public nuisance, and contempt of court, now statutory under the Contempt of Court Act 1981.

19.2.13.1   Which crimes?

In contrast, many regulatory offences in areas of public safety, where the law is statutory, and especially if the criminal nature is relatively trivial, contain strict liability. Examples include many offences in food safety (for example the Food Safety Act 1990) and consumer protection legislation (for example the Trade Descriptions Act 1968), an example of the former being the sale of bad meat where the butcher has no reasonable means of checking for bacteria (*Hobbs v Winchester* (1910)). Many offences under the Licensing Act 1964, for example selling liquor to a drunken person (who did not appear to be so in *Cundy v Le Coq* (1884)), and many of the more trivial offences under the Road Traffic Act 1988 are strict.

Increasingly, there is also strict liability in the field of pollution. In *Alphacell Ltd v Woodward* (1972) the House of Lords held a river-side company guilty of pollution when an overflow channel became clogged up even though it was not negligent in allowing it to happen or in failing to appreciate that it was happening, because otherwise, if fault were required, 'a great deal of pollution would go unpunished'. In *Atkinson v Sir Alfred McAlpine* (1974) the Divisional Court held a company guilty of using crocidolite, prohibited under the Asbestos Regulations, though they neither knew, nor were negligent in not knowing, that it was using it. Clearly, the message for industry is: find out what you are using, or suffer for it.

We have already seen that the courts presume a requirement of *mens rea* (*Sweet v Parsley* (1969), at the introduction to this chapter). But Wright J in *Sherras v De Rutzen* (1895) said that 'that presumption is liable to be displaced either by the words of the statute creating the offence or by the subject matter with which it deals'.

19.2.13.2   The presumption of fault

Thus words such as 'knowingly', 'permitting' or 'possession' are usually taken to require *mens rea*, but those such as 'using' or 'causing', or phrases such as 'no person shall', are usually taken to denote strict liability. The case of *James & Son Ltd v Smee* (1954) emphasises that the prosecuting authorities must choose their offences carefully: the defendant, who was ignorant of a lorry's faulty brakes might nevertheless have been convicted of 'using' it in its defective state, but was not surprisingly acquitted of 'permitting' it to be driven.

The subject matter of the offence will also influence the court in whether to impose strict liability. In *Gammon (UK) Ltd v AG of Hong Kong* (1984) Lord Scarman, speaking for the Privy Council, said that 'the presumption [of *mens rea*] is particularly strong where the offence is 'truly criminal' in character'. Thus, the courts will be more inclined towards strict liability where the purpose of the offence is merely to enforce a regulation, usually by imposition of a fine, and with little likelihood of causing disgrace.

However, the courts do maintain that social protection weighs more than injustice to the defendant. The Privy Council in *Gammon (UK) Ltd v AG of Hong Kong* (1984) stated that the court could rebut the presumption of *mens rea* in statutory offences of grave social concern, for example public safety, especially if it would encourage observance of the statute.

19.2.13.3 Problems of strict liability

Strict liability is not without its problems. In practical terms, if the harshness of strict liability is to deter bad practice, might it not go further to deter a trader from trading at all? The case of *Hobbs v Winchester Corporation*, above, deters the selling of bad meat; but for the butcher unable to tell whether his meat is good or bad, might it not be easier for him to stop selling meat at all?

The second problem is that, quite simply, strict liability is unfair. Under its principle, those who are blameworthy and blameless are convicted alike. And strict liability means ignoring the degree of blame when considering liability (as opposed to sentence). Thus all persons, whether intentionally harmful, recklessly or negligently so, or not at fault, are convicted alike.

19.2.13.4 Statutory defences

Perhaps it is because of these elements of unfairness that statutory defences are becoming more common. They are usually of three types: that a third party caused the thing, and the defendant exercised all due diligence to avoid the *actus reus*; secondly, the unavoidable consequence of the process of collection or preparation, for example of food; and thirdly, that the defendant did not know, nor could reasonably have known, of the *actus reus*. Some of the offences in the Food

Safety Act 1990 also provide for these defences. Thus, decisions such as in *Parker v Alder* (1899) would now result in acquittals. In that case, a milk salesman delivered milk to a station for carriage to London, the contract stating that ownership passed on delivery in the capital. It was there found to have been adulterated with water to the extent of 9%, and the defendant milk salesman was convicted of selling adulterated milk.

But rather than rejoicing in the provision of these defences, Smith & Hogan (in *Criminal Law*) are sceptical: 'they usually impose on the defendant a burden of proving both that he had no *mens rea* and that he took all reasonable precautions and exercised all due diligence to avoid the commission of an offence', and that while the provision of a defence is better than none at all, 'they are still a deviation from the fundamental principle that the prosecution must prove the whole of their case [ie including *mens rea* and the absence of any defence raised]; and an extensive use of offences of strict liability, even when so qualified, is to be deplored'.

Chapter 20

Homicide

Homicide, the killing of a person pure and simple, is not a crime. It is an act or omission which might be criminal or not depending on circumstances.

Execution by criminal process, killing in self-defence, suicide: these are all *justifiable*, or at least *excusable* homicide, and, accordingly, not criminal. Here, we are concerned with *unjustifiable* homicide, of which there are several types. These range from murder and manslaughter to infanticide (the killing of a born child in its first year by the mother, still suffering mentally from the childbirth, contrary to the Infanticide Act 1938), child destruction the killing of an unborn child capable of being born alive, ie illegal abortion, contrary to the Infant Life (Preservation) Act 1929, and procuring a miscarriage, contrary to the Offences against the Person Act 1861.

We shall consider here murder and manslaughter, which, it should be noted, share the same *actus reus* and differ only in *mens rea*.

20.1 Murder

Sir Edward Coke, Chief Justice of the Court of King's Bench under King James VI and I, defined murder thus:

> '... when a man of sound memory, and of the age of discretion, unlawfully killeth within any county of the realm any reasonable creature in *rerum natura* under the king's peace, with malice aforethought, either expressed by the party or implied by law, so as the party wounded, or hurt, etc.'

In short, it is the killing of a person who has been born (wholly expelled from the mother, even though still connected to her) and is not an enemy alien ('in the heat of war, and in the actual exercise thereof' (Hale Cn)) and of whatever mental state, with malice-aforethought. The English courts have jurisdiction in murder and manslaughter committed by a British citizen anywhere in the world. Given the advances in forensic medicine and the greater ease in proving the cause of death, the requirement that the death must occur within a year and a day of the last act causing death was abolished by the Law Reform (Year and a Day Rule) Act 1996.

However, the consent of the Attorney General is required to a prosecution commenced after three years of the last act causing the death or where the defendant was convicted and sentenced to at least two years' imprisonment for the act or omission now alleged to have caused the death.

We shall look first at the joint *actus reus* of murder and manslaughter and then at the *mens rea* of each crime. (It is usually good sense to look first at the *actus reus* of a crime, since to determine *mens rea* first is to determine his intention to do what has not yet been determined.)

20.1.1   *Actus reus* of murder and of manslaughter

- The defendant

  The defendant must be 'of sound memory', not able to plead the defences of insanity and diminished responsibility, and 'of the age of discretion', not able to plead the defence of infancy.

- The victim

  The victim must be bom, as described above, but not dead. In *R v Malcherek, R v Steel* (1981), the court was faced with victims of assaults who were on life-support machines. The question for the court was whether the switching off of the machine caused the death of the victim, or whether it was the original wound which did. The Court of Appeal said that 'There is, it seems, a body of opinion in the medical profession that there is only one true test of death and that is the irreversible death of the brain stem, which controls the basic functions of the body such as breathing. When that occurs it is said the body has died, even though by mechanical means the lungs are being caused to operate and some circulation of blood is taking place.' Thus, the victims in these two cases were already dead, killed by their wounds.

20.1.2   Causation of the death

The defendant must be proved to have caused the death, or rather, since man is after all mortal, 'The proper question to have been submitted to the jury was whether the prisoner accelerated the death by the injuries which he inflicted' (*R v Dyson* (1908)). Causation is an issue of fact, therefore to be decided by the jury, but the jury must apply the principles of law in the judges' direction.

The prosecution must prove that but for the defendant's act, the death would not have happened as and when it did. In *R v White* (1910) the defendant intended to kill his mother by putting potassium cyanide in her drinks. She was found dead, killed not by her drink, which it was not proved she had taken, and which was too weak to kill her, but by a heart-attack completely independent of the poison. Although what he intended had indeed happened, it was not his administration of poison which had caused the death, and he was accordingly acquitted. (However, he was convicted of attempted murder, see below.)

The defendant's act need not be the sole or main cause of death. There might be a contributory natural event: for instance, in *R v Dyson* (1908) the two contributory factors were the defendant's striking the victim and meningitis, neither of which would have killed alone. Similarly, the behaviour or condition of the victim might contribute to the death, but 'the defendant must take his victim as he finds him'; so the fact that the old age of the person whom the defendant ran over also contributed to his death operated against the defendant in *R v Swindall & Osborn* (1846). It follows that the contributory behaviour of a third party will not relieve the defendant of liability.

Thus in *R v Benge* (1865), a foreman whose failure to order the carrying out of safety measures while the track was up (at Staplehurst, in Kent), thereby causing a railway crash, could not argue that other employees also failed to take care.

The criminal law usually refrains from imposing liability for an omission, but, as we have seen, a failure to act where there is a duty or responsibility to act will amount to an *actus reus*.

20.1.3   Omissions

Thus, in the following two cases a failure to care for the victim amounted to manslaughter in *R v Stone & Dobinson* (1977), where a bed-ridden elderly sister of one of the defendants was allowed to die, and murder in *R v Gibbins & Proctor* (1918), where a seven year old daughter of the first defendant was starved to death.

In cases of doctors who allow their patients to die, the House of Lords in *Airedale NHS Trust v Bland* (1993) said that though there is a duty to keep patients alive, such that allowing them to die would normally constitute this actus reus, in this case it was in the 'best interests' of the patient that his life, in a persistent vegetative state since the Hillsborough football disaster, should be allowed to expire.

A *novus actus interveniens*, a new intervening act, will break the chain of causation. Thus, if the fire I cause is brought under control but it is your throwing paraffin on the embers which causes further damage, I will not be responsible for that further damage, but you alone will. But it will not be a *novus actus interveniens* if the defendant's original act is still 'an operating cause and a substantial cause' (*R v Smith* (1959)). Thus, the switching off of a life-support machine which was keeping an assault victim alive did not break the chain of causation leading from the assault (*R v Malcherek, R v Steel* (1981)).

20.1.4   *Novus actus interveniens*

Similarly, medical mistreatment will only break the chain of causation of death if the treatment was 'palpably wrong' and the original assault was no longer a threat to the victim's life, as in *R v Jordan* (1956) where the drug administered to the patient was given to him in abnormal quantity, and moreover, after it was discovered that he was intolerant of it. But this case was distinguished in *R v Smith* (1959) where the victim was stabbed in the lungs with a bayonet in a barrack-room fight. Here, the victim was twice dropped from his stretcher; oxygen was given him even though this was bad for pierced lungs; the doctors were harassed by having other victims to attend to. The result was that the victim died two hours after the stabbing; but what caused it: the stabbing or the poor treatment?

Similarly, in *R v Cheshire* (1991), the victim was shot in a fish and chip shop and was taken to intensive care. He had breathing problems, and a tracheotomy was performed (a hole cut at his throat to get direct access to his windpipe). Two months later a rare but not unknown complication set in (a narrowing of the windpipe), from which he died. The same question arose: what caused his death, especially as there was expert evidence at the trial that the wounds were no longer a threat to his life?

In these two cases the courts hearing the appeals took a more robust stance, refusing to allow the defendants to offload their liability onto hard-pressed doctors, who, after all, were acting to preserve their victims' lives. The wounds in both *R v Smith* (1959) and *R v Cheshire* (1991) were still 'an operating cause and a substantial cause' of the death and both defendants' convictions were upheld.

In discussing the effect of a *novus actus*, the question also arises, as in tort, as to whether the victim's unreasonable behaviour breaks the chain of causation. In the next two cases the victims of assaults refused to undergo treatment, and consequently died.

In *R v Holland* (1841) the treatment was amputation of a gangrenous finger, and in *R v Blaue* (1975) the wounded girl was a Jehovah's Witness who refused a blood transfusion. In both cases the victims were told that the treatment would save them. But, as in tort, you take your victim as you find him, so that both juries found that the victims' behaviour was reasonable, and did not break the respective chains of causation leading from the wounds.

But, further, if the defendant's original act, is not an 'operating cause', but causes a foreseeable natural consequence which causes the death, is the defendant liable for that consequence?

In *R v Pagett* (1983), the defendant, knowing that the police who were after him were armed, held his pregnant girlfriend in front of him before shooting at the police. The police shot back, in self-defence, killing the girlfriend. The Court of Appeal held that it was a foreseeable natural consequence of his own shots that the police would fire back, so that he was liable for the death of the girl.

On the other hand, if the consequence is not foreseeable, it is a *novus actus interveniens*. Thus, in a case from Kentucky, *Bush v Commonwealth* (1880), where the defendant's gunshot put the victim in hospital, where a doctor innocently infected the victim with scarlet fever, the defendant was not liable for the death caused by the infection.

Sometimes the fright of the victim forms part of the chain of causation. In *R v Towers* (1874) the defendant assaulted a girl who screamed as a result. The baby in her arms went black in the face, had convulsions and died two months later. The defendant was held to have caused its death. And in *R v Hayward* (1908), a husband who chased his wife, threatening her, was liable for her injuries when she jumped out of a window to escape him.

20.1.5   Causation and fright

The *mens rea* of murder is called *malice aforethought*, though it need be neither malicious nor pre-meditated. Malice aforethought is the intention to kill or cause grievous bodily harm.

20.2   *Mens rea* of murder

As we have seen above, there are two forms of intention. The first form is the state of mind where it is the defendant's purpose to bring about the death or grievous bodily harm. Thus, if the defendant admits, or if the jury infers from all the evidence under s 8 Criminal Justice Act 1967, that he or she killed or caused grievous bodily harm on purpose, or deliberately, then he can be said to have intended that result. But Lord Bridge's example of a man intentionally going to Manchester, in *R v Moloney* (1985), above, shows also that purpose need not always coincide with desire.

The second form of intention arises where it is not the defendant's purpose to bring about that result (or so he says), but the result is something that could have been expected in the circumstances. Neither in *R v Moloney* (1985) where a soldier at a family party shot his step-father's head off, and in *R v Hancock & Shankland* (1986), where some striking miners dropped a concrete block from a bridge onto a taxi passing underneath, did the defendants purposefully or deliberately cause the deaths. Both cases discussed a second form of intent which the jury can infer, based on foreseeability of natural and probable consequences. But it was in *R v Nedrick* (1986), where the defendant caused death by pouring petrol through the victim's letter-box, and setting light to it that Lord Lane CJ refined this definition of 'intention', namely of causing an *actus reus* where there was no purpose in causing it. He explained it as the defendant's 'appreciation' that causing the *actus reus* was a 'virtual certainty' of his act or omission.

| 20.3 | *Mens rea* of manslaughter |

As we have seen, manslaughter has the same *actus reus* as murder. It is clearly going to be the case that a defendant will cause death but without intending it; sometimes he may intend some harm, but not serious harm, by his act; and sometimes he will intend no harm at all but is in some degree careless. But the fact is that he has caused death, and the criminal law must recognise that fact.

There are two broad groups of manslaughter.

| 20.3.1 | Voluntary manslaughter |

Here, malice aforethought is present; but because there is a special defence the voluntary and intended killing is excused, and a conviction for manslaughter brought in.

The special defences are diminished responsibility, under s 2 Homicide Act 1957; provocation, under s 3 of that Act; and killing in pursuance of a Suicide Pact, under s 4 of that Act.

The first two are special defences only to murder, but are considered in the part of this chapter dealing with defences. (Section 4 is mentioned for completeness, but is not considered further.)

| 20.3.2 | Involuntary manslaughter |

Here, there is no malice aforethought, but there is some lesser *mens rea*.

There are two types of involuntary manslaughter:

• Constructive manslaughter

This occurs where the defendant kills by an unlawful and obviously dangerous act.

A criminal assault would certainly constitute an 'unlawful act', for example, pushing into a post-office queue, knocking an old man into the elderly victim, who fell and later died (*R v Mitchell* (1983)), or criminal damage, eg children throwing a paving stone from a bridge onto the cab of a railway engine (*DPP v Newbury & Jones* (1976)).

The act of the defendant must also be 'one which inevitably would subject the other person to the risk of some harm from the act itself. Thus, in *R v Dalby* (1982) (from which case the preceding quotation was taken), the mere act of handing a syringe with illegal drugs in it to the victim was held not to fall within this rule, whereas the injecting of an illegal drug into the victim by the defendant was held to be so (*R v Cato* (1976)).

The unlawful act must also be obviously dangerous, or 'such as all sober and reasonable people would inevitably recognise must subject the other person to, at least, the risk of some harm resulting therefrom, albeit not serious harm' (*R v Church* (1965)). An assault would therefore be sufficient, for example, that in *R v Mitchell* (1983) and the criminal damage in *DPP v Newbury & Jones* (1976), above. Again, the test is objective ('all sober and reasonable people').

The *mens rea* of constructive manslaughter is the intention to do the act that kills (though not the intention to kill) and the fault of the crime which constitutes the unlawful act.

- Gross or criminal negligence manslaughter

  Before *R v Caldwell* (1981) it was generally accepted that there existed manslaughter by gross (or criminal) negligence. For example, there were convictions in both *R v Finney* (1874), where a nurse intended to get a mental patient out of the latter's bath by turning the cold tap on, but in switching the hot tap on, scalded him to death, and in *R v Stone & Dobinson* (1977) where the defendant allowed his infirm sister to take to her bed and die. In the latter case, Geoffrey Lane LJ said that 'the defendant must be proved to have been indifferent to an obvious risk of injury to health, or actually to have foreseen the risk but to have determined nevertheless to run it'.

  But the question arose, namely: were there two types of involuntary manslaughter (in addition to constructive manslaughter), or one? Was there reckless manslaughter and was gross (or criminal) negligence manslaughter separate? Or since *R v Caldwell* had reckless manslaughter swallowed up gross negligence manslaughter?

  Nor was this an purely academic question: for instance if, on facts similar to *R v Lamb* (1967), a youth shot and killed his friend with a revolver, which he thought was not dangerous as he had checked and seen that the bullet was in the revolving chamber, but not opposite the barrel. Under the recklessness test, the defendant would be acquitted under the loophole; but if the defendant had been 'criminally negligent', he would have been convicted under the gross (or criminal) negligence test.

  Interestingly, the Criminal Law Revision Committee has recommended that the whole of involuntary manslaughter be abolished and replaced by a new offence of causing death recklessly; but the Parliamentary draughtsman of the

Road Traffic Act 1991 was taking no chances: 'reckless driving' was abolished. But the question still remained unanswered: was there, since *R v Caldwell*, still manslaughter by gross or criminal negligence?

The answer came in *R v Adomako* (1994), where the House of Lords confirmed that this type of manslaughter still existed; it required proof of:

- a duty;

- breach of that duty and causation of death; and

- gross negligence which the jury considered justified a criminal conviction.

Lord Taylor CJ in the Court of Appeal without purporting to give an exhaustive definition, had said that its *mens rea* might be any of:

- indifference to an obvious risk of injury to health;

- actual foresight of the risk coupled with the determination nevertheless to run it;

- an appreciation of the risk coupled with an intention to avoid it but also coupled with such a high degree of negligence in the attempted avoidance as the jury considered justified the conviction; or

- inattention or failure to advert to a serious risk which went beyond mere inadvertence in respect of an obvious and important matter which the defendant's duty demanded he should address.

20.4 Offences ancillary to murder

Before leaving murder and manslaughter, it is perhaps useful to note two offences which relate solely to murder.

Under the first, called solicitation to murder, it is, by s 4 Offences Against the Person Act 1861, an offence to 'solicit, encourage, persuade or endeavour to persuade or ... propose to any person, to murder any other person'. All of the words used in s 4 imply that the defendant must reach the mind of the person solicited etc.

Secondly, it is an offence under s 16 of the same Act to threaten to X to kill X, or a third person, intending that X would 'fear' its being carried out. But the threat must be made 'without lawful excuse'; thus it might be reasonable to threaten to kill in self-defence, even where it would not be so to kill in the same circumstances. So, in *R v Cousins* (1982), where the defendant thought that a violent man was after him to assault him, such that the defendant took a gun and went to the man's parents' home, and made threats to them to kill the man, the threat was held justifiable.

An important crime causing death is s 1 Road Traffic Act 1991. As we have noted above, there are certain problems caused by the definition of 'recklessness' in *R v Caldwell* (1981). Parliament has recently removed that problem from the road traffic legislation. Section 1 of the 1991 Act, replacing the previous s 1 Road Traffic Act 1988, now contains a crime of causing death by dangerous driving (as defined in s 2A), with s 2 constituting simple dangerous driving (as defined in s 2A).

20.5   Road Traffic Acts 1988–91

The key to both sections is therefore s 2A, which states that driving is 'dangerous' where:

> '(a) the way he drives falls far below what would be expected of a competent and careful driver, and (b) it would be obvious to a competent and careful driver that driving in that way would be dangerous.'

Further, s 2A(3) states that to determine what is 'dangerous':

> '... regard shall be had not only to the circumstances of which he could be expected to be aware but also to any circumstances shown to have been within the knowledge of the accused.'

Chapter 21

General Assaults

This part, unlike the last, looks at those offences against the person which do not cause death. There are many criminal assaults ranging from the well-known 'grievous bodily harm' offences to the more esoteric assaults on seamen or a clergyman in the midst of holding a service or burial. An example of these last offences is s 89(1) Police Act 1996, of assaulting a policeman in the execution of his duty. Clearly, the *actus reus* or *mens rea* of these last will apply to very few assaults actually committed, and it is for general offences of assault and personal injury that most assaulters are convicted.

The Criminal Justice Act 1988 caused changes in this area. The following general offences now exist. (Henceforth, OAPA means Offences Against the Person Act 1861):

- common assault (or assault);

- battery;

- 'assault occasioning actual bodily harm' (s 47 OAPA 1861);

- wounding or inflicting grievous bodily harm (s 20 OAPA 1861);

- wounding or causing grievous bodily harm with intent (s 18 OAPA 1861).

Note that a jury acquitting a defendant indicted for s 18 can convict him of s 20 or s 47, and if acquitting him when indicted for s 20 can convict him of s 47.

There are certain problems in identification. Firstly, it is unfortunate that, while the civil lawyer treats the two torts separately, under their separate names, the criminal lawyer tends to run the assault and the battery together, in the phrase 'criminal assault'. It is clearer to keep them separate by the use of their correct names. Not surprisingly, in *R v Lynsey* (1995) the Court of Appeal confirmed that assault (also known as common assault) and battery are separate offences. A charge of 'assault and battery' in this case was duplicitous, ie it disclosed two offences, and could not therefore proceed. The Court of Appeal also confirmed that 'assault' in s 47 OAPA 1861 includes 'battery'. Secondly, the question arises from the Divisional Court's judgment as to whether s 39 converted common assault and battery from common law crimes to statutory ones. Smith and Hogan suggest that s 39, which does convert them from indictable offences to summary ones, is accordingly procedural only and does not alter the substance or source of either offence.

Further, note that only s 18 is a specific intent crime; the other four can also be committed recklessly and accordingly are crimes of basic intent.

21.1	**Common assault (or assault)**	An assault is an intentional or (by analogy with battery in *R v Venna* (1975), below) reckless act which causes a victim to apprehend immediate unlawful touching of the victim's person, however slight.

The *actus reus* of common assault is much the same as in tort, and is considered more fully in Part II of this book. It is sufficient here to say that it is causing the victim to apprehend the immediate unlawful touching. This could be by gesture or words, or in *R v Ireland* (1997) the making of a telephone call. In this case the defendant said nothing after the women victims picked up the telephone, but the Court of Appeal said that 'The act [sc of assault] consists in the making of the telephone call, and it does not matter whether words or silence ensue'. The defendant had made a series of calls of this nature to three women, but the court made it clear that even a single call could amount to an assault, and that 'repetitious telephone calls of this nature are likely to cause the victims to apprehend immediate and unlawful violence'.

The *mens rea* of common assault was confirmed by the House of Lords in *R v Savage, R v Parmenter* (1991) as 'an intention to cause the victim to apprehend immediate and unlawful violence or recklessness whether such apprehension be caused'.

As this is an offence against the person the form of recklessness here is the actual foresight of some harm (*R v Cunningham* (1957)).

21.2	**Battery**	According to the Court of Appeal in *R v Venna* (1975) a battery is committed when 'the defendant intentionally or recklessly applied force to the person of another'.

The force must be unlawful.

The *actus reus* consists of a voluntary touching of the victim without consent or other lawful excuse. It is more fully considered in Part II on Tort.

There has been much judicial discussion as to whether a battery must be hostile. In *Faulkner v Talbot* (1981), where a woman invited a 14 year old boy to bed with her, and forced him to commit sexual intercourse with her, thus committing 'indecent assault on a man', Lord Lane CJ said: 'It need not necessarily be hostile or rude or aggressive, as some of the cases seem to indicate.' Lord Lane CJ repeated this view in the Court of Appeal in *R v Brown* (1992), a case involving sadomasochistic practices between men, but in the House of Lords Lord Jauncey refers to hostility as 'a necessary ingredient of assault' (meaning here, battery). Thus, as in tort, the issue is undecided, although the opinions of a Lord of Appeal (Lord Goff in *F v West Berkshire Health Authority* (1989)) in tort, and of the Lord Chief Justice, are very influential.

As in tort, not all physical contact with other people is criminal; Lord Goff in *F v West Berks HA* (1989) excluded 'all physical contact which is generally acceptable in the ordinary conduct of everyday life', such as the tap on the shoulder by a policeman to attract that person's attention (*Donnelly v Jackman* (1970)).

The *mens rea* of battery was discussed in *R v Venna* (1975), where the defendant, while being arrested, thrashed out with his legs and broke a policeman's arm. The statement set out in 21.1 above shows that intention or *Cunningham* actual foresight of some harm is required.

The victim's lawful consent will obviate an assault or a battery.

21.3 Defences to assault and battery
21.3.1 Consent

The problem over consent to assault or battery is the same as in tort: whose burden of proof is it? Is it part of the prosecution's burden of proof that the victim did not consent? Or is it for the defence to argue that there was consent?

In the sado-masochism case of *R v Brown* Lord Lane CJ, in the Court of Appeal in 1992, said:

> 'Generally speaking, the prosecution in order to bring home a charge of assault must prove that the victim did not consent to the defendant's action, an assault being any unlawful touching of another without that other's consent.'

But Lord Jauncey, in the House of Lords in 1993, said: '... I would hold that consent was a defence to but not a necessary ingredient in assault ...', though he points out that his opinion on this issue was not necessary to decide the appeal under consideration. There is clearly a doubt over this issue; we have followed the Lord of Appeal here (but followed by Lord Lane in Part II on Tort). However, this is unsatisfactory; the burden should be the same in both areas of law.

- Consent must be real

    As in tort, the consent can be vitiated by duress, fraud etc, but ignorance, non-disclosure, or misrepresentation as to the effect or consequences of the touching is immaterial if the victim understood the nature of the act. Thus, in *R v Clarence* (1888) a wife who contracted venereal disease after having sexual intercourse with her husband, claiming that she had not consented to getting the disease, lost her claim as she had consented to the sexual intercourse.

• Physical contests

Controversially, the courts have held, as a matter of policy, that consent is not available to certain activities where consent would be argued by the participants as existing. Thus, consent is no defence where two men fight each other (*AG's Reference (No 6 of 1980)* (1980); this was 'not in the public interest'), or in taking part in prize fights (*R v Coney* (1882)).

Recently, this principle has been applied to deny this defence to some homosexual men engaging in sadomasochistic behaviour, involving the application of hot candlewax, nettles, scrubbing-brushes and so on to their genitals (*R v Brown* (1993)). But in *AG's Reference (No 6 of 1980)* (1980), there was 'accepted legality of properly conducted games and sports'. This is a troublesome area; why are sports such as rugby acceptable, but prize-fighting not so? And is what a group of men does to each other not their own affair, if they all agree to it?

After all, a husband's branding with a hot knife of his initials on his wife's buttocks, at her instigation and by her consent and done at home, was quite acceptable in *R v Wilson* (1996). The Court of Appeal, distinguishing the behaviour in *R v Brown*, commented that the branding was no more harmful than a tattoo (which the wife had wanted, but which the defendant had not known how to do) and was 'perhaps in this day and age no less understandable than the piercing of nostrils and even tongues for the purposes of inserting decorative jewellery'. The court said that the law 'should develop upon a case-by-case basis rather than upon general propositions'.

21.4 'Assault occasioning actual bodily harm' – s 47 Offences Against the Person Act 1861

It was noted above that 'assault' in s 47 includes 'battery' (*R v Lynsey* (1995)). The *actus reus* is an 'assault', which causes actual bodily harm. Occasioning raised solely a question of causation, 'an objective question', so said Lord Ackner for the House of Lords in *R v Savage; R v Parmenter* (1991). Guidelines issued to the Crown Prosecution Service in 1994 describe actual bodily harm as 'loss or breaking of a tooth or teeth, temporary loss of sensory functions, extensive or multiple bruising, displaced or broken nose, minor fractures, minor –

but not merely superficial – cuts, psychiatric injury which is more than fear, distress or panic'.

An example is *DPP v K* (1990), where a schoolboy took some acid from the science laboratory, to a toilet. Hearing footsteps, he hid the acid in the warm-air hand-dryer. Another boy came in and tilted the dryer upwards towards his face (as is permissible), with the result that the acid flew out into his face, injuring him. Further, in *R v Savage* (1991), the defendant threw her beer over another woman she did not like and was found to have let go of the glass as the glass broke, cutting the other woman's wrist. In both *DPP v K* (1990) and *R v Savage* (1991), the defendants were convicted under s 47.

The *mens rea* of s 47 is simply the *mens rea* of assault. So said the House of Lords in *R v Savage, R v Parmenter* (1991), approving *R v Venna* (1975), above. But the occasioning of the actual bodily harm was simply a matter of causation of *actus reus*, 'an objective question which does not involve inquiring into the accused's state of mind'.

The serious crime s 18 and s 20, involve either wounding or causing or inflicting grievous bodily harm.

21.5 Wounding

The *actus reus* of s 18 and s 20 are similar, only differing in one particular.

21.5.1 *Actus reus*

Each section is divided into two offences:

- wounding; and

- causing (s 18) or inflicting (s 20) grievous bodily harm.

In fact, the variants of the specific intent of s 18 create even more separate offences.

- Wounding

  This requires a break in both layers of skin. Thus, a broken collar-bone alone was insufficient in *R v Wood* (1830), and a rupture of blood vessels in the eye caused by an air pistol shot was insufficient in *JCC (a minor) v Eisenhower* (1983).

  In *R v Sheard* (1837) it was accepted that the wound could be caused by striking apparel which then caused a wound, in this case a hat which when struck caused its peak to cut the skin.

- Causing or inflicting grievous bodily harm

  'Bodily' harm needs no explanation. 'Grievous' means no more and no less than 'really serious' (*DPP v Smith* (1960)). The jury should consider the totality of the injuries: no one injury need be grievous (*R v Grundy* (1989)), and grievous bodily harm will include harm not within 'wounding'.

Causing (s 18) or inflicting (s 20) before 1983 it was unclear whether 'inflicting' required an assault.

Then in *R v Wilson* (1983) on a procedural matter, it was held that 'inflicting' did not need an assault; it was narrower than 'causing'; and unlike 'causing', it required a direct application of force.

Thus, there have been convictions under s 20 in *R v Halliday* (1889), where the defendant frightened his wife, who jumped through a window, injuring herself, and in *R v Martin* (1881), where the defendant blocked the exit from a theatre, put the lights out, and shouted 'fire'. Not surprisingly people were injured and in *R v Burstow* (1996) the infliction of psychiatric damage by nuisance telephone calls, visits and solvent poured over the victim's car, all by the defendant, who would not accept that the victim had ended their relationship: again a conviction ensued. But there is no liability for transmitting a disease to another person (*R v Clarence* (1888)).

21.5.2   *Mens rea*

'In order to establish an offence under s 20 the prosecution must prove either that the defendant intended or that he actually foresaw that his act would cause harm.'

(*R v Savage; R v Parmenter* (1991)).

Under *R v Cunningham* foresight usually means that the prosecution must prove that the defendant knew the circumstances and intended or foresaw the results prescribed by the *actus reus*. But in *R v Mowatt* (1967), it was said that on a charge of s 20 (a basic intent crime), the prosecution need only prove intention or actual foresight that some harm might be inflicted.

Similarly, where the jury is directed on a charge of s 18 (the higher offence) that if it cannot convict of s 18, it may convict of s 20, again, the prosecution need only prove intention or actual foresight of some harm in order to convict of s 20.

(Why on a charge of s 18, cannot the prosecution simply prove that defendant intended or foresaw lesser harm? Because s 18 demands proof that defendant caused grievous bodily harm 'with intent ... to do some ... grievous bodily harm', so only this specific intent will suffice for a s 18 conviction.)

The case of *R v Mowatt* was approved in *R v Savage, R v Parmenter* (1991). Thus in *W (a minor) v Dolbey* (1983) where the defendant shot his victim in the forehead thinking there was no slug-pellet in his gun, because he had thought about whether there was a risk but had decided (albeit wrongly) that there was none, he had no actual foresight of any harm, and was acquitted on appeal.

'Intent' must be proved (on the lines of *R v Moloney* (1985) and *R v Nedrick* (1986)). Recklessness will not suffice, nor that the defendant is 'capable' of forming the intent. And the word 'maliciously' in s 18 must be otiose; actual foresight is not enough.

The specific intent (that is whether he intended to cause grievous bodily harm, or to resist arrest etc) mentioned in the indictment must be proved. So, if the defendant is indicted with the 'intent to do some grievous bodily harm', but in fact has the 'intent to resist or prevent apprehension', he must be acquitted, but he may be convicted if he means to cause grievous bodily harm in order to escape arrest.

A defendant's mistake as to the lawfulness of the arrest (s 18) was held in *R v Bentley* (1850) to amount to ignorance of the criminal law, and was therefore no defence. But honest belief in facts which, as believed, would make the arrest unlawful will, on the principle of *DPP v Morgan* (1975), negate the defendant's intent to resist arrest (so held by the Privy Council in *Beckford v R* (1987)).

There are other assaults capable of being committed solely while resisting arrest, for example, s 38 OAPA 1861, 'assault with intent to prevent arrest of himself or another', and s 89(1) Police Act 1996, 'assault of a policeman in the execution of his duty'. The common law offence of breach of the peace still exists, defined (for present purposes) in *R v Howell* (1981) as 'whenever [unlawful] harm is actually done or is likely to be done to a person ... or a person is in fear of being so harmed through an assault, an affray, a riot ... or other disturbance.'	**21.6** **Closely-related offences to the person**
Sections 23 and 24 are not assaults, but are nevertheless ways of causing personal harm. The *actus reus* of each offence requires the defendant to 'unlawfully and maliciously administer to or cause to be administered to or taken by any other person any poison or other destructive or noxious thing'.	**21.7** **Administering 'poison or other destructive or noxious thing'**

'Taken' requires the poison etc to be taken into the stomach, but 'noxious' need not necessarily imply injury to bodily health. In *R v Marcus* (1981), where a sedative and sleeping tablets were put in milk, it was held that a substance harmless in small quantities is 'noxious' if administered in sufficient quantity to injure, aggrieve or annoy, and it would include a snail in a ginger-beer bottle! However, s 23 contains the further provision: 'so as thereby to endanger the life of such person, or so as thereby to inflict upon such person any grievous bodily harm ...'.

The *mens rea* of s 23 requires the actus reus to have been committed 'maliciously', that is to say intentionally or recklessly. In *R v Cunningham* (1957), the defendant broke a gas meter off the wall to steal money, thereby causing gas to seep into next door where it was breathed in by the victim, who was asleep, causing her life to be endangered. It was held that 'maliciously' does not mean 'wickedly', but with actual foresight of harm.

The *mens rea* of s 24, however, is 'with intent to injure aggrieve or annoy such person'; s 24 is therefore a crime of specific intent.

21.8 Offensive weapons

Many assaults are committed with weapons. In an attempt to nip an assault in the bud the Prevention of Crime Act 1953, at s 1(1), says, 'Any person who ... has with him in any public place any offensive weapon' commits an offence.

'Offensive weapon' means 'any article made or adapted for use for causing injury to the person, or intended by the person having it with him for such use by him or by some other person'. A knuckle-duster, or flick-knife would clearly fall in the first category, and a bottle intentionally broken for this purpose would be 'adapted for use for causing injury to the person', but any article could fall within the third category as 'intended by the person having it with him for such use by him'.

Thus, if the article can be proved to have been 'made' or 'adapted' etc, the prosecution need only prove possession in a public place, but in the third category the prosecution must prove the specific intent that it was carried with intent to injure.

But the *actus reus* is having it with him in a public place; that is, not use, but before use. Thus, in *Ohlson v Hylton* (1975) a carpenter who took a hammer from his tool bag in a fight and hit his victim was acquitted, as the hammer was neither 'made' or 'adapted' for personal injury, nor did he have it with him while intending to cause personal injury. The *mens rea* is actual knowledge of possession (*R v Cugullere* (1961)), but forgetfulness is immaterial.

Section 1(1) provides for defences of 'lawful authority or reasonable excuse', putting the burden of proof on the defendant. But these are narrow. 'Lawful authority' means carrying by soldiers or the police, while 'reasonable excuse' requires 'an imminent particular threat affecting the particular circumstances in which the weapon was carried' (*Evans v*

Hughes (1972)). Regularly carrying it for self-defence is, therefore, not 'reasonable excuse'. A woman who wears a hat pin which she intends to use on an assailant commits an offence.

A further offence is that contained in s 139 Criminal Justice Act 1988, whereby any person 'has with him in a public place any article which has a blade or is sharply pointed except a folding pocket knife' (but including a folding pocket knife with a cutting edge exceeding three inches). There are defences 'that he had good reason or lawful authority for having the article with him in a public place, or that he had it with him 'a) for use at work; b) for religious reasons; or c) as part of any national costume'.

Clearly this overlaps with the Prevention of Crime Act; would it not have been better to have created a single new offence, instead of perpetuating this piece-meal legislation? Indeed, the Offensive Weapons Act 1996, enacted after the Dunblane massacre, has created an offence, s 139A, consisting of an offence under the 1953 or 1988 Act committed 'on school premises'.

There are many sexual offences, formerly mainly in the Offences Against the Person Act 1861, now mainly in the Sexual Offences Act 1956.

21.9   Sexual offences

Section 1(1) Sexual Offences Act 1956 says simply 'It is an offence for a man to rape a woman or another man'. 'Rape' was not statutorily defined until the Sexual Offences (Amendment) Act 1976 was enacted, following *DPP v Morgan* (1975), below.

21.9.1   Rape

The Criminal Justice and Public Order Act 1994 expanded rape to cover male victims. Since 1994 the new s 1 Sexual Offences Act 1956 defines rape as:

'a) ... sexual intercourse with a person (whether vaginal or anal) who at the time of the intercourse does not consent to it; and [where] b) at the time he knows that the person does not consent to the intercourse or is reckless as to whether that person consents to it.'

- *Actus reus*

  The age-old rule that a man could not rape his wife was abolished by the House of Lords in *R v R (rape: marital exemption)* (1991) saying that 'in modern times the supposed marital exception in rape forms no part of the law of England'. In short, a man can now be charged with raping his wife.

- Absence of consent

  The burden is on the prosecution to prove, not that the intercourse was against the victim's will (ie forcible), but that the victim did not consent. Thus, it is rape to have intercourse with a sleeping woman (*R v Mayer* (1872)). And consent obtained by fraud is void. But, as elsewhere, it is only rape if he deceives the victim as to the nature of the act. The latter's mistake as to the effect of the sexual intercourse is immaterial. In the aptly named *R v Flattery* (1877), where the defendant told her that he was undergoing a surgical operation on her, and in *R v Williams* (1922), where he told her it would improve her singing.

  It is important to note that these two women 'were persuaded to consent to what he did because she thought it was not sexual intercourse' (Lord Hewart CJ in *R v Williams*). Had she in each case been mistaken only as to the effect of the sexual intercourse there would have been no rape.

- *Mens rea*

  This is an intention to have normal sexual intercourse with a person: either if he 'knows that the person does not consent', or is 'reckless as to whether that person consents'. The type of recklessness is actual foresight of *R v Cunningham*.

  In *R v Satnam* (1983) the distinction was drawn between recklessness in assaults or criminal damage as to the consequences of the criminal act, and recklessness in rape as to the state of mind of the woman. The Court of Appeal approved a model direction based on the 1976 Act, and which incorporated *DPP v Morgan* (1975) and ended:

  > 'If they [the jury] carne to the conclusion that he could not care less whether she [or now, he] wanted to or not, but pressed on regardless, then he would have been reckless ... guilty.'

  Clearly, to have come to a conclusion implies having considered the matter of her consent, which is the actual foresight of *R v Cunningham*.

  The reader will be reminded of the case of *DPP v Morgan*, where three airmen were honestly mistaken in believing that the woman, who protested against the sexual intercourse, was in fact consenting. As her lack of consent was a circumstance part of the *actus reus* their honest ignorance that she was not consenting negated *mens rea* as to that part of the *actus reus*.

Chapter 22

Criminal Damage

The Criminal Damage Act 1971 provides a complete general code. There are some specialised offences which still exist under the previous statutes, such as placing objects on a railway line with intent to overturn the train; but these are simply doing acts with intent to cause damage: no actual damage need be proved.

The offences are:

- s 1(1) – intentionally or recklessly destroying or damaging property of another;

- s 1(2) – intentionally or recklessly destroying or damaging property with intent (or reckless) to endanger life;

- s 1(3) – the aforesaid offences by fire, charged as arson; s 2 – threats to commit s 1(1) or (2);

- s 3 – custody or control with intent to destroy or damage.

The forms of *mens rea* required here are generally intention and recklessness, but whereas actual foresight recklessness was the form recognised in the assaults area, here both actual and reasonable foresight are prominent.

Section 1(1) is the offence in its simple, unaggravated form.

22.1   Section 1(1)

- 'Destroy or damage'

  According to Smith and Hogan, in *Criminal Law*, this would be 'some physical harm, impairment or deterioration which can be usually perceived by the senses'. The cases interpreting the same phrase in the repealed Malicious Damage Act 1861 are persuasive, for example, it included trampling grass down (*Gayford v Choulder* (1898)).

More recently, in *Lloyd v DPP* (1992), it included breaking a wheel-clamp to remove it from the defendant's car wheel, although the original disabling of the car by clamping on it was said, *obiter*, not to be damage where there was no evidence of real damage. But in *R v Henderson & Battley* (1984), the judge, Cantley J, said that it included also 'an obstruction temporarily rendering a machine useless for the purpose for which it was intended to be used can be damage'. In that case, rubbish was dumped on land which made the land unusable.

22.1.1   *Actus reus*

But in *Morphitis v Salmon* (1990) something similar to Cantley J's example actually occurred. A barrier consisted of a scaffold bar, a clip and an upright. The defendant removed the bar and clip. He was convicted of damage to both of these parts, but his appeal was allowed. It was held that damage is a question of fact and degree. Thus, if the whole structure (ie the barrier) were damaged or impaired by the removal, that would be damage and a charge of criminal damage to the whole barrier would have succeeded; but there was no damage to the individual parts removed.

It would appear from this case that a physical item can be 'property' (see below) either individually or as part of a complex structure. Damage by dismantling would agree with the opinion in *Samuels v Stubbs* (1972), an Australian decision, that a 'temporary functional derangement' can be damage, in that case a policeman's cap which had been jumped on and thereby knocked out of shape.

- Removable items

  If a defendant affixes something to the property, for example, a sticker, does that amount to damage? In tort, it would certainly be trespass to goods. Here, it seems that if cost must be incurred in removing the item then damage has occurred, for example, the removal of the rubbish in *R v Henderson & Battley* (1984), and the removal by high water jets of pavement drawings in *Hardman v Chief Constable of Avon & Somerset Constabulary* (1986); both cases resulted in convictions. On the other hand, if the item can be removed simply, damage would not have occurred. So, in *A (a juvenile) v R* (1978) a defendant who spat on a policeman's coat, but which left no stain on it, was acquitted.

- Property

  Property is defined by this Act as 'of a tangible nature, whether real or personal, including money'. Wild animals and birds which have not been tamed or 'reduced into possession' are not included. Note that land can be damaged (though it cannot be stolen). I would therefore 'damage' my neighbour's lawn if I let loose a mole on it while he was away on holiday.

  But intangible property cannot be damaged (though it can be stolen). In *Cox v Riley* (1986), the defendant erased the suggested programs on a card which operated a computerised saw, thereby rendering the saw inoperable by computer. He was guilty on appeal to the Divisional Court of damaging the plastic card (but not of erasing the programme). *R v Henderson & Battley* (1984), above, was approved; here the saw was rendered inoperable, which constituted damage. Further, the Court of Appeal in *R v Whitely* (1991), upheld the conviction of a defendant who deleted files on a disk; this was damage to tangible property. In this area, however, a prosecutor should also consider the offence of 'unauthorised modification of the contents of any computer' offence under s 3 Computer Misuse Act 1990 and s 13 Theft Act 1968 (dishonestly abstracting electricity).

While these offences would cover computer damage, other forms of intangible damage are not covered. For instance, a person who removes a film from a camera into broad daylight will spoil the photographs, but leaving the film strip intact; this will normally make the film unusable, thus bringing the act within the principle of *R v Henderson & Battley* (1984), above.

- Belonging to another

   The other must have a proprietary right over the property, that is (a) custody or control, or (b) some proprietary right or interest (though some equitable interests are excluded), or (c) a charge on the property.

   Section 1(1) (as opposed to s 1(2)) does not cover damaging or destroying the defendant's own property, but other statutes cover such damage, for example, demolition, cruelty to animals, destruction of wild plants, bat roosts, birds' nests, badgers' setts etc.

Section 1(1) prescribes that the defendant must commit the *actus reus* both (a) 'intending to destroy or damage ... or being reckless' and (b) 'without lawful excuse'.

22.1.2   Mens rea

- 'Intending to destroy or damage ... or being reckless'

   We have seen that there are two forms of intention: 'purpose' intention and 'awareness of the virtual certainty' intention (see *R v Moloney* (1985) and *R v Nedrick* (1986), above). An intention to do the act, which in the event destroys or damages, is not enough: he must intend to damage etc. Further, in determining whether he intended or foresaw the result of damage or destruction s 8 Criminal Justice Act 1967 no longer requires the court to infer that the defendant intended or foresaw the natural and probable result of his act; it must determine this after a consideration of all the evidence.

   Similarly, he must intend the circumstance of the property being 'of another'. But an honest but mistaken belief as to this circumstance would, on the principle of *DPP v Morgan* (1975), negate *mens rea* as to the circumstance. Thus, in *R v Smith* (1974) the defendant, a tenant, put in some wiring for his stereo. When he quit the flat he ripped it all out. Unfortunately, he did not realise that the wiring had become the landlord's property; he honestly thought it was his. The Court of Appeal, in a judgment presaging *DPP v Morgan*, said: 'Honest belief, whether justifiable or not, that the property is the defendant's own negatives the element of *mens rea*.' His appeal was therefore allowed.

A charge of 'with intent' alone, is one of a crime of specific intent.

The Law Commission had intended that 'reckless' would mean actual foresight only. But in the notorious case of *R v Caldwell* (1981), the defendant, developed a grievance against a hotel owner for whom he had been working. The defendant got drunk, and in the early hours set fire to the occupied hotel. As Lord Diplock put it: 'At his trial he said that he was so drunk at the time that the thought that there might be people in the hotel whose lives might be endangered if it were set on fire had never crossed his mind.' But his conviction was upheld on the basis of Lord Diplock's well-known dictum, with which Lords Keith and Roskill agreed, that there is liability if:

> '(1) ... he does an act which in fact creates an obvious risk that property will be destroyed or damaged and (2) when he does the act either has not given any thought to the possibility of ... risk or has recognised that there was some risk involved and has none the less gone on to do it.'

It should be remembered, however, that in Chapter 19, 19.2.6 above, we saw that the House of Lords had refined Lord Diplock's *dictum* to mean 'actual foresight of some risk', here of property damage or destruction, whether obvious or not, and reasonable foresight of an obvious risk.

Reference should be made to two cases dealt with earlier in this section, namely *Chief Constable of Avon & Somerset v Shimmen* (1986) on actual foresight: the karate expert who when showing off, had recognised the risk of breaking the window, though he thought he had eliminated it, and on reasonable foresight, *Elliott v C* (1983), where the 14 year old, mentally sub-normal girl, set fire to the shed. The defendants in both cases were convicted after appeal.

But it should be remembered that Lord Diplock's test presupposes the chance of the defendant's thoughts falling into the loophole or lacuna: the defendant considers it but decides there is no risk, or only a negligible one.

Finally, the doctrine of *transferred malice* will apply from one type of property to another. A charge of recklessness, or intent or recklessness, is one of basic intent.

* Without lawful excuse

Section 5(2) provides two statutory defences of honest belief. The first defence is his honest belief that he had the actual consent of the owner, or assumed consent in the circumstances, to the defendant's act.

Thus, in *R v Denton* (1982) a defendant who thought his employer had encouraged him to burn the employer's mill down, to enable the employer to make a fraudulent claim, was acquitted. The second defence concerns the defendant's honest belief in the immediate need to protect property (or a right or interest), and that the means are reasonable in the circumstances, for example, shooting a dog which is worrying the defendant's livestock.

Section 5 also recognises the common law defences of self *defence, necessity* and *claim of right*. And honest mistaken belief that although he is not owner, he nevertheless has a right to damage or destroy the property will either negate the mens rea altogether (*R v Smith* (1974)), or provide a defence (*Beckford v R* (1987)). However, an attempted defence to a charge of damaging a wheel clamp based on the self-help remedy of recaption of chattels failed in *Lloyd v DPP* (1992).

The discussion above on s 1(1) applies to destroying or damaging property with intent to endanger life, or recklessly as to endanger life, to a large extent. But there are important differences. Whereas s 1(1) is simply the intentional or reckless damaging or destruction of property belonging to another, s 1(2) firstly adds a specific *mens rea*, that of intention or recklessness as to whether life would 'be thereby endangered' (this intention or recklessness is additional to the intention or recklessness required concerning the damage or destruction of property); and secondly, s 1(2) applies to all property, even that of the defendant's. Clearly, it should not be allowable to set fire to the defendant's own property while he has guests staying.

22.2 Destroying or damaging property with intent to endanger life, or recklessly as to endangering life (s 1(2))

But, while, as a matter of *mens rea*, there must be intention or recklessness as to causation of destruction or damage leading to the endangering of life, he need not be proved, as a matter of *actus reus*, to have actually endangered any life. Further, on the anticipated causation of the endangering, in *R v Steer* (1987), the defendant took a gun in the early hours of the morning to the house of a man he had a grudge against.

When the man and wife looked out of their bedroom window the defendant fired a shot which was aimed at the window (but not at them). He was charged with s 1(2). The House of Lords had to decide whether the *mens rea* as to endangering life should consist of intention or foresight of the endangering arising from the defendant's act, or from the damage or destruction of the property. Lord Bridge, with whom the other Lords of Appeal agreed, adopted the latter, that the defendant should intend or foresee that life should be endangered by the damage or destruction. In this case, while it was clear that his act of shooting might be intended to endanger life, or be reckless as to that result, this defendant would not have intended or been reckless, as Lord Bridge required, as to whether the breaking window would endanger life. Thus, the defendant was acquitted.

Staying on the subject of recklessness, the question arises as to which type of recklessness is meant by s 1(2). Section 1(2) could be viewed as either a personal injury offence (inviting the actual foresight test of *R v Cunningham*), or a criminal damage offence. As it is contained in this Act, it is properly a criminal damage offence, and *R v Caldwell* makes it clear that both forms of foresight described by Lord Diplock in that case, namely actual and reasonable foresight, should apply.

The 'lawful excuse' of s 5(2) does not apply to s 1(2). It is no justification in endangering a life to say that you have the owner's consent, nor that you were protecting property. Nor does the damaging under claim of right apply. It cannot be right to damage your own property if that entails endangering life.

22.3 Arson (s 1(3))

Arson comprises the offences within s 1(1) and s 1(2) where the damage or destruction is by fire. But arson is not a third offence, merely a compulsory way of charging the offences of s 1(1) and s 1(2) by fire. As in s 1(2), there must be intention or recklessness as to causation of endangering life by fire, but no actual causation need be proved. But as in s 1(1) and (2) some damage must be proved, though as for those offences it may be slight (*R v Parker* (1839), mere charring of wood).

22.4 Threats to commit acts within s 1

It is an offence without lawful excuse to make a threat 'intending that another would fear it would be carried out' to commit s 1(1) or (2). The lawful excuses of s 5(2) do not apply; though the common law excuses do.

Note that the offence is committed on the threat, notwithstanding the person addressed not being impressed at all by the threat.

This offence consists of having 'anything in his [the defendant's] custody or under his control intending without lawful excuse to use it or cause or permit another to use it' to commit s 1(1) or (2).

Thus, the principles already seen in the Prevention of Crime Act 1953 apply, namely, that the offence is one of possession with intent, not use, and that possession of innocent or common items would be caught, for example, a box of matches or two sticks. As in the 1953 Act, intention is all important.

22.5 Custody or control with intent to destroy or damage (s 3)

Chapter 23

Theft and Related Offences

One of the serious attempts at codification in modern times has been the Theft Act 1968, which covers most, but not all, of the property offences amounting to a denial of another's right to property (as opposed to the property damage offences dealt with by the Criminal Damage Act 1971).

1968

The 1968 Act has survived with only two major problems. One section, called in one case, 'a judicial nightmare', was repealed and replaced by the three offences of the Theft Act 1978. And a hole made by the House of Lords was plugged by the Theft (Amendment) Act 1996. (In this part, all section numbers refer to the Theft Act 1968 unless otherwise stated.)

1978

We shall consider:

23.1 The offences

- theft – s 1, with passing comparison with s 13 (abstracting electricity) and s 12 and s 12A (taking a conveyance without owners consent and aggravated vehicle taking);

- robbery – s 8;

- deception offences (the first four below except s 3 which does not require deception): obtaining property by deception – s 15; obtaining a money transfer by deception – s 15A; dishonestly retaining a wrongful credit – s 24A; obtaining a pecuniary advantage by deception – s 16; obtaining services by deception – s 1 Theft Act 1978; evasion of liability by deception – s 2 Theft Act 1978; making off without payment (by deception or not) – s 3 Theft Act 1978;

- burglary – s 9, with passing comparison with s 10 (aggravated burglary) and s 25 (going equipped for stealing etc); and

- handling stolen goods – s 22

Three offences, ss 8, 12A and 10, are simply aggravated forms of other offences (that is, instances of the simple offence but accompanied by violence).

23.2 Theft (s 1 Theft Act 1968)

23.2.1 Definition

Section 1(1) states:

'... a person is guilty of theft if he dishonestly appropriates property belonging to another with the intention of permanently depriving the other of it; and "thief" and "steal" shall be construed accordingly.'

Criticize

Sections 2–6 explain, though they do not always define, the terms used in s 1(1).

Any assumption or interference with the owners rights

'Appropriates' – s 3(1) explains this as an 'assumption ... of the rights of an owner', including 'where he has come by the property (innocently or not) without stealing it, any later assumption of a right to it by keeping or dealing with it as owner'.

23.2.2   Actus reus

1970 + 80's cases

A matter only settled recently is: must the interference be adverse, or can it be authorised by the victim?

It was decided in *Lawrence* v MPC (1971) that an appropriation could indeed be authorised by the victim. In this case the defendant, a taxi-drive, was paid £1 for a fare, but also took an extra £6 in notes from his Italian customer's wallet. At the trial the Italian said, via an interpreter, that he had 'permitted' it. The question was whether a conviction under s 1(1) required proof of the owner's lack of consent. It was held that it did not; consent to the taking will not rule out s 1(1).

Taxi driver - Italian ⟶

71
83
93

It was only because the House of Lords in *R v Morris; Anderton v Burnside* (1983), a 'label-switching' in supermarkets case, had decided that a consensual taking could not be 'appropriation', that the position was put in doubt. This doubt was removed by the House of Lords' decision in *R v Gomez* (1993), where the defendant employee knew that a certain client's cheques were stolen, but persuaded his shop manager to accept them in payment for some goods. The shop handed over the goods by consent under a voidable contract. The House held that this dealing with the goods amounted to an appropriation, despite its having been with the victim's consent. *Lawrence v MPC* was followed, and cases such as *R v McPherson* (1973) approved. In the latter case, where the defendant put goods in his own shopping-bag, appropriation took place on the taking from the shelf.

Label switching ⟶
Appeared to directly contradict Lawrence

Conflict btwn prev. 2 ⟶
cases brought out -
overturned Morris + declared
appropriation" occurred
when D2 became legal
owner. It had taken place
when D2 took the goods off of
the shelves with intent to steal

The decision in *Eddy v Niman* (1981) was not mentioned in *R v Gomez*. Here the defendant put the supermarket's goods m a basket with intent to steal, but lost his nerve and left the basket in the shop. He was acquitted, but since *R v Gomez* the position is not clear. Lord Roskill in *R v Morris* said that such behaviour as in *Eddy v Niman* was not an appropriation, as the shopkeeper consented to that behaviour; but this principle, in *R v Morris*, has gone, and this behaviour might now be 'appropriation'; at least Lord Keith, in *R v Gomez* thought so:

> 'There was much to be said in favour of the view that it did, in respect that doing so gave the shopper control of the article and the capacity to exclude any other shopper from taking it.'

This, after all, would amount to an assumption of one of the rights of an owner, namely the right of control, and Lord Keith in *R v Gomez* confirmed that 'assumption by the defendant of any of the rights of an owner could amount to an appropriation within s 3(1)'.

The approval in *R v Gomez* of the rule that there can be an appropriation even where the victim consents has confirmed too that an unlawful removal of funds from a company the director or majority shareholder of which is the defendant, amounts to an appropriation of those funds; the case of *R v Philippou* (1989), which had previously held to that effect, was approved by *R v Gomez*.

At least the appropriation discussed so far involves a positive act, but it can also take place by omission, as in *R v Monaghan* (1979), where the defendant put some money in the till, but failed to ring it up, intending to take it later. Presumably, her failure to ascribe the money to her employer by ringing it up on the till amounted to an appropriation of it to herself. At least in that case the defendant had had *mens rea* at the time of receipt, but it can happen that the defendant receives goods without *mens rea* but forms *mens rea* later; it would constitute an appropriation 'by keeping or dealing with it as owner'.

However, there can be an appropriation without having possession of the property or without acquiring it.

An example of the first is *R v Pitham & Hehl* (1976), where E was held to have appropriated the furniture of a friend (who was in prison) by showing the furniture to the defendants, and inviting them to buy it. An example of the second is *Corcoran v Anderton* (1980) where grabbing a handbag and pulling it away from the owner such that it fell onto the ground, was held to be appropriation even though the thief did not acquire possession of it. Indeed, since *R v Gomez*, does the appropriation take place on the grab or the pull?

Finally, by s 3(2), where an innocent and *bona fide* purchaser assumes the rights of an owner, which he assumed he had already bought, such an assumption will not 'by reason of any defect in the transferor's title' be theft.

Section 4 states that 'property' includes money and all other property, real or personal, including things in action and other intangible property', but that 'a person cannot steal land'. (It is clear that while land, buildings, crops, can be criminally damaged it is nonsense to say that it can be stolen (except by severing from the land.) The Dutch paid the Red Indians a pittance for Manhattan Island: how can you purport to acquire the Earth? English land law agrees; a landowner does not own the land, but a title in it.) Nor can confidential information, as opposed to the paper or disk it is recorded on, be counted as 'tangible'. Thus, in *Oxford v Moss* (1978), there could be no theft of the questions set out on a copied examination paper.

It is also interesting that while gas is within s 1, electricity, being intangible, is not. But s 13 makes it an offence to 'dishonestly use without due authority, or dishonestly cause to be wasted or diverted, any electricity'.

Section 5 states that 'belonging to another' involves 'possession or control of it, or having in it any proprietary right or interest'. It may be that the property is the defendant's, but in another's control, and capable of being stolen when reclaimed by the defendant, unless he can show an honest belief that he had the right to take it. In *R v Philippou* (1989), above, it was held possible to steal from a company of which the defendant is a director. The fact that the defendant owns the company is immaterial; the money is the company's property.

It is possible to steal from your own company – money is company's property.

23.2.3   *Mens rea*

Two elements to it.

Section 1 prescribes two forms of *mens rea*, both of which are required: firstly, 'dishonesty', and secondly the 'intention of permanently depriving the other (ie the person to whom the property belongs) of it'.

Dishonesty is not defined in the Act, though s 2 gives three instances where the defendant would not be dishonest. These are: a claim of right – that is a belief he could deprive the other of it, for himself or another; a belief that the other would consent if the other knew of the appropriation and the circumstances; and a belief that the owner 'cannot be discovered by taking reasonable steps'. On the other hand, it is immaterial that the defendant does not intend himself to gain (s 1(2)), and it can be dishonest even if defendant is willing to pay (s 2(2)). Thus, you cannot claim to be accepting what is an invitation to treat (if that).

3 exceptions to dishonesty

But these explanations are not exhaustive, and in cases outside these specific situations, a general test of dishonesty is needed.

But should it be subjective, whether the defendant thought he was being honest, or objective, whether the jury (as right-thinking members of society) think he was being honest?

CA laid out a two limbed test in Ghosh 1983

After contradictory cases, *R v Ghosh* (1982) appeared in the Court of Appeal (in fact on a charge of s 15, dishonestly obtaining property, as opposed to appropriating it). The defendant doctor maintained he was entitled to claim payments for jobs he had not done. Lord Lane CJ, for the court, said that the test was, firstly, whether it was it dishonest by the standards of 'reasonable and honest people' (ie the jurors), and secondly, if so, did the defendant realise that it was dishonest by those standards?

Lord Lane used two examples: one, a man from abroad in whose country public transport is free, and who in England gets off a bus without paying, and Robin Hood, who steals from the rich, and ardent anti-vivisectionists who steal animals from laboratories. The prosecution of the man from abroad would fail on the second point, but Robin Hood and the others would be convicted. Their subjective beliefs in the righteousness of their causes would not displace the facts that they each are aware that by ordinary standards they are dishonest.

An intention to permanently deprive the other of the property is also required (although no actual permanent deprivation need be proved as part of the *actus reus*). Even if the defendant does intend to repay, but in different notes and coins, he will be convicted (*R v Velumyl* (1989)). And 'treating the property as the defendant's own', though intending to return it is no defence, nor 'borrowing or lending for a period and in circumstances making it equivalent to an outright taking or disposal' will.

For example, taking an unused train ticket intending to use it and return it 'in such a changed state that it can truly be said that all its goodness or virtue is gone'. See also Lord Lane CJ in *R v Lloyd* (1985), where films were taken and copied, though the originals were returned. And in *R v Beecham* (1851) a railway ticket was indeed taken to use and return afterwards.

Finally, note that it is the latter *mens rea*, that of intending to permanently deprive the other of the property that prevents a prosecution under s 1 for 'joyriding', where this intention is often absent. The Act therefore contains s 12, an offence of 'taking' another's 'conveyance' without his consent. 'Conveyance' means motorised or not, and while 'taking' requires some movement, this might be slight. In *R v Bow* (1976) the defendant was convicted for coasting a vehicle without its engine on for some 200 yards to remove an obstruction.

Interestingly, Bridge LJ (*obiter*) said that pushing a car out of the way a 'yard or two' would not be a use as a conveyance. Section 12A was enacted in the light of increasing 'joy-riding' offences (s 12) in cars involving young lads and sometimes causing bystanders' deaths. Section 12A was introduced by the Aggravated Vehicle Taking Act 1992. It is an offence if after the defendant commits the offence of s 12 either personal injury or

[handwritten note in left margin: joyriding constitutes an offence if death or prop. damage take place. s. 12 + 12a]

death or property damage occurs, by fault or otherwise, or merely if the vehicle is 'driven dangerously on a road or other public place'.

23.3   Robbery (s 8 Theft Act 1968)

[handwritten note in left margin: Theft with violence.]

Robbery is committed when a person 'steals, and immediately before or at the time of doing so, and in order to do so, he uses force on any person or puts or seeks to put any person in fear of being then and there subjected to force'. It is therefore aggravated theft, or theft by violence. Because of the aggravating factor robbery carries a higher maximum sentence than does theft under s 1.

Theft is essential. In *Corcoran v Anderton* (1980) the defendant snatched a handbag from his victim's grasp, which fell to the floor. The defendant made off without it. He was convicted. And as s 3 defines appropriation as 'any assumption ... of the rights of an owner', it will constitute an appropriation even if the property is merely touched. Clearly, from this case, the force need not be applied to the victim's person.

The *mens rea* required for robbery comprises the *mens rea* of theft, as discussed above, and an intention to use or threaten force in order to steal.

23.4   Deception offences

The modern position is set out in the Theft Acts 1968 and 1978 offences discussed here. These offences involve the three elements of deception, (apart from s 3 Theft Act 1978: making off without payment, which might or might not involve deception, but does not require it), dishonesty, and obtaining something, or getting away with paying.

The offences are:

* Section 15 Theft Act 1968: 'dishonestly obtaining property belonging to another' by deception

    These words have the same meaning as in s 1, and 'obtaining' means the acquisition of 'ownership, possession or control of it', even for the benefit of a third party.) The *mens rea* is as in s 1 (therefore *R v Ghosh* will apply; it is in fact a s 15 case). And in *R v Gomez* (1993) it was said that there may be an overlap between s 1 and s 15, allowing a prosecution under both sections on the same facts as those occurring in *R v Gomez*. (But do not confuse this offence with blackmail under s 21 where property is obtained by 'menaces');

    But in *R v Preddy* (1996) the House of Lords held that a defendant who by deception obtains a bank transfer of money to his bank account did not obtain the 'property of another'; rather the payer's legal interest (a chose in action) was extinguished, and the defendant's interest (a separate chose in action) was created in his own bank. This loophole in s 15 was quickly filled by the Theft (Amendment) Act 1996, which created the next two offences.

- Section 15A Theft Act 1968: dishonestly obtaining a money transfer by deception

  This occurs when a debt and a corresponding credit are made in separate bank or similar accounts. Thus the bank transfer in *R v Preddy* would fall into this offence, as would the obtaining of a simple cheque by deception.

- Section 24A Theft Act 1968: dishonestly obtaining a wrongful credit

  A credit is wrongful if it is the credit referred to in s 15A, or 'derives from theft, blackmail or stolen goods'.

- Section 16 Theft Act 1968: 'dishonestly obtaining for himself or another a pecuniary advantage'

  The words have the same meaning as above, but 'pecuniary advantages' covered by s 16 are merely being allowed an overdraft, or taking out a policy of insurance or an annuity, or obtaining an improvement of those terms, or being given the opportunity to earn remuneration or greater remuneration in an office or employment, or to win money by betting;

- Section 1 Theft Act 1978: 'dishonestly obtaining services from another' by deception

  Again, the words have the same meaning as above, and 'services' means 'causing or permitting some act to be done'. The services must be done for reward and as with s 1 willingness to pay is no defence. Obtaining a loan falls within 'services'.

- Section 2 Theft Act 1978: dishonestly by deception evading liability to pay an existing or future debt

  Thus in *R v Jackson* (1983) where the defendant got petrol from his payee by producing a stolen credit card, he was convicted because his payee would now look to the bank for payment; the defendant had therefore secured remission from his own liability.

The words 'deception' and 'obtaining' are defined in s 15 (and applying to all these crimes) as 'any deception (whether deliberate or reckless) by words or conduct as to fact or as to law, including a deception as to the present intentions of the person using the deception or any other person'.

23.4.1   'Deception' and 'obtaining'

Thus if a defendant states what he thinks is untrue, but is in fact true, he does not deceive (*R v Deller* (1952)) but he may be guilty of an attempt (later).

Examples of deception are wearing a cap and gown in Oxford and obtaining credit, though not an undergraduate (*R v Barnard* (1837)) and, especially fraudulently, writing cheques. It was held by the House of Lords in *R v Charles* (1976) that the representation is that a cheque will be honoured on presentation, and it was held in *R v Lambie* (1981) that in the case where a cheque-card is produced to the payee, the defendant is authorised by his bank to use the card (ie his credit has not been stopped, or the card re-claimed).

There is generally no duty to correct a self-deception, eg as to the fitness of goods being sold by the defendant. But if a payer is entitled to assume some fact and he is not put right on the matter then there will be a deception. In *R v Rashid* (1977) the defendant, a British Rail catering steward, took his own bread and tomatoes on to the train to sell to customers as sandwiches. The Court of Appeal held that he had impliedly represented to the customer-travellers that the food was British Rail's own, and had not corrected their misunderstandings. He had therefore deceived them.

Finally, it should be noted that the obtaining must be *caused* by the deception. Thus, if the payee buys, not in reliance on the deception, but for another reason, then causation is not proved. In *R v Laverty* (1970) the defendant sold a stolen car with changed number plates. The buyer had not relied on the supposed authenticity of the number plates, so the defendant was acquitted.

23.4.2	The timing of the fraudulent intent

In all these deception offences the timing is important. Clearly a man who orders food intending not to pay for it does 'obtain property by deception' under s 15. But what if he orders it intending to pay, but decides after the meal not to. Here, there has been no prior deception. If he deceives in evading liability, then s 2 of the 1978 Act is suitable, but if he merely disappears without paying then the following offence is the proper (and simpler) charge:

Section 3 Theft Act 1978: '... a person who, knowing that payment on the spot for any goods supplied or service done is required or expected from him, dishonestly makes off without having paid as required or expected and with intent to avoid payment' commits an offence.

The making-off 'may be an exercise accompanied by the sound of trumpets or a silent stealing away after the folding of tents' (*R v Brooks and Brooks* (1983)).

'Dishonesty' has the same meaning as in s 15, above, but he will not 'know that payment on the spot ... is required or expected from him' if he honestly believes that the goods are free, or that it is a credit transaction, or that someone else is going to pay.

Further, it was held by the House of Lords in *R v Allen* (1985) that there must be an intent to avoid payment permanently. In that case an Australian left an English hotel without paying his bill of £1,286. He was in financial difficulty, but genuinely hoped to be able to pay. He arranged to call back and leave his Australian passport as security. As his intent was to defer payment temporarily he was acquitted of s 3 (even though a prosecution under s 2 would have failed on account of the lack of deception).

There are two forms of burglary. A person commits it if either:

- s 9(1)(a): he 'enters any building or part of a building as a trespasser and with intent to commit' either theft (s 1 Theft Act 1968), or infliction of grievous bodily harm (ss 20, 23 Offences Against the Person Act 1861), or rape, or 'unlawful' damage; or

- s 9(1)(b): 'having entered a building or part of a building as a trespasser' either he steals (s 1 Theft Act 1968) or inflicts grievous bodily harm, or attempts either of these.

(a) Actus reus

Actus reus offence can be committed by day or night. The defendant must 'enter', but definitions in the cases differ.

In *R v Collins* (1972) the Court of Appeal said that if the entry was 'effective and substantial' before consent was given, it would constitute entry as a trespasser. In this farcical case a youth, the defendant, drunk and intending to 'have a girl, by force if necessary', climbed up a ladder and found a naked young woman asleep at the other side of the window sill. He descended, stripped (apart from his socks, which he kept on 'to effect a rapid escape' if the young woman's mother appeared), and mounted the ladder again. The young woman, also drunk and thinking him to be her boyfriend paying her an 'ardent nocturnal visit' allowed him to join her in bed, where sexual intercourse took place until she realised that this youth was not her boyfriend. His conviction was quashed as it was not proved at the trial whether he had already entered as a trespasser by the time she woke up, or whether he had not and therefore entered by her consent.

23.5   Burglary (s 9 Theft Act 1968)

Arm through window suff. entry

In *R v Brown* (1985), the defendant leant the top half of his body through a broken shop window. The Court of Appeal this time held that the test is one of 'effective' entry only, and here an arm through a break in the pane would be effective and therefore sufficient entry.

As to the trespass, the criminal courts are reluctant to enter into matters of definition in tort as to the meaning of this word in s 9. Trespass implies lack of consent or other lawful authority. But in tort the consent can only be given by the person in possession of the property, ie not the girl, but the mother, in *R v Collins*. The Court of Appeal thought that application of this point to criminal law was 'unthinkable'. Was it? Wasn't the mother the right person to give any consent? Would she have consented to Collins' entry?

In *R v Jones & Smith* (1976) the defendants stole two televisions from Smith's father's home. Smith's father had said Smith would never be a trespasser in his house. In upholding the conviction the court held that the defendant must either know or be reckless in not knowing that he is 'entering in excess of the permission that has been given to him'. Had the father known of the intended thefts he would not have consented to the defendants' entry.

As to the definition of 'any building or part of a building' the Act is silent. In pre-Theft Act cases, it was required to be 'of considerable size and intended to be permanent' (*Stevens v Gourley* (1859)). But in *R v Walkington* (1979) a till area in a shop, bounded by a moveable three-sided counter, from which the public was excluded, was held to suffice. A higher penalty applies if the building is a 'dwelling'.

(b) *Mens rea*

The prosecution must prove intention to enter as a trespasser (ie knowing, or reckless as to the facts which make his entry a trespass (*R v Collins* (1972)), and either

- in s 9(1)(a) cases, 'intent' to commit theft (s 1), inflict grievous bodily harm (ss 20, 23 1861 Act), commit rape (s 1 Sexual Offences Act 1956) or do unlawful damage to the building or anything therein (any Criminal Damage Act 1971 offence); or

- in s 9(1)(b) cases, intent to commit theft (s 1), or intent or recklessness to inflict grievous bodily harm (ss 20, 23 1861 Act), or, in the case of an attempt, the intent to commit s 1 or ss 20 or 23 (s 1 Criminal Attempts Act 1981, dealt with later).

Many burglaries are committed by desperate men. It is not surprising that Parliament has tried to discourage burglary by violence, by establishing it as a separate crime justifying a more severe sentence.

This offence occurs when the defendant commits 'any burglary and at the time has with him any firearm or imitation firearm, any weapon of offence, or any explosive'.

'Weapon of offence' is a wider definition than those covered by the Prevention of Crime Act 1953. Here it must be made or adapted or intended 'for causing injury to or incapacitating a person'; this would include a gag, sleeping pills, pepper or even an aggressive dog, to keep the occupant in a corner.

The defendant must be aware of his possession of the thing 'at the time' of commission of the burglary: in s 9(1)(a), at the time of entry; but in s 9(1)(b), at time of the theft or infliction of grievous bodily harm (or attempt of either).

The following cases are s 9(1)(b) prosecutions. In *R v Francis* (1982), the defendants had sticks on entry, but had discarded them by the time they stole, and were accordingly acquitted. In *R v O'Leary* (1986), the defendant entered as a trespasser, but only then picked up a kitchen knife, and went upstairs and obtained property from the occupant at knifepoint; he was convicted. In these s 9(1)(b) cases the operative time for ascertaining possession of the thing is at the time of the theft.

The Theft Act 1968, like the Criminal Damage Act 1971, tries to prevent crime by making it an offence that a person 'when not at his place of abode ... has with him any article for use in the course of or in connection with any burglary, theft or cheat' (the latter defined as burglary (s 9), theft (s 1), taking a conveyance (s 12), and obtaining property by deception (s 15)).

Clearly there need be nothing dangerous about these things and they will range from marked playing cards to the bread and tomatoes *R v Rashid* (1977), above.

The *mens rea* is the knowledge of possession, and the intention to use the article 'in the course of or in connection with any burglary, theft or cheat'. The possession must be before the burglary etc, but the intended use might be before, at, or after the burglary, as in *R v Ellames* (1974), the possession of masks and guns for use after a robbery.

Section 22 states that 'a person handles stolen goods if (otherwise than in the course of the stealing) knowing or believing them to be stolen goods, he dishonestly receives the

23.5.1 Aggravated burglary: s 10 Theft Act 1968

23.5.2 Going equipped for stealing, etc: s 25 Theft Act 1969

23.5.3 Handling stolen goods: s 22 Theft Act 1968

goods, or dishonestly undertakes or assists in their retention, removal, disposal or realisation by or for the benefit of another person, or if he arranges to do so.'

(a) *Actus reus*

'Goods' includes money 'and every other description of property except land', though land may be 'handled' after severance. 'Stolen' means stolen by theft (s 1) or obtained by deception (s 15) or blackmail (s 21) or by some foreign equivalent of these.

Thus, if the alleged thief is not guilty, there are no stolen goods, as in *Walters v Lunt* (1951), where parents were charged with handling a tricycle 'stolen' by their seven year old son (who in law is irrebuttably presumed incapable of crime, and who would more sensibly be called the innocent agent of the criminal parents).

If the 'handler' believes them to be stolen when they are not, he can be convicted of an attempt (see the Criminal Attempts Act 1981; these were essentially the facts of *Anderton v Ryan* (1985), which was held to have been wrongly decided by *R v Shivpuri* (1986)).

(b) Ceasing to be stolen

Goods cease to be stolen after they have been restored to the person from whom they were stolen, or to other lawful possession or custody, or after that person, or any person claiming through him, have ceased to have any right to restitution.

But as to what is restoration may be a difficult decision, often depending on the intention of the police. In *R v King* (1938) a policeman examined the goods to decide whether to seize them; this was held not to amount to restoration, and the goods were still 'stolen'. But in *AG's Reference (No 1 of 1974)* (1974) a jury acquitted in a case where a policeman who suspected that goods in a car were stolen, immobilised the car by removing the rotor arm in the engine: thus the goods were restored, and no longer 'stolen'. Lord Widgery CJ (for the court) said, 'In our judgment it depended primarily on the intentions of the police officer'. Had he made up his mind that he would take them into custody, or was he still of an entirely open mind at that stage?

Finally, proceeds or goods in the hands of the thief or a handler which represent the stolen goods, are included in the term 'stolen goods'.

(c) Forms of handling

By s 22 these are receiving, undertaking or assisting in the retention, removal, disposal or realisation – or arranging to do any of the aforesaid.

In *R v Karwar* (1982) the defendant's husband stole some furnishings. She furnished their home with them, knowing of the theft; she was convicted of dishonestly assisting in their retention. But in *R v Coleman* (1986) a wife was stealing from her employer. The money went to support them both, and into the purchase of their flat in joint names. The husband knew that the money was stolen but was acquitted. Deriving benefit is insufficient. 'Assisting' means helping or arranging, he did neither.

(d) Innocent receipt

If the defendant receives the goods innocently, ie without knowledge that they are stolen, or with knowledge but intending to restore them to the true owner, he commits no offence. But if, on the other hand, he has received them innocently, but later forms the intention to retain or dispose of them, he may commit an offence under s 22.

(e) *Mens rea*

The *mens rea* consists of both knowledge or belief that the goods are stolen, and dishonesty.

(f) Knowledge or belief

It is not enough that the defendant suspected: that the goods were stolen, nor that he should have known (ie that he is reckless or negligent), nor that he thinks it more likely than not that they are stolen. Knowledge and belief can be based on the defendant's first-hand knowledge. In cases where the defendant's mind is acting upon what is reported to him, the guidelines in *R v Hall* (1985) of the Court of Appeal are useful. Knowledge is being 'told by someone with first hand knowledge'; belief is 'I cannot say I know for certain ... but there can be no other reasonable conclusion'.

As to knowledge of the type of goods, once the defendant knows he has goods and knows or believes that they are stolen, it matters not that he knows what type of goods they are (*R v McCullum* (1973)).

(g) Dishonesty

Probably, the test in *R v Ghosh* (1982) applies. And if the defendant is being prosecuted solely under s 22, other than for receiving, evidence is admissible of his commission of the same act relating to a theft in the last 12 months, or of a conviction of s 1 or s 22 in the last five years.

Chapter 24

Defences in Criminal Law

The following defences apply to most crimes:

- infancy;

- insanity;

- diminished responsibility (not a general defence, but only a defence to murder);

- provocation (not a general defence, but only a defence to murder);

- intoxication;

- private (or self) and public defence;

- duress;

- necessity.

The above-listed are general defences, with the exception of 'diminished responsibility' and 'provocation'. These two are only defences to murder, under the Homicide Act 1957, and have the effect of reducing the charge of murder to a conviction for manslaughter (called 'voluntary manslaughter', as the defendant has in truth acted with *mens rea* of murder, albeit under special circumstances). In 1957 a person convicted of murder would normally have been sentenced to death, but these two defences offered a compromise to the defendant. The other defences listed are, where they apply, complete defences.

Since the Family Law Reform Act 1969 the term 'infancy' has been generally superseded by 'minority', which covers birth to the start of the 18th birthday. But the age of minority is not coextensive with the two age-groups protected by this defence, as now follows.

Firstly, there is an irrebuttable presumption that an child of less than 10 years cannot commit a crime (either *actus reus* or *mens rea*). Thus, a person who acts through an a child of less than 10 years, eg by telling him to 'steal' in a shop, is himself a principal acting through an innocent agent. And a person cannot 'handle stolen goods', contrary to s 22 Theft Act 1968, by receiving the goods from an child under 10 who has taken them since the child has not stolen them (*Walters v Lunt* (1951)).

24.1   Infancy

Secondly, there is a rebuttable presumption that 10–13 (inclusive) year olds cannot commit a crime (either *actus reus* or *mens rea*). To rebut this presumption the prosecution must prove, as well as *actus reus* and *mens rea*, that the child had 'a mischievous discretion'.

In *C v DPP* (1994) the Divisional Court stated its disapproval of the doctrine of mischievous discretion, and purported to abolish it. In this case a 12 year old boy was seen tampering with a motor bike on a private driveway, using a crowbar. The House of Lords allowed his appeal, confirming that the doctrine still applied and required proof that 'he knew that it was a wrong act as distinct from an act of mere naughtiness or childish mischief'. The boy had run away when seen by police officers, but this does not prove mischievous discretion, as Lord Lowry said, because it can 'as easily follow a naughty action as a wicked one'.

In the case of homicide by an infant, the infant must stand trial in the normal way, as exemplified by the trial in 1993 of the murderers of two year old James Bulger.

24.2   Insanity

A defendant found, or presumed, to be fit to plead, can put forward this defence of insanity. The legal test for insanity are the *M'Naghten* Rules 1843, set out in *R v M'Naghten* (1843), where the defendant shot and killed the Prime Minister's secretary, mistaking him for the Prime Minister. After M'Naghten was acquitted on the ground of his insanity, there was public outrage and debate, after which the judges of the Court of Queen's Bench met and formulated the present Rules.

The Rules are that, firstly, 'every man is presumed to be sane'; and that to have a defence 'it must be clearly proved that, at the time of the committing of the act, the party accused was labouring under such a defect of reason, from disease of the mind, as not to know the nature and quality of the act he was doing; or, if he did know it, that he did not know he was doing what was wrong'. (In fact, the judge can introduce the issue of insanity of his own volition provided he can raise a *prima facie* case and allows both sides to call evidence on it.)

24.2.1   'Disease of the mind'

This is decided by a legal, not a medical, test. Devlin J in *R v Kemp* (1956) said, 'It seems that any disease which produces a malfunctioning of the mind is a disease of the mind. It need not be a disease of the brain.' And in *R v Quick* (1973), where a nurse, charged with actual bodily harm to a spastic patient pleaded hypoglycaemia (not enough blood sugar in the diabetic nurse), Lawton LJ (for the court) said:

'In our judgment the fundamental concept is of a malfunctioning of the mind caused by disease. A malfunctioning of the mind of transitory effect caused by the application to the body of some external factor such as violence, drugs, including anaesthetics, alcohol and hypnotic influences cannot fairly be said to be due to disease.'

This test is now followed: that a disease of the mind can only be caused by an internal factor. Internal factors have included sleepwalking in *R v Burgess* (1991); hypoglycaemic episode in *R v Quick* (1973); epilepsy (*R v Sullivan* (1983)); and stress caused by a woman's rejection (*R v Burgess* (1991)).

In *R v Burgess*, the test was defined as being that if the cause is an Internal factor, which manifests itself in violence, and is prone to recur, and for which defendant ought to be detained in hospital, rather than acquitted outright, then, it is insanity. In this case it was recognised that the label of 'insanity' was perhaps unfair to some of these defendants, but that the answer lay rather with Parliament.

The powers of reasoning must be impaired. In *R v Clarke* (1972), an old woman in a supermarket forgot to pay for some items, and put them in her own bag. The trial judge said she was insane, but on her successful appeal Ackner J said that the Rules 'do not and never have applied to those who retain the power of reasoning but who in moments of confusion or absent-mindedness fail to use their powers to the full'.	24.2.2 'Defect of reason'
Writers' examples of a person not knowing the nature and quality of his act have been: killing under the 'delusion that he is breaking a jar', or cutting a throat 'under the idea that he was cutting a loaf of bread'. In these cases the prosecution is necessarily relieved of the burden of having to prove that defendant has *mens rea* (here, knowledge) of the conduct part of the *actus reus*.	24.2.3 'Does not know the nature and quality of his act'
That a person does not know that he was doing what was wrong, means, in this sense 'legally wrong'.	24.2.4 'Does not know that he was doing what was wrong'
The verdict, if insanity is proved (along with *actus reus* and any *mens rea* still left to be proved), is 'not guilty by reason of insanity', but even though the special verdict is technically an acquittal, the defendant has an appeal against it. It is also worth noting that since 1991, if the defendant is too insane to plead to the charge (ie to say 'guilty' or 'not guilty' to it), the jury must still hear evidence to decide whether the alleged *actus reus* is proved.	24.2.5 The 'special verdict'
Before 1957 in England, a person who could not secure an acquittal for murder, was either convicted and hanged or	**24.3 Diminished responsibility**

found insane within the *M'Naghten* Rules. Section 2 Homicide Act 1957 now provides a defence to murder (either as principal or as secondary party) where, although malice aforethought exists, there is an 'abnormality of mind'.

An early case was *R v Byrne* (1960), where the defendant, suffering from 'violent perverted sexual desires which he finds it difficult or impossible to control', killed and mutilated a woman in a YWCA hostel. Three doctors called by the defence all agreed that he was not insane within *M'Naghten* Rules. He was convicted of murder, but successfully appealed against conviction. Lord Parker CJ said:

> 'It appears to us to be wide enough to cover the mind's activities in all its aspects, not only the perception of physical acts and matters and the ability to form a rational judgment whether an act is right or wrong, but also the ability to exercise will-power to control physical acts in accordance with that "rational judgment", and that s 2 should be interpreted in a "broad common-sense way".'

The jury must decide both whether there was an 'abnormality of the mind' and whether the abnormality of mind 'substantially impaired (the defendant's) mental responsibility', and can disagree with the doctors on both issues.

24.3.1   The cause of the 'abnormality of mind'

Section 2 says '(whether arising from a condition of arrested or retarded development of mind or any inherent causes or induced by disease or injury)'. Clearly, whereas defendants before had to plead insanity they will now plead diminished responsibility. The proportion of mental acquittals (ie insanity before; diminished responsibility now) has been the same. Courts allow s 2 to be used in cases of insanity; the other causes specified in s 2; inability or difficulty (provided it is more than trivial) to control will-power (*R v Byrne*); in mercy-killing by distressed relatives (*R v Gray* (1965)); deserted spouses or disappointed lovers, persons with chronic anxiety states. In *R v Ahluwalia* (1993) a woman who had suffered from a long history of battering and degradation from her husband, but was not able to succeed with the defence of provocation, was allowed this defence.

It is acceptable, if not anomalous, for the defence to be seeking a conviction of manslaughter, and for the prosecution to be seeking an acquittal on grounds of insanity in the same case. A defendant convicted of manslaughter can be given one of many sentences, some benign, whereas insanity means detention at Her Majesty's pleasure.

24.4   **Provocation**

It is always open to a defendant to raise provocation in mitigation of sentence. But it is a defence to murder (only), reducing the charge to a conviction of manslaughter. The issues raised are decided by the jury and a judge may raise the issue of his own volition.

Section 3 Homicide Act 1957 states that the provocation can be caused 'by things done or by things said or by both together'. These words have their ordinary, natural meaning, thus a lawful act or statement might suffice, such as a baby crying in *R v Doughty* (1986). Indeed, the defendant himself may have provoked the provocative words or behaviour which provokes a defendant to kill. In *R v Johnson* (1989) the defendant threatened V & V's woman friend; a struggle ensued in which he killed V with a flick-knife. The Court of Appeal allowed the defence. Moreover, the provocation can have been made either to or by a third party.

24.4.1   What is a provocation?

Was the defendant actually provoked into losing his self-control or did he keep his self-control, and kill premeditatedly? The defence protects provoked, impulsive retaliation, not carefully planned revenge. Relevant, therefore, are the nature of the provocative act, the sensitivity or phlegmatism of the defendant, the time elapsed between the act and the killing.

24.4.2   Was the defendant actually provoked into losing his self-control

There must be a 'sudden and temporary loss of self-control' (Devlin J in *R v Duffy* (1949)). This was approved in *R v Ibrams* (1981), where the provocation occurred on 7 October, the retaliation was planned on 10 October and it was carried out on 12 October, and could hardly be said to have been 'sudden'. In *R v Thornton* (1996), where there had been a history of domestic violence ('battered woman syndrome'), followed by the wife killing the husband by stabbing, the defence succeeded, as she did suddenly snap at the end of the provocative battering. (In *R v Ahluwalia*, as we have seen, the defence under s 2 was available, the sudden snapping being absent.)

The decision as to whether provocation was 'enough to make a reasonable man do as he did' posed by s 2 raises two issues: would the reasonable man have reacted at all? Would the reasonable man have reacted in this way?

24.4.3   Was the provocation 'enough to make a reasonable man do as he did?'

Formerly, at common law, the defendant's behaviour was gauged by that of the reasonable man (on which the judge could instruct the jury), even if defendant was not mentally or physically like the reasonable man. But this ignores the very characteristics that triggered off the defendant's response, such as the impotency of the 18 year old defendant in *Bedder v DPP* (1954), jeered at and kicked in the genitals by the prostitute he killed. The judge directed the jury to compare the defendant with the reasonable man, even though the reasonable man is not impotent and would have ignored the taunt. In *DPP v Camplin* (1978), a 15 year old boy who had been forcibly buggered and laughed at by his assaulter, killed him with the assaulter's own chapati pan. The judge followed Bedder's test, refusing a reasonable 15 year old test. Lord Diplock in the House of Lords stated the test:

> '... the reasonable man referred to in the question is a person having the power of self control to be expected of an ordinary person of the sex and age of the accused, but in other respects sharing such of the accused's characteristics as they think would affect the gravity of the provocation to him.'

'Characteristics' need not be permanent or part of the defendant's character or personality. In *R v Morhall* (1995) the defendant stabbed and killed a friend who criticised the defendant's addiction to glue-sniffing. Allowing the defence, the House of Lords stated that the defendant's history and circumstances at the time of the killing, and the 'entire factual situation', were relevant.

As to the second issue, would the reasonable man have reacted in this way; s 3 gives this decision to the jury. The judge cannot therefore instruct them on whether the response must be in proportion to the provocation; the jury must decide for themselves.

24.5 Intoxication

This defence mainly concerns the influence of drink; but in *R v Lipman* (1969), where, after taking LSD, the defendant thought he was fighting snakes in the centre of the earth but killed his girlfriend, it was held that drugs should be treated in the same way. But in *R v Bailey* (1983) and *R v Hardie* (1984) a distinction was made between drugs commonly known to cause dangerous or unpredictable behaviour, and drugs not commonly known to cause this.

24.5.1 Intoxication caused by alcohol or dangerous drugs

There is no automatic defence of intoxication. The sole issue is whether the intoxication prevented the defendant from forming mens rea or not. Evidence of intoxication is only relevant, therefore, to prove the presence or absence of *mens rea* (*DPP v Majewski* (1976)).

Crimes of specific intent are murder, s 18 Offences Against the Person Act 1861, theft, robbery, burglary with intent to steal, handling stolen goods, criminal damage in its intentional form, attempts, and possibly aiding and abetting.

In these cases the requisite specific intent might be proved to have been absent through intoxication, but if intent is present, it is no defence that the defendant became drunk involuntarily. In *R v Kingston* (1994) the jury convicted K of indecently assaulting a boy after he had had his drink laced with sedative by others, the jury decided that he still had the intent to assault. The House of Lords upheld his conviction; his lack of blame for being intoxicated was immaterial. And if the intoxication is self-induced with the intention of committing a crime ('Dutch courage'), as in *AG for Northern Ireland v Gallagher* (1961), where the defendant had *mens rea* to kill his wife before drinking whisky and stabbing her to death, the *mens rea* is assessed at the time he decided to intoxicate himself.

It follows that drink or drugs taken, for pure enjoyment, cannot create such a defence to a crime of basic intent. These are manslaughter, rape, s 20 Offences Against the Person Act 1861 and other assaults, taking a conveyance etc, criminal damage alleging recklessness. This is so, even if, because of the intoxication, the defendant does not have *mens rea* for all circumstances of the *actus reus*, or was in a state of automatism (*DPP v Majewski*). Further, on a charge of a basic intent crime committed during voluntary (or self-induced) intoxication, the prosecution need not prove any intention or foresight, whatever the definition of the crime may say, nor indeed any voluntary act (*R v Lipman*; *DPP v Majewski*).

It has, however, been stated that where statute allows a particular belief to amount to a defence, 'intoxication' or at least 'drunkenness' shall not defeat that defence. In *Jaggard v Dickinson* (1980) a drunken woman broke her way into a house, believing it was her friend's, who would consent: it was not. Her defence, under statute, that the friend would consent was held to be available despite her drunken state, as Parliament had not decreed otherwise.

24.5.2 *Majewski* and statutory defences

But consider the anomaly posed by Smith and Hogan in *Criminal Law*:

> '... where the defendant did not intend any damage to property he may be held liable because he was drunk [drunkenness no defence to a basic intent crime]; but where he did intend damage to property but thought the owner would consent he is not liable, however drunk he may have been [a statutory defence, which must be allowed].'

The distinction between intoxication caused other than by alcohol or drugs was established in *R v Bailey* (1983), where a diabetic failed to take enough food after insulin, and was charged under both ss 18 and 20 Offences Against the Person Act 1861 and *R v Hardie* (1984), where he took valium, and was charged under s 1(2) Criminal Damage Act 1971.

24.5.3 Intoxication caused otherwise than by alcohol or dangerous drugs

Here, to convict, the test is whether the defendant was reckless in taking the drug, ie could actually foresee 'aggressive, unpredictable and uncontrollable conduct' (*R v Bailey*), whether or not there is any foresight of *actus reus*.

24.6 Private (or self) defence and public defence

Both common law and statute allow reasonable force to be used against an aggressor in private, or self defence and in public defence. This is a complete defence.

(The defendant must in logic have acted intentionally; a defendant cannot say that he acted recklessly or negligently in order to save himself.)

There are two tests in all situations:

• it must be reasonable to use force, though the defendant's honest belief as to the circumstances is relevant (see below); and

• the force used must be reasonably necessary.

In self-defence or defence of property the courts must consider the facts as the defendant saw them, even if prompted by a mistaken though honest belief. In *Beckford v R* (1987), the defendant, a policeman, was looking for a dangerous man in Manchester, Jamaica. He saw a man run out of a house and honestly believing himself to be in danger he shot the man dead. The Privy Council applied the decision in *DPP v Morgan* (1975), the rape case. A man who honestly believes himself to be in danger believes that the harm he causes his victim is covered by this defence.

As to whether the force must be reasonable has been clarified by the House of Lords in *R v Clegg* (1995), where a soldier in Northern Ireland fired shots at a car which was speeding through a checkpoint. The fourth shot, which killed a passenger, was fired after the danger to Private Clegg had passed, and the car already 50 feet down the road. This defence failed on the point above. But the Lords reconfirmed, *obiter*, the Privy Council decision in *Palmer v R* (1971), another Jamaican murder appeal, that when the defendant either was in danger (or as in *Beckford v R* believed himself to be) the amount of force used by the defendant in self-defence must be reasonable.

Section 3 Criminal Law Act 1967 also states that reasonable force can be used in preventing crime or arresting offenders. Probably *Beckford v R* and *Palmer v R* apply here also. This defence overlaps with the defence at common law (above), but s 3 would not be available, say, if the assailant were an infant under 10 years old or insane, both being incapable of committing a crime. And in a situation such as that in *R v*

Renouf (1986), where a defendant could claim that his reckless driving was justifiable to arrest a car by forcing it off the road, but where the danger had passed, only s 3 would be available.

In either the common law or the statutory defence the defendant must have been aware at the time of the *actus reus* of the circumstances which justify his taking measures. The principle of *R v Dadson* (1850), above, still applies. The policeman there who shot a felon who was stealing wood, was ignorant of his being a felon, and thus could not plead this as a defence to the shooting.

24.6.1 Unknown circumstances of justification

The same principles as set out above would apply here. Thus, if a defendant assaults an aggressor, the defendant can as appropriate plead self-defence or s 3. If the defendant commits a relevant criminal damage offence he can plead the defence of reasonable protection in s 5 Criminal Damage Act 1971. But as the remoteness of the property increases, so the amount of justifiable harm decreases.

24.6.2 Defence of property

Duress is the overbearing of the defendant's will by a third party's threat such that he commits an offence while in that state. But his acts are his voluntary acts; he has chosen to carry out those acts to avoid the effect of the threats.

24.7 Duress

In *Lynch v DPP for Northern Ireland* (1975) a man told, under threat, to drive a gunman to a killing was allowed the defence on a charge of aiding and abetting murder. But in murder trials since then there has been a hardening of judicial attitude. In *Abbott v R* (1976) the defendant, under threat, held a woman as she was stabbed by another. The defendant then helped to bury her still live body. The defendant had no defence to a charge of principal to murder. In *R v Howe* (1987) the defendant and two others lured two youths into the Goyt Valley in the Peak District, where the youths were beaten, tortured and strangled. It was held that a threat was no defence on a charge of principal to murder (confirming *Abbott v R*), nor on a charge of aiding and abetting murder (overruling *Lynch v DPP for Northern Ireland*).

24.7.1 Which crimes?

Further, in *R v Gotts* (1992), where a 16 year old son stabbed his mother, on threat of being shot by his father, it was held to be no defence to attempted murder. (The Court of Appeal in *R v Gotts* did not, however, equate conspiracy and incitement with attempt: those crimes are 'a stage further away from the completed offence than is the attempt'. The defence may be a defence to other crimes, however.)

| 24.7.2 | The threat | Threats accepted by the courts are usually threats to the person. Probably 'the more dreadful the circumstances of the killing, the heavier the evidential burden of an accused advancing such a plea, and the stronger and more irresistible the duress needed' (Lords Wilberforce and Edmund-Davies in *Abbott v R* (1976)). |

It was once said that the threat must be immediate or imminent, but in *R v Hudson* (1971) there was opportunity to inform the police of a threat to 'cut her up' if she gave evidence at a trial, and the defence still held on a charge of perjury.

| 24.7.3 | Withstanding the threat | The test of whether the defendant could be expected to withstand the threat is mainly objective. 'The law should ... require him to have the steadfastness reasonably to be expected of the ordinary citizen in his situation', according to Lord Lane CJ, in *R v Graham* (1982), approved by the House of Lords in *R v Howe* (1987), above. Lord Lane CJ said that this defence and provocation were analogous, and stated that the defendant must have been compelled to act by what he 'reasonably believed', have had 'good cause to fear' the threat, and his response must have been that which 'a sober person of reasonable firmness, sharing the characteristics' of the defendant, would have made. |

24.8 Necessity

Whereas in self-defence and duress the threat is from an aggressor who threatens harm to the defendant, here the threat is from circumstances, including nature (indeed, this defence is sometimes called 'duress of circumstances').

In some cases threats might in fact be made by a third party, but these would not import harm against the defendant. So in *R v Conway* (1988), the defendant had assumed the existence of threats against his passenger, and in *R v Martin* (1989), where the defendant's wife had suicidal tendencies; the defendant had assumed her threat to commit suicide if the defendant did not drive her son to work, to be real.

It is uncertain whether such a defence exists. The two cases described above were both driving cases, with no actual victim. In *R v Conway* the charge was one of reckless driving and in R v Martin it was driving while disqualified. And in *R v Pommell* (1995) the charge of illegal possession of a firearm came about after Pommell had dis-armed a gunman and slept with the gun, intending to hand it to the police in the morning. His conviction was quashed on appeal.

But in *R v Dudley & Stephens* (1884) there was indeed a victim. Three men and a cabin boy had been 18 days adrift on a raft on the high seas. Two men then killed the boy and all three ate him. The three men were later picked up alive and the two who had killed the boy were tried for murder at the Exeter Assizes. They were convicted (but not hanged). Lord Coleridge wondered if there was a necessity on the facts; but apart from this, the court doubted the existence of the defence as a matter of law, because of the morality of it all, the difficulty in measuring the necessity (after how many days was it 'necessary'? As Cardozo J said off the bench, 'Who shall know when masts and sails of rescue may emerge out of the fog?'), and the difficulty of selecting the victim.

In *United States v Holmes* (1842), where men were thrown overboard to save women and children (and the crew!) the defence failed. The judge stated that lots should have been drawn. But Cardozo J, again off the bench, has replied that 'Where two or more are overtaken by a common disaster, there is no right on the part of one to save the lives of some, by the killing of another.' On the other hand, the corporal who was reported in the press as having thrown, possibly to his death, a man paralysed with fear and blocking an escape ladder on the *Herald of Free Enterprise*, was not prosecuted, and might conversely be congratulated for saving the lives he led to safety up the ladder. Who is to weigh in the balance the lives of men?

If a defence does exist, and in *R v Conway*, *R v Martin* and in *R v Pommell* it was held to do so, at least where no other person is harmed, then the test is that stated by Lord Lane CJ in *R v Martin*, as:

'... was the accused impelled to act as he did out of fear of the situation he "reasonably" thought to exist, and if so, would a sober person of reasonable firmness, sharing the characteristics of the accused, have responded to that situation by acting as the accused did?'

The similarity of Lord Lane's test in duress is noticeable.

Chapter 25

Parties to Crime

To say, 'Bloggs is liable for theft' is not sufficient; it should also explain how, or in what capacity, Bloggs is liable. Section 8 Accessories and Abettors Act 1861 says that any person who aids, abets, counsels or procures the commission of an indictable offence is liable in all respects as a principal offender. Section 8 also applies to either way offences, and s 44 Magistrates' Courts Act 1980 applies similarly to summary offences. It is important to understand that this discussion depends on a crime in fact being committed.

Prima facie, therefore, for each crime there must be a principal (called 'principal in the first degree' at common law). But any person listed in s 8 will also be liable as a secondary party, or accomplice or accessory (called at common law a 'principal in the second degree'). Even in strict liability cases, secondary parties must be proved to have *mens rea*; in some cases only a member of a specified class can be liable as principal, eg a licensee; and the defendant might be vicariously liable for the act of a principal, but cannot be so for the act of a secondary party. (Vicarious liability, dealt with later, is the liability of a person, 'the master', for the crime of another, 'the servant'.)

A principal is the person whose criminal act is the most immediate cause of the *actus reus*. There can be several principals of the same crime, as in Caesar's assassination, where many people stabbed him, each being a contributing cause of his death. If an innocent agent is used by the defendant, the defendant will be the principal.

25.1 The principal

A crime may be committed, and a defendant convicted as secondary party for it, even though the principal participant is acquitted. In *R v Cogan & Leak* (1975) a husband was convicted as secondary party to his wife's rape by another man. The husband had convinced that man that his wife would be consenting despite her protestations. That man had honestly believed this to be so (as in *DPP v Morgan* (1975)) and was therefore acquitted. In *R v Bourne* (1952) a husband had forced his wife to commit buggery with an alsatian dog. She was acquitted of being principal to the offence, because she participated under duress, but this did not prevent his conviction as secondary party.

25.2	**Secondary parties**	A crime will usually be committed by a principal, ie someone who takes the main part, or who personally commits the *actus reus*. But he might be assisted in various ways by other people. Those others are called 'secondary parties'.
25.2.1	The conduct	Section 8 (and s 44) states that a person will be guilty of a crime as secondary party who 'aids, abets, counsels or procures' that crime.

'Aid' means assist before or during the commission of the crime; 'abet' means encourage at the time of commission of the crime. To 'procure' means to 'produce by endeavour'. In *AG's Reference (No 1 of 1975)* (1975), a defendant had been wrongly acquitted of procuring a drink-driving offence after lacing his friend's drink with alcohol, knowing that the friend would drive home over the limit (which he did do).

'Counsel' means 'advise, solicit, or something of that sort', but as opposed to abetting, the counselling must take place before the commission. In *R v Calhaem* (1985) a woman (the defendant) in love with a man, hired a 'hit-man' to kill another woman, also in love with the same man. The hit-man killed that other woman and the defendant was convicted of counselling the murder.

Some of the four forms imply consensus: some do not (anonymous encouragement would suffice). Some imply causation, but it is immaterial, say, that an abettor or counsellor's encouragement was in fact disregarded by the principal, who had himself made up his mind to commit the crime. 'To sum up – the law is probably that:

(i) 'procuring' implies causation but not consensus;

(ii) 'abetting' and 'counselling' imply consensus but not causation;

(iii) 'aiding' requires actual assistance but neither 'consensus nor causation' (Smith and Hogan, *Criminal Law*).

25.2.2	Time of assistance	Assisting before or during an offence by the principal may create secondary liability for that offence. But assistance after the completion of the principal's offence will not.
25.2.3	Presence at the crime	There is no offence of being present at a crime but doing nothing to prevent it. Further, even if there is causation, eg encouragement, it must be wilful. Mere presence, even if intentional, is not abetting, no matter how encouraging to the defendant. In *R v Clarkson & Carroll* (1971) the defendants, soldiers, had entered their barrack hut to find a rape in progress; they stood quietly and watched. It might indeed be that their presence acted as an encouragement to the rapists or

as a discouragement to the girl, but there was no wilfulness in either, so there was no liability as secondary parties.

On the other hand, if there is an intentional assistance or encouragement, this will be *prima facie* (but not conclusive) evidence of abetting the offence, for example, spectating at an illegal boxing match in *R v Coney* (1882), or meeting an illegally-visiting jazz saxophonist, and attending and writing about his concert, in *Wilcox v Jeffery* (1951). But encouragement does not require presence. In *R v Rook* (1993) a defendant's prior agreement to the crime was effective encouragement to the principals who committed it, even though the defendant was not present. And if the defendant has a right of control and fails to exercise it, this may be aiding and abetting by encouragement. In *R v Russell* (1933), an Australian case, a father stood by as the mother drowned their children.

If one must have been principal and the other aiding and abetting, both can be convicted. But if it cannot be proved that the other (whichever one it was) was at least aiding and abetting, both must be acquitted.	**25.2.4** Difficulty in deciding who was principal
The prosecution must prove that the defendant intended to participate in the acts of assistance or encouragement, knowing that they *would* assist or encourage. He need not intend the ultimate crime to be committed. Thus, in *DPP for Northern Ireland v Maxwell* (1978) a defendant who drove X to a public house knowing X would shoot or bomb there was guilty of aiding in the offence.	**25.3** *Mens rea* **of secondary parties**
An aider and abettor must 'at least know the essential matters which constitute the offence'. In *Ferguson v Weaving* (1951) a landlord was unaware of after-hours drinking or at least be 'wilfully blind'. But provided the defendant knows of the type of offence being planned, or that it is to be committed against a particular person or thing, then he or she has sufficient knowledge on which to convict. In *R v Dunning & Graham* (1985) the defendant counselled X to burn Y's house; he burnt Y's car instead. This was within the agreed plan to destroy Y's property.	**25.3.1** Knowledge
If there is no common design to kill or cause grievous bodily harm, but the defendant is aware that the principal 'may' act with malice aforethought, both are guilty of murder. This amounts to authorisation, or lending himself to the enterprise with foresight of some physical harm (manslaughter) or of grievous bodily harm (murder).	**25.3.2** Unforeseen killings

In *Hui Chi-Ming v R* (1991) the defendant joined a gang who were going to assault a man. The defendant knew that one of them was carrying a length of heavy piping. The man was killed with it, and the defendant was held guilty of murder as secondary party.

But, on the other hand, if the crime requires *mens rea*, and one party goes beyond what was agreed, and the secondary party is not aware that the principal 'may' go beyond the common design the other is not liable for the unforeseen consequences of the principal's unauthorised act. In *Davies v DPP* (1954) in a gang-fight with fists, one man pulled out a knife and killed a man with it. The defendant was not aware that he had the knife and was not liable as secondary party for the murder but on account of his *mens rea* for 'some' harm he would be liable for manslaughter. Even if it is impossible to prove which had gone beyond the common design (by acting with intent to commit grievous bodily harm), both can be convicted if each has at least lent himself to the common venture with foresight of grievous bodily harm by himself or the other.

25.4 Withdrawal by a secondary party

To withdraw, the defendant-secondary party must act, and not merely make a mental turn-around. He must give his co-criminals clear notice of his withdrawal, and must neutralise, or take all reasonable steps to neutralise, the aid already given. Thus in *R v Becerra* (1976), shouting 'Come on, let's go!' and leaving through the window, was not enough, and in *R v Rook* (1993) not turning up at the criminal rendezvous was not either. But in *R v Grundy* (1977), the continuous attempt over two weeks to stop the principal from committing the crime was sufficient to relieve the defendant of liability.

The secondary party's arrest is not his withdrawal. And an arrested person might still be held to abet a principal still at large. In *R v Craig & Bentley* (1952), an arrested man shouted to his armed colleague, 'let him have it, Chris'. Unfortunately, Chris took this to mean 'shoot the policeman', rather than 'hand over the gun'. Chris shot the policeman. Chris was convicted of murder as principal, but was too young to hang, whereas the defendant under arrest was held to be secondary party and was hanged.

25.5 Victims as parties to crimes

Where a statute creates an offence, it is implied that it is also an offence to aid, abet, counsel or procure that offence. But if the statute is intended to protect a certain class, it is implied that a victim, a member of that class, who does aid etc, shall not be liable. The only class to which this rule applies is victims of certain sexual offences. In *R v Tyrrell* (1894), a girl who aided a man to commit unlawful sexual intercourse with her was in truth his victim, and for that reason she acquitted on the charge of secondary party to his offence.

Where a master delegates to his servant certain statutory duties imposed on the master, the master will be vicariously liable for crimes committed by the servant in performing those duties. In *Allen v Whitehead* (1930), statute forbade the owner of cafes to allow prostitutes to gather there. Unknown to him, his servant, to whom he had delegated the management of the cafe did allow them to gather, but on this delegation principle the owner was convicted of the offence.

25.6   Vicarious liability

A corporation can be liable vicariously for the acts of its servants and agents, or through the acts of those in the corporation who are the 'brains' of the company and control it. Their minds are, in effect, that of the company.

In *Tesco v Nattrass* (1971) the House of Lords stated that the 'brains' are the board, managing director, and possibly others 'in actual control of the operations', or 'entrusted with the exercise of the powers of the company'. But the culprit branch manager here was one of the 'hands', and therefore allowed Tesco to escape personal liability by pleading that the criminal price misdescription was the act of 'another person' (ie the branch manager).

The corporation can only be convicted of crimes punishable by a fine; this excludes murder. There are others which it cannot commit, for obvious reasons, eg rape, assault etc, though it can now commit manslaughter, *per R v P&O European Ferries (Dover) Ltd* (1990), the *Herald of Free Enterprise* trial in which P&O was acquitted.

25.6.1   Corporations

Under the Interpretation Act 1978, these are 'persons', and therefore capable of liability where statute uses that word.

25.6.2   Unincorporated associations (including partnerships)

Chapter 26

Inchoate Offences

'Inchoate' means incomplete. These three offences are preliminary stages in committing crimes. They are, however, quite independent, self-standing crimes in their own right, and can be committed even though the crime they are leading up to is not itself committed.

The three inchoate offences are:

- incitement of a person to commit an offence (dealt with by the common law);

- conspiracy to commit an offence (dealt with partly by the common law, but mainly by statute);

- an attempt to commit an offence (dealt with by statute).

The first two may sound similar to counselling or possibly abetting, but the difference is that a person who counsels etc is a secondary party to the offence he counsels someone to commit, and is in general only liable as such if an offence is ultimately committed by the principal; here, incitement, conspiracy and attempt are three independent crimes.

Thus, he who incites someone to commit an offence, or who conspires or attempts to commit an offence is a principal of the crime of incitement etc, whether or not the crime he incites, conspires or attempts is committed (though if it is committed, he can be prosecuted as both principal of the inchoate offence and secondary party of the ultimate offence).

26.1 Incitement

This is expressly or impliedly persuading (or seeking to persuade) someone to commit a crime, by suggesting, cajoling or by threat.

Whether the incited person commits the crime is irrelevant. But the crime the defendant is inciting someone to commit must be a crime if committed by the person incited. Thus in *R v Whitehouse* (1977) where the defendant tried to persuade a 15 year old girl to commit incest with him, there was not liability for incitement as the girl would not have committed any offence according to the wording of the statute.

The person incited must have had *mens rea* to commit his offence. Thus, in *R v Curr* (1967), where a man persuaded several women to take part in a social security fraud, but the women all thought that it was above-board, again there was no liability.

It is possible to incite someone to commit any crime, whether summary, either way, or indictable.

26.2   Conspiracy

A conspiracy is an agreement to do an unlawful act, or a lawful act by unlawful means, whether or not the ultimate crime is ever committed.

The Criminal Law Act 1977 provides for a crime of (statutory) conspiracy to commit any offence. The Act abolished the offence of conspiracy at common law, but the following common law conspiracies were preserved: conspiracy to defraud; conspiracy to corrupt public morals; conspiracy to outrage public decency. The Act states that an agreement to commit a crime involving fraud can be either a statutory conspiracy or a conspiracy to defraud, or both. (The common law conspiracies to corrupt public morals and to outrage public decency are dealt with in Part IV on Civil Liberties.)

26.2.1   *Mens rea*

The *mens rea* required by the ultimate offence is not necessarily sufficient to support a charge of conspiracy to commit that ultimate offence *(R v Siracusa* (1989)). However, the defendant must intend the crime to be carried out – consider the wording of s 1, and *Yip Chiu-Cheung v R* (1994). Here the defendant was charged with conspiring with a carrier to move illegal drugs from Hong Kong to Australia. The carrier was an undercover agent who would not have been prosecuted, so the defendant claimed that the carrier was not a conspirator, and so neither was he. The Privy Council held that as the carrier had the intent to have the plan carried out (ie the carrying of the drugs to Australia), he was a conspirator and so, therefore, was the defendant. But he need not intend to take part *(R v Siracusa)*. In *R v Siracusa* it was held necessary only to prove that the defendant knew it to involve the commission of an offence. To convict a defendant of conspiracy the Act requires him and at least one other conspirator to know of all the facts and circumstances which make it criminal, even those it is not necessary to prove (eg in strict liability crimes) to convict an individual of the crime itself.

26.2.2   'Course of conduct'

Section 1 requires that the conspirators agree 'that a course of conduct shall be pursued'. This must either 'necessarily amount to or involve the commission of any offence ... by one or more of the parties ... or would do so but for the existence of facts' which make the crime impossible.

Smith and Hogan argue that a 'course of conduct' agreed now, to be carried out in the future must include consequences, including those out of the control of the conspirators, and circumstances. To exclude such consequences and circumstances from the 'course of conduct' element of the *actus reus*, would mean that in a charge of conspiracy to murder by poisoning the victim's tea, there could be liability simply on the agreement to poison the cup of tea. The prosecution would have to prove agreement that the victim would drink it and die from it.

Mens rea as to all 'circumstances' of the *actus reus* is required in all cases of conspiracy, ie intention, knowledge or belief. Recklessness as to circumstances is not sufficient *mens rea* in conspiracy (though it might be for the ultimate offence) and is in attempted rape, see *R v Khan* (1990), below.

A conspiracy exists on the basis of an agreed 'course of conduct', including circumstances and consequences. There cannot be liability under the original agreement, for unforeseen consequences, as they would not have been agreed.

26.2.3   Liability for unforeseen consequences?

The prosecution must prove that the defendant conspired with another person (though the other person need not be identified). A defendant is not guilty of statutory conspiracy if the only other conspirator was his spouse, or an infant (lacking criminal responsibility), or an intended victim.

26.2.4   The other conspirators

Section 1 of the Criminal Attempts Act 1981 states that:

> 'If with intent to commit an offence to which this section applies, a person does an act which is more than merely preparatory to the commission of the offence, he is guilty of attempting to commit the offence.'

26.3   Attempts

Thus, even though liability for the ultimate crime might be based on a lesser *mens rea* (eg intention to commit grievous bodily harm in murder; recklessness in most non-fatal offences against the person, criminal damage etc), generally, intention is required for the attempt of these. But in *R v Khan* (1990) convictions for attempted rape were upheld where the judge had directed the jury that they could convict even where the defendant had only been reckless as to whether the victim was consenting. Section 1 only means that the defendant must have intended to have intercourse with a woman (ie the conduct), while the circumstance of her consenting needs only proof of recklessness. The Court of Appeal, however, pointed out that a division of actus reus into 'conduct' and 'circumstances' is not possible for all ultimate offences. Thus, *R v Khan* interprets the phrase as: with intent to commit the conduct and result elements of the *actus reus*, and with intent or recklessly (ie with actual foresight) as to the circumstances.

26.3.1   Mens rea of an attempt

26.3.2	*Actus reus* of an attempt	The *actus reus* of an attempted crime is committed when: 'a person does an act which is more than merely preparatory to the commission of the (ultimate) offence' (s 1). This is essentially a question of fact, and the court should decide it without referring to pre-Act cases, according to the Court of Appeal in *R v Gullefer* (1986) and *R v Jones* (1990).

In *R v Gullefer* the defendant had tried to stop a greyhound race by jumping onto the track, so that he could get his stake back; he was acquitted. But in *R v Jones* a defendant who had bought a gun, sawn off its barrel pointed it at a victim, was held to have attempted to assault that victim. The defence arguments that he needed to remove the safety catch, put his finger on the trigger, and pull the trigger created a too-fine analysis of what might be a quick action. Taylor J in *R v Jones* said that the decision was one for the jury, based on the wording of s 1 and their applicability to the facts of each case. (The reader will now reconsider whether a prosecution for attempt would now succeed on the facts of *R v Deller* (1952) and *R v White* (1910).)

26.3.3	Which offences can be attempted?	An attempt can be made to commit any indictable or either way offence, but not summary ones, nor conspiracy, nor acting as secondary party (though you can be a secondary party to an attempt, as in the failed robbery in *R v Dunnington* (1984)), nor for a 'pure omission', nor an offence which may only be committed recklessly or negligently, eg involuntary manslaughter, nor where the *actus reus* is a state of affairs (either the state of affairs exists or it does not). But it is a crime to attempt to incite a person to commit a crime.

26.3.4	The effect of withdrawal	Once the *actus reus* of attempt has been committed, with *mens rea*, the defendant's withdrawal is irrelevant to liability for attempt. Thus in *R v Taylor* (1859) a man who struck a match to burn a haystack but saw that he was being watched and desisted, was properly convicted of attempted arson. Today, the jury would have to decide whether the acts were 'more than merely preparatory to the commission of the offence'.

26.4	**Impossibility of the ultimate offence envisaged in any inchoate offence**	This concerns the situation where a defendant incites X to commit, or conspires to commit, or attempts to commit a crime that is impossible because of some fact as to which he is ignorant or mistaken.

At common law, the defendant must have incited someone or conspired to commit acts which amount to a crime. Thus, if the ultimate crime cannot be committed, the incitement or common law conspiracy is not a crime.

In the case of a statutory conspiracy (under the Criminal Law Act 1977) and in the case of an attempt (under the Criminal Attempts Act 1981), a person can conspire to commit an impossible offence or attempt to commit one, provided in each case the person accused of the conspiracy or attempt intends the ultimate crime to be committed.

Thus, where D and E agree that they will murder P, D shoots at P's heart, but P is already dead; D and E are guilty of statutory conspiracy to murder, and D of attempted murder. In *Anderton v Ryan* (1985) a defendant bought goods she thought were stolen, but which were not. Unexpectedly, the House of Lords allowed her appeal against conviction. But within a year the House had used the Practice Direction of 1966 to correct its own previous *ratio decidendi*. This was the case in *R v Shivpuri* (1986), where the defendant thought he was illegally importing drugs into the UK. In fact he had a suitcase of snuff! He was convicted of attempting the offence he thought he was committing. The House of Lords only discussed the law of attempts but presumably this decision on attempts would apply by analogy to statutory conspiracy.

Criminal Law

The existence of a criminal law is a confirmation that a society exists. The criminal law marks out the boundaries of acceptable conduct, so that, ideally, everyone can refer to the law when planning his affairs, in order to keep himself within those boundaries, and not outside them. This is not to say that all undesirable conduct should be made criminal. Adultery is an activity which has adverse consequences for society, but is not at present deemed a legal wrong.

The criminal law sets out to identify criminal conduct. The *actus reus* of each crime identifies the conduct, circumstances and consequences which are forbidden and the *mens rea* identifies the accompanying fault which completes the crime. It is important to recognise that it is only when these coincide that there should be criminal liability. A taking of another's property should not be criminal if done innocently, nor should there be liability for criminal thoughts, or *mens rea* alone. But as in tort, the law seeks to nip criminal activity in the bud and allows the criminal process to run when there has merely been an incitement, conspiracy or attempt. It would be a foolish system indeed which could not prevent the planning of crimes.

The reader will have noticed that crimes can be classed in many ways, all useful. There are statutory and common law crimes; crimes of intention, recklessness and negligence, or of no fault at all; crimes of basic and specific intent. Further, as this law is an attempt at balancing the competing interests of the state and of citizens, there are the defences. These again are divided between those which, when applicable, deny or negate *mens rea* and those which recognise the existence of mens rea but which justify the commission of the crime.

However, in all cases there will be an *actus reus* and a *mens rea*, and each crime should be approached accordingly, looking systematically in the crimes definition for the prohibited conduct, circumstances and consequences, and the prescribed fault, and checking that definition against the facts of any set problem to see if the whole *actus reus* and *mens rea* is proved on those facts.

PART IV

THE LAW OF CIVIL LIBERTIES

Chapter 27

The Nature of Civil Liberties

'It is the common fate of the indolent to see their rights become a prey to the active. The condition upon which God hath given liberty to man is eternal vigilance.' John Philpot Curran, 1790

'The price of freedom is eternal vigilance.' Edmund Burke

27.1 Introduction

It is interesting that writers in the area of civil liberties have stressed this element of watching. Nowhere else in law, save perhaps in the neo-European bureaucracy, are we told to watch for Byron's Assyrian, coming 'like a wolf on the fold'. Nowhere else is there an unease about the changes being made. So what are the changes we are advised to watch out for, and why are these changes so important?

The answer lies in the very subject matter of civil liberties. It goes without saying that the law consists of duties and rights: duties of care, duties to drive carefully, rights to sue for a debt, rights to return goods, and so on. But we are concerned here with rights which are more important than commercial rights, or even than rights of safety perhaps. Here, we are considering rights so important, so fundamental, indeed so necessary to the human condition, that whereas the commercial rights mentioned above might justifiably be excluded or otherwise lost, these should be regarded as inalienable.

But straightaway we run into problems of terminology. This Part is headed civil 'liberties', Curran uses both 'rights' and 'liberty'. In *Malone v MPC (No 2)* (1979), the applicant sought a declaration that the tapping of his telephone by the police had been unlawful. Megarry VC refused the application saying that in the absence of any restriction, English law allows everyone to do as he likes. Thus, he said, a man can smoke cigarettes, not because there is an express right to do so, but because there is no provision saying he cannot do so. Thus, there is a liberty to smoke (or at that time, to tap telephones: now changed, see later), without the need for an express right to do so.

The problem arises when the state seeks to impose a restriction. Let us use another example: the liberty or right to carry a gun. Presumably, English law being silent, Englishmen were at liberty to bear arms in the 18th and earlier centuries. At sometime, before or after then, restrictions were passed to cover highwaymen, poachers and possibly even dwellers, until today, in a heavily regulated field of law, our liberty to carry a loaded firearm is very narrow. Compare the citizen of the US Amendment 2 to that Constitution says, '... the right of the people to keep and bear arms shall not be infringed'. Thus no inroad can be made on that right by the state.

In summary, then, a liberty does not need express creation, but it can be eroded; a right does need express creation, but once created it is inalienable (unless the constitution itself allows for this). We have to remember, then, that English law consists mainly of liberties. (The supporters of the European Convention on Human Rights will point to its 'rights' in justification of its becoming law in the UK, but these are qualified by let-out clauses, and can in any case be removed in times of unrest: more about this later.)

Having established part of the nature of the subject matter, we can now review that subject matter itself. Perhaps the most fundamental liberty, or freedom, is that of the person, from unjustified arrest, search and detention; this Part will then consider freedom of property, from entry, search and seizure by the police; freedom of association, assembly and demonstration, to meet and protest, within the bounds of public order; freedom of expression, to speak, write, caricature, paint or draw, dance or play music, without hindrance or censorship; freedom of information to know what information is held and used which concerns you, and to pass it on (linked to this is a right to privacy, keeping information about you from others); and, increasingly curtailed, freedom of access to the courts. There are others, not covered here: freedom of family life, religion etc, and freedom from discrimination (though on what grounds: age? political view? dress?). Indeed it should be remembered that freedoms usually reflect current value-judgments either the community's or even the world's. Consider here the status of females in the UK and across the world, and whether the Sex Discrimination Act 1975, the Abortion Act 1967 and the Prohibition of Female Circumcision Act 1985 are examples of western enlightenment and moral confidence or of moral corruption and decline.

It is argued, then, that these rights are so important that they should be treated differently from other legal rights; further, that the people should not be deprived of them, either at all, or at least without some special, cautionary process.

27.1.1   Constitutional law

As well as being part of the civil and criminal laws, these rights are also part of the Constitutional law, ie the law that defines the position of a person within the legal state to which he belongs (or aspires to belong). These rights will clearly cause friction between the individual and the state, and not surprisingly it is after times of extreme social unrest that these rights are entrenched into a *Constitution* or *Declaration*.

> 'We hold these truths to be self-evident, that all men are created equal, that they are endowed by their Creator with certain unalienable Rights, that among these are Life, Liberty and the pursuit of Happiness.' *Declaration of Independence of the 13 United States of America* (1776)

> 'Recognition of the inherent dignity and of the equal and inalienable rights of all members of the human family is the foundation of freedom, justice and peace in the world.' *Universal Declaration of Human Rights* (1948) (United Nations)

> 'Fundamental freedoms which are the foundation of justice and peace in the world are best maintained on the one hand by an effective political democracy and on the other by a common understanding and observance of the human rights upon which they depend.' *European Convention on Human Rights* (1953)

States having a Charter or Declaration of fundamental rights are said to have a 'written constitution'. The UK does not have a written constitution, its constitution consisting of the 'ordinary law of the land' (AV Dicey, a Victorian constitutional lawyer), that is, common law and statute. It is said to have an unwritten constitution. Nor is the British judiciary bound by the United Nations Declaration or the European Convention. The nearest the UK comes to a written constitution are Magna Carta 1215, the Bill of Rights 1688 and the Act of Settlement 1700, although the European treaties are also now part of our constitution.

How are such fundamental rights and liberties safeguarded in the UK?

In the US, where there is a true separation of powers, between the legislature (who make the laws), the executive (who implement them), and the judiciary (who adjudicate on and interpret them), the Supreme Court has power to declare a statute unconstitutional, and void, if it contravenes the fundamental rights of the constitution. But in England, it was said by Lord Reid in *BRB v Pickin* (1974) that:

> 'In earlier times many learned lawyers seem to have believed that an Act of Parliament could be disregarded in so far as it was contrary to the law of God or the law of nature or natural justice, but since the supremacy of Parliament was finally demonstrated by the Revolution of 1688 any such idea has become obsolete.'

Thus, statute law, British, or European Community, is supreme. It is only when considering foreign law that the court has the luxury of declaring it to be against human rights. In *Oppenheimer v Cattermole* (1975), the question arose: should the English courts recognise a Nazi law that deprived German Jews resident abroad of their nationality and which confiscated their property? A majority of four Lords of Appeal condemned it as 'so grave an infringement of human rights that the courts of this country ought to refuse to recognise it as a law at all'. But the other Lord of Appeal and two Lords Justices of Appeal (in the Court of Appeal) felt bound to yield to the 'supremacy' of the Nazi legislature.

A further problem: If there is a body of fundamental laws, should it override every inferior type of legislation? How fundamental should it be?

The main problem arising out of a declaration of fundamental rights is that if there is general fundamental rule giving the people an absolute power, for example, Article 10(1), European Convention on Human Rights:

'Everyone has the right to freedom of expression (which) shall include freedom to hold opinions' etc, then government of a modern state would be almost impossible. It is not therefore surprising that such rules are hedged in by numerous restrictions, leaving the general rule very little scope. For example, Article 10(2) continues:

'The exercise of these freedoms ... may be subject to such formalities, conditions, restrictions or penalties as are prescribed by law and are necessary in a democratic society, in the interests of national security, territorial integrity or public safety, for the prevention of disorder or crime, for the protection of health or morals, for the protection of the reputation or rights of others, for preventing the disclosure of information received in confidence, or for maintaining the authority and impartiality of the judiciary.'

Such restrictions admit one very important point: that whether under a written constitution, or under the English system, freedom in any area is bound, realistically, to be relative.

When we talk of freedom, we therefore mean freedom under the law. (The excuse of state necessity within the defence of necessity in Part II on Tort makes an interesting study here.)

27.1.2   The European Convention of Human Rights and English law

We have mentioned the European Convention Human Rights several times. The UK has signed it, but has not ratified it. The problem for the courts is then: is the Convention binding on

English courts? In *R v Secretary of State for the Home Department ex p Brind* (1990), a judicial review of the banning of transmission on television or radio of interviews with members of the Provisional Irish Republican Army (IRA), Lord Ackner said:

> 'The treaty, not having been incorporated in British law, cannot be a source of rights or obligations and the question – did the Secretary of State act in breach of Article 10 – does not therefore arise ...'

To impose a duty under Article 10

> 'would be to incorporate the convention into domestic law by the back door.'

Further, in *Derbyshire County Council v Times Newspapers* (1993) it was said that the Convention could only be used in the case of an ambiguity in English law, which was not the case there. And in *R v Khan (Sultan)* (1996), where the police obtained incriminating evidence that Khan was involved in the importation of illegal drugs by bugging private premises which Khan visited, and where Khan then claimed a breach of his right to privacy under Article 8 of the Convention, Lord Nolan in the main speech in the House of Lords said 'we are not concerned with the view which the European Court of Human Rights might have taken of the facts of the present case. Its decision is no more part of our law than the convention itself'. But as he had said earlier, 'That is not to say that the principles reflected in the convention are irrelevant ... They could hardly be irrelevant, because they embody so many of the familiar principles of our own law and of our concept of justice'.

It is noteworthy that, in his first interview since taking office, Lord Irvine of Lairg, the Lord Chancellor (*The Observer* 27 July 1997) stated that the European Convention would be incorporated into the law of the United Kingdom in the present Parliamentary session. He added that a model closer to that in New Zealand (where the courts cannot strike down Acts of Parliament) would be adopted rather than that in Canada (where they can).

However, the result of a case can prompt the British government to introduce legislation. Thus, when the European Court of Human Rights (sitting at Strasbourg; not to be confused with the European Court of Justice, of the European Community, sitting at Luxembourg) decided that the House of Lords' imposition of an injunction to prohibit press discussion of the thalidomide affair was in breach of Article 10, the government passed the Contempt of Court Act 1981, s 5 of which allows discussion. And when the European Court decided that telephone-tapping was in breach of the Convention the government passed the Interception of Communications Act 1985 which made it a crime.

Chapter 28

Freedom of the Person

Under English criminal law a person is generally only liable to custody after conviction. However, earlier than this, and while still presumed innocent, he can be arrested for an offence. Article 5(1)(c) of the European Convention recognises that:

> 'Everyone has the right to liberty and security of person. No one shall be deprived of his liberty save in the following cases and in accordance with a procedure prescribed by law: ... (c) the lawful arrest or detention of a person effected for the purpose of bringing him before the competent legal authority on reasonable suspicion of having committed an offence or when it is reasonably considered necessary to prevent his committing an offence or fleeing after having done so.'

28.1 Arrest

Arrest can be made with or without a warrant obtained from a magistrate. A policeman is protected from action in tort provided he acts within the terms of the warrant (ie arrests the right man etc), but he need not have the warrant on him at the time of arrest, so long as he can show it to the arrested person as soon as practicable.

28.1.1 Arrest without a warrant

As it would be ridiculous to insist that a policeman who sees a robbery must go to seek out a magistrate for a warrant, it is reasonable to allow summary arrest (ie without judicial intervention) in certain circumstances.

Thus, summary arrest may be made:

(a) primarily under the Police and Criminal Evidence Act 1984; and

(b) at common law for breach of the peace; and

(c) under certain specific statutes (for example, terrorists under the Prevention of Terrorism (Temporary Measures) Act 1989); these last need not detain us here.

(a) Police and Criminal Evidence Act 1984

It was intended that this Act would contain all the police powers of arrest without warrant, other than those in categories (b) and (c), above. But the Public Order Act 1986 and the Criminal Justice and Public Order Act 1994 have since created further powers of arrest specific to those Acts. The 1984 Act covers two situations:

(i) *Summary arrest by a policeman or private citizen*

Section 24 (re-enacting previous law in s 2 Criminal Law Act 1967) gives a power to arrest for an 'arrestable offence'. This is an offence where the sentence is fixed by law (eg murder), or the offence carries a sentence of at least five years' imprisonment, eg most Theft Acts, Criminal Damage Act and Offences against the Person Act (plus manslaughter and rape) offences and the Protection from Harassment Act 1997 (but not the common law offences of common assault and battery) or for certain other offences which escape the five-year net, eg all Official Secrets Acts offences, ss 12 ('joyriding') and 25 (going equipped for stealing or burglary or cheating) Theft Act 1968. Section 24 extends to the inchoate offences of these offences (incitement, conspiracy and attempt).

A policeman can arrest any person who is committing, has committed, or is about to commit an arrestable offence, or whom he has reasonable grounds to suspect to be committing, about to commit, or to have committed an arrestable offence. The House of Lords in *O'Hara v Chief Constable of the RUC* (1997), an action in tort for a wrongful arrest, has confirmed that s 24 requires the arresting officer to have in his own mind the reasonable grounds for suspicion. This was the fact of that case, where the officer had attended a briefing by his superior officer about a murder. The information given at the briefing was held at the trial to have been sufficient to give the officer reason to suspect the plaintiff. The Lords said that s 24 is more stringent than Article 5(1)(c) (see the start of this chapter) which is more flexible and requires simply that there is 'reasonable suspicion' as an objective test.

As to what is 'reasonable' the case of *Castorina v Chief Constable of Surrey* (1988) assists. Here a company's premises had been burgled. The police thought it was an 'inside job'. A director told the police that the plaintiff had just been dismissed, and the papers taken would have been useful to someone with a grudge, but that he did not think it was the plaintiff. The plaintiff had no criminal record, but was arrested. She sued and won damages at the trial, the judge saying that the police should have made further enquiries. But the Court of Appeal reversed the decision, saying that there was no need to 'probe every explanation' or 'make all presently practicable enquiries'.

A private citizen can arrest any person who is committing an arrestable offence, or he has reasonable grounds to suspect to be committing an arrestable offence, also, where an arrestable offence has in fact been committed, a person who has committed it or whom he has reasonable grounds to suspect has committed it.

In *Walters v WH Smiths* (1914), Smiths suspected an employee was stealing books from their bookstand. Having marked some books, Smiths visited his home, to find the marked books. Smiths arrested him, and in due course the employee stood trial. Surprisingly, however, the jury believed him when he said he intended to pay for them. Thus, no offence had in fact been committed, so no power of arrest was available, and Smiths were held liable in tort. A similar case is *R v Self* (1992), where a store detective wrongly assumed that a shopper had stolen a chocolate bar he picked up off the floor and walked out of the shop with.

(ii) *Arrest by a policeman for a non-arrestable offence*

Section 25 is a new power in so far as it extends to the whole country. If a policeman has reasonable grounds to suspect that a person is committing or has committed a non-arrestable offence (attempts included) he can still arrest that person if he thinks that service of a summons on him will be impracticable because either the policeman does not know that person's name, or the policeman reasonably suspects whether the person has given his true name, or the person has not given a satisfactory address for service, or the policeman reasonably thinks arrest is necessary to prevent the person causing injury or damage, or committing an offence against public decency in a public place, or an obstruction of the highway, or the policeman reasonably thinks arrest is necessary to protect a child or other 'vulnerable person'.

In *Nicholas v Parsonage* (1987), a boy who persisted in riding his bike with no hands after being told by two policemen not to, and who refused to give his name and address when asked by them, was held to have been correctly arrested after the policemen had informed that he was committing a road traffic offence (for which he was subsequently convicted). It was not necessary to say why they wanted his name and address.

(b) Arrest at common law for breach of the peace

> '... there is a breach of the peace whenever harm is actually done or is likely to be done to a person or in his presence to his property or a person is in fear of being so harmed through an assault, an affray, a riot ... or other disturbance' *(R v Howell* (1981)).

> The harm 'must be unlawful harm' *(McBean v Parker* (1983)).

A private citizen (including a policeman) in whose presence a breach of the peace is being committed, or who reasonably expects one to be committed immediately (whether or not one has yet been committed) can take reasonable steps to prevent it (including by arrest) *(R v Howell* (1981)). All citizens have this power. It is no defence for the person arrested to say that he did not believe the person arresting him was a policeman. Thus, in *Albert v Lavin* (1981), it was no excuse for a man pushing into a bus queue to justify resisting his arrester because he did not believe him when he said he was a policeman. As the House of Lords said, it would have been a valid arrest whether by policeman or by private citizen.

28.1.2	**The use of force at the time of arrest (whether with or without a warrant)**

Two statutes justify the use of reasonable force when making the arrest. Both s 117 of the 1984 Act and s 3 Criminal Law Act 1967 cover policemen, but s 3 covers anyone who makes an arrest:

> 'A person may use such force as is reasonable in the circumstances in the prevention of crime, or in effecting or assisting in the lawful arrest of offenders or suspected offenders or of persons unlawfully at large.'

In the remarkable case of *R v Renouf* (1986) the arrest was made by forcing another car off the road. The occupants of the arrested car had thrown something at the arrester's car, who gave chase and made the arrest as mentioned above. His conviction for reckless driving was quashed on appeal on account of s 3.

Another matter concerns the information to be given on arrest. Section 28 mainly re-enacts the common law. The person detained must be told as soon as is practicable that he is under arrest and the ground for the arrest. He must be told even where the fact of arrest or the ground is obvious (formerly there was no need). Until he is told the arrest is not lawful. If he escapes before being told, he will still be taken to have been lawfully arrested.

It is interesting to compare s 28 with Article 5(2), which says, 'Everyone who is arrested shall be informed promptly in a language which he understands of the reason for his arrest'. In *Wheatley v Lodge* (1971) the arresting policemen did not realise that the man they were speaking to was deaf, and did not realise that he was being arrested (which the court held that he had been).

Clearly, the correct ground for arrest must be told. Thus, in the former leading case, *Christie v Leachinsky* (1947), an arrest of a man suspected of wartime theft was held invalid as the policemen, instead of telling him this reason, told him that they were arresting him under the equivalent of the present s 25, as they did not know his name. In fact, they knew full well who he was; thus the 's 25' power was not available, and the policemen had thus committed a tort against him.

But s 28 does not require any particular form of words. In *Christie v Leachinsky* Lord Simon said: 'The requirement that he should be so informed does not mean that technical or precise language need be used.'

This was applied in *Abbassy v MPC* (1990), where the reason was acceptably given as 'for unlawful possession' of a car.

One final matter which can arise at this stage is the caution. Code of Practice C.10.4 requires a person being questioned with a view to obtaining evidence to be cautioned in these words:

> 'You do not have to say anything. But it may harm your defence if you do not mention when questioned something which you later rely on in court. Anything you do say may be given in evidence.'

(Research in 1995 cited by The Law Society found that when the caution was said in full, 86% of the general population did not understand the second sentence.)

The effect of ss 34–37 Criminal Justice and Police Act 1994 required this new caution. This new Act allows adverse comment at the trial where, after caution, a suspect fails to mention either a fact relied on in a later defence or a 'fact which [he] could reasonably have been expected to mention' (s 34), or after arrest, a failure to 'account for the presence of an object, substance or mark' (s 36) or, after arrest, a failure to account for his presence at a place where and at a time at which an offence is alleged to have been committed (s 37). (See further at 28.8.2 below – the right to silence.)

Clearly the first thing a policeman will want to do after an arrest is search the arrested person. Section 32 of the 1984 Act states that where the arrest takes place other than at a police station, a policeman can search the arrested person, if he thinks

28.2   After the arrest

he may be dangerous, or for anything which might be used in making an escape, or which might be evidence of 'an offence'. The policeman may only order the removal of outer clothing, and he may seize any dangerous items or evidence.

The arrested person must then be taken as soon as practicable to a police station designated by the Chief Constable as one for the detention of arrested persons.

But a policeman on his own when he arrests someone can take him to any station if the person is dangerous, but he must be taken to a designated station within six hours. The policeman can also carry out reasonable investigations first. Thus, in *Dallison v Caffery* (1964), it was acceptable to arrest a man in Clapton, take him 34 miles to Dunstable, where the alleged offence had taken place, to a house to verify his alibi then to search his own house and, finally, after seven hours, to a police station.

Where the arrest is made by a private citizen he must deliver the arrested person to a policeman or a magistrate within a reasonable time, but even here a delay might be justifiable. In *John Lewis & Co Ltd v Tims* (1952) a person arrested by a 'store detective' was detained in the chief detective's room to await his arrival and that of a manager, who would make the decision whether they would be handed over to the police, which they were after about an hour. It was held reasonable to wait for the arrival of a senior employee to make the decision.

28.3 Where a person is not under arrest

We have so far looked at the process of arrest. At one time, at common law, a person was either under arrest or he was not, and if not he could not be 'detained for questioning', or made to answer any questions. If the police wanted to divert him from his business, they had to arrest him. In *Rice v Connolly* (1966), two policemen saw Rice loitering in an area where there had been some burglaries; they asked him his name and address, where he had come from and where he was going to. He gave his surname and the street he said he lived in. When asked to accompany them to a police box to check the information, he refused, and was arrested for wilfully obstructing a policeman in the execution of his duty (now s 89(2) Police Act 1996, below). Lord Parker CJ, quashing his conviction, said:

> '... the sole question here is whether the defendant had a lawful excuse for refusing to answer the questions put to him. In my judgment he had. It seems to me quite clear that though every citizen has a moral duty or, if you like, a social duty to assist the police, there is no legal duty to that effect, and indeed the whole basis of the common law is

the right of the individual to refuse to answer questions put to him by persons in authority, and to refuse to accompany those in authority to any particular place, short, of course, of arrest.'

Stirring words indeed, and s 29 reinforces this by confirming that where a person attends voluntarily at a police station he is free to leave at will. But Parliament has gradually filled in the once clear gap between arrest and complete freedom.

We have seen that Rice could not be forced to give information without arrest, but some statutes impose a duty to volunteer information (Prevention of Terrorism (Temporary Measures) Act 1989): any person with information relating to terrorist activities who fails to inform the police is guilty of an offence, or at least a duty to answer questions (under the Road Traffic Act 1988, if a driver is asked by a policeman).

Furthermore, under s 1 of the new Act can stop and search, without arrest, any person, vehicle or thing in or on a vehicle for stolen or prohibited articles such as knives or implements for use in burglary or theft. The stop and search must take place in public and on the ground that he reasonably suspected he would find such articles. If he finds such articles, he can seize them.

Section 66 Metropolitan Police Act 1839 contained a similar provision. So did many local Acts. However, because the power was not national, and the police were sometimes at a disadvantage when they did not have the power (eg at football matches), it was decided to replace s 66 and the local Acts with the national s 1.

There are, however, safeguards to s 1. Before the search the policeman must, if not in uniform, show proof that he is a policeman; he must give his name, station, the purpose of the search and his grounds for suspicion; but he cannot require the person to remove more than outer clothing. After the search, he must make a full record of the search (including purpose, grounds and what was found). The person searched, or owner of a vehicle searched, can request a copy; and the annual report of each police force must contain the number of s 1 searches made and the number of persons arrested (by months).

But did we think Parliament would stop there? Section 60 Criminal Justice and Public Order Act 1994 allows a police superintendent or above to allow stop and search of persons and vehicles where 'serious violence' may take place. This power lasts for 24 hours (extendible by six hours). And the same Act added s 13A to the Prevention of Terrorism (Temporary Measures) Act 1989 (see 28.7 below), allowing stop and search of vehicles and passengers for 28 days (extendible by another 28 days) in a specified locality, in order to prevent acts of terrorism. Section 13B was added (by the Prevention of Terrorism (Additional Powers) Act 1996 and rushed through Parliament in 24 hours) to allow stop and search of pedestrians for 28 days (ceasing if the Home Secretary does not confirm the superintendent's order within two days).

The reader may ask: but what do s 60, s 13A and s 13B add to s 1? There is erosion of liberty in two ways. Firstly, these powers are capable of being invoked where it is 'expedient' to do so to prevent serious violence or acts of terrorism. What does 'expedient' mean? How close is it to 'convenient'? Why is 'necessary' not used, a word commonly used in the European Commission on Human Rights (see Chapter 27, 27.1.1 above)? Secondly, the two safeguards are missing from these new powers: the requirements of 'reasonable grounds for suspicion' and of making a full record afterwards. After s 1 of the 1984 Act we thought these requirements were essential to getting the balance right. Were we wrong? Are these safeguards too lenient?

And as if that was not enough, the road check powers are evolving into easier powers merely to divert people away (see Chapter 29, 29.3 below).

It is of course open to a person subjected to these powers to object or resist, but this would be unwise. Section 89(2) Police Act 1996 makes it an offence to wilfully obstruct a policeman who is acting in the execution of his duty; but it is not always clear when he is doing so. A policewoman was not doing so in *Collins v Wilcock* (1984); she had unlawfully taken the defendant's arm so that resistance by assaulting her was justified.

But it seems to be within a policeman's duty to attract a person's attention by tapping him on the shoulder (*Donnelly v Jackman* (1970)). And there also seems to be a difference between peaceful refusal to communicate, as in *Rice v Connolly*, above, and an aggressive refusal. In *Ricketts v Cox* (1982), where police tried to question a black youth in an area where an assault had just been committed by a black youth. The defendant was not simply uncooperative, but aggressively and rudely so, walking away from the policemen eventually, before they could finish their questions. The defendant was convicted of the predecessor of s 89(2). (Actually touching the policeman would be the offence of assaulting a policeman who is acting in the execution of his duty (s 89(1) Police Act 1996). Note, however, that neither offence under s 51 contains a power of arrest without warrant that must be found within s 25 or the law on breach of the peace, both above.)

A recent further error of *Rice v Connolly* is mentioned at 28.1.3 above. The fact that adverse comment can now be made at trial on a failure to answer police questions after caution (even before arrest: see s 34 Criminal Justice and Public Order Act 1994) also means that pressure to speak is eroding the principle of that case.

The sole authority for police detention is the 1984 Act. Under s 41 the maximum police detention without charge is 24 hours.

28.4   Detention

But for 'serious arrestable offences', there are extensions where detention is necessary to get or preserve evidence (from arrested person or elsewhere), and the 'investigation is being conducted diligently and expeditiously'. (Would a police report admit to the contrary?)

Thus, under s 42 a police superintendent can order a further detention of 12 hours (the detained person or his solicitor can make 'representations' to the superintendent). Under s 43 a magistrates' court can order a further detention of 36 hours (there is a right to attend and instruct solicitor in order to address the bench). Under s 44 the magistrates' court can order a final 24 hours detention, making 96 hours in total for 'serious arrestable offences'. These are, of course, maximum periods. The maximum period before the new Act was about 48 hours, so the general 24 hour maximum is an improvement; but how many offences fall within 'serious arrestable offences'?

By s 116, 'serious arrestable offence' fall into two categories:

- those serious by their very nature, such as treason, murder, manslaughter, rape, kidnapping, hostage-taking, hijacking and a few others; and

- any arrestable offence causing, intended or likely to cause, or a threat which if carried out is likely to cause serious harm to national security or public order, or serious interference with administration of justice or investigation of offences, or death or serious injury, or substantial financial gain or serious financial loss. (The word 'serious' is not defined, and is therefore left to be interpreted by the court, but loss is 'serious' if it is serious for the victim.)

At the end of the time-limit, he must be charged, or let free, or released on bail without charge. But if at any time he is charged but detained by the police, he must be taken before the magistrates the same day, or the next day (s 46).

28.5 Treatment while in police detention

Before the 1984 Act some of the following matters were dealt with by the Judges' Rules, first formulated in 1912. These were not rules of law, breach of which would rule evidence inadmissible, but rules of practice, breach of which would give the trial judge a discretion to refuse to admit the evidence as he saw fit. The Act and codes of practice replace the Judges' Rules on treatment, cautioning, questioning and other matters.

An arrested person has a right to contact a friend or relative 'if he so requests'. But a superintendent can delay it for 36 hours in the case of a 'serious arrestable offence' where he reasonably thinks that allowing it 'will' cause interference with evidence or persons, or lead to other suspects being alerted, or hinder the recovery of property (s 56). The arrested person must be informed of this right. He also has a similar right to consult a solicitor 'if he so requests', subject to the same delay for 36 hours (s 58). In *R v Samuel* (1988), access to a solicitor was refused on the ground that he might inform, albeit unwittingly, an accomplice. The conviction was quashed on appeal; s 58 says that the risk must be that the solicitor 'will' inform someone. The Court of Appeal thought it unlikely that an experienced solicitor would be hoodwinked by a 24 year old into passing a message on. It is interesting that ss 56 and 58 refer only to police custody, but not to custody under court order. In *R v Chief Constable of South Wales ex parte Merrick* (1994) right to access in that circumstance was held to exist at common law.

Further, at the European Court of Human Rights in *Murray v UK* (1996), the unjustified delay in allowing access to a solicitor during questioning was a breach of Article 6(3) of the European Convention on Human Rights, which guarantees the 'minimum right' of 'legal assistance ... when the interests of justice so require'.

There are powers of search (s 54) and intimate search (s 55), fingerprinting etc.

28.6 The effect of a breach of the Act or of a code of practice

No action in false imprisonment or battery may lie, but any evidence obtained in breach may be excluded as unfair evidence (s 78), which the court has a discretion to exclude. It was held that inventing evidence and hoodwinking both defendant and his solicitor was unfair and inadmissible (*R v Mason* (1987)). The police had falsely told both that the defendant's fingerprints had been found on a bottle which had been used for carrying inflammable liquid.

While the court still has a discretion whether to admit unfair evidence, evidence in the form of a confession will be subject to the more definite s 76, by which the court 'shall not allow it in evidence against the (defendant)' unless the prosecution proves, beyond reasonable doubt, that it was not obtained by either 'oppression of the person who made it'. For example, in *R v Hudson* (1980), a 59 year old man, with no convictions, employed in town and country planning, was arrested at 6.30 am on a Sunday, for accepting bribes. He was detained for 108 hours, was posed 700 questions, and after 105 hours confessed. The confession was disallowed. Although this was a pre-Act case, such oppressive interrogation (as took place in the more recent *R v Gopee* (1992)) would clearly be ruled as inadmissible. Section 76 also covers circumstances making the evidence 'unreliable', such as an inducement by reward or by threat.

Increased activities of the Provisional Irish Republican Army (IRA) and others, in particular, the Birmingham pub bombing in 1974 in which 21 died, prompted the passing of the Prevention of Terrorism (Temporary Measures) Act 1974, reenacted in 1976, 1984 and 1989. The Act is renewable by Parliament each year, after an initial life of five years. A 1996 Act made further provisions.

28.7   Arrest without warrant of suspected terrorists

The Act contains novel quasi-criminal sanctions and powers of arrest: For example, exclusion orders may be made excluding a person from entry into the two geographically separate parts of the UK, namely from Northern Ireland into Great Britain, or vice versa. Thus, a British citizen can be banned from a part of his own country, without conviction of any terrorist offence.

Further, s 14 gives a policeman power to arrest without warrant a person about whom he has reasonable grounds to suspect to be or to have been 'concerned in the commission, preparation or instigation of acts of terrorism'. (In this case it is recognised that the policeman need not have a specific offence in mind when making the arrest.) As to when an officer can claim to have 'reasonable grounds for suspicion', see *O'Hara v Chief Constable of RUC* (1997), at 28.1.1 above.

Significantly, too, the period of detention by the executive (and accordingly without judicial order) is two days without charge, extendible by the Home Secretary for a further five days. In *Brogan v UK* (1988), in the European Court of Human Rights, four Northern Irishmen who had been held for between four and six days complained that this was a breach of Article 5(3) of the Convention, which states that they 'shall be brought promptly before a judge'. Their claim was upheld (but the British government chose to derogate from its obligations under Article 15). But against four days, seven days does not seem so bad; indeed, against seven days, four days does not seem so bad. It must be remembered that the ordinary period of detention of a person arrested in 1974 was two days.

It is incidentally, unlikely that the Act will be replaced now that the situation in Northern Ireland has improved. The Act has also been used to arrest and detain terrorists of other countries and groups, and will continue to be useful in those cases.

| 28.8 | **Traditional bulwarks of English liberties** | We have, in this chapter, become aware that the erosion in civil liberties is a gentle, sometimes hardly perceptible process. Two areas which have received political attention, and still do, are trial by jury and the right to silence. |

28.8.1   The criminal jury

In the common law world, trial by jury has been regarded as a means of ensuring that a man was tried and punished, not merely by the state, whose motive has over the centuries been the cause of mistrust, but by his equals. Patrick Devlin, later a Lord of Appeal, in his Hamlyn Lecture of 1956, put it thus:

> 'Trial by jury is more than an instrument of justice and more than one wheel of the constitution it is the lamp that shows that freedom lives.'

The rise of summary justice, in the magistrates' courts, has caused the decline of the number of jury trials. At present about 97% of criminal trials are tried summarily; one might have thought that the modern state could afford to keep what few jury trials remained. But Blackstone, the eminent 18th century judge and writer, had already seen the future:

> '... the liberties of England cannot but subsist so long as this Palladium remains sacred and inviolate; not only from all open attacks (which none will be so hardy as to make), but also from all secret machinations, which may sap and undermine it ... Though begun in trifles, the precedent may gradually increase and spread, to the utter disuse of juries in questions of the most momentous concern.'

The post-war history of the jury is a case-study of 'sapping and undermining'.

- 1948 Abolition of the Grand Jury, its function now taken over by committal proceedings;

- 1972 In Northern Ireland jury trial is abolished in terrorist cases, recommended by the Diplock Commission;

- 1974 Juries Act 1974: majority verdicts introduced;

- 1977 Criminal Law Act 1977 made some offences summary, which were formerly either way or indictable, eg s 51(1) Police Act 1964;

- 1977 Trial of criminal damage below £400 (1992 figure) is made summary;

- 1978 Vetting of jurors admitted by Attorney General after disclosure in the 'ABC Trial' (an official secrets trial);

- 1984 Juries (Disqualification) Act 1984: prohibited people in receipt of a custodial sentence in the last 10 years, or probation in the last five years from serving as jurors;

- 1986 Roskill Committee on Fraud Trial recommends abolition of jury in fraud trials, and transfer to a tribunal system (though not implemented);

- 1988 Right of Peremptory Challenge by defence (ie without showing cause) abolished (after reductions in 1949 and 1977);

- 1980s Several recommendations to make small thefts triable summarily only;

- 1993 Royal Commission on Criminal Justice recommends curbs on jury trials, by allowing the magistrates, not the defendant, the decision on whether either way offences (including those involving dishonesty, such as theft) should go before a jury.

- 1994 The Criminal Justice and Public Order Act increased the criminal damage limit in summary trial (see 1977, above) to £5,000;

- 1994 s 40 of same Act prohibited those remanded on bail from jury service;

- 1977 Home Secretary expressed proposal to remove defendant's right to jury trial.

The 1993 recommendation produced a foreseeable polarisation of views. Lord Taylor CJ, and Lord Scarman, once Lord of Appeal, have expressed strong opposition to further tampering; but Lord Woolf, present Lord of Appeal, regarded it, in the current economic climate, as an 'undesirable necessity'. It is worth noting the Seventh Amendment to the American constitution, which preserves the right to jury trial.

The 1997 proposal was supported by evidence that one of 89,000 trials (one in about 200) in 1995 was for the theft of £2. But what sort of career does a conviction of dishonesty destroy?

28.8.2   The right to silence

In criminal cases the accused is presumed innocent: the burden of proof is on the prosecution to prove his guilt. In *Woolmington v DPP* (1935) this principle was called the 'one golden thread ... throughout the web of the English criminal law'. No-one would dispute this. The issue is, however, can the prosecution enlist the help of the defendant to prove his own guilt. The Fifth Amendment to the American Constitution prevents questioning which might cause self-incrimination.

This is broadly the position in the UK; thus, a suspect who is questioned for evidence must be cautioned, as must a person who is arrested. But since the enactment of ss 34–37 Criminal Justice and Public Order Act 1994, a criminal court may draw adverse inferences from a failure to mention a relevant fact during police questioning; or failure to account for possession of a substance or for his presence near the scene of a crime; or for failure to give evidence at trial (see 28.1.3 above).

To balance this, s 38(3) of the same Act states that a conviction cannot be based 'solely on an inference drawn from ... a failure or refusal' to answer or give evidence. In *R v Cowan* (1995) Lord Taylor CJ stated that trial judges must direct juries that the burden of proof remained on the prosecution, that the defendant was entitled to stay silent, that s 38(3) applied, and that it was only once the prosecution had proved all elements of the crime (both *actus reus* and *mens rea*: see Chapter 19) that the jury could draw inferences from the defendant's silence. In *R v Argent* (1997) Lord Bingham CJ reminded solicitors that they could advise clients not to answer if the question was not related to discovering whether or by whom a crime had been committed; other questions could be ignored. But the European Court of Human Rights, in *Murray v UK* (1996) took a weaker line on the Northern Ireland equivalent of ss 34–37, conceding that it allowed 'common sense implications to play an open role in the assessment of evidence'.

In fraud cases the pressure to speak is even greater. In the UEC at large, s 2 Criminal Justice Act 1987, empowers the director of the Serious Fraud Office, in fraud cases, to ask questions or to insist on production of documents, in either case on pain of criminal prosecution. The Royal Commission on Criminal Justice in 1993 has recommended that the s 2 power be extended to the fraud investigation group of the Crown Prosecution Service, the police, and even to foreign investigating authorities. Serious fraud is of course an important matter: the Maxwell case shows that. However, it remains to be seen whether this is the start of another saga of 'sapping and undermining'.

Certainly the next step has been taken. The Criminal Procedure and Investigations Act 1996, in all contested cases, requires that, once the prosecution has disclosed to the defence evidence which might help it, the defence must disclose to the prosecution the nature of the defence, the matters on which the defence takes issue, the reasons for its doing so, and any alibi defence (ie evidence to support a defence that the defendant was elsewhere when the crime was committed). The reward for the defence is that the prosecution must then disclose any evidence which might assist the defences which the defendant has stated its intention to use.

Chapter 29

Freedom of Property

Article 8 of the European Convention states that:

> 'Everyone has the right to respect for his private and family life, his home and his correspondence.'

And Article 1 of the First Protocol to the Convention states:

> 'Every natural or legal person is entitled to the peaceful enjoyment of his possessions. No one shall be deprived of his possessions except in the public interest and subject to the conditions provided for by law and by the general principles of international law.'

However, entry onto premises to search for evidence of crime can be made with or without a search warrant. The warrants are issued under various statutes, but by s 15 of the 1984 Act, all must contain certain details: the name of the policeman applying for it, the statutory power being used, the premises to be searched, the articles sought, and the date of issue. But, surprisingly, not the offence also. Surprisingly, because in *Entick v Carrington* (1765) 'general warrants', that is, blank warrants, were declared unlawful. But in *Inland Revenue Commissioners v Rossminster Ltd* (1980), where Revenue men staged a 'military style operation' based on a warrant for 'tax fraud', the House of Lords held this to be satisfactory. The Revenue could not specify an exact offence until they saw what evidence they seized.

The old rules of seizure were confused, but in no-nonsense style, s 19 now empowers he who is 'lawfully on any premises' to seize anything where he reasonably believes the thing is stolen, or evidence of any offence, and seizure is necessary to prevent it being concealed, lost, altered etc.

Warrants issued after a 'serious arrestable offence' are subject to greater control. Under s 8 a magistrate can issue a warrant to enter, and search for and seize evidence 'of substantial value to the investigation' of a serious arrestable offence', but not 'excluded material' which is held in confidence, namely personal records, human tissue or fluid for diagnosis, journalistic material, or 'special procedure material', that is, material acquired or created in the course of trade, profession etc and held in confidence, or journalistic material other than documents or records. These materials require the decision of a Circuit Judge.

The code contained in s 8 and s 9 is quite liberal, but the courts have been faced with issues of whether the suspect should be informed of an application relating to his documents in the custody of his bank or solicitors, but behind his back. Clearly, a suspect who is so informed can remove his documents, and the decisions have borne that fear in mind. A s 8 application is *ex parte* (the applicant only appears); a s 9 application is *inter partes* (both sides can appear); but *partes* means the police and the person holding the material, not the suspect (*R v Leicester Crown Court ex p DPP* (1987)). Nor is there a duty on a banker to tell his or her customer that a s 9 application is being made against the bank in respect of that customer (*Barclays Bank v Taylor* (1989)).

Further, lawyers' communications, between a person, his solicitor and his barrister, are privileged. However, in *R v Central Criminal Court ex p Francis and Francis* (1988), such documents were held subject to access if there was an intention to use them for criminal purposes, even if the purpose is that of third party.

Finally, in *R v Bristol Crown Court ex p Bristol Press and Picture Agency Ltd* (1986) press photographs of riots at St Paul's, Bristol were ordered to be produced, despite the fear among photographers that once it was known that a man was filming a riot, and that the police now had access to the film, the safety of the photographer would be put in jeopardy.

Entry can also be made without a warrant, under s 17 to make an arrest, and under s 18, after an arrest (with or without warrant) for an arrestable offence (not serious), for evidence of that arrestable offence, or any other arrestable offence 'connected with or similar to that offence'. But once he is 'lawfully on the premises', s 19, above, will apply. Lawyers' communications are excluded from ss 18 and 19. And entry to stop or prevent a breach of the peace can be made, even on private premises (*McConnell v Chief Constable of Greater Manchester Police* (1990)), but not to stop and search under s 1.

But will this scheme fall into disuse given the arrival of police powers to give themselves authorisation to 'interfere with property', as s 93 Police Act 1997 puts it? 'Interference' here means 'such action [as a chief constable or his deputising assistant] may specify' and 'such action as he may specify in respect of wireless telegraphy'. In short, a chief constable can authorise his force to enter, seize property or 'bug' premises, vehicles and other things and places. The evidence to be gained must not be reasonably obtainable by other methods and must be of 'substantial value in the prevention or detection of serious crime' (ie involving violence, substantial financial gain, or offences of at least three years' imprisonment for a first offence, or a 'large number of persons in pursuit of a common purpose'). High Court judges may be appointed Commissioners, but their leave is only required to get knowledge of matters concerning legal privilege, personal or journalistic confidentiality, or to enter or 'bug' an office, dwelling or bedroom. A Chief Commissioner must make an annual report to the Prime Minister, who may censor it if need be, before laying it before Parliament. No appeal can be made in any court against a Commissioner (s 91).

The reader may wonder at the daring of these police self-authorisation provisions, and note the low threshold of three years' imprisonment (compare this with five years for an 'arrestable offence': see 28.1.1 above), and wonder why a judge cannot perform these functions as a judge rather than as a Commissioner of three years' tenure (see too the start of this trend of ousting the jurisdiction of the courts, at Chapter 31, 31.11.2 below).

Chapter 30

Freedom of Assembly

Article 11 of the European Convention says that:

'Everyone has the right to freedom of peaceful assembly and to freedom of association with others.'

But sub-article (2) concedes that:

'No restrictions shall be placed on the exercise of these rights other than such as are prescribed by law and are necessary in a democratic society in the interests of national security or public safety, for the prevention of disorder or crime ... or the protection of the rights and freedoms of others.'

Even the Convention recognises that any right of assembly will be the result of compromise. Indeed, Lord Scarman in the *Red Lion Square Disorders – Report of Inquiry* (1974) said:

'A balance has to be struck, a compromise found ... Violent demonstrators by creating public disorder infringe a fundamental human right which belongs to the rest of us: excessively violent police reaction to public disorder infringes the rights of the protesters. The one and the other are an affront to civilised living.'

It is noteworthy that Lord Scarman assumed a right to protest to exist; he said elsewhere in the Report: 'Amongst our fundamental human rights there are, without doubt, the rights of peaceful assembly and public protest.' In *Duncan v Jones* (1936), however, Lord Hewart CJ said, 'English law does not recognise any special right of public meeting for political or other purposes.' Clearly, it is not at all clear that there is any right to assemble, or whether this is a liberty. Certainly, the law is restrictive rather than establishing rights or privileges.

30.1 Restrictions on the place of assembly

Bailey, Harris and Jones in *Civil Liberties: Cases and Materials* usefully separate the law into restrictions on the place of assembly, and on its conduct. Thus, the first hurdle is: where to assemble? The highway is the most obvious place, but both the criminal law and the civil law impose restrictions.

An assembly which wilfully obstructs the highway is an offence under s 137 Highways Act 1980. In *Hirst & Agu v Chief Constable of West Yorkshire* (1986) the convictions of two animal rights supporters who were arrested while handing out leaflets or holding a banner outside a fur shop in a busy pedestrian precinct were acquitted on appeal as the wilfulness, or deliberateness, of their obstruction had not been proved. But in *Arrowsmith v Jenkins* (1963) the defendant was held to have committed this offence (under a previous statute) by attracting a crowd to hear her speak, partially obstructing a street for some 20 minutes at a place where others had spoken in the past with impunity. This was part of her complaint, that her prosecution was a form of victimisation, but, as Lord Parker CJ put it, 'that ... has nothing to do with this court'.

Another offence committed when unreasonably obstructing the highway is public nuisance. In *R v Clark (No 2)* (1964), the defendant, a member of the Campaign for Nuclear Disarmament, was acquitted on appeal for inciting crowds to block London streets during a visit of the King of Greece. At his trial, the distinction had not been drawn between mere obstruction and reasonable user, the latter being necessary for a conviction of public nuisance. Clearly, therefore, prosecutions for the former can be expected to be more common than under the latter.

Wrongful use of the highway might also amount to the torts of trespass to land and private nuisance. In *Harrison v Rutland* (1893) the plaintiff sued the Duke of Rutland, whose servants had manhandled the plaintiff, who was on a road, the subsoil of which was owned by the Duke. He had been frightening away grouse by opening and shutting his umbrella, a use of the road hardly consistent with the 'right to pass and re-pass ... for the purpose of legitimate travel'. Interference by obstruction of access to premises is also a private nuisance. In *Hubbard v Pitt* (1976) protesters paraded with placards in front of an estate agent's office to protest against property development. However, these rights in tort are only exercisable by those whose rights have been infringed; the police would have no right to intervene unless criminal offences were likely.

The use of public open spaces, for example parks, is also restricted. Under the Local Government Act 1972 a local authority can make by-laws, for example, creating an offence to hold a meeting without the local authority's consent. In *Brighton Corporation v Packham* (1908) the space was a beach.

The Public Order Act 1986 has also increased police control in this area. Section 14 controls public assemblies by empowering the police to impose conditions as to place, maximum number of persons and maximum duration. Sections 11–13 of the same Act controls processions. Section 11 requires seven days' written notice to the police, stating date, time, route, and organisation. The police can then, under s 12, impose conditions which include re-routing. Further, if the police think s 12 is inadequate, they can apply to the local authority, who with the Secretary of State's consent can prohibit for three months either all, or a 'class' of processions (s 13). Section 70 Criminal Justice and Public Order Act 1994 created s 14A which now controls 'trespassory assemblies', especially on land of 'historical, archaeological or scientific importance', or on the highway *per DPP v Jones* (1997). In this case a demonstration on a roadside verge near Stonehenge, even though peaceable and non-obstructive, was 'nothing whatever to do with the right of passage' and therefore an offence under s 14A.

These powers of control, over public and trespassory assemblies and processions, are only available if either:

- 'it may result in serious public disorder, serious damage to property or serious disruption to the life of the community' (which is inevitable in most cases of Procession); or

- the purpose is to intimidate others into refraining from doing an act or compelling them to do an act. A political procession or assembly not having such an aim would be rare indeed! Should the police be concerned with appraising the motive behind a gathering? Summary offences abound in these sections where the gathering is unlawful, and powers of arrest are available to policemen in uniform.

Section 68 Criminal Justice and Public Order Act 1994 has created 'aggravated trespass', where a person trespasses in the open air with the intent of intimidating, obstructing or disrupting people carrying out a lawful activity there. This could apply where people stand in the way of bulldozers about to destroy a wood, or even to parents trying to dissuade school governors from making an opt-in or opt-out decision.

It is, of course, possible to hold meetings on private land with the consent of the landowner. However, 'raves' are now controlled by ss 63–66 Criminal Justice and Public Order Act 1994 and might be classed as a public nuisance, as in *R v Shorrock* (1993). Section 77 Criminal Justice and Public Order Act 1994 also allows a local authority to remove unauthorised motorised campers from its land or from the highway. Whether by consent or not, as we have seen, the police have a right of entry to stop or prevent a breach of the peace (*McConnell v Chief Constable of the Greater Manchester Police* (1990)). However, a person whose land has been invaded by squatters no longer has, at his own expense, to apply for an injunction based on trespass to land if he can now enlist the help of the police under s 61 Criminal Justice and Public Order Act 1994.

Under s 61 the police can ask trespassers to leave, if they have the purpose of residing there, and the landowner has asked them to leave, and either there has been damage to property on the land, or threatening, abusive or insulting words or behaviour to the landowner or his family or servants, or at least six vehicles have been brought onto the land. Summary offences exist of refusing to leave or re-entering the land, and a power of arrest is available to a policeman in uniform.

30.2   Restrictions on the conduct of the assembly

It should also be realised that the new trespass and assembly provisions in the Public Order Act 1986 and the Criminal Justice and Public Order Act 1994 ensure compliance by criminal sanction.

The enactment of the Public Order Act 1986 has caused some rationalisation in this area. The Act was seen necessary after the debacle of the Miners' Strike 1984–85, and the wholesale acquittals and withdrawals of prosecutions from juries which followed. There could, of course, be several explanations of these: the miners' behaviour was anti-social, but not criminal; it was criminal but in the confusion of the struggles, evidence was unclear or simply lacking; or the law was too strict to allow convictions in most cases. The government assumed the latter, revising several offences and discarding another. The Act's appearance allows an examination of this area in two parts: offences under the Act, and other offences which, despite the arrival of the Act, should not be underestimated as a means of breaking up unlawful gatherings.

Recent racial assaults and harassment has resulted in a new offence s 4A Public Order Act 1986, which is, however, not restricted to purely racially motivated behaviour.

The Public Order Act 1986 contains two groups of offence: four violence offences (ss 1, 2, 3), and two 'threatening, abusive or insulting words or behaviour' offences (ss 4, 5, s 4A 18). All seven can be committed in private as well as in public.

The three violence offences are riot (s 1), where 12 at least must assemble or use or threaten violence for a common purpose, violent disorder (s 2), where three at least must assemble or use or threaten violence, and affray (s 3), committed by one person who uses or physically threatens violence towards another. In each section the violence must be 'such as would cause a person of reasonable firmness ... to fear for his personal safety'. (But no such person need be present.) Sections 1 and 2 are 'arrestable offences'; for s 3 a policeman has power of arrest where he reasonably suspects someone 'is committing' the offence.

The 'threatening, abusive or insulting words or behaviour (or sign or writing)' offences are s 4, which must be committed with intent to cause fear of, or provoke, immediate violence, or causing such fear; s 5, the behaviour of which must be 'disorderly', and must be committed within hearing or sight of a person likely to be caused harassment, alarm or distress; s 4A (added by the Criminal Justice and Public Order Act 1994), which is a mix of ss 4 and 5, as it contains a requirement of both intent to cause, and causation of, harassment, alarm or distress; and s 18, which must be committed with intent to stir up racial hatred, or likely to cause it. All four are summary offences.

Section 4 is the successor to the old s 5 Public Order Act 1936, which was the main public order offence (it was 40% of Miners' Strike offences in 1984–85; and 70% of offences at Oxford United's football ground in 1974–75). The old s 5 could be committed in public only. However, more menacing is the new s 5. At its more sensitive extreme this has the capability of catching much behaviour which is likely to distress the old lady next door, such as calling her dog a mangy, flea-ridden bag of bones, or shaking a fist at it, neither of which would distress the cat itself. Section 4A is intended to cover racial harassment which does not amount to incitement to racial hatred within s 18. Section 4A is not, however, restricted to racially motivated behaviour.

Fortunately, there are defences, such as the behaviour being reasonable, but the burden of proof of reasonableness is on the defendant. Section 6 provides a defence to s 5, that the defendant neither intended his words or behaviour to be threatening, abusive or insulting nor was aware that it might be. This defence was successful in *DPP v Clarke* (1992), even though the defendant's display of pictures and models of aborted foetuses was objectively unreasonable.

Another issue which has arisen concerned whether a policeman could be the person 'likely to be caused harassment, alarm or distress'. In *DPP v Orum* (1988) held that in law and theory he could be; but that the magistrates must treat each case separately to decide whether in that case it was likely. It is noteworthy that 'disorderly behaviour' is part of the *actus reus* of s 5, as the Court of Appeal in *R v Howell* (1981), above, when defining 'breach of the peace' were at pains to emphasise that 'the word 'disturbance' when used in isolation cannot constitute a breach of the peace'. Has 'disturbance', thrown out at the back door, merely re-appeared at the front as 'disorderly conduct'?

The Protection of Harassment Act 1997 develops the harassment, alarm or distress theme commenced by s 5 above.

Section 2 of the new Act creates an offence of twice pursuing conduct (or speech) which causes a victim harassment, alarm or distress, and which he knows or ought reasonably to know amounts to any of these states.

Other public order offences outside the Public Order Act include breach of the peace and the two summary offences in s 89 Police Act 1996 of assaulting (s 89(2)) and wilfully obstructing (s 89(2)) a policeman in the execution of his duty, all of which are considered above.

30.3 Preventive powers

One of the main aims in a set of laws intended to keep the public order is clearly to prevent disorder from arising in the first place. Road checks, whereby vehicles can be 'selected by any criterion', are possible under s 4 Police and Criminal Evidence Act 1984. This area, too, is widening. The 1994 Act created two police powers to direct people away: under s 65, from a 'rave' (if within five miles from it) and under s 71 (creating a new s 14C of the 1986 Act), from a trespassory assembly. The police have power of dispersal when they reasonably apprehend a breach of the peace, failure to disperse being an offence against s 89(2) Police Act 1996. Arrest is permissible to prevent a breach of the peace. Magistrates can bind over a person to keep the peace whether or not he has been convicted of an offence.

In his *Brixton Disorders Report* 1981, Lord Scarman thought that these powers were adequate. However, we have seen that powers to require advance notice of processions and to control them and public assemblies have been given to the police by ss 11–14 Public Order Act 1986, and police assistance under s 61 of that Act is available in a civil matter against squatters or so-called new-age travellers, instead of having to obtain an injunction and the Criminal Justice and Public Order Act 1994 continues the criminalisation of, not just the out-casts of our society, but also ordinary people trying to stop a motorway or a decision which intimately affects their lives. But perhaps the most insidious preventive power is that of revocation of general permissive rights nothing to do with public order. Thus, public rights enjoyed by everyone over Greenham Common were revoked by Newbury District Council in an attempt to prevent women from remaining there to protest against the presence of cruise missiles in 1983. A rather over-zealous case of throwing the baby out with the bath water.

Chapter 31

Freedom of Expression

Article 9(1) of the European Convention states, 'Everyone has the right to freedom of thought and conscience and religion' and Article 10(1), 'Everyone has the right to freedom of expression' but we have already seen that Article 10(2) allows restrictions where 'necessary' in a democratic society (see Chapter 27, 27.1.1 above); Article 9(2) is restrictive in the same manner.

An immediate issue is: should unpopular views be protected? In *Verrall v Great Yarmouth BC* (1980) the Court of Appeal enforced a contract by the Council which allowed the National Front, a right-wing organisation, to hire a public hall for the purposes of an annual meeting, and s 43 Education Reform (No 2) Act 1986 obliges universities and colleges 'to take such steps as are reasonably practicable to ensure that free speech is secured' for employees and outsiders alike. Such provisions only ensure a hearing, of course; what is said at the hearing is covered by the Public Order Act 1986 in the usual way, but does freedom of expression extend to those who despise such a freedom?

It should also be observed that although much censorship is brought about by the criminal law (in the fields of obscenity, public order, contempt of court, official secrets and criminal libel) and civil law (tort: defamation, equity: breach of confidence), there is also much private censorship. Quasi-official bodies, often attempting to regulate a field of publication, include the Press Council, and the British Board of Film Censors, but money, power and influence often go hand in hand to influence news coverage in the form of politically biased newspapers.

We have seen (in the introduction to this chapter) that Article 10(2) lists the areas in which the Convention allows censorship. We shall consider the extent of English legal censorship, using those headings.

31.1 **'Protection of health or morals'**

The present law is the Obscene Publications Act 1959. Section 2 makes it an offence to 'publish' an article, or to have one in possession 'for publication for gain'. 'Obscene' means that 'its effect is ... if taken as a whole, such as to tend to deprave and corrupt persons who are likely, having regard to all relevant circumstances, to read, see or hear the matter' (s 1(1)). The meaning of 'deprave and corrupt' is a decision for the jury.

The Act was intended as a balanced code, incorporating three beneficial tests. Hopefully, these would prevent decisions such as the destruction orders of copies of Boccaccio's *Decameron* (reversed on appeal). These tests are:

- that an article is considered having regard to its likely audience (but it is no defence that the likely audience is already corrupted; it can be re-corrupted);

- that the article is considered as a whole: a selection of juicy bits to disgust the jury is not possible; and

- s 4 contains a defence of 'public good', ie 'publication is justified as being for the public good on the ground that it is in the interests of science, literature, art or learning, or of other objects of general concern', or in the case of a film 'in the interests of drama, opera, ballet or any other art, or of literature or learning'.

The first trial under the new Act was *R v Penguin Books Ltd* (1961) in which the publisher of *Lady Chatterley's Lover* by DH Lawrence was acquitted.

But this balanced code can be by-passed by both common law and statutory provisions. The agreements preceding publication might be, firstly, a conspiracy to corrupt public morals. In *Shaw v DPP* (1961) a 'Ladies' Directory', an illustrated list of prostitutes was the subject of a successful prosecution. Viscount Simonds set the moral standard:

> 'I entertain no doubt that there remain in the courts of law a residual power to enforce the supreme and fundamental purpose of the law, to conserve not only the safety and order but also the moral welfare of the state ... It matters little what label is given to the offending act. To one of your Lordships it may appear an affront to public decency, to another considering that it may succeed in its obvious intention of provoking desires, it will seem a corruption of public morals.'

The offence led to a conviction as recently as 1985.

Secondly, and quite apart from liability under the first conspiracy, there is the common law offence of outraging public decency. In *Knuller v DPP* (1972) advertisements for homosexual men to meet resulted in a conviction. Homosexual practices had been legal since 1967, 'but no licence is given to others to encourage the practice' (Lord Reid).

In *R v Gibson* (1990), 'human earrings' made from aborted human embryos were exhibited in an art exhibition, resulting in conviction. The Court of Appeal neatly side-stepped s 2(4) of the Act, which prevents prosecution for the conspiracy instead of under the Act (thus by-passing the three tests) where essentially the article is 'obscene'. The court said that 'obscene' here had the technical meaning of tending to 'deprave and corrupt' ascribed by s 1(1) (rather than a general meaning of 'obscene'); and as the earrings would not have this tendency, they were not 'obscene', so the charge was not caught by s 2(4); thus prosecution for conspiracy was possible; thus the three beneficial tests were not applicable.

Thirdly, Customs and Excise have powers under s 42 Customs Consolidation Act 1876 which says:

> 'The goods described in the following table ... are hereby prohibited to be imported: Indecent or obscene prints, paintings, photographs, books, cards ... or any other indecent or obscene articles.'

The three tests are not applicable and the burden of proof as to indecency and obscenity by statute lies on the defendant. Finally the Post Office Act 1953 makes it an offence to send through the post any 'indecent or obscene' articles.

It is noticeable that these two statutes refer to 'indecent' articles; it was held in *R v Stanley* (1965) that an article might be indecent, while not being obscene. Under both statutes, and indeed under the 1959 Act, the articles can be forfeited, ie seized without compensation following exercise of powers to enter and search.

The Theatres Act 1968 abolished theatre censorship. However, it is an offence to put on an obscene play, but there is the defence of 'public good'. Prosecution requires the Attorney General's consent. But in *R v Bogdanov; Re The Romans in Britain* (1982), after he refused to prosecute in respect of scenes depicting forcible buggery of an Ancient Briton by Roman soldiers, Mrs Mary Whitehouse, who professed before her retirement to represent the moral views of most people, prosecuted the director under s 13 Sexual Offences Act 1956 whereby it is an offence 'to procure ... an act of gross indecency with [a] man'. Confusion reigns as the prosecutrix abandoned her case once the judge had pronounced that a *prima facie* case existed, but before the defence had had its say. If such a prosecution were now possible the defence of 'public good' would, of course, not be available.	**31.2 The theatre and obscenity**
Close to the obscenity laws is the crime of blasphemous libel. The last conviction had been in 1922 and Lord Denning in 1949 during a lecture had said it was obsolete, when a prosecution by the same Mrs Mary Whitehouse resulted in *R v Lemon Gay News Ltd* (1979). This concerned a poem depicting Jesus as a homosexual. It was held that the *actus reus* of the offence was	**31.3 Blasphemous libel**

the publication of material tending to outrage and insult a Christian's religious feelings, and that the *mens rea*, as in all libels, was merely the intent to publish that which was blasphemous; there need not be an intent to blaspheme.

This prosecution has caused new interest in this offence; in *R v Lemon*, Lord Scarman said:

> 'I do not subscribe to the view that the common law offence of blasphemous libel serves no useful purpose in the modem law. On the contrary, I think there is a case for legislation extending it to protect the religious beliefs and feelings of non Christians. The offence belongs to a group of criminal offences designed to safeguard the internal tranquillity of the kingdom.'

And the Law Commission in 1981 recommended an offence of publicly wounding or outraging the feelings of religious believers, the *mens rea* being the intent to wound or outrage rather than the strict liability of the present offence. But in *R v Chief Metropolitan Stipendiary Magistrate ex p Chaudhury* (1991) Tasker Watkins LJ refused to find the book *The Satanic Verses* by Salman Rushdie criminally blasphemous as claimed by Muslims. He saw that to try to protect all religious beliefs 'would encourage intolerance, divisiveness and unreasonable interferences with freedom of expression. Fundamentalist Christians, Jews or Muslims could then seek to invoke the offence of blasphemy against each other's religion'.

31.4	**'Prevention of disorder or crime'**	Sections 4, 4A, 5 and 18 of the Public Order Act 1986, described in Chapter 29, 29.2 above, apply equally to words and signs as they do to behaviour, and thereby constitute a restriction on freedom of expression also. Section 6 Theatres Act 1968 and s 20 Public Order Act 1986 also make it an offence to use 'threatening, abusive or insulting words or behaviour' in the public performance of a play which are intended or likely to cause breach of the peace (s 6) or are intended or likely to stir up racial hatred (s 20).
31.5	**'Protection of the reputation or rights of others'**	The tort of defamation is clearly allowed by Article 10(2). Briefly (it is dealt with in detail in Part II on Tort), it is the publication to a third party of a defamatory (though not necessarily false) statement which refers to the plaintiff. Damages are at large, leading to very high awards, and an injunction might be awarded or agreed in a settlement. Legal aid is not available. There are several defences, eg justification; fair comment on a matter of public interest. But note that the burden of these, and other defences, is on the defendant. In *Goldsmith v Sperrings* (1977) the plaintiff, as well as proceeding

against the magazine *Private Eye*, issued writs against some 37 of its distributors, hoping thereby to snuff out the magazines distribution lines, but falling short of committing the tort of intimidation.

It was thought, until 1977, that criminal libel was obsolete. This is a clear-cut libel so serious that the public interest demands that criminal proceedings are instituted. Unlike the law of tort, the defence of justification is not available unless publication was in the public interest (Leigh Hunt was convicted for exposing the Army practice of flogging); publication to a third party is not required; and the libel is actionable even though it is against the dead.

It was re-used in a private prosecution in *Goldsmith v Pressdram Ltd (Private Eye)* (1977) where the satirical magazine had suggested that the prosecutor, a well-known City tycoon had engineered the disappearance of Lord Lucan, wanted by the police (still), in connection with the violent death of his child's nanny.

In 1980 the Attorney General stopped a criminal libel trial; thus, as in other areas of expression, it is uncertain how potent this area of law remains.

Contempt of court takes several forms. It can be committed in the face of the court, as in 1631 at the Salisbury Assizes where a prisoner 'Ject un Brickbat a le dit Justice que narrowly mist' and had his 'dexter manus ampute & fix al Gibbet' for his trouble.

31.6 'Maintaining the authority and impartiality of the judiciary'

However, more common is a statement or behaviour which prejudices a fair trial. Thus, any trial, civil or criminal, which is *sub judice* might be prejudiced by interference, say, from the press. Thus, in *AG v Times Newspapers* (1973) (*The Thalidomide injunction*) the court prevented *The Sunday Times* from publishing an article unfavourable to Distillers in its treatment of the parents of the English thalidomide children. The test was whether there was a 'real risk of interference' with the case. If so, then that outweighed the public interest in discussion. *The Times* took the case to the European Court of Human Rights, pleading that this exception to Article 10 did not apply in this case. The court agreed that it did not.

To comply with its obligations under the Convention the government enacted the Contempt of Court Act 1981, which creates a strict liability rule of contempt if a publication creates a 'substantial risk' of the case being 'seriously impeded or prejudiced'. However, the beneficial sections for commentators are, firstly, s 3 which excuses a publication while ignorant that relevant proceedings are active and a distribution while ignorant that it might be contemptuous. Secondly, s 5:

> 'A publication is not to be treated as a contempt of court if the risk of impediment or prejudice to particular legal proceedings is merely incidental to the discussion.'

In *AG v English* (1982), two separate stories happened to appear in the same issue of the *Daily Mail*, 'The vision of life that wins my vote' (on an election campaign on 'the sanctity of life and the right of every person, however severely handicapped, to be cherished and encouraged to live'), and 'The Mongol Murder Baby Trial' (on the then current jury trial of Dr Arthur indicted for attempted murder for allowing a baby to die with parental consent). It was held in the House of Lords that by s 5 the risk of the first article prejudicing the criminal trial was only incidental; there was therefore no contempt of court. Further, in a decision already beneficial to the press, the House held that the burden of proof in s 5 lay on the prosecution.

AG v Times Newspapers would, however, be decided the same today, because 'there the whole subject of the article was the pending civil actions against Distillers ... and the whole purpose of it was to put pressure on that company in their defence in those actions' (Lord Diplock in *AG v English*).

31.7 **'Preventing the disclosure of information received in confidence'**	A development in equity over the last century and a half has been a law which prevents, by injunction, a breach of confidence (it seems, however, that damages are not available). In *Prince Albert v Strange* (1849) the Prince Consort prevented publication of private etchings of the Royal children by the employee of a printer to whom the etchings had been given for copies to be made; in *Argyll (Duke of) v Argyll (Duchess of)* (1965) the Duke prevented the Duchess from selling the secrets of the bedchamber to the press to make some money after their rather heated divorce. Modern instances include the duty of confidentiality to the state established as being owed by current and past civil servants in *AG v Guardian Newspapers Ltd (No 2)* (1988).

But equity will not act in vain, so if the information is already in the public domain then an injunction will be refused; thus, in *AG v Guardian Newspapers Ltd (No 2)* (1988) a final injunction was refused because the information was already known to the rest of the world, where the book *Spycatcher* was freely on sale. And 'delay defeats equities', as shown in *AG v Jonathan Cape Ltd* (1975) Lord Chief Justice only refused an injunction to stop publication of the Crossman Diaries because the Cabinet secrets they revealed were stale, being 10 years old.

Further, 'just cause or excuse' (*Fraser v Evans* (1969)) will justify breaking the confidence, as in *Lion Laboratories Ltd v Evans* (1984), where a breath test machine known to be faulty was exposed by employees of the manufacturers sending copy documents to the press.

But it is not always clear where the public interest lies. In *X v Y* (1988) the court had to decide between the public interest of allowing public knowledge of names of doctors with AIDS, and the public interest of keeping the names secret, so as to encourage sufferers to come forward without fear of public exposure. The court decided that the latter public interest was most important and refused to allow publication of the names. But the development in this field of equity has also taken an unwelcome turn, in *AG v Times Newspapers* (1991), where a newspaper (*The Times*) was held to be in contempt by ignoring an injunction (which bound *The Guardian* and *The Observer*) to which the contemnor was not a party to the injunction, but was aware of its gist. The House of Lords made the point that in other actions (eg in *Mareva* proceedings), a third party will often interplead in an action to which he is not a party; so why not here? But this net spreads far wider than a *Mareva* injunction (which freezes a defendant's assets in the hands of a third party, to prevent an action against the defendant from being frustrated). And in *X v Morgan-Grampian & Goodwin* (1990) a journalist (Goodwin) used, but not criminally by himself, information leaked to him about a company's financial plans by a friend who worked in the company. The House of Lords held the journalist in contempt when he refused to divulge his confidential source as required by s 10 Contempt of Court Act 1981, 'in the interest of justice'. But the European Court of Human Rights disagreed; his refusal was within his right to freedom of expression protected by Article 10 of the European Convention of Human Rights.

Traditionally, the national security has been protected by criminal offences such as treason, sedition, and the Incitement to Mutiny Act 1797 or Incitement to Disaffection Act 1934 (both applicable to incitement of members of the armed forces), and the similar disaffection provisions in the Police Act 1964. However, national security has also caused much statutory activity through the 1980s, and justifies separate treatment.

31.8   'National security or public safety'

31.9 National security

An increasing restriction on freedom of expression in national security.

31.9.1 The concept

There has always been executive and legislative concern over the national security; indeed, only if a nation is secure will it remain as a nation. But several issues arise in connection with it; the first problem arises as to who is to say whether a measure which impinges on the civil liberty of a whole nation or simply one person is truly in the interest of national security. In *The Zamora* (1916) Lord Parker said:

> 'Those who are responsible for the national security must be the sole judges of what the national security requires. It would be obviously undesirable that such matters should be made the subject of evidence in a court of law or otherwise discussed in public.'

But that was in 1916, and the country was at war, and it is now accepted that in general, decisions of the executive are subject to judicial review or, where appropriate, *habeas corpus*. However, if the executive raises the issue of national security, the question arises as to whether the judiciary challenge the decision. In both *R v Civil Service Minister ex p Civil Service Unions (GCHQ case)* (1984) and *R v Home Sec ex p Cheblak* (1991), the rule of natural justice, *audi alterem partem* (hear the other side) had to give way to a claim of national security. In the first of these, the minister decided without consultation that trade unions were to be banned at Government Communications Headquarters (GCHQ), and in the second that an Iraqi subject, resident in Britain for some time, and now with British children, was a threat to Great Britain at the time of the British-Iraqi conflict. In each case no reasons were given to the subjects, or to the court, as to the reasons for supposing trade union membership or Cheblak's continued presence here was a threat to national security.

National security also justifies (*inter alia*) trials in camera, jury-vetting, and dismissal from employment. The strange affair of the prosecution of directors of the company Matrix Churchill over the sale of arms to Iraq has taken the time and expense of a Lord Justice of Appeal in an attempt to work out why ministers allowed a prosecution of men who had Government backing for the sale.

Amid such secretive goings-on, it is refreshing and reassuring to find such influential and independently-minded persons as Lord Atkin and Lord Bridge who speak out against the abdication of the judicial role. In *Liversidge v Anderson* (1941) Lord Atkin, the sole dissenter, called his four fellow Lords of Appeal 'more executive than the executive' when straining a wartime regulation allowing internment to meet a minister's interpretation of it. And in *AG v Guardian Newspapers* (1987) Lord Bridge, one of two dissenters against granting the government an interlocutory injunction to restrain newspaper publication of *Spycatcher*, said that he had hitherto had 'confidence in the capacity of the common law to safeguard the fundamental freedoms essential to a free society', but that 'My confidence is seriously undermined by your Lordships' decision', and in a notable finale:

> 'Freedom of speech is always the first casualty under a totalitarian regime. Such a regime cannot allow the free circulation of information and ideas among its citizens. Censorship is the indispensable tool to regulate what the public may and what they may not know. The present attempt to insulate the public in this country from information which is freely available elsewhere is a significant step down that very dangerous road. The maintenance of the ban, as more and more copies of the book *Spycatcher* enter this country and circulate here, will seem more and more ridiculous. If the government are determined to fight to maintain the ban to the end, they will face inevitable condemnation and humiliation by the European Court of Human Rights in Strasbourg. Long before that they will have been condemned at the bar of public opinion in the free world.'

It is, of course, well known that rather than sensibly and quietly accepting the inevitable defeat, the government went on in its obsession to achieve the condemnation and humiliation which Lord Bridge, supported by Lord Oliver, could foresee.

We shall now consider some recent examples of the exploitation of national security, and, in particular, the increasingly frequent statutory examples of the executive, with the legislature's connivance, ousting the jurisdiction of the courts.

One of the main manifestations of national security and of the secrecy perceived by government to be necessary, is the Official Secrets Acts 1911–89. Section 1 of the 1911 Act concerns true espionage, and generally covers matters which most would regard as necessary to state security, for example, an offence of passing to any other person any information, thing, document or information which might be of use to them, and with 'a purpose prejudicial to the safety or interests of the state', the burden being on the accused to prove the purpose was not so prejudicial.

It was s 2 of the same Act that for years had caught the passing over of ridiculous and trivial information, such as in *R*

31.9.2   Official secrets

v Lowther (1985), where at the Central Criminal Court charges were dropped against a civil servant who passed government information about children's toy typewriters to another civil servant who already knew it and had helped to compile it.

Opposition parties boldly promised its repeal, but this only took place on the government's humiliation caused by the acquittal against the direction of the judge in *R v Ponting* (1985) (a civil servant who passed documents to a Labour Member of Parliament showing that ministers had lied to the Commons about the first sighting of an Argentinian warship, the General Belgrano, later sunk in controversial circumstances), and its being replaced by the 16 sections of the Official Secrets Act 1989. Significantly, the judge in *R v Ponting* had said, 'Maybe it suits all governments to keep it as it is'. The government had always been selective in prosecution; Cecil Parkinson MP and Leon Brittan QC, MP, both then Ministers of the Crown, were not prosecuted for alleged disclosures in the Belgrano and Westland helicopters affairs.

Now, under the Official Secrets Act 1989, a civil servant, secret service agent or government contractor commits an offence if he makes a disclosure relating to security and intelligence (s 1), defence (s 2), international relations (s 3), or which would interfere with the criminal process (s 4); nor must contractors officially entrusted with information by the Crown disclose that information (s 5). There is a defence based on reasonable ignorance of its being secret information, but the *R v Ponting* defence (of making the disclosure to a Member of Parliament, 'in the interest of the state') has disappeared: disclosure is lawful now 'only if it is made in accordance with his official duty' (s 7(1)).

So what does a conscience-troubled civil servant, such as Ponting, aware of ministerial deception and chicanery, do now? Under the Armstrong Memorandum of 1985 and 1987 he must follow a procedure through a superior officer, or the permanent head of his department, with appeal to the Head of the Home Civil Service. (But what if they are in on the deception?)

31.9.3   A civil servant's duty of confidentiality to the state

We have already seen that civil servants are additionally under a duty of confidentiality to the state, recognised by the House of Lords in *AG v Guardian Newspapers Ltd (No 2)* (1988).

31.10   Restrictions on the media ('DA' notices, broadcasting and injunctions)

These exist alongside the criminal offences of the Official Secrets Acts, but the 'DA' Notice system is entirely voluntary and has no legal force. The government issues a 'DA' Notice, relating to 'naval, military or air matters the publication of which would be prejudicial to the national interest' to guide the media on what information the government does or does not want it to publish. Sir John Donaldson MR in *AG v Guardian Newspapers (No 2)* (1988), the *Spycatcher* interlocutory injunction application, recommended that the system be placed on a statutory footing.

On another, related subject, the Home Office can issue a direction to the BBC under its Charter, or to the IBA and independent radio under the Broadcasting Act 1990 (with legal effect), requiring it to refrain from broadcasting on any specified matter. The Home Office did so to the BBC and the IBA prohibiting the direct broadcasting of statements made by representatives of proscribed Northern Irish organisations. The House of Lords in *R v Home Secretary ex p Brind* (1991) held that the prohibition was reasonable. (In 1995, the prohibition was lifted, as matters had improved in Northern Irish affairs.)

We have also already seen that a newspaper (or anybody else) can be held to be in contempt of court by ignoring an injunction to which contemnor is not a party, but is aware of its gist (*AG v Times Newspapers* (1991)).

An important matter increasingly is the acquisition of information about the subject by both the state and industrial and commercial concerns.

31.11 Personal information

31.11.1 Data on computers

For good or ill, we live in a technological age. Much personal information is now on computer, or can easily be put on. Records held by central or local government include the files of the Department of Social Security on most of the population; Council Tax registers; DVLA records on all drivers at Swansea; three and half a million further education students' files held by the Department of Education; census returns; votes; public library records of books taken out by each individual, and so on.

In 1979 *The Guardian* newspaper revealed that 19 out of the 93 potential jurors for a 'political' trial had been vetted. The information identified those who had friends or relations with criminal records, had complained against the police, were squatters, had 'spent' convictions, or had been victims of crime. And yet despite Article 8 of the European Convention proclaiming a 'right to respect for his private and family life', there was no specific British control over the amassing of personal information. The Data Protection Act 1984 seemed to provide the answer.

The Act requires holders of such information to register with the Data Protection Registrar. Such holders must follow certain principles such as that the data must be accurate, and kept up to date, must not exceed what is necessary for the purpose for which it is held, and must not be used or disclosed for any purpose incompatible with the main purpose for which it is held. The subject, on whom data are held, has rights of access to his entry, and remedies available of rectification or erasure, and compensation.

But the Act has serious weaknesses. It only applies to information on computer, not on microfilm, microfiche, or simply on files or documents. A serious set-back was the House of Lords' decision in *R v Brown (Gregory)* (1996) that the offence of unauthorised 'use' of data was not committed merely by someone calling up data onto a screen to allow a friend to see it in order to use it for his own purposes. A policeman had called up addresses from the Swansea data base on car registration numbers, to enable his friend, who ran a debt-collecting firm, to chase debtors. Further, data held for the purpose of safeguarding national security are exempt from the access rights, all the remedies and the non-disclosure principle. Further, whether any data are held for that purpose is to be decided by a Minister, whose certificate that it is held for that purpose is conclusive evidence of the fact (s 27); thus the jurisdiction of the court is ousted in an important area.

31.11.2   Interception of communications

In response to the European Court in *Malone v United Kingdom* (1984) declaring telephone-tapping as an invasion of privacy, contrary to Article 8 of the Convention, the Government passed the Interception of Communications Act 1985, covering both interception of telephone and postal communications. Under s 1 it is an offence to intentionally intercept communications unless the Home Secretary has issued a warrant of authority, or the interceptor reasonably believes the sender or receiver consents (s 1(2)). Thus, the Home Secretary, not a judge, can issue the warrant (*cf* the issue of search warrants by a circuit judge under s 9 Police and Criminal Evidence Act 1984), on the grounds of 'national security', or to detect or prevent 'serious crime', or to safeguard the 'economic well-being' of the UK. None of these terms are defined.

Such an exercise of executive power would normally be subject to judicial review: but not here (s 7). The only safeguards are a tribunal and a commissioner. The tribunal, of five lawyers, can check procedure, but not the merits, of issuing warrants; nor can it tell an ignorant person his communications are being intercepted. There can be no appeal from, or judicial review of, its decision, and whereas a judge has security of tenure, the tribunal members do not. The tribunal reports to the Prime Minister. The Commissioner, a present or past senior judge, keeps the Home Secretary's execution of his functions under review, but again, can only report to the Prime Minister. Section 9 makes it clear that no suggestion of illegal interception by the state may be made in any court proceedings (except, of course, the tribunal). Ironically, this would now prevent *Malone v Metropolitan Police Commissioner* in the Chancery Division, ie the case that caused the Act could not now be heard because of it.

A serious defect in this Act is that bugging is not within its ambit. Thus, whatever other issues were raised in *R v Khan (Sultan)* (1996) (see Chapter 27, 27.1.2 above) the application of this Act to the case was not one of them.

The Security Service (MI5) was in existence before 1989, but was 'continued' by the Security Service Act 1989, which sets out its function, namely 'the protection of national security and, in particular, its protection against threats from espionage, terrorism and sabotage, from the activities of agents of foreign powers and from actions intended to overthrow or undermine parliamentary democracy by political, industrial or violent means ... and to safeguard the economic well-being of the UK'. The Security Service Act 1996 adds the function of MI5's liaison with the police 'in the prevention and detection of serious crime'. As with the Interception of Communications Act, complaints about the Service are heard by a tribunal of five lawyers, again lacking security of tenure, and review of the service is by a Security Service Commissioner. Again, the tribunal's decisions 'shall not be subject to appeal or liable to be questioned in any court' (s 5(4)).

The Intelligence Service Act 1994 'continues' the intelligence service of MI6. The Act provides for the usual tribunal and commissioner and for a committee of (removable) Members of Parliament, and contains the now customary ouster section, that the courts have no jurisdiction over the Act.

31.11.3 The activities of the Security and Intelligence Service

We have seen that national security is the means whereby the government can safeguard the military, civil and economic well-being of this country. Or is it merely the executive's cloak to hide a multitude of sins and goings-on in Whitehall? The late Harry Street, whose 'Freedom, the Individual and the Law' was the pioneering work in this field of law, saw the Emperor's new clothes only too clearly: 'Usually the crux of the matter is not national security – it is ministerial embarrassment.'

31.12 National security – an appraisal

In the face of these secret and technological means of acquiring information about the subject, this is increasing pressure for a right of privacy.

31.13 Privacy and freedom of information

31.13.1   Privacy

Article 8 of the European Convention says that 'Everyone has the right to respect for his private and family life, his home and his correspondence.' Notwithstanding this, English courts have persistently denied the existence of a general right of privacy. In *Malone v Metropolitan Police Commissioner (No 2)* (1979) no tort had been committed against the applicant when his telephone was tapped by the Post Office, on instructions from the police. And in *Kaye v Robertson* (1991) an actor was unable to prevent publication of photographs taken of him as he lay in a hospital bed with head wounds; the photographs were taken without his consent by press photographers who entered his room despite a no-entry sign on the door. We have also seen that access to the court is being restricted in areas where, traditionally, an aggrieved could at least go to the High Court.

Indirectly, it is true that some areas of the law do provide some incidental protection from interference with our privacy: battery; trespass to goods and conversion; trespass to land (*Harrison v Rutland* (1893)); nuisance and intentional physical harm (*Khorasandjian v Bush* (1993)); defamation (*Tolley v Fry* (1931)); breach of confidence (*Prince Albert v Strange* (1849) and *Argyll v Argyll* (1965)).

However, these torts and the equitable relief do not prevent intrusion in all cases, for example, by taking photographs ('The eye cannot by the laws of England be guilty of a trespass' (*Entick v Carrington* (1765), approved in *Malone v MPC (No 2)* (1979))); lawful but undiscovered phone-tapping, ie permitted by the Interception of Communications Act 1985; bugging; using a person's name or voice, either recorded or by mimicry; unfavourable publicity by digging up a person's past; or harassment of a person, even in sickness (*Kaye v Robertson* (1991), where the plaintiff failed in libel, battery, and passing-off and only obtained his injunction to stop publication of the photographs through injurious falsehood, a tort more connected with protection of business interests rather than private ones). Even the offences created by s 7 Conspiracy and Protection of Property Act 1875 of 'persistently following', 'watching or besetting a house', or 'following a person' require the specific intention of seeking to compel the victim to do or not do something.

31.13.2   Could the courts not develop a tort of privacy?

In the US a tort of right to privacy was developed by the judges from an article in *Harvard Law Review* (1890), written by two future Supreme Court judges after one had been shocked at the press invasion at his daughter's wedding. This right has been called 'the right to be let alone'. Thus, in the American case of *Melvin v Reid* (1931), the plaintiff, who, when a prostitute, was acquitted of murder, but who then abandoned her former ways, becoming respectable and keeping her past dark, was able by injunction to restrain a film ('*The Red Kimono*') not from mentioning her role in the trial (this was a matter of record), but from mentioning her former life as a prostitute. The defence of justification would cover mentioning both pieces of information in England.

The surprising thing about the American development is that the *Harvard Law Review* article was based on English case law. Could the English judges not do the same? Could not a judge in the mould of Lord Atkin in *Donoghue v Stevenson* (1932) derive some principle, say, from the case law in breach of confidence to set the ball rolling? The late Harry Street in *Freedom, the Individual and the Law* had no illusions:

> 'There is no spirit of adventure or progress, either in judges or counsel, in England today. Today's English judges are not the innovators that some of their distinguished predecessors were; in the hands of modern judges the common law has lost its capacity to expand.'

And in *Malone v Metropolitan Police Commissioner (No 2)* (1979) Megarry VC said that the judiciary should only legislate in established legal areas, not in brand new fields, as such a new area of law would have to spring 'fully fledged with all the appropriate safeguards'; he further commented that such a right (against the applicant's telephone being tapped) would even go beyond the right of privacy envisaged by Article 8, which in *Klass v Federal Republic of Germany* (1978) was merely interpreted by the European Court as being a right to adequate safeguards, not a right not to be tapped (an example of Street's lack of 'spirit', and which dearly did not deter Lord Atkin). In *Kaye v Robertson* (1991), too, the Court of Appeal said that 'This right has so long been disregarded here that it can be recognised now only by the legislature'.

Thus, legislation seems to be the only answer. Certainly, the press seem unable to regulate themselves in this area, a circumstance which, according to the '*Report of the Committee on Privacy and Related Matters (Calcutt Committee)*' (1990 Cm 1102), should invoke the threat the report suggested of criminal control if self-regulation through a Press Complaints Commission did not work.

But at the time of the 1997 General Election these moves had come to nothing short of the Protection from Harassment Act 1997, and indeed was proceeding to still suppress rights of privacy (see Police Act 1997, at Chapter 29). And in contrast to the uncertain start towards some form of tort of protection from harassment which we see in *Khorasandjian v Bush* (1993), we can contrast the bold moves in the criminal law to control harassment in *R v Johnson* (1996) (see Chapter 13, 13.1 above),

R v Ireland (1997) (see Chapter 20, 20.1 above) and *R v Burstow* (1996) (see Chapter 20, 20.5.1 above).

31.14   Freedom of information

Another matter which, like a right of privacy, would reverse the flow of information which at present flows from the individual to the state, is the area of freedom of information. Much information that does pass to the individual from the state is still regulated by, for example, the Public Records Act 1958–67, which delays the deposit of state documents in the Public Record Office for 30 years, or in some sensitive areas for up to 100 years. Thus, it was only in 1988 that the press learned of the fire in 1958 at the Windscale (now Sellafield) nuclear reprocessing plant.

The trials in the mid 1980s under s 2 Official Secrets Act 1911, especially *R v Ponting* (1985), prompted several private members' bills: to ensure that genuine matters of national security were protected, but otherwise, to ensure that other matters of either genuine public concern, or sometimes of private concern, were available.

However, in the absence of general rights, legislation is haphazard and piecemeal: on public matters, the Local Government (Access to Information) Act 1985; and in private matters, the Access to Personal Files Act 1987, the Access to Personal Files (Social Services) Regulations SI 1989/206, the Access to Medical Reports Act 1988, and the Access to Health Records Act 1990. But these contain let-out clauses, such as being applicable only to records made since the passing of the Act, or allowing doctors to withhold records if to reveal them would in his or her view be detrimental to the physical or mental health of the patient.

In *R v Norfolk County Council ex p M* (1989), a 13 year old girl told her teacher that she had been sexually abused by M, a 55 year old married plumber doing work at her home. A few days earlier she had made a similar complaint about another man. She was unsettled at school, and sometimes lived with her mother and sometimes with other relatives, and attended school 'inappropriately dressed in tight jeans and high heels'. M was arrested but no prosecution was brought because of the lack of evidence. She then complained of another man's approach. A local authority committee, sitting in his absence, put M's name on a register as a 'known/suspected abuser', and M was informed. But the committee also secretly told M's employer, who suspended M from work. On judicial review of the committee's decision, which was made in his absence, Waite J said that it was 'too chillingly reminiscent of 17th century Salem to be tolerated in a free society' and *certiorari* was granted of the committee's decision.

Chapter 32

An English Bill of Rights?

Great Britain has an 'unwritten constitution'. Its constitution is contained in case law, statute law and conventions of the constitution, and is 'the result of the ordinary law of the land' (AV Dicey). That being so, it is proper to consider whether, within that constitution, the judiciary and the legislature are checks on the executive, the state; in other words, whether they are capable of preventing the executive from 'riding roughshod over the rights or liberties of the subject'.

Sir Leslie Scarman, in his Hamlyn Lecture in 1974, made this stark observation:

> 'When times are normal and fear is not stalking the land, English law sturdily protects the freedom of the individual and respects human personality. But when times are abnormally alive with fear and prejudice, the common law is at a disadvantage: it cannot resist the will, however frightened and prejudiced it may be, of Parliament.'

And the late Harry Street, in *Freedom, the Individual and the Law*, observed that:

> '... there are obvious limits to what the judges can be expected to do in moulding the law of civil liberties. Two factors stand in their way: their reluctance to have clashes with senior members of the government ... and their unwillingness to immerse themselves in problems of policy.'

That both men were correct in their assessments is borne out by a study of the national security cases, already reviewed, where the unwillingness of the House of Lords to challenge this plea in *R v Civil Service Minister ex p Civil Service Unions (GCHQ)* (1984) and in *AG v Guardian Newspapers* (1987) and of the Court of Appeal in *R v Home Secretary ex p Cheblak* (1991) is shown in true relief by the lone dissenting speeches of Lord Atkin in *Liversidge v Anderson* (1941) and Lord Bridge in *AG v Guardian Newspapers* (1987).

Parliament's record in matters of civil liberties shows a willingness to connive with the executive. The Official Secrets Act 1911 (with its infamous s 2, now repealed) passed through the Commons in one hour and the Prevention of Terrorism (Additional Powers) Act 1996 in one day. Street pointed out

32.1 The judiciary as a check upon the executive

32.2 The legislature as a check upon the executive

that in 1976, 188 statutory powers existed to enter private premises; and *Salmond on Torts* cited a reference from *Hansard* House of Lords Debates that in 1952, there were 3,887 statutory and common law powers to enter private premises without a warrant. Do our electoral representatives not protest at the executive's attempts to pass such legislation?

The truth is that power has shifted from Westminster to Whitehall. Parliament is controlled by the executive. The party Whips keep Members of Parliament in check (the First Sea Lord's personal Parliamentary code of practice in Gilbert's *HMS Pinafore* libretto, 'I always voted at my party's call/And never thought of thinking for myself at all', is, when it comes to a Commons' vote, as generally true now as then).

An obstinate House of Lords can be by-passed under the Parliament Acts 1911–49 (rarely used, but was so to enact the War Crimes Act 1991, which retrospectively imposes on war criminals criminal liability in English law for 'crimes' not existing when supposedly committed). Thus, the executive controls the Commons, which controls the Lords. Small wonder that Lord Hailsham, former and later Lord Chancellor, said in a lecture in 1976 that Parliament had become 'an elective dictatorship'.

Sadly, then, neither the judiciary nor Parliament can lay claim to be the protector of our civil liberties. Let us now explore the matter of a Bill of Rights.

32.3 What are the options for a Bill of Rights?

Three options have emerged. The first is an entrenched statute. But entrenchment could only be effected by making the Bill incapable of repeal, whether in whole or in part, or by allowing repeal only after a specified, very large majority of votes in Parliament. But the 'Doctrine of Sovereignty' of Parliament does not allow Parliament to bind itself. A second option is enactment of the European Convention on Human Rights. This is the most popular option but, again, the Act of incorporation cannot bind later Parliaments. A third option is a Civil Rights Commission, as suggested by Street, and by Ewing and Gearty in Freedom under Thatcher. Generally, it would have power to analyse problems and propose legislation and codes of practice. But if, like the Equal Opportunities Commission and the Commission for Racial Equality, or for that matter the Law Commission, its legislative proposals could be ignored by the executive, would it not become a 'show-court'?

32.3.1 Is a Bill of Rights desirable?

In favour of a Bill, it can be said:

- A bill creates 'rights', which cannot be eroded as can liberties (though they can be qualified by let-out clauses);

- Neither the judiciary nor the legislature are complete checks on the power of the executive;

- The UK would be spared the embarrassment of being 'defendant-in-chief' at the European Court of Human Rights. Twenty-three Council of Europe Member States are party to the European Convention.

  All of them allow individual applications direct to the European Court; but the UK is defendant in one quarter of successful applications (37 cases taken against the UK, of which 24 were upheld (1990)).

  Granted, this might be because the others also allow their domestic courts to hear applications based on the Convention, thereby cleverly restricting publicity of their own breaches; but this greater domestic judicial access is itself an argument in favour. Further, hearings at the European Court of cases such as *Ireland v UK* (1978), in which the UK was found guilty (under Article 3) of inhuman and degrading treatment of IRA suspects, can be said to show just the wrong example to countries indifferent to human rights, and to give them rare encouragement in their oppression.

- A Bill of Rights would create a better awareness in the UK of human rights:

  > 'The [Convention] seems likely to have far more practical effect on administrators, the executive, the judiciary and individual citizens, as well as legislators, if it ceases to be only an international treaty obligation and becomes an integral part of the United Kingdom law' (House of Lords' Select Committee).

- A Bill of Rights would be permanent. But would it? Consider Parliament's inability to bind itself; the ability to derogate from its obligations under Article 15, dealt with below. Further, might it become outdated? The 'right of the people to keep and bear arms', enshrined in the Second Amendment to the United States Constitution was probably seen as a welcome civil right in 1791, when the 'wild west was just that'; but how embarrassing a right in the 1990s when anyone can buy a gun and go on the rampage, killing President and citizen alike.

  Against a Bill, it can be said:

- A Bill of Rights does not of itself guarantee civil rights. As Lord Hailsham stated in a House of Lords' debate:

  > 'Show me a nation with a Bill of Rights and I will show you a nation which has fewer actual human rights than England because the escape clauses are used, often quite ruthlessly, by the executive of the time.'

The discussion of Freedom of Expression above, using as sub-headings the let-out clauses of Article 10(2) of the Convention, shows that much of English law might well be unchanged after incorporation of the Convention. It is noticeable that phrases such as 'necessary' (Milton's 'tyrant's plea') and 'national security' are safely enshrined in Article 10(2)!

- The English Judiciary is ill-suited to the role it would have to play. A Supreme Court would have to take political decisions.

  On the other hand, the courts do so already, *R v Civil Service Minister ex p Civil Service Unions (GCHQ)* (1984) being an example, and judges are used for inquiries of a political nature, for example, Lord Justice Scott on the Matrix-Churchill affair. A Supreme Court would also involve the judiciary, who of course are not elected, having the final say on what may well be political issues, and perhaps over-ruling legislation created by our democratically elected representatives. Or should political judges be appointed, on the American pattern? Would judges seen as political lose some of their standing?

- There would never be agreement on what rights are fundamental. For example, should there be a right to equal education or health care, or the right to private education or health care? A right to security of a job, or a right to dismiss staff. Do we want a right to 'keep and bear arms'? Would either political party enshrine the right to jury trial, or the right to silence? Why has the Government failed since 1983 to sign the Sixth Protocol to the European Convention, Article 1 of which says, 'The death penalty shall be abolished.' Does it want to keep its options open? Is a Bill of Rights likely to end up the lowest common denominator between political (and in the UK), party political views?

- Parliament would lose its sovereignty. Some might argue that this has been handed over to the European Community anyway; but that argument does not overcome the English view that Parliament cannot bind itself.

- What use is it if there can be derogation of rights at the crucial times? Any Bill of Rights is likely to allow derogation. Article 15 of the European Convention says:

  'In time of war or other public emergency threatening the life of the nation any state may take measures derogating from its obligations under this Convention to the extent strictly required by the situation.'

The judiciary is unlikely to question the derogation, as derogation is bound up with matters of national security (see the national security cases, above). In any case, some statutes expressly oust the jurisdiction of the courts in national security cases (for example, the Data Protection Act 1984, the Interception of Communications Act 1985, and the Security Service Act 1989), and spreading elsewhere (see Police Act 1997, in Chapter 29).

In *Brogan v UK* (1989), at the European Court of Human Rights, the British government, when held in breach of the Convention in 1988, over the length of summary detention under the Prevention of Terrorism (Temporary Measures) Act 1984 (now 1989), did not hold back from derogating from its obligation under Article 5(3) to bring the persons arrested 'promptly' before a court. The Act allows detention without judicial sanction for up to seven days.

Thus, given Article 15, it is sensible to ask: of what use is a Bill of Rights which can be suspended at the very time when it is most needed, as it is in that part of the UK called Northern Ireland?

The Law of Civil Liberties

History is full of examples of man controlling man, from the Old Testament to the mediaeval English system of land law and the use of concentration camps in Germany in the 1930s and 1940s. Many states have felt compelled, to ensure that tyranny and oppression do not arise again, to enshrine into their constitutions a bill of citizens rights. The reader will, of course, be aware of the many failures world-wide of these bills, or charters, and may divert his attention to what has over the centuries become one of the most stable of the worlds states, the UK, and its unwritten constitution. In this chapter the reader will have been presented, not with a charter, neatly set out and easily referable by citizens, but with a haphazard collection of common law and statutory provisions, intended to protect the citizen's civil liberties.

It is in the concept of a liberty as opposed to a right that the strength and weakness of an unwritten constitution are shown. Liberties do not have to be created; they exist because no-one has curtailed them. English law recognises liberties, if only by virtue of the fact that it is constantly eroding and curbing them. A liberty can thus be eroded completely, either over time, or by the sudden stroke of a statute. It is therefore interesting that the models of written constitutions, both national and international, choose to declare rights, say to freedom from arbitrary arrest, which are declared by the constitution itself to be inalienable. The reader will have followed the content of this chapter comparing the English liberty on a certain matter, in some cases well eroded by now, with the rights declared by the European Convention on Human Rights.

At first attractive by their inalienability, these rights are balanced by the charters themselves with the let-out clauses, whereby restrictions necessary in a democratic society are justified. Thus a right declared by the above-mentioned Convention starts its existence with a mechanism for erosion already in place. Indeed Article 15 of that Convention allows for derogation of citizens rights in time of civil unrest. Is this not erosion by another name? For most of the time a citizen does not worry about his rights, but when he is frightened and looks to those rights, they may well have been removed! It is against this background that the reader will have tried to assess the balance of competing interests, official secrecy, public order and national security on the state's side, against the various freedoms of assembly, expression, information and privacy and so on, on the citizen's. As Lord Scarman is quoted in this chapter, civil liberties or civil rights are the end-result of a balance; they are a compromise between total freedom and total oppression. It is important to ascertain how level each compromise is, and how tilted in any direction.

In performing these tasks, the extent of protection of these rights and liberties by, separately, the judiciary and Parliament will have been observed.

Both bodies show a mixture of protection and oppression. It is hard to discern a pattern in many areas, but in the field of national security and official secrecy, both have shown a reluctance to support the citizen's rights and liberties against encroachment by the state. The judiciary have refused to peer through the veil of national security raised by many ministers, and Parliament has, perhaps learning from the judiciary's stance, gone on to remove the right of access to the courts in some areas. The 1980s particularly were a time of increase of both tendencies. It is important, therefore, in assessing whether an unwritten constitution is suitable and fair, to bear in mind the varying degrees of support shown by these two important parts of the state.

It is against these criteria, then, that the fairness of an Englishman's rights and liberties will be assessed: whether there is a fair balance and compromise; how the judiciary and Parliament each influence that balance and compromise; and, frankly, is the idea of a Bill of Rights, especially the European Convention on Human Rights, an improvement on the Englishman's present rights and liberties? Or does the Englishman, despite the constant erosion, enjoy a comfortable position still as against his state?

PART V

FAMILY AND WELFARE LAW

Chapter 33

Family Law

Family law looks at the legal basis of relationships of a particular kind. The relationship can either be that of 'matrimony' or 'cohabitation' ie two people living together being married or cohabiting (living together as though they were married).

Family law is very difficult to define but in English law it concerns the family unit itself. This unit consists of a husband and a wife and their children. The law here is concerned with the rights and obligations within the relationship that come from the fact that the couple are married or living together as though they were married. Society has traditionally placed some value upon marriage and families and it can be seen that the regulation of the relationship is of concern to society as families themselves are one of the fundamental organisations that make up the organisation we call 'society'.

The concerns of the law, however, go beyond this because the law is also concerned with other aspects of the family relationship, whether the couple be married or not married, such as the care of children and the resolution of disputes. This chapter will concentrate on some of the major concerns of the law in the broad sphere of the area of family law.

Family law is a very 'dynamic' area of law because it is changing to meet the needs of the society in which it operates. Our family law is obviously not the same as that found in other countries, yet as society changes (the increasing number of couples living together as though they were married is just one example of the sort of changes taking place) the law is reformed to take account of those changes. The ecclesiastical courts were the forum for legal matters to do with family law before the Reformation and the principles of the law were those found in Canon law. It was not until 1857 that jurisdiction in matters relating to family law was transferred from the ecclesiastical courts to the newly created Divorce Court. This happened because Parliament passed the Matrimonial Causes Act 1857 thus making it possible to divorce other than by using the nullity provisions or a private Act of Parliament. As a result of the Judicature Acts of 1873 and 1875 the jurisdiction of the Divorce Court was transferred to the Probate, Divorce and Admiralty Division of the High Court. As you may know, this division was renamed the Family Division in 1970.

33.1 Legal bases behind marriage and cohabitation

33.1.1 Developments in family law

Acts of Parliament after 1857 gradually extended the grounds or 'reasons' for divorce and for nullity and the positions of the spouses when the relationship was breaking down was made more 'equal', so that the same grounds applied to husband and wife.

One of these major changes was that in the Divorce Law Reform Act 1969 and in the Matrimonial Causes Act 1973. There have been others, but they will be introduced when we reach that part of the chapter.

Currently, we should be looking at the Family Law Act 1996, which will have a dramatic effect upon how divorces are conducted under UK law. The domestic violence provisions in Part IV of this Act are due to come into force in the Autumn of 1997, but the provisions relating to divorce (although *due* in July 1998) are unlikely to be in force before the turn of the century.

The development of family law has not just been in the grounds for the 'legal' ending of the marriage; there have been changes in the law relating to the property rights of parties to the marriage and in relation to the children of the marriage, to note but two main areas. In many respects these changes reflect alterations in the ways that society has tried to amend 'inequalities' between the sexes (for example, giving fairer 'shares' in family property after divorce), and in the recognition that children do not 'belong' to their parents but have certain 'rights' of their own – even from a quite early age – and that parents have parental responsibility for their children (see 33.3.1 below and others).

Thus, family law is still concerned with the rights, duties and remedies of those who live together (or did so at one time) and with that most intimate of relationships.

| 33.1.2 | The institution of marriage |

This usually results in the rather old joke that no-one in their rights minds would live in an institution! However, consideration of the definition given in *Hyde v Hyde* (1866) where Lord Penzance said:

> 'I conceive that marriage as understood in Christendom, may ... be defined as the voluntary union for life of one man and one woman to the exclusion of all others.'

helps us to perceive what sort of 'institution' we are talking about.

A marriage has to be 'voluntary' and must be heterosexual and monogamous for the purposes of English law. Many marriages are not, however, for life (otherwise family law would probably be a lot shorter!). In addition we must remember that we see many marriages now within a society that tolerates relationships which 'reflect' marriage, though not being 'married' – either because the partners are simply living together, or because they *cannot* marry as they are of the same sex.

Our primary concern within this chapter, though, is to look at family law in terms of heterosexual relationships and the legal consequences of those relationships.

Special rules apply to those who are 'engaged' to marry and prior to the Law Reform (Miscellaneous Provisions) Act (LR(MP)A) 1970 an engagement to marry was considered as a contract and it was possible to sue on the basis of Breach of Promise. The LR(MP)A 1970 abolished this action for damages. Sometimes, though, when couples break off their engagement to marry there may be disputes about the ownership of property. Engaged couples have some rights in relation to property because of the application of the LR(MP)A 1970 and under s 37 can apply for a beneficial interest in property which they have substantially improved for example, a house which the engaged couple bought with a view to marriage, but only one of them has their name on the deeds of the property itself.

The 1970 Act also makes provisions about engagement gifts which can cause difficulties when an engaged couple decide not to marry. Who owns the items given as presents or gifts may depend upon the intention of the person who actually made the gift itself. In the absence of any clear intention (for example, that it was intended simply as a gift to be kept by one or both of the parties) it can be presumed that the gift should be returned to the person who gave it, on the basis that it was a gift given in anticipation that the couple were going to get married. An engagement ring is presumed to be an absolute gift unless it is a family heirloom and given in anticipation of the marriage actually taking place (*Samson v Samson* (1982)).

There are a number of important differences between marriage and cohabitation. Many of these differences are best viewed in the section of this chapter that deals with the difference between the two 'states'. There are major differences like the legal requirements of the formalities of the marriage itself these will be looked at in 33.1.4 and 33.1.5 below – and the usage of the law when certain provisions relating to property disposal are employed. Many have suggested that it is time that the law reflected the fact that large numbers of couples choose to live together (sometimes for a long period prior to marriage itself) and more children are born outside marriage, often to stable relationships. Greater statutory protection

33.1.3   Some comparisons with cohabitation

should, perhaps, be accorded to cohabiting couples. There have been changes in the statutory provisions in recent years, among them the greater 'recognition' that the Children Act 1989 gives to the unmarried father, but as we shall see for many the changes have not yet gone far enough and for many cohabiting couples there can be extra difficulties when their relationship breaks down and yet they find that they have very similar disputes to resolve and family law fails to provide as much statutory provision and guidance as it does for the married couple.

Some countries have enacted legislation that specifically deals with cohabiting situations that have resemblance to marriage – that is, they seem to have the same 'commitment' or other characteristics that are traditionally attributed to marriage situations. These countries include Australia where the *De Facto* Relationships Act 1984 was enacted in New South Wales.

Among the major differences between those who marry and those who cohabit are:

- requirements of formalities prior to marriage yet not for cohabiting;

- cohabitees are subject to the ordinary law of property both during and after their relationship which can be compared to the married couple for whom special rules exist to protect rights simply because they are married (see *Burns v Burns* (1984));

- ownership of real property and personal property of cohabitees is governed by the law of contract and trusts and it may be necessary for non-owning cohabitees to establish an interest in the property and to apply to the court for a declaration (see *H v M (Property – Beneficial Interest)* (1992); *Lloyds Bank plc v Rossett* (1990)) where a trust was found after the cohabitee was able to establish that there was evidence of a common intention that she should have an interest in the property;

- the cohabitee must establish that a substantial contribution (preferably in money or very substantial other contribution) was made to the property and this can be difficult to prove;

  Note: The Trusts of Land and Appointment of Trustees Act 1996, which gives effect to recommendations in the *Law Commissions Report on Transfer of Land: Trusts of Land* (Law Com No 181 (1989)) will, when brought into force, abolish the trust for sale and substitute a new system of a trust for land. This Act will replace s 30 Law of Property Act 1925 with more detailed guidelines.

- statutory rights of occupation differ considerably and are far less helpful to the cohabitee than to the person who is married to the other party with whom they live (see the Matrimonial Homes Act 1983 which gives a spouse a statutory right of occupation in the matrimonial home). If the cohabitee possesses a right of occupation because they own the home, then there will be no problem. They are otherwise obliged to demonstrate that there was such a right through a trust or a licence to occupy (ie that they were led to believe that they could stay there for a period sometimes a long period – or until the children were older);

- rights upon death are different – anyone may leave their property to whom they wish after they die so long as the will complies with legal requirements such as those within the Wills Act 1837. Surviving cohabitees are not necessarily entitled to their partner's property after death (unless a will was left) although any children they have are entitled to make a claim. Generally, illegitimacy is no longer important in considering succession. Only when a surviving cohabitee was dependant upon the dead cohabitee can a claim be made under the Inheritance (Provision for Family and Dependants) Act 1975 for reasonable financial provision out of the dead partner's estate. A declaration could be sought to settle any dispute as to property under these circumstances. The Law Reform (Succession) Act 1995 amends s 46 Administration of Estates Act 1925 so that a spouse does not inherit unless he or she survives the deceased for at least 28 days;

- married parents have an automatic parental responsibility for their children (see Chapter 1, 1.3 above) but where the couple are cohabiting only the mother has this automatically, although the father of the child is able to either make an agreement with the mother (which is subsequently registered in court) or can acquire parental responsibility by using s 4 Children Act 1989. See *Re H (A Minor) (Parental Responsibility)* (1993) for the importance that having parental responsibility has for the 'rights' that it gives to the unmarried father. It is particularly important for the major decisions (like adoption) in regard to the child, although the law does recognise that the cohabitee can be a 'parent' for the exercise of many of the responsibilities within the Children Act 1989. Many believe that further reforms of the law to recognise claims made by cohabitees are required;

- just like married partners, cohabitees can use the criminal law to protect them against violence from their partner. The civil law can also be used, but the range of powers open to the cohabitee is more limited (see Chapter 1, 1.5 above). Cohabitees cannot make use of the powers within matrimonial proceedings and do not have statutory rights of occupation like married partners, so they must make use of other provisions to protect themselves and their children from domestic violence. It should be noted that Part IV of the Family Law Act 1996 extends considerably the provisions relating to domestic violence and the protection afforded to the cohabitee. These provisions are due to come into force in the Autumn of 1997;

- an important difference in the law relating to married and unmarried partners is that apparent in financial provision. Cohabitees generally have no obligation to maintain one another unlike spouses who may use the statutory provisions to seek financial support of various kinds. The law says, though, that both partners are liable to maintain any children they have so that the Children Act 1989 and the Child Support Act 1991 (as amended by the Child Support Act 1995) can be used to enforce financial support for children of the relationship even though the partners (or erstwhile partners) are not married. Cohabitees are entitled to claim welfare benefits and their partner could be a liable relative if, for example, income support is claimed, as could a married partner.

The law itself seems to provide the married couple with a ready-made 'living together' contract because the married couple are subject to many more already-provided statutory and common law provisions regulating their relationship – or at least providing for what ought to happen if the relationship does not 'work'. Cohabiting couples are beginning to draft 'agreements' to cover situations which might arise and the agreed actions that should happen in the eventualities listed. These agreements or contracts are subject to the same 'rules' as contracts in general, except that statutory provisions cannot be 'ousted' and the contracts could easily be misunderstood and misconstrued, as well as being an 'alien' idea under English law. It is not possible to oust the jurisdiction of the court, and attempting to do so where cohabitees have children is futile.

33.1.4   Capacity to marry

For a valid marriage to exist the parties must have the capacity to marry and the appropriate formalities must have been complied with under the relevant laws at the time in force.

Capacity is governed by the laws of the country in which the parties are domiciled, ie where they live and regard as their home.

Capacity under English law requires that:

- the parties are not within the prohibited degrees of relationship set out in the Marriage Acts from 1949 onwards;

- both parties are 16 years or over;

- both parties are 'single';

- both parties are of the opposite sex;

- the marriage (if celebrated abroad) is not actually or potentially polygamous since under English law you can only be married to one person at any one time.

16 years and over?

Section 2 Marriage Act 1949 and s 11 (a)(ii) MCA 1973

Otherwise, you can get married if you are over 16 but under 18 if you obtain parental permission or the permission of the court.

Both 'single'?

A party must not already be married, otherwise the marriage is void and the partner who knowingly goes through a ceremony of marriage may be committing bigamy. A marriage must be terminated by death or by the decree of *nullity* or *divorce*. (After the implementation of the divorce provisions in the Family Law Act 1996 there will be a divorce order.)

Of the opposite sex?

See s 11(c) of the MCA.

Usually having to be of the opposite sex will not cause a problem, but it is not possible under English law to contract a homosexual or lesbian marriage and a person is regarded as the sex they were designated at birth for their sex at the time of their marriage (see *Corbett v Corbett* (1970); *Rees v UK* in the *Rees case* (1987) and *Cossey v UK* (1991)). In some countries, like Denmark, Norway and Sweden, same sex couples may register their partnerships and their relationship is given limited legal protection similar to traditional marriage.

Foreign marriages?

See below.

33.1.5   Validity of marriage

Foreign marriages may create some complications with respect to the law and are outside the scope of this text but the formalities which must be complied with are those prescribed by the laws of the country where the marriage is celebrated. There are exceptions, and sometimes a marriage will be regarded as valid even though its formalities did not comply with the law of that country.

The marriage formalities are somewhat complicated at first glance but for the purposes of Advanced Level study the details often found in family law textbooks are not required.

Basically, there are two 'types' of marriage:

- ecclesiastical marriages; and

- civil marriages.

The aim of formalities is to create the certainty that following particular rules gives those involved. Proof is provided that the marriage actually took place, and the legal entitlements that follow marriage can be claimed. Financial and property implications follow marriage, as do some important differences in parental obligations, though actual obligations towards children are no less for cohabiting parents than they are for married parents.

Failure to comply with some preliminary requirements may not only render the marriage invalid but could be a criminal offence.

- *Ecclesiastical marriages*

    Church of England marriages can be celebrated according to the rites in force at the time. They require:

    (a) Publication of Banns

        ie a 'notice' of marriage requiring notice and registration in parishes of the parties concerned inviting any objections to the marriage to be declared.

        If no-one objects then the marriage can take place.

    (b) Common licence

        ie a special licence granted by the bishop which allows the parties to marry in church without banns so long as time limits are respected.

    (c) Special licence

        ie for exceptional circumstances only where the marriage can take place at any time and place according to the rites of the Church of England.

    Either (a) (b) or (c) must be followed for a Church of England marriage to be solemnised.

Non-Anglican religious marriages can also take place and comply with legal formalities.

Unless it is a Quaker or Jewish marriage, the civil preliminaries must first be followed (see below) and the ceremony basically requires the declarations that there are no lawful impediments to the marriage and that they each take the other to be their lawful wedded whatever it is! See *R v Registrar General ex p Segerdal* (1970) for what is regarded as a place of religious worship. It is possible to get married in another place under new provisions in the law.

All marriages other than those to be solemnised in the Church of England have to be preceded by preliminary formalities for which the superintendent registrar of the relevant district is responsible.

- *Civil marriages*

  This is a non-religious marriage ceremony requiring the authority of a superintendent registrars certificate (with or without a licence) or the registrar-general's licence. Religious marriages which are celebrated in other than a Church of England will require one of the following:

  - Superintendent registrar's certificate

    This is a commonly used procedure requiring notice to the local registrar for the area in which you reside, a fee and a declaration that there is no impediment to the marriage.

    If there is no objection then the marriage can take place.

  - Superintendent registrar's certificate and licence

    In this instance only one party needs to give notice and it avoids public display of intentions to marry. The same declaration as to the absence of impediment to the marriage is required.

  - The registrar general's licence

    This is used for exceptional circumstances only (eg serious illness where a person cannot be moved) and it authorises the solemnisation of a marriage in a place other than a registered building or registered office.

  - 1994 Marriages Act

    From April 1995 onwards couples celebrating a civil wedding ceremony will be able to make their vows in a range of premises which have licenses for the solemnisation of marriage, not just register offices. Civil marriages are, accordingly, permitted to take place on 'approved premises'.

| 33.2 | **Ownership of property** | Husbands and wives have property rights and the law provides mechanisms for the resolution of any disputes that occur. For cohabiting couples, generally, the ordinary law that relates to the ownership of property must be used and the law does not have the discretion that it possesses in respect of those who are married. |

Until a couple are ending their marriage similar property principles apply as may apply to any other persons, but the main difference is that married persons have right to occupy the matrimonial home. Cohabiting couples have more restricted rights. That is why it is very important to establish a beneficial interest in the home if the person concerned is cohabiting rather than married to their partner. This may appear unfair, but it is how the law has been developed, although there is evidence to suggest that there is a growing recognition of the needs of cohabiting couples and this is reflected in legal provisions.

| 33.2.1 | Family relationships and property | Most disputes relate to property in the matrimonial home itself. That will be looked at 33.2.2 and 33.2.3 below. Entitlements to property do sometimes arise even though there is no actual marriage breakdown. This might be because a third party is attempting to establish an 'interest' in the house the couple live in. |

- Legal ownership

  This occurs where a person is the 'legal' owner in name on the deeds of the house, for example.

- Equitable (or beneficial) ownership (see note below under Reform)

  This occurs where the person who is the legal owner is holding the property 'in trust' for themselves and for their partner so that while the partner is not the legal owner their 'interest' in the property is recognised under English law.

  Many couples who are married own their home as co-owners both at law and in equity.

  Spouses who own as joint-tenants each own the whole interest in the property and as individuals own no separate share, and will gain the whole property upon the death of the other.

  Spouses who own as tenants-in-common each own a separate share of the property and on the death of one party their share passes to the person named in the will or under the rules of intestacy (the legal provisions where there is no will).

Reform

Trusts of Land and Appointment of Trustees Act 1996:

This Act makes changes to s 30 Law of Property Act 1925 and abolishes the settlement of the Settled Land Act 1925. The 1996 Act replaces trusts for sale and strict settlements with a single system of co-ownership known as 'trusts of land'. A joint beneficial interest in land is treated as an interest in land rather than in the proceeds for sale which most closely indicates the purpose of co-ownership itself as the provision of a home.

Husbands and wives, like cohabiting couples, have separate legal personality and as such can own their own property. This has not always been so and it was not until the end of the last century that there has been recognition of the 'right' of a wife to own property in her own name (see s 1 Married Women's Property Act 1882).

There have been a number of other reforms in the time since then, among them the provisions under the Matrimonial Proceedings and Property Act 1970 which was passed to enable a non-owning spouse to have a beneficial interest in the matrimonial home where a substantial contribution in money or money's worth (like labour) had been made to improving the property. Since divorce courts do have wide discretionary powers in respect of matrimonial property (like the erstwhile couple's home), the necessity for some of the statutory provisions has diminished. Perhaps one of the most important provisions in this area has been the Matrimonial Homes Act 1983 which gave the non-owning spouse the right to occupy the family home (see later).

Most spouses today own their homes jointly.

There are a number of methods of resolving problems and these include:

33.2.2   Property disputes; solving problems

- s 17 Married Women's Property Act 1882 (see below);

- s 30 Law of Property Act to declare the rights in the property;

- using the Matrimonial Homes Act 1983;

- proceedings to restrain a breach of trust;

- by using proprietary estoppel;

- by way of a licence to occupy the property.

Some of these methods are more usual than others and it will not be necessary to go into all of the above in detail.

Couples can apply under s 17 Married Women's Property Act 1882 or a declaration under the law to establish interests under trusts by using the High Court or the county court.

Matrimonial misconduct is irrelevant under s 17 although the behaviour of the parties may be relevant if the couple are getting divorced and s 23 Matrimonial Causes Act 1973 is used instead (see later).

Applications for orders were made under the provisions of the Matrimonial Homes Act 1983 and were more commonly used where there was domestic violence. From the Autumn of 1997 the provisions of Part IV of the Family Law Act 1996 will be in force. The provisions of s 1(1) Matrimonial Homes Act 1983 are reproduced in s 30(2) Family Law Act 1996.

The method used to resolve property disputes may depend upon whether the couple are married or not, and, if married, whether they are in process of ending their marriage.

Where one spouse has a right to occupy the matrimonial home (the owning spouse) and the other spouse has no such right s 30 Family Law Act 1996 gives statutory rights of occupation.

Statutory rights of occupation mean that:

• if not in occupation the spouse has a right to occupy;

• and the right to re-occupy if not in occupation at that time.

These rights exist until the marriage is ended, either by divorce or by death.

These powers are often used where there has been 'domestic violence' (see 33.5 below).

These rights are only for spouses who do not already have rights of occupation, as they would do if they were 'owners' and create a 'charge' on the home and any subsequent purchaser of the home will take the house subject to this right of occupation.

However, the purchaser could, like the other spouse, apply to the court to discharge the order.

See *Kashmir Kaur v Gill and Another* (1988) was a case in which the court was asked (and did) take the circumstances of the purchaser into account even though the wife had registered a notice for the registered land interest she had.

Section 30 Family Law Act 1996 only applies to a dwelling house intended to be occupied by the spouses as their dwelling house (see s 30(7)).

33.2.3   Financial provision during marriage

We know that spouses have a right to the property that is their own when they marry. The position with respect to bank accounts illustrates the law here – if both spouses 'pool' their resources then there is an assumption that they own the property in the account 'equally' unless the relationship is ended by the death of one and the surviving spouse retains all the property in the account. There is a presumption that property bought from money in the joint bank account belongs to the purchaser but this can be rebutted by evidence to the contrary (see *Jones v Maynard* (1951)) and if only one partner pays into the joint account then there may be a presumption that they intended the other to benefit from the use of the account. See *Hoddinott v Hoddinott* in 1949 where the account was maintained for household expenses only.

Gifts given to one spouse belong to that person; gifts given 'jointly' are 'shared'.

A person in a relationship has the right to own that item unless it can be shown that there was an intention that it was to be 'shared'. Usually, there is no problem, unless the couple argue when the relationship breaks down, or the item is particularly valuable, or of sentimental interest, or a third party is involved.

At common law the husband was bound to maintain his wife in the necessities of life because she did not have the capacity to do so herself – there were restrictions on her holding property and entering into contracts. The common law rules have been largely replaced by statutory provisions in the Domestic Proceedings and Magistrates' Courts Act 1978 which makes a person liable to provide reasonable maintenance.

Note, though, that there is a *mutual duty* to maintain imposed by the Social Security Act 1986 which, by s 26, imposes this duty to maintain both spouse and children which is used when one spouse claims a welfare benefit like Income Support and there is another person (like as spouse) who is liable to maintain the claimant. A magistrates' court order can reclaim the money from the 'liable relative' under s 24 of the Act.

You should also note that liability to provide for the 'natural' and adopted children of the partnership is now covered by the Child Support Act 1991 where a formula is used to calculate the maintenance requirement for each child of the couple (even if they were never married, or even not a 'couple' in the usual sense!). Much of the legal power of the courts in dealing with child maintenance has been removed by the extensive powers within this Act and given to the Child Support Agency to 'manage' where one of the parents is 'absent' according to the Act – usually where they are separated or divorced.

The DPMCA can be used where decree proceedings to end the marriage are not being contemplated.

Section 22 MCA can also be used for 'maintenance pending suit' which will cease on decree absolute, but see later for comment on the reform of divorce law.

The magistrates' court can be used to obtain financial provision when the marriage has not ended. There are a range of provisions:

- Domestic Proceedings and Magistrates' Courts Act 1978

  No matrimonial offence has to be proved and the court has powers under ss 2, 6 and 7 to make orders for financial provision.

  The applicant must establish that there has been a failure to maintain (for s 2 periodical payments of money) or to maintain a child of the family, or that the respondent has behaved in such a way that the applicant cannot reasonably be expected to live with them, or that the respondent has 'deserted' the applicant.

- What can the applicant obtain?

  Periodical payments of money or a lump sum agreed by the parties or ordered by the court, a periodical sum for any children of the family, or a lump sum for child(ren).

  There is a limit of £1,000 for the lump sum.

  The parties can come to an agreement and have a 'consent order' under s 6 if the court is satisfied that there is proper agreement and that the sums are appropriate.

  Section 7 can be used where the parties have been separated for three months and neither is in 'desertion' and payments have been made already. This section 'regulates' payments made, including lump sums to third parties.

  Statutory Guidelines are used (in s 3 of the Act, as amended by the Matrimonial and Family Proceedings Act 1984) and are very similar to the criteria set out in the MCA 1973 (see 33.2.4 below). In addition to the circumstances of the case the court has regard to:

  (a) income, earning capacity, property and other financial resources of the parties;

  (b) financial needs and obligations;

  (c) standard of living enjoyed by the parties;

  (d) age of the parties and duration of the marriage;

  (e) any physical and mental disabilities suffered by the parties;

(f) contributions made by the parties to the welfare of the family;

(g) conduct of the parties if that is relevant

and in considering these the court will take into account not just the past, but any future responsibilities, contributions, etc.

In making orders under s 7 the financial needs, resources disabilities of the child and the standard of living of the family will be taken into special consideration.

Such financial responsibilities extend to children whom the respondent treated as a child of the family – that is, had assumed a responsibility for them.

The act gives guidance on the amounts to be regarded as appropriate and orders cannot extend beyond the receiver's remarriage nor beyond the death of either party.

Reform

The DPMCA, ss 16–18 and parts of s 1 providing grounds for maintenance orders during a marriage are repealed upon the Family Law Act 1996 coming into force.

Orders can be enforced in the magistrates court under s 32 through a warrant of distress, attachment of earnings order or imprisonment. Arrears can also be enforced through a higher court.

- Maintenance and separation agreements

  These can be made by parties to a marriage and these can contain provisions of maintenance for both spouses and children. Such agreements can contain other clauses covering not living together, not taking proceedings for past matrimonial misdemeanours and other financial arrangements.

- Section 15 Children Act 1989

  A range of financial orders may be granted for the benefit of a child. The applicant here is the parent or guardian of a child and it does not matter with this order whether the parents are married or not. Again, the provisions of the Child Support Act 1991 will be used where a parent who is not living with a child is not paying sufficiently for the child's maintenance.

Many of the provisions already noted can be used when a couple are ending their relationship.

The important provision, though, for couples terminating their relationship permanently is within the MCA 1973 where by ss 23 and 24 the following may be obtained:

33.2.4 Provision upon termination of marriage

- Periodical payments and secured periodical payments

  Under s 23 for a specific amount of money weekly or monthly, usually.

  Secured payments may depend upon alternative incomes for the payer and may go on beyond the payer's death, if the payment comes from property still in existence, for example.

  Wachtel v Wachtel (1973) is often used as a starting point for the calculation as Lord Denning put forward in this case. This is known as the 'one-third' rule as one-third of joint earnings and assets is initially allocated for the wife. The court will then consider whether this is an 'appropriate' sum in all the circumstances, bearing in mind the factors which are outlined here.

  The court can specify the duration of orders and is required to consider the 'Clean Break' situation as a result of the amendments to the act in 1984. Often there is a specified period, especially if there are no children, the marriage was of short duration or both parties are able to earn reasonable salaries.

- Lump sum orders

  Under s 23 can be paid in 'instalments' or secured on property owned by the payer. Often used to repay debts accrued during the separation and decree period.

- Transfer of property

  Under s 24 the court may order that one party transfer property to the other party.

  This can include items like jewellery, shares, furniture, land and the matrimonial home.

  Rented property can also be transferred so that the interests which parties have in the property is moved from, for example, the husband to the wife; this may also be in the best interests of the party who has the daily care of any children.

- Settlement of property and variation of settlement order

  Under s 24 the court may order that one party transfer interests for the benefit of the other party and this allows the court to be 'creative' in the kinds of arrangements that can be made when a marriage relationship breaks down.

  The case of *Mesher v Mesher* (1980) was such a case where the house was in joint names and the court ordered that it could not be sold until the youngest child reached 17 and the court gave the wife exclusive rights to occupation until that point. Usually, if the house is held in joint names we say that it is held on a trust for sale, and that it would have to be sold to raise the necessary 'liquid' interest in the house. In *Brown v Pritchard* (1975) the wife received a transfer of the property but had to grant the husband a charge over the property equal to half its value. Property adjustment orders can be sophisticated to take into account the various factors and the individual circumstance of each family situation.

This was done in *Harvey v Harvey* (1982) where the wife was not in a position to look forward to buying her own place and the equity in the family home was transferred with two thirds to the wife, who was to pay the husband an occupation rent for the house. There was to be no sale until the wife died, remarried or voluntarily left the house. To order that the house be sold when their youngest child reaches 18 would merely have postponed the problem.

- Order reducing or ending an interest in a settlement

  Under s 24 and this related to less common nuptial settlements.

  None of these orders can be made until a decree of divorce, nullity or judicial separation has been made (see 33.1.4 above).

- Factors taken into account

  These are covered by s 25 and were mentioned above.

  The court has to consider all the circumstances of the case and the welfare of the minor children of the family are given first consideration (not necessarily, then, the children in the 'new' family that one or both partners may be joining).

  Children of the family can have the same types of orders made in their favour which can direct that payment be made to them or to a third party for their use. Periodical payments and lump sums can be made (which can be made before a decree is granted) and must end when the child reaches 17 unless the court considers otherwise.

  In *Suter v Suter and Jones* (1987) it was held that giving children this 'first consideration' did not mean that the welfare of the children was actually more important than any other consideration (as it would be under the Children Act 1989 when the welfare of the child is of paramount consideration when considering the upbringing of the child). The courts have noted that a result should also be 'just' as between the husband and wife.

  Section 25(2) MCA 1973 provides for a list of factors.

(a) *Income, earning capacity, property and other financial resources*

The court will not necessarily make use of all such resources.

Parties are also expected to maximise their potential earnings – so that a wife, for example, would be expected to take steps to earn an income at some point in the future, and an income could be 'attributed' for that purpose. See *Delaney v Delaney* (1990) where the problem of taking state benefits into account in making awards was discussed.

(b) *Financial needs, obligations and resources*

This will include what the parties have had in the past and could be expected to have in the future. This includes living expenses as diverse as household bills, rents, income tax, and other reasonable liabilities. The court will also have regard to what could be regarded as the reasonableness of such expenses, in order to avoid a person inflating bills to gain an advantage over their erstwhile partner. Resources of new partners are not regarded as the 'income' of the party but account would be taken of their resources. Children are not the first consideration of the court but if, for example, the husband has a new partner who has children he may be contributing to their welfare even though he has no legal obligation to support those children.

(c) *Standard of living*

The standard of living enjoyed before the breakdown is taken into account although it may be difficult to ensure that the parties are not affected by the breakdown!

(d) *Age of the parties and duration of the marriage*

This can be relevant since it may affect employment prospects of a former spouse asked to maximise their prospects by seeking work after the ending of maintenance, or the ability to raise a mortgage. A short marriage will generally mean that the parties will have less 'call' upon one another than those who have been married for a long time – although the exact length that the courts regard as being 'short' or 'long' has not been defined.

There is no agreement that the period of time spent together (even living together) before marriage adds to this period.

(e) *Any disabilities*

Any disabilities will be taken into account since the parties may have special needs.

(f) *Contributions to the welfare of the family*

These are taken into account, whether they be present or future; this factor includes looking after the home and the family.

(g) *Conduct of the parties*

Conduct of the parties is taken into account since it would be 'inequitable' to ignore the conduct. The courts have considerable discretion here and Lord Denning said in *Wachtel v Wachtel* (1973) that such conduct could be taken into account if it was 'gross and obvious'.

See *Kyte v Kyte* (1988) where the behaviour of the wife towards the depressive husband was regarded as a factor to be taken into account – she encouraged him to commit suicide because she wanted to inherit his money and share it with her lover.

Extreme conduct is required, and it is examined in the context of the conduct of both parties.

(h) Value of lost benefits

Value of lost benefits such as pension rights which could be lost to one party as a result of the decree. (See note on Pensions.)

Reform

The Family Law Act 1996 has made changes to the ancillary relief provisions of the MCA 1973. The existing law has been amended to require ancillary relief to be settled before the grant of the new divorce or separation order. A new s 21 to the MCA 1973 redefines types of orders which can be made and are contained in new ss 22A and 23A.

It is interesting to note here that s 25(2)(g) MCA 1973 is being altered from reference to conduct which is 'inequitable to disregard' to 'whatever the nature of the conduct and whether it occurred during the marriage or after the separation of the parties, or (as the case may be) dissolution or annulment of the marriage'.

Exactly what effect this will have is to be wondered at! However, it should be noted at this point that existing law remains until amendment and the implementation awaits trial periods of the new provisions due prior to 2000.

Section 25(2)(h) MCA 1973 ceased to apply on 1 August 1996 when s 166 Pensions Act 1995 came into force. This applies to petitions filed from 1 July 1996.

The Pensions Act 1995 and ss 25B–D MCA 1973 imposes a duty on the court in considering pension provisions after divorce. These include benefits a party to a marriage would lose the chance of acquiring upon dissolution of the marriage. Section 25B applies to divorce petitions presented after 1 July 1996 and petitions presented before that date permit the court a discretion, rather than a duty, to consider the pension provision. Section 25(2)(h) MCA 1973 ceased to apply on 1 August 1996 when s 166 of the Pensions Act 1995 came into force. This applies to petitions filed from 1 July 1996.

Dealing with pensions may involve:

(i) compensating via lump sum payments;

(ii) varying a post-nuptial settlement;

(iii) pension 'earmarking' as a deferred settlement under ss 25B–D via maintenance or lump sum payments to former spouses upon the retirement;

(iv) pension splitting under s 16 FLA 1996 – not yet in force, but accepted as a principle. This adds provisions to the MCA 1973 and permits a court to make a pensions adjustment order. Rules are to be enacted to deal with the technicalities.

33.2.5	The 'clean break' principle

The exercise of the court's powers has the objective of making the parties financially independent of each other. This principle was introduced in to the MCA by the Matrimonial and Family Proceedings Act (MFPA) 1984 and gave a new s 25 (A) and applies only where the parties are granted a decree of divorce or nullity.

The court has to *consider* whether it would be appropriate to make an order to terminate the financial obligations of the parties towards one another immediately or at some time in the future, as the court thinks fit. This might mean making no order for financial provisions at all or stating a time in the future when such periodical payments might cease. There is no duty to order a dean break – only a duty to consider such an order under the circumstances.

Making use of this provision of the MFPA 1984 added to the 1973 provisions and the range of orders available means that the court is able to 'mix and match' and put together a 'package' to meet the needs of the parties according to their circumstances – in so far as the court is able to do so. For example, more 'generous' capital settlements (whereby, perhaps, the value of the house goes to a wife who has the daily care of the children of the family) might be 'balanced' by nominal periodical sums which are to cease when the wife has seen the youngest child to school and is able to return to the employment she had before having children. It may, for example, be more appropriate that the wife pay the husband a sum of money in settlement for his share of the house.

A clean break is not appropriate in every situation and is not intended to be a clean break between parent and child, for the obligation to maintain a child continues.

The 'social' problems after the ending of marriages is apparent here because it is often women who are not in a position to return to jobs, or who were 'disadvantaged' in the job market because of having more responsibility for looking after children. If orders for periodical payments were not made many women would simply have to use the welfare benefit system and rely upon the state. This is partly why the government introduced the new Child Support provisions in the 1991 Act. See *Waterman v Waterman* (1989) and *Whiting v Whiting* (1988) where Balcombe LJ stated that to realise the clean break principles in many instances would simply mean that wives were forced onto Income Support because there were no alternatives. Sometimes the loss of periodical payments results in a substitution of lump sums but these are only used where there is the possibility of there being such a sum of money in the first place – if the family has no money, the court cannot make the award!

See *Gojokovic v Gojokovic* heard in the Court of Appeal in 1990 where a large sum of money from a hotel business was used so that the wife was able to obtain a substantial lump sum settlement.

Cases like *Harvey v Harvey* show that there is a conflict in considering the 'clean break' situation, especially where there may not be sufficient resources or where there are children who are still quite young, and for whom provision has to be made.

In *F v F* (1996) the wife was 56 and the husband 57. The wife had no assets, apart from her joint interest in the matrimonial home. The husband's net assets were some £3.4 million. After a marriage of 23 years, the court considered that the wife should receive a net income of £36,000 a year. To achieve this, a Duxbury calculation (from *Duxbury v Duxbury* (1987)) was made so a lump sum of £575,000 was ordered to give the required annual income.

The Department of Social Security can ask for a 'liable relative' to contribute where a child's adult carer is claiming benefits. This order would effectively mean that the 'advantages' of 'clean breaks' would be lost to such payers.	33.2.6 Liable relatives and the department for social security

33.2.7   The Child Support Act 1991

The implementation of the Child Support Act also reduces the attraction that the 'clean break' principle seemed to have. By this provision, which came into effect in April of 1993, natural (or adoptive) parents, whether married or not, who no longer live with their children (often fathers who have left the matrimonial home after a divorce) are still obliged to pay maintenance for their children under the system established under the Act. This system is a formula which takes into account a maintenance requirement calculated on the number and ages of the qualifying children, the income of both parents, a limited range of 'allowances' for the parents with a 'safety net' of a protected income for the paying parent.

When the Act first came into effect there was a hostile reception because of its effects upon the financial arrangements of parents, its approach to maintenance and allegations that the provision was aimed at reducing Treasury expenses and payments from the Social Security system rather than 'putting children first' by ensuring that those 'absent' parents who did not pay towards their children's upbringing began to do so. There were accusations of 'targeting' already paying 'middle class' fathers who were easily traceable, and claims that the Child Support Agency, established to run the formula system, was slow and inefficient. These claims were borne out after the first year or so of operation, during which time there were large numbers of documented cases of administrative problems.

One of the major criticisms was that the system increased maintenance payments for most payers and overturned previous arrangements, many of which involved so-called 'clean break' approaches under the MCA as amended by the 1984 Act. Reduced Benefit Directions (to reduce the payments of welfare benefits to carers of children who would not comply with the requirements of the Child Support Acts 1991 and 1995 or assist the Child Support Agency (CSA) in obtaining maintenance payments from the absent parent) were criticised. Changes to the Act from 1994–96 reduced the severe effects which many of these changes had upon erstwhile couples who thought they had settled their financial and property arrangements after they divorced or simply went their own ways. Among the changes are increased 'allowances' for absent parents and their second families and a new allowance to attempt to take into account clean break settlements made when the courts were assisting couples to settle their arrangements which frequently involved reduced child maintenance payments as an 'offset' for any loss of capital interest in the home. The full extent and effect of these changes remains to be seen.

The workload of the CSA has dramatically increased since the implementation of the original legislation in April 1993. The provisions for planned take-on of maintenance on a phased basis virtually collapsed under the pressure of claims. Court maintenance orders made in favour of parents with care of children and who are not on benefit *prior* to April 1993, remain in force.

From December 1996, parents can apply to the CSA for a Departure Direction under provisions inserted into the 1991 (s 28A–H) Act by the 1995 Act. A much wider range of expenses/allowances can be taken into account in calculating the income of the parent *not* looking after the child(ren) so that there is potential for *reducing* the child maintenance paid under the legislation. Among these allowances (not fully taken into account – or, in some situations, not at all – under the 1991 Act) are travel to work expenses, contact-with-children expenses and pre-1993 capital or property transfers. There is also provision to consider cases where there is conflict between parents about 'inconsistent lifestyles' which allegedly do not reflect declared income (for the purpose of calculating child maintenance) or where the parent with care alleges that the absent parent is diverting income to avoid payment.

Much of the law relating to children is now found in the Children Act 1989.	**33.3** **Parents and children**

During the 20th century children have acquired more rights as individuals and these rights have been 'recognised' in the international sphere by the United Nations (1959 Declaration and the 1989 Convention on the Rights of the Child), the Court of Human Rights and international provisions such as that covering the abduction and return of children taken abroad contrary to court orders.

33.3.1 Legal status of the child

Unfortunately, it is not easy to try to list all the supposed rights that children do have, as they are not universally recognised and applied throughout the world. Such lists are not useful, either, when one considers the application of them in practise.

Children, Rights and the Law by Alston, Parker and Seymour (published by Clarendon) discusses these rights if you are particularly interested.

One starting point is *Re Agar-Ellis* (1883) where the position of both the wife and the child in law and in relation to the father of the family was illustrated. The court felt that it had no jurisdiction to interfere when a 16 year old daughter wanted to spend the holidays with her mother when the father removed the children from the mother in a dispute about upbringing.

At common law the rights to control custody and upbringing vested with the father. No longer are children regarded as the chattels of fathers – nor of their mothers! The welfare of the child and the role of the state, alongside the recognition of the growing maturity of the child as they approach (though not having reached) adulthood ensures this legal situation.

Compare the earlier case with *Gillick v West Norfolk and Wisbech Area Health Authority* (1986) where the right of the child were seen to 'grow' as the rights of the parents diminished as the child grew older and acquired the essential 'maturity' to make its own decisions. Lord Scarman's statements in the judgment are revealing in that they seemed to be recognising that whilst there must by some date by which a child was no longer a child (presumably by the time the child reached 18 when the law regards them as adults) it was not possible to state categorically when this 'maturity' was reached. The case did not actually give children absolute rights and the scope of these rights will depend upon the circumstances of the case. The *Gillick*-competency of the child is only one factor to be taken into account of parents and child cannot agree and the court is asked to step in and make a decision. See *Re R (a minor) (Wardship – Medical treatment)* (1992) where the court said that the views of the Gillick-competent child could be overridden if the circumstances demanded it.

Many children are born outside of marriage but it is no longer true to say that these children are treated less favourably than those who are born within marriage. There are some differences in the way they are viewed in law but the Family Law Reform Act 1987 removed unjustifiable legal discrimination against non-marital children. The major differences that remain include questions of nationality and automatic parental responsibility for unmarried fathers (see later). Non-marital children can be legitimised by the subsequent marriage of the parents to each other or by being adopted. It is important to note whether a child's parents are married or unmarried because the legal effects may be different (see s 1 Family Law Reform Act 1987) although the Family Law Reform Act 1987 has given a new construction on the meaning of the phrase and no more children born to unmarried parents have to be included expressly in a statute for that statute to refer to them. If it does not refer to them, the statute must expressly state this. The social effects of 'illegitimate' children being legally labelled will diminish completely in the future.

33.3.2   Who are 'parents'?

The Human Fertilisation and Embryology Act 1990 helps to us to see the legal relationship of parents and child, which is established at birth between the child's birth mother and her husband (if she is married) who is assumed to be the father of the child unless this presumption is rebutted by contrary evidence. The area of surrogate births and donated eggs and sperm is beyond the syllabus.

The question of paternity can be dealt with in court where evidence can be adduced from court admissions or registration at birth, or by evidence suggesting the existence of a sexual relationship at the time of conception. Blood tests are also used, as are DNA fingerprinting techniques, and any refusal to comply with tests may mean that the court will draw its own conclusions in any dispute.

Re H (A Minor) (Blood Tests: Parental Rights) (1996)

Blood test directions can be made even where a parent refused to undergo blood testing herself and for the child. Inferences may be drawn from a refusal to undergo the blood test. The child's welfare was paramount on such matters as parental responsibility and on contact but not so when deciding whether to direct a blood test. A court will normally refuse to direct a blood test if satisfied that it would be against the child's interests.

Child of the family?

This is a legal phrase that refers to s 105 Children Act 1989 and means, in relation to parties to a marriage:

- a child of both parties; and

- any other child (not placed as a foster child) who has been treated by both parties as a child of the family;

- and the definition can be found referred to in the MCA 1973.

It means that the law recognises the relationship between the child and married adult who are not necessarily the natural parents of that child. There does not have to be a blood tie and the adults will not automatically have parental responsibility for that child but are able to apply for some of the orders under the Children Act 1989.

Parental responsibility defines the legal relationship between parent and child and is found in s 3 Children Act 1989 as:

33.3.3   Parental responsibility

> 'all the rights, duties, powers, responsibilities and authority which by law a parent has in relation to the child and his property.'

However, the idea is not 'new' and reference to it is found in the *Gillick* judgments but it is a new concept in that it is enshrined within statute for the first time in the Children Act 1989. Rights of parents exist for the benefit of the child and the concept includes such items as:

- maintaining the child;

- providing for the child's education;

- protecting the child from physical and moral danger;

- administering the property that belongs to the child,

among others.

Those parents who have parental responsibility may exercise that power alone (s 2(7)) although there are limitations if the parental responsibility is given with just a residence order, or if a separated father wanted to exercise power as part of parental responsibility he might find it a problem without the agreement of his wife, if she had the regular care of the child.

References are to the Children Act 1989:

- s 2(1) says that parental responsibility belongs to both parents of they are married at the birth of the child;

- s 2(2) says that if the parents are unmarried then only the mother has automatic parental responsibility.

It was not considered appropriate to give automatic parental responsibility to every unmarried father where there was no way of knowing the stability of the union.

Section 4 allows the unmarried father to attain parental responsibility either by agreeing with the child's mother and registering a parental responsibility agreement with the court in prescribed form, or by seeking a court order. Both can be ended by court order and are therefore not permanent.

A court should not be using its power to make a parental responsibility order as a 'weapon' to force a father to pay child maintenance. In *Re H (Minors) (Parental Responsibility Order: Maintenance)* (1996), the father had shown genuine concern for the child's welfare and had maintained contact. Failure to pay maintenance was not regarded as a good reason for refusing a parental responsibility order.

There is no limit on parental responsibility since others may exercise it, ie:

- a guardian appointed by a parent;

- a 'residence' order may vest parental responsibility in the person in whose favour the residence order is made so that the welfare of the child in a particular instance is maintained.

Parents do not 'lose' parental responsibility just because someone else exercises it. It can be delegated under s 2(9) and can only be terminated by a court order – for example by an adoption order.

Obviously, parental responsibility will terminate automatically when the child reaches the age of 18 because they are then legally an 'adult', although remember that, as was discussed earlier, children do not simply acquire all the rights of adulthood just at 18, their rights 'mature' and the exercise of parental responsibility diminishes according to the approach adopted in *Gillick*. The general view now is that parental responsibility terminates when the child is able to make the decisions, but there is some dispute about when this might be!

There are some principles within the Children Act 1989 that help the court in making decisions where parents cannot agree:

33.3.4 Disputes over upbringing between parents of children

- Non-intervention principle under s 1(5)

  The court will not make an order unless making an order is better than not making an order. The idea behind this is that court orders do not always resolve difficulties and can make matters worse by not allowing parents to reach appropriate agreements themselves.

- Welfare of the child is paramount

  See s 1(1) where it states that in determining any question in relation to the child and his property the child's welfare is the paramount consideration.

  There are other references in different statutes to what is meant here – the welfare is not always 'paramount' and may be 'first' in other provisions. In the Children Act 1989, however, the paramountcy principle is very important in making decisions relating to children. Lord McDermott in *J v C* (1969) referred to the welfare of the child being a determining factor in decisions.

- The checklist

  In making decisions the court uses the statutory list of guidelines found in s 1(3) Children Act 1989. The contents of this list have been derived from previous cases where the courts have found particular factors to be important considerations in making decisions about children. The checklist should be carefully read and includes:

  (a) ascertainable wishes and feelings of the child considered in the light of his or her age and understanding;

(b) his or her physical, emotional and educational needs;

(c) likely effect upon him of any change in his or her circumstances, such as living somewhere else;

(d) age, sex, background and any other characteristics of his or hers which the court might consider relevant;

(e) any harm he has suffered or is at risk of suffering;

(f) how capable each of his parents, and any other person the court considers relevant is in meeting the child's needs;

(g) the range of powers available under the Children Act 1989.

All these factors are taken into account as the court considers applicable to the question, but all courts must use them and some might be given more weight than others.

- The resolution of disputes?

  Here we will look at the disputes between individuals rather than parents and local authorities, which is more easily dealt with under 33.1.3 above.

  The Children Act 1989 replaces all previous legislation in relation to orders relating to children and creates a new guardianship system, parental responsibility orders and four new orders (called 'section 8' orders) to deal with problems that arise.

  Only parents or guardians or persons with parental responsibility may apply for any s 8 order unless leave of the court is granted.

- Residence order

  This settles the arrangements as to with whom a child will reside and can be made in favour of anyone (and more than one) but not a local authority. The order can specify periods of time that are to spent in each place. If granted to a person who does not have parental responsibility then parental responsibility vests in the person named in the order but does not extend to adoption or appointment of a guardian for the child. This type of parental responsibility lasts for as long as the residence order is in force.

  (a) Who may apply?

     Spouses and ex-spouses may apply in relation to whom the child is a child of the family, or a person with whom the child has lived for three years, and a person who has the consent of a person with a residence, the local authority (if the child is in care although a residence order cannot be made in favour of a local authority) and in any other case, a person with parental responsibility.

- Contact order

This requires the person with whom the child lives to allow the child to visit or stay with the person named in the order and this order can be made in favour of any person, but not a local authority. Contact is not specified and could be deemed by the court to be by letter, telephone, visits or staying contact.

(a) Who may apply?

As for a residence order (see above).

- Prohibited steps order

This directs a person named in the order not to take a specified step in relation to the child without the consent of the court. The 'specified step' is one which a parent would be able to take in relation to the child in exercising parental responsibility.

- Specific issue order

This determines a specific step in relation to a child which, again, might be an issue in the exercise of parental responsibility like which school the child attends.

Section 9 prevents the last two orders being used to achieve a result which could be achieved by a residence order or contact order and all s 8 orders can be made subject to directions in s 11 of the Children Act 1989.

None of the orders can be made in relation to a child over 16 years unless there are exceptional circumstances, and all cease when the child reaches 18 (s 91).

It is possible to resolve difficulties by using proceedings under the Children Act 1989 and asking for one of the orders outlined above.

Under s 5 it is possible to apply for an order appointing a guardian of the child, or for an unmarried father to apply for parental responsibility under s 4. Most disputes are dealt with via s 8 orders either through applications under s 10(2) or as part of 'family proceedings' which includes jurisdiction to deal with a wide variety of problems relating to the upbringing of children. Persons other than parents may apply to obtain orders relating to the upbringing of the child and the court, once proceedings have begun, may decide to make use of powers it has under the Children Act 1989 to make an order the applicants did not specifically apply for in the first instance.

33.4 Local authority social services and children

The Children Act 1989 gives responsibilities to local authorities as part of their duties to ensure the welfare of children within their areas whom they know are 'in need' or who come to their attention. This responsibility is wide-ranging and is the subject of separate texts.

The major areas for the syllabus concern the responsibilities under adoption situations and, more importantly, the responsibilities which local authorities have where the criteria for 'need' have been satisfied.

33.4.1 Adoption

Although the Children Act 1989 is still relevant (especially since alternative orders may be made when the courts are approached in adoption proceedings) the law is contained within The Adoption Act 1976 and section references, unless stated otherwise, are to that statute in this part.

Adoption severs the legal relationship between parent and child. The court may add directions that it thinks fit (see *Re C (Minor – adoption conditions)* (1988) where the agreement required was that the adopters would facilitate contact with the 'first' family).

The court in family proceedings may make use of s 8 orders as an alternative to granting the adoption.

The adoption gives parental responsibility to the adopters and ends parental responsibility that is held by others. The child is treated as though born to the person or persons who adopt the child and any claims in succession apply as though the child is a natural child of his adoptive parent(s).

Adoption is regulated by the Adoption Act 1976 and by s 6 the court or adoption agency must have regard to all the circumstances, first consideration being given to the need to safeguard and promote the welfare of the child. Adoption law is currently under review and it is likely that the welfare of the child will be designated as 'paramount' in adoption matters, which would bring it into line with the Children Act 1989. The Draft Adoption Bill 1996 clause 1 referred to 'The paramount consideration of the court or adoption agency must be the child's welfare, in childhood and later'.

The child's wishes and feelings are ascertained and due consideration is given to them so far as it is practicable to do so and bearing in mind the age and understanding of the child. The child's welfare in this instance is not paramount and will not override other considerations if they are felt to be relevant.

- Criteria:

    (a) the child is under 18;

    (b) the child is at least 19 weeks old;

(c) the child has had a home with the applicant for at least 13 weeks if either applicant is the child's parent, step-parent, relative, or the child was placed with the applicant by an adoption agency or by order of the High Court;

(d) if the preceding prospective adopters are not related as described then the child must be at least 12 months and must have lived with the applicants during that period;

(e) the adoption must be of a person who has never been married;

(f) there must be parental agreement to the adoption under s 16 or the child must have been freed for adoption.

- Parental agreement?

    See s 16.

    (a) Parental agreement is required of each parent or guardian and must be given with full understanding and unconditionally (although adoption agencies must have regard to reasonable wishes of the parents with respect to the child and its religious upbringing).

    (b) A mother's agreement is ineffective if given less than six weeks after the birth of the child.

- Dispensing with parental agreement?

    See s 18.

    Parental agreement may be dispensed with if:

    (a) A parent cannot be found or is incapable of giving agreement.

    (b) The parent is unreasonably withholding their agreement in cases where adoption would advance the child's welfare, for example, although this alone would be insufficient and in determining this the court will have regard to all the circumstances of the case.

    See *Re W* (1971) where the House of Lords suggested that the test is not the welfare of the child as such but what the reasonable parent would have done in respect of the child's welfare, although welfare as such is obviously to be considered.

    (c) The parent has persistently failed without reasonable cause to discharge parental duties.

    (d) The parent has abandoned or neglected the child and the court interprets this accordingly.

    (e) The parent has persistently ill-treated the child.

(f) The parent has seriously ill-treated the child (this avoids having to demonstrate that the ill-treatment is persistent) and rehabilitation within the household is unlikely.

A child can be freed for adoption but the parents may withdraw their agreement for this declaration any time before the adoption order is made. However, s 18 means that once agreement has been given parental permission for adoption is not required. See *Re A* (1993) where Butler Sloss LJ talks about the effect of the freeing order being to extinguish parental responsibility and bring an end to the relationship between the child and his natural family (see s 12(3) Adoption Act 1976). An application for freeing cannot be made unless at least one parent or guardian consents or an adoption agency is applying for the agreement to be dispensed with and the child is in the agency's care and for these purposes the local authority constitutes such an agency. Parental responsibility would vest in the adoption agency if agreement was dispensed with or a freeing order was made so long as the court was satisfied that parents and guardians had been given the opportunity to express their views or that their agreement was freely given to the making of the order.

Reform of the grounds for dispensing with agreement are discussed in the Department for Health and Welsh Office document, Review of Adoption Law, Report to Ministers of an Inter-departmental Working Group, 1992. The Draft Adoption Bill 1996 set out new conditions for dispensing with parental consent which, under clause 46, could be dispensed with if the parent or guardian could not be found or the court was satisfied that the welfare of the child required it.

• Who can adopt?
  (a) A married couple under s 14 of whom at least one is domiciled in the UK;

  (b) A parent and step-parent – the parent must be at least 18 and the spouse at least 21;

  (c) Any unmarried person 21 or over (see s 15);

  (d) One married person aged 21 or over (see s 15 for additional requirements in the absence of the spouse).

• Suitability?

  The adoption agency or local authority has the duty to ensure that the environment where the child is to be living is appropriate and that the adopters themselves are suitable people.

Additional rules are used under The Hague Convention for adoptions where persons not domiciled in the UK apply.

Again, most of the law in the area of local authority responsibilities and family disputes is to be found in the provisions of the Children Act 1989.

Despite the principle of the Children Act 1989 that there should be no 'intervention' unless there are reasons for intervening in the way in which children are being brought up there are occasions when it might be appropriate for the state to intervene in order that the welfare of the child is maintained. It might be helpful at this point to refer back to the notes on parents and children and the legal status of the child.

Protection for children (when this is not occurring through the child's parents) is usually by means of the local authority, although wardship proceedings can be used.

Section 17 of the Children Act imposes a general duty on the local authority:

- to safeguard and promote the welfare of children within their area who are in need; and

- where this is consistent with that duty, to promote the upbringing of such children by their families by the provision of a range of services to that end.

Only the Children Act 1989 may be used unless the provisions of wardship are used which are very limited.

In general, these applications are Family Proceedings within the Children Act 1989 and the court can therefore decide to substitute its own order (like a s 8 order) for the order being sought.

By s 31(4) (see later) an application for a Care Order or a Supervision Order can be made on its own or within other proceedings as defined by s 8(3) but the remaining major orders may be made alone without other proceedings.

Section 17(10) and (11) says that a child is in need if that child is unlikely to achieve or maintain a reasonable standard of physical or mental health, or physical, intellectual, or emotional social or behavioural development without the provision of services, or if the child's development or health is likely to be significantly or further impaired or he is disabled.

Under s 20 a child in need may be 'accommodated' by the local authority if that is the way in which his needs can be met and that child is under 18 years; the local authority may provide services for those over 18 years.

The range of orders available to the local authority is wide, although the powers are not as extensive as they were under the old 1980 Child Care Act which the Children Act 1989 swept away.

33.4.2 Local authority responsibilities and family disputes

33.4.3 Responsibilities of the state

33.4.4   Range of orders

- Care order under s 31

  This commits a child to the care of the local authority and the child may live in a community home, with foster parents, etc. The local authority has parental responsibility so long as the care order is in force but there are restrictions on what the local authority can 'permit' in respect of the child – it cannot give permission for adoption, for example.

  Others who have parental responsibility will not cease to have this but cannot exercise it in any way incompatible with the care order. The child must be under 17 at the time.

  Only a local authority or the National Society for the Prevention of Cruelty to Children (NSPCC) may currently apply.

- Supervision order under s 31

  The local authority or a probation officer will supervise the child. Parental responsibility does not follow this order and the child cannot be removed from his or her home. The duty is to 'advise, assist and befriend' and the order can have conditions attached to it. This order cannot be made if the child has reached 17 and is often viewed as one step before a care order.

  Only the local authority or the NSPCC may currently apply.

- Education supervision order under s 36

  This places a child under the supervision of the local education authority and does not give that authority parental responsibility. It is used where the child is not attending school regularly and is registered to do so, or where there are indications that the child is not benefiting from school attendance.

  Only a local education authority may apply.

- Child assessment order under s 43

  This is a 'new' concept to ensure that where a local authority fears a child may be as risk and yet has no proof of harm being done to it. This order provides a resolution to the problem of immediately applying for a care order or some form of immediate protection for the child by providing, where granted, a period of seven days to give the local authority or NSPCC to carry out an assessment and any person who has the care of the children is obliged to permit access to the child for the purposes of the assessment. The order can permit the temporary removal of the child and does not give parental responsibility.

  Only a local authority or the NSPCC may apply.

- Emergency Protection Order under s 44

  This is designed for emergency situations where the local authority (or the NSPCC) feel that the only way to protect a child is to remove that child from its home. The order gives parental responsibility and the application can be made *ex parte* – that is without the presence of the parents – and very quickly since notice would not have to be given. the order lasts for only eight days in the first instance but may be extended for a period of a further seven days in specified circumstances. It can be challenged after 72 hours under s 45 and the order specifies that the local authority must only take such steps as are reasonably necessary to safeguard or promote the welfare of the child.

  Any person may apply but in practice this will usually be the local authority.

Section 34 places the local authority under a duty to ensure that the child who is the subject of an order is afforded reasonable contact with his parents. The court can make an order for directions regulating contact if necessary, although there is an assumption within the Act that this will take place unless there are reasons for not doing so and these have been presented to the court.

33.4.5   Contact between parents and children

Care and Supervision Orders under s 31 have the ground set out in s 31 and the court must be satisfied of the following, known as the threshold criteria.

33.4.6   The grounds for orders?

- that the child is suffering or is likely to suffer significant harm; and

- that the harm or likelihood of harm is attributable to:

  (a) the care given to the child, or likely to be given to him if the order were not made, not being what it would be reasonable to expect a parent to give to him; or

  (b) the child's being beyond parental control.

  Section 31(9) defines 'harm'.

  These are the only grounds upon which a child may be taken into care.

  See *Re M (A Minor)* (1994) for a discussion on significant harm and its application, including the use of threshold conditions.

  Education supervision orders under s 36 require that a child is of compulsory school age and is not being properly educated suitable to his age, aptitude and ability, and to any special educational needs he or she has.

Child assessment orders under s 43 require the court to be satisfied that the applicant has reasonable cause to suspect significant harm to the child which can only be determined by an examination of the child which is unlikely to take place unless an order is made.

Emergency protection orders under s 44 require three separate criteria to be applied:

- where a local authority is making enquiries already then if they can show that their enquiries are being frustrated and they need emergency access to the child;

- if the NSPCC, already making enquiries, can demonstrate that their enquiries are being frustrated and they need to get access to the child, and that they have reasonable cause to suspect that the child about whom they are concerned, is suffering, or is likely to suffer, significant harm;

- any other applicant must show reasonable cause to suspect significant harm if the child is not removed as a matter of urgency.

Section 1 of the welfare principle applies, but for emergency protection orders it is not necessary to show the application of the s 1(3) guidelines.

In *Nottinghamshire CC v P (No 2)* (1993) a local authority was prevented from applying for a prohibited steps order to exclude an abuser from the home. This problem, identified in *Re S (Minors) (Inherent Jurisdictions: Ouster)* (1994), was provided with a solution by the Family Law Act 1996 (not yet in force). In future a court may, when making an emergency protection order under s 44 Children Act 1989, or an interim care order, make an 'exclusion requirement'. This requires a named individual to leave the home shared with the child. To make such an order the court must be satisfied that there is reasonable cause to believe that if the person is excluded the child would cease to suffer (or cease to be likely to suffer) significant harm, and that the parent who remains at home can provide reasonable care and consents to the exclusion requirement. A power of arrest can be attached to the order, and the court has the power to accept undertakings in place of the exclusion requirement.

33.5   Domestic violence

Violence in married and unmarried relationships is very common. The law does provide some means of dealing with the problems, but these are merely legal solutions (if solutions they be) to what are social and psychological problems.

Currently, injunctions and orders can be used in the civil courts to attempt to remedy the problems.

The ordinary criminal law can be used but for various reasons (often evidential, or reasons of accommodation) this is not necessarily the most appropriate resolution.

The law of tort could also be used to bring a case of assault and battery but since this is most often used to obtain compensation for wrongs it is not regarded as being the best solution in domestic violence where what is required is protection from further violence for the victim.

It is also true that injunctions or orders can add to rather than reduce problems in situations where relationships may be breaking down and there are orders which can be used to separate the parties to avoid further violent events in the household. These are called ouster orders and can order a person from particular rooms in the house or from the home altogether. Orders can also be made to allow a person free access to the home.

Orders can be sought by adult or child victims of the violence which can take many forms and may be physical, mental or emotional violence.

In 1992, the Law Commission published its report 'Family Law, Domestic Violence and the occupation of the Family Home' (No 207) which criticised existing law on domestic violence. It was recommended that there be a single and uniform provision with a consistent remedy for domestic violence covering all courts and a wider range of perpetrators and victims. The first attempt to reform the law (the Family Homes and Domestic Violence Bill of 1994–95) met with opposition and failed.

The proposals in the abandoned Family Homes and Domestic Violence Bill were incorporated into the Family Law Act 1996 which was passed in July 1996. The Act is not yet in force, and Part IV concerns domestic violence. The major part of the Family Law Act 1996 concerns divorce and provisions for the facilitation of mediation and the legal aid provisions for this. Part IV of the Family Law Act 1996 is due to come into force in the Autumn of 1997. When in force it will repeal the Domestic Violence and Matrimonial Proceedings Act 1976, the Matrimonial Homes Act 1983 and ss 16–18 Domestic Proceedings and Magistrates' Courts Act 1978.

The court has a general power to grant an injunction in cases where it seems appropriate in the view of the court to do so. This is referred to as 'inherent' power and does not depend upon the statutory definition of a situation having arisen; the court may use its power in any proceeding where it considers it appropriate to do so.	33.5.1 Injunctions and orders

A person who is not married to their partner must use the county court to seek an injunction, whereas married couples may make use of the magistrates' court for orders in addition to their use of the injunctions.

There are three main statutes:

• Matrimonial Homes Act 1983;

• Domestic Violence and Matrimonial Proceedings Act 1976;

• Domestic Proceedings and Magistrates' Courts Act 1978

and a brief note will be given on each. A few points must be made first.

There are a number of cases in relation to domestic violence and these include:

Patel v Patel (1988);

Montgomery v Montgomery (1965);

Wilde v Wilde (1988).

An important case to read is *Richards v Richards* (1983) in which the court indicated that there were limits upon the powers of the court since it was not open to litigants to use a general power of the court when specific powers were available to cover situations relating directly to the problem they had. The court decided that when the regulation of the occupation of the matrimonial home was in question then the specific statute enacted to deal with that problem had to be used. *Note*, though, that the provisions under this Act are replaced by Part IV of the Family Law Act 1996.

• The Matrimonial Homes Act 1983

If a spouse has a right to occupy a home that has been or still is the matrimonial home then the court can make an order regulating those rights by restricting, terminating, prohibiting, suspending or restricting those rights or requiring the other to permit the exercise of the right.

This Act applies only to those who are married and does not extend to the area around the house.

The grant of ouster injunctions requires the application of s 1(3) MHA 1983 and the court will make an order that it thinks just and reasonable and will have regard to:

• conduct of the spouses in relation to each other;

• their respective needs and financial resources:

• the needs of any children;

• all the circumstances of the case.

See *Richards v Richards*.

In *Wiseman v Simpson* (1988) the Court of Appeal pointed out that to remove a person from their home was a serious matter and an order was refused despite the violent outbreaks.

- Domestic Violence and Matrimonial Proceedings Act 1976

  Section 1 allows the following:

  (a) a non-molestation injunction for the applicant;

  (b) one relating to any child living with the applicant;

  (c) an ouster injunction from home or environs;

  (d) an injunction to permit the applicant to enter and remain in the home or part of it.

  In practice most injunctions will have a time limit of three months since there is an expectation that the couple will resolve their difficulties or seek a decree of divorce.

  This Act will apply to cohabitees as well as married couples.

  See *Davis v Johnson* (1978) where the House of Lords discussed the application of the provisions to cohabitees.

  Those who have domestic violence problems but have never lived together may not use this provision. Such people must use the inherent jurisdiction of the court to seek an injunction within an application under the law of tort, or the criminal law provisions.

- Domestic Proceedings and Magistrates' Courts Act 1978

  Section 16 allows a spouse to apply for an order not to molest or threaten violence against the applicant or child of the family (this is called a personal protection order or family protection order) or for an order that the spouse should leave or not enter (or permit the other to enter) the home (this is called an exclusion order).

  This Act does not cover the broader 'molestation' and means 'violence' done to the applicant.

  Conditions must be fulfilled which prove the use or threat of violence and that the order is necessary to protect. The threat can be against the applicant or child, with actual violence to another party.

Breach of injunction granted by the High Court or county court is contempt and a person may be fined or imprisoned. The provisions give the magistrates court power to fine or imprison.

33.5.2   Enforcement

Powers of arrest can be attached to orders and this can reduce the anxiety felt by many victims for whom the prospects of taking a case to court again is too much. There are limitations on the grant of this power due to its severe results for the alleged transgressor.

33.5.3   The future?

Plans to reform the law relating to domestic violence because it was felt that the law was unnecessarily complicated in this area have already been introduced. There is confusion about what orders/injunctions are available to whom, whether married or unmarried, and that there appeared to be little protection outside the immediate 'family' – none from violent children, for example, and none for the protection of the wider family. The main issues were the differences in the level of protection afforded to married and unmarried and the different procedures and requirements in the courts themselves. What follows is a brief summary of the new provisions found in Part IV of the Family Law Act 1996.

Occupation of the matrimonial home

Provisions in s 1(1) MHA 1983 are now found in s 30(2) Family Law Act (FLA) 1996. Statutory rights of occupation are to be called 'matrimonial home rights' – if one spouse has a legal right of occupation and the other does not then that spouse is given rights not to be evicted or excluded unless via a court order. This provision also gives rights with leave of the court to occupy the home. The new provisions also give a spouse with an equitable interest rights of occupation under s 30(2) FLA 1996.

Rights of occupation under s 30 will continue as long as the marriage does and as long as the other spouse is entitled to occupy.

Orders

Applications for occupation and non-molestation orders can be made to the High Court, county court or magistrates' court. It is likely that there will be rules directing that applications commence in the magistrates' court (cheaper and quicker) and more difficult cases will be transferred to county courts. It is also likely that disputes concerning entitlement to occupy property by virtue of a beneficial interest are likely to be dealt with at a county court. *Ex parte* orders (s 45) will be made where the court considers it just and convenient to do so.

Appeals against the making of orders lie to the High Court under s 61 FLA 1996, or the Court of Appeal if the decision was made in the county court or High Court. Section 62 FLA 1996 gives *definitions* of those to whom the new provisions apply. As was stated earlier, one of the criticisms of previous provisions under domestic violence was that they covered limited situations. Under the new provisions cohabitants (a man and a woman, although not married to each other, but living together as husband and wife) and former cohabitants are covered. 'Relevant children' are also covered, and this group includes any child whose interests the court considers relevant, so long as they are under 18 years. 'Significant harm' is referred to in s 63 FLA 1996, and this has the same meaning of that found in the Children Act 1989. There are 'associated' persons in the new provisions who may make applications if they:

- are or have been married to each other;

- cohabitants or former cohabitants;

- have lived or live in the same household (but not as employees, tenants, lodgers or boarders);

- they are relatives (as defined in s 63(1) FLA 1996);

- they are or have been engaged to marry each other (proof is required);

- they are the parents of a relevant child, or have parental responsibility for the child;

- they are parties to the same family proceedings.

Applications for occupation orders may be made by the above groups.

Occupation orders in FLA 1996:

1   Application by a person with occupation rights or with matrimonial home rights against an 'associated' person (under s 33).

2   Application by a former spouse with no existing right to occupy against the other former spouse who has a right to occupy (under s 35).

3   Application by a cohabitant or former cohabitant with no right to occupy against a cohabitant or former cohabitant with a right to occupy (under s 36).

4   Application by a spouse with no right to occupy against a spouse who also has no right to occupy (under s 37).

5   Application by a cohabitant or former cohabitant with no right to occupy against a cohabitant or former cohabitant who also has no right to occupy (under s 38).

Different considerations apply in each case (although there are similarities) but important factors are as follows.

In No 1, s 33 looks at needs/resources, the likely effect on any child and the conduct of the parties (see s 33(6) FLA 1996). The 'balance of harm' test applies – s 33(7).

In No 2, similar consideration to s 33 apply, but also the length of time that may have elapsed and any pending proceedings for an order under s 23A or 24 MCA 1973. The 'balance of harm' test applies and an order under s 35 must be limited to a period not exceeding six months, although it may be extended for a further period not exceeding six months on one or more occasions.

In No 3, a s 36 order is limited to a period not exceeding six months but may be extended. In deciding whether to make an order, the court will also have regard to all the circumstances, as for s 33.

In No 4, the same considerations for s 33 apply, as does the 'balance of harm' test. A s 37 order is limited to a period not exceeding six months but, again, can be extended on one or more occasions for a further period. The order will not affect a third party who is entitled to occupy the property.

In No 5, the order is again limited to a six month period but may be extended for one further period under s 38(6) FLA 1996.

Occupation orders may be made in other family proceedings or without any being instituted. The court has power to make orders about repair, maintenance of the property, payment of rent or mortgage (only under ss 33, 35 and 36). In deciding how and whether to exercise its powers, the court must have regard to all the circumstances of the case, including financial needs and resources of the parties, present and future financial obligations to each other or to any relevant child.

Non-molestation orders

This order prohibits the respondent molesting another person 'associated' with the respondent and/or prohibits the molestation of a relevant child (see s 42 FLA 1996). In deciding whether and in what manner to exercise power, the court will have regard to all the circumstances of the case (s 42(5)). The order can be made for a specified period or ceases if, when made in other family proceedings, those proceedings are withdrawn or dismissed.

Applications by children: occupation orders or non-molestation orders.

Under 16 – a child may not apply for an order except with leave of the court, granted if the child has sufficient understanding (s 43 FLA 1996).

Over 16 – a child may apply in their own right.

Undertakings

Under s 46 FLA 1996 a court may accept an undertaking (a very 'serious' promise which can be enforced) from any party to the proceedings. Powers of arrest cannot be attached (s 46).

Power of arrest

Under s 46 the court can consider attaching a power of arrest to the order. If the respondent has used or threatened violence against the applicant or a child it must attach a power of arrest unless satisfied that the applicant or child will be adequately protected without it. Where there is a power of arrest a constable may arrest without a warrant a person reasonably suspected of being in breach of an occupation or non-molestation order. The arrested person must be brought before a court to be dealt with.

Where there is no power of arrest, the applicant can apply to the court for the issue of a warrant for the respondent's arrest if there has been a failure to comply with the order. The courts have power to commit to prison a respondent who disobeys an occupation or non-molestation order.

33.6   Family break-up and the law

Much of what has been written has explained the situation with respect to the break-up (or is it break-down?) of the family. This section is concerned with the law that relates to the legal ending of the marriage that was dealt with at 33.1 above.

Note on reform

The Family Law Act 1996 was passed in July 1996 and radically changes divorce law. Sections 1–7 MCA 1973 will be repealed and replaced by Parts I, II and III FLA 1996. This law is not yet in force and awaits further detailed regulations. It was anticipated that the new divorce law would be in force by 1998, but it is unlikely to be so until the turn of the century. The law regarding nullity remains basically unchanged.

33.6.1   Nullity

Section 11 MCA 1973 states four grounds for the decree of nullity which declares that a marriage is either void or voidable. In one sense this does not end the marriage because it is saying that there was no marriage but it means that the parties are free to marry after the decree without there being a doubt cast on the legal end of the 'marriage'.

A void marriage was never a marriage because there was some 'error' but the granting of a decree allows for a claim under ss 23 and 24 for ancillary relief.

Voidable marriages are valid marriages until annulled by decree.

Four grounds for declaring a marriage void:

- not a valid marriage under the Marriage Acts;

- either party was already married at the time of marriage;

- parties are not respectively male and female;

- a polygamous marriage entered into outside England and Wales where either part was domiciled at the time in England or Wales.

See s 11 MCA.

Six grounds for declaring a marriage voidable:

- non-consummation due to incapacity of either party;

- non-consummation due to wilful refusal of the applicant for the decree;

- lack of valid consent by either party;

- either party was suffering from a mental disorder;

- the respondent was suffering from a venereal disease in a communicable form at the time of the marriage;

- that the respondent was pregnant by someone other than the petitioner at the time of the marriage and the petitioner did not know or consent.

See s 12 MCA.

Non-consummation is the most common ground relied upon.

Consummation of a marriage requires one act of intercourse after the celebration of the marriage and it does not matter for this purpose if the couple lived together before they married, or never have intercourse again.

The act must be 'ordinary and complete, not partial and imperfect' and whether the incapacity is due to physical or psychological reasons does not matter but it must be 'incurable' or curable only by a dangerous operation or refused by the party suffering the incapacity.

A spouse may petition upon their own incapacity.

Where there is wilful refusal the decision must be 'settled' and have been arrived at because of no just cause for the decision (see *Horton v Horton* (1947)).

Void marriages have no bars or defences since the marriages never existed unless it can be established that the ground does not exist.

Section 13 MCA deals with bars and defences which includes:

- the respondent satisfying the court that he or she was led to believe that the petitioner would not petition and it would be unjust to grant the decree. This belief must have been reasonably held.

  See *D v D* (1979) where the parties had adopted a child.

Divorce is now a very common event in a society and the number of divorces has steadily grown since the end of the Second World War. There have been increases at times when the law has been reformed (as in the early 1970s) but current estimates suggest that one person in three will, on at least one occasion in their life, get divorced. The law relating to divorce has been 'accused' of creating many social problems and discussions on this issue are really the subject of other texts.

What follows is the current law on divorce. A brief summary of the reformed provisions will be given later.

33.6.2   Divorce

There is only one ground for divorce and that is that the marriage has irretrievably broken down (see s 1(1) MCA 1973).

Section 1(4) requires the court to be satisfied of this.

The court may grant a petition for divorce if the petitioner can show one of five facts, which are often confused with the ground for divorce itself. A petitioner has to prove one of the five facts before the decree could be granted, even if it is clear that the marriage has broken down.

33.6.3   The ground for divorce

- Section 1(2)(a)

  The respondent has committed adultery and the petitioner finds it intolerable to live with him.

  There are two parts to this requirement:

  Adultery is consensual sexual intercourse with another person of the opposite sex, the one not being the other's spouse.

  In *Clarkson* (1930) the raped wife of the petitioner had not committed adultery.

  See *Cleary v Cleary* (1974) where it was established that the intolerability of the situation does not have to be caused by the adultery.

  The test for intolerability is subjective (see *Goodrich* (1971) where this was confirmed) and the petitioner might have to give explanations for the feelings in order to persuade the court.

33.6.4   The five facts

- Section 1(2)(b)

  The respondent has behaved in a way that the petitioner cannot reasonably be expected to live with them.

The test applied in Livingstone-Stallard in 1974 where Dunn J said:

> 'Would any right thinking person come to the conclusion that this husband had behaved in such a way that the wife could not reasonably be expected to live with him ...'

and the court will take into account the circumstances of the case.

Behaviour here is likely to refer to drinking, gambling, behaviour that falls short of adultery, or more trivial behaviour which has occurred over a longer period of time.

Both acts and omissions suffice and it is unnecessary that the parties actually intended this behaviour to cause distress.

One case concerned an epileptic wife with a neurological disorder whose 'behaviour' included bedwetting, setting fire to the house, wandering the streets at night and inability to feed herself. Her failure to 'keep house' prior to her illness was also taken into account.

In *Katz* (1972) behaviour was defined as action or conduct that affects the other party.

A state of mind might then be insufficient to establish the situation as described in *Buffery v Buffery* (1988) where the parties had simply grown apart and had nothing in common.

It is problematic as to whether the court would regard something as a state of affairs or 'behaviour' and it is not always possible to predict.

For example, not consummating the marriage could be used in nullity, but whilst subsequent refusal of sex (after consummation) would not be 'satisfactory' it would not necessarily be regarded as 'behaviour'.

- Section 1(2)(c)

  The respondent deserted the petitioner for at least two years immediately before the petition.

  This is not often used and requires:

  (i) the parties to be living apart in a physical sense;

  (ii) with the intention that the respondent wished to live apart permanently;

  (iii) and the desertion did not take place as a result of agreement (despite any sense of relief if one party does leave!);

  (iv) there being no 'good cause' for leaving arising from the petitioner's behaviour using the test in s 1(2)(b) to result in 'constructive' desertion because the supposedly deserting spouse was 'forced' to leave.

Desertion only begins when all the conditions are satisfied and can be brought to an end by one of them ceasing to apply.

The section requires a period of continuous desertion of two years immediately preceding the petition.

- Section 1(2)(d)

The parties have lived apart for two years and the respondent consents to the decree.

Both living apart and consent are required here but the difficulties occur where the parties 'share' the same building yet attempt to live separate lives – are they 'apart' for the purposes of the legislation? Signs of communal life must certainly be absent for this purpose, so that it is much easier to demonstrate if the parties are actually living in separate homes.

In *Mouncer v Mouncer* (1972) the parties had separate bedrooms and the wife did not do the husband's washing. She cooked for the family and they all had meals together and shared the cleaning. The husband did not leave because he wanted to see the children, but the court said that they were not living separate lives!

Compare this with *Fuller v Fuller* (1973) where the husband was 'taken in' by the wife and her boyfriend and was looked after because he was ill and had nowhere else to go. The wife performed similar duties to that of Mrs Mouncer but the court said they were not living together as husband and wife.

One of the parties at least must recognise that the marriage is at an end so merely being apart does not suffice for the purposes of this section.

The court can only grant a decree where the marriage has irretrievably broken down and the parties have lived apart (as described) for two years immediately preceding the petition.

Both parties must consent to the decree.

- Section 1(2)(e)

The parties have lived apart for five years immediately preceding the petition.

This is very similar to the previous fact except that the period of time is longer and it does not require the consent of both parties. The two are used for different situations often, since (e) does not need the consent and (d) is used where the parties agree there should be a divorce. Proceedings under (e) occur more often where one party does not wish there to be a divorce!

See *Santos v Santos* (1972) which involved a petition under the previous section it was emphasised that at least one party must feel that the marriage is at an end and this applies to five years apart too.

33.6.5   Defences?

Defences are as follows:

- That the fact does not exist.

- That the marriage has not irretrievably broken down.

- Section 5 MCA (only for s 1(2)(e) five years' separation) so long as the petitioner cannot find another fact that applies to his or her situation then the petition is refused on the ground that the respondent would suffer a 'grave financial or other hardship' resulting from the dissolution of the marriage but not the mere fact of the separation of the parties. This is rare and not very successful as a pleading. Usually it has been anticipated that the loss of pension rights might be what is thought of here, or severe social ostracism. If successfully pleaded the marriage is not terminated.

  K v K (1996): in this financial provision case concerning the s 5 special defence of grave financial hardship, the law seemed inadequate to deal with the pension, leaving the wife to suffer grave financial hardship. The husband had made proposals, but they did not fully compensate for the loss of a widow's pension.

33.6.6   Bars to divorce?

- Section 3 MCA requires the parties to have been married for at least one year before a petition can be filed. There can be reference to matters occurring prior to that date.

- A six month 'kiss-and-make-up' applies in s 1(2)(a) if the parties have lived together for a period of six months after the discovery of the last episode of adultery.

- In s 1(2)(b) a similar provision applies which is a discretionary bar because the court will take into account the parties living together for a period of six months or more in deciding whether the criteria have been made out.

- The period of six months (which is noted in s 2) applies only if the period is not less than six months and any period shorter than this will not prevent, for example, the continuous period applying in separation – but longer than six months and it will.

- If the parties live together for any number of periods not exceeding six months but added together exceeding the six month period then s 2 will operate.

Section 10 MCA 1973 enables the respondent whose divorce is based upon (d) or (e) separation to apply after decree nisi but before absolute for the financial arrangements to be examined so that the court can be satisfied that they are appropriate.

    Section 41 (as amended by the Children Act 1989) protects children under 16 years of age and the court considers whether any powers under the Children Act 1989 should be used in respect of any relevant children. The court will then direct that a decree absolute should not be granted without a further court order.

    Two conditions are to be applied – that the court is not in a position to exercise its powers without considering the case and there are exceptional circumstances concerning the welfare of the children.

33.6.7   Delays?

Decrees of judicial separation do not end the marriage but recognise that there has been a 'marital breakdown' and allow for ancillary relief under s 24 MCA 1973 to be made. All the arrangements that can be made in the case of divorcing couples can be made for those obtaining a judicial separation, except that neither party is free to remarry since they are still married. The decree is now infrequently used, but where it is it is either because one or both parties have a fundamental objection to getting a divorce, or they wish to take a stage akin to divorce and cannot (perhaps because they have not been married long enough) actually divorce at the time.

33.6.8   Judicial separation

Section 17 MCA 1973, the five grounds for a decree of judicial separation, correspond with the five facts for divorce in s 1(2) MCA 1973.

    The major difference is that there is no need to show that the marriage has irretrievably broken down.

33.6.9   Grounds

The respondent may defend on the basis that the ground has not been made out but the defence of grave financial or other hardship is unavailable for this decree.

33.6.10   Defences?

Section 2 applies but there is no bar on applying for a decree before the marriage has lasted for one year.

33.6.11   Bars?

Section 41 MCA 1973 applies and the decree itself may not be granted on the basis that the court may wish to make a further order relating to the protection of children.

    Section 10 does not apply.

33.6.12   Delays?

33.6.13 Reform of divorce law

The Law Commission Report on the Ground for Divorce No 192 was published in 1990 and a number of possible proposals were put forward by interested groups.

The proposal which received the most support is one involving 'divorce over time' allowing for a period of 'reflection' and consideration of the implications and practicalities of divorce for the couple and the children.

The one proposed ground is that the marriage has irretrievably broken down, proved by the parties having gone through the 'period of reflection' which effectively abolishes the facts as set out in s 1(2) MCA 1973.

All references are to the FLA 1996.

The new law on divorce (not yet in force) sets out general principles in s 1. These include the support of the institution of marriage, the encouragement of reconciliation and, when a marriage has broken down, the bringing to an end of the marriage with minimum distress to the parties and children, with regard being had to continuing relationships, and without unreasonable cost being incurred and the avoidance of risk of violence.

Divorce orders are applied for using s 2 FLA 1996 and s 3(1) states that a divorce order may only be made if the marriage has broken down irretrievably (demonstrated by the passage of a period for reflection and consideration) where requirements in s 8 (on information meetings) are met, and parties' arrangements for the future are satisfied, according to s 9 FLA 1996.

A party may not begin the process (by making a statement of marital breakdown) until at least three months after that party has attended an information meeting (s 8(2) FLA 1996). This meeting provides relevant information in connection with the divorce, and may include financial matters and marriage counselling opportunities. Where one party has made a statement, the other must attend a meeting if they wish to make or contest an application to the court relating to a child or financial matters.

Statements are required by ss 5 and 6 which permits the court to direct the parties to mediation on disputes.

Section 7 FLA 1996 relates to the period of reflection and consideration. This gives an opportunity for reconciliation and a consideration about future arrangements. It begins with the fourteenth day after the statement of marital breakdown is received by the court (which is not less than three months after attendance at an information meeting) and lasts nine months. This nine months will be 18 months where there are children of the family under the age of 16.

The period of reflection may be extended (under regulations to be specified) and the clock can be stopped where the parties give notice of an attempted reconciliation. An interruption lasting longer than 18 months can only be followed by an application by either party for a divorce order by reference to a new statement of marital breakdown.

Section 5 provides that applications cannot be made using a statement if the parties jointly give notice withdrawing the statement, or if more than one year has elapsed since the end of the period of reflection and consideration.

The statement of marital breakdown and the application for a divorce order do not have to be made by the same party.

A divorce order cannot be made unless a court order dealing with financial arrangements (or a declaration by the parties) can be produced. No divorce order can be applied for unless one year has expired from the marriage date (see s 7).

Section 11 provides specifically for the welfare of any children (compare s 41 MCA 1973) and the court must treat this as paramount in considering whether powers under the Children Act 1989 are to be exercised. What must be considered are the wishes and feelings of the child(ren) in the light of their age and understanding, conduct of the parties in the upbringing of any child, the maintenance of good continuing relationships between children and parents, and any risk to the child(ren) from arrangements for residence, contact care and upbringing (see s 11(4)).

Section 14 permits the court to adjourn proceedings to allow the parties to comply with mediation directions.

Section 10 provides a special defence on the grounds that the dissolution of the marriage would result in substantial financial or other hardship, including loss of a future benefit, to the other party or to a child of the family, and that it would be wrong in all the circumstances for the marriage to be dissolved.

Separation order (previously judicial separation)

Under the FLA 1996 irretrievable breakdown is the sole ground for judicial separation. It will be known as a 'separation order' (see s 2(1)(b)). The procedure is the same as for a divorce order (s 3) and the order remains in force while the marriage continues unless cancelled. Under s 4 a separation order can be converted to a divorce order but not before the marriage is two years old, neither can it be converted if there is an order preventing divorce under s 10 or there is a child of the family under 16 when the application is made. (But see s 4(5) relating to domestic violence.)

33.7   Inheritance and family provision

Marriage affects the entitlement to property after the death of the other spouse. A spouse, like any other person may make a will leaving their property to any person they wish (subject to the rules of the Wills Act 1837 to prevent fraud 18 – or over, will in writing and signed by the testator with two witnesses to attest to the signature). If a spouse dies intestate (not having made a will) then the surviving spouse receives an entitlement under intestate succession but cohabitees are not so well treated.

Where a spouse makes a will they can leave their property to whom they wish, except for property in joint names since that goes to the survivor under survivorship. Marriage automatically revokes a will made prior to marriage unless made in contemplation of marriage. On divorce or nullity the will does not take effect in so far as it involves the former spouse as the recipient of a gift or a trustee (unless there is a contrary intention in the will) but this does not prevent claims under the Inheritance (Provision for Family and Dependants) Act 1975.

Where a spouse does not make a will (intestacy) special rules apply. Provision is made for the surviving spouse, then for the children and then other surviving relatives if there is no spouse, children or issue of children. Only where there is a substantial estate will anyone other than the spouse receive money. Personal representatives of the dead person must pay debts and expenses and distribute the remainder according to the Administration of Estates Act 1925 (amended) and the law on intestacy is complex.

Whilst the law is complex the following is a summary of the provisions upon intestacy:

If the person is unmarried and has no children the estate upon intestacy goes to the person's parents or surviving brothers and sisters or other close relatives.

If there are no relatives then the estate goes to the Crown.

If the person was married but had no children the spouse gets the first £200,000 and half of the remainder. The other half of the remainder goes to the dead person's parents and if they are dead, to the brothers and sisters.

If the person was married and had children the spouse gets the first £125,000 and a life interest in half of the rest. This would then pass to the children on the death of the surviving spouse. The other half will go to the children immediately.

If there are children but no spouse then the estate is shared equally between the children.

The law is found in the 1975 Act noted above.

The court has jurisdiction to make provision for certain family members and dependants where there has not been provision either because the deceased dies without a will, or the will did not make provision.

Applications are made within six months of the death otherwise leave of the court is required.

The following may apply:

- surviving spouses;

- former spouses who have not remarried;

- children of the deceased;

- any person treated as a child of the family;

- anyone who was being 'maintained' wholly or partly by the deceased immediately before the death of the deceased (this would include cohabitees, for example).

Note here *Cameron v Treasury Solicitor* (1996) where the Treasury successfully appealed the award of an estate to an ex-wife after her ex-husband died intestate, having already agreed to a clean break settlement upon divorce. The question was whether in all the circumstances it was reasonable for the (ex) husband to have made financial provision for the (ex) wife. The court considered it relevant to consider whether there were any obligations towards the (ex) wife and special circumstances would have to be demonstrated to justify giving her an award.

Various orders could be made where provision had not been made by the deceased and where the applicant is a spouse (but there was no decree of judicial separation which does not legally end the marriage) which results in reasonable financial provision in all the circumstances of the case for the husband or wife to receive. Other relatives receive 'maintenance' as their reasonable financial provision.

Section 2 of the Act covers the orders that could be made and they are similar to ancillary relief under the MCA 1973. For example, periodical payments, property transfer, lump sums, and settlements could all be available to the court.

Section 3 sets out criteria by which decisions are made and the court must consider all the circumstances of the case. Included among the criteria are actual and potential financial resources, obligations and responsibilities of the deceased, other applicants under the Act, size and nature of the net estate, physical and mental capacity of applicants and any other relevant matter agreed by the court. Spouses and

33.7.1   Provision from the estate of a deceased family provider

children of the deceased have additional criteria to recognise their position in respect of the deceased. These might include the duration of the marriage, age, contributions to the welfare of the family and what the surviving spouse might have expected to receive if on the date of death the marriage had been terminated by divorce rather than by the death (see *Re Moody (deceased)* (1992)).

The 1975 Act also allows the court to vary or discharge secured periodical payments orders made on divorce.

Under s 15 of the Act financial obligations can be restricted in accordance with the MFPA 1984 as part of the clean break approach (see *Whiting v Whiting* (1988) where the husband made an application).

See *Re Krubert (deceased)* (1996) concerning a surviving spouse making claims under the 1975 Act. There was a conflict between using 'presumed entitlement' as a starting point or simply only one of the factors. The court preferred to use 'presumed entitlement' as only one of the factors.

Chapter 34

Welfare Law

It is a question of philosophical, moral and socio-legal interest as to whether a person is 'entitled' to receive welfare benefits from the state.

34.1   The legal basis of welfare

Here we are concerned with legal entitlements in a complex benefit system where the law makes provision for certain groups of individuals who fall within a category to receive a financial 'benefit' as a result of qualifying for that benefit through the basis set out in statutory provisions.

Much of the law in this area is complex and this chapter contains an outline of the provisions. The law was to be found in some 15 Acts of Parliament now consolidated in two major provisions – The Social Security Contributions and Benefits Act (SSCBA) 1992 and the Social Security Administration Act (SSAA) 1992. There is a lot of technical detail (unnecessary for the purposes of the syllabus) in Statutory Instruments which allow for the essential alterations each year that take changes like amounts and criteria into account without having to alter the parenting Act of Parliament.

Under the relevant rules and regulations a person is entitled to a benefit if he meets the qualifying criteria set out for the benefit. These are laid down under headings and a person can lose the right to receive the benefit in certain circumstances. The right may be suspended according to the rules, for example, if there is doubt about entitlement, or circumstances change, or a person can no longer claim because they no longer meet the criteria. It all depends on the nature of the benefit itself!

The right to the benefit is 'inalienable', that is, it attaches to the individual who cannot nominate another to claim instead.

Some 'benefits' within the system are not 'rights' but may be claimed and awarded on a discretionary basis. Some benefits depend upon the existence of funds which may be exhausted when a person applies and will thus not be available.

Benefit rates and limits are revised annually, and information about current benefits and the rates that apply is readily available from material distributed by the Department for Social Security through a range of outlets like local offices and post offices, job centres and so on. The major leaflets are FB2 *Which Benefit?* and those available on the major benefits themselves, like unemployment benefit, sickness benefits and benefits for babies and children.

The Social Security system is recognised as being complex. Some rules are common to all benefits, or to many of a 'type' of benefit, such as contribution and residence qualifications, special rules for those in hospital or prison, and how earnings are calculated.

34.1.1	Types of benefits	Benefits fall into two main categories: contributory and non-contributory.

The criteria for receipt of the benefit thus depends upon this basic division.

Some benefits are only payable for those who have made a contribution through the national insurance scheme (see below) through deductions from their earnings which entitles them to make a claim to see if they qualify for the benefit according to the criteria for that benefit.

Benefits which are contributory include contribution-based jobseekers allowance and maternity allowance. Contribution benefits are paid from the National Insurance Fund funded by National Insurance Contributions.

Other benefits are non-contributory and are based on whether the set of circumstances has arisen which entitles the person to claim the benefit – these include child benefit and attendance allowance. Non-contributory Benefits are paid out of general taxation and have a residence qualification.

Means-tested benefits specify that a benefit will only be paid if the claimant's income or resources are low enough to qualify for making a claim. This is a monetary limit.

This is favoured as a means of ensuring that the benefits reach those most in need, but it does mean that a redefinition of 'right' to claim is needed since a person might otherwise either meet the claiming criteria, or be paying into the system through tax or national insurance contributions without necessarily ever being able to receive a welfare benefit.

Some benefits exist to compensate those unable to work through unemployment, sickness, pregnancy or old age. Others are designed to meet specific needs, like being disabled, or having children.

34.2 The National Insurance system

Most of those who work between the ages of 16 and retirement age will pay a proportion of their earnings to the National Insurance (NI) system as contributions (NICs).

These NICs are a requirement of a claim is to be made on NI benefits.

There are the following classes of contributions:

Classes 1 and 1A if you work for another person.

The more you earn the more you will pay as a percentage of your earnings up to a maximum amount. This gives entitlement to all benefits with contribution conditions.

NICs are taken out of the pay received.

Classes 2 and 4 are paid if you are self-employed.

Class 4 is paid if the earnings rise above the current limit (limits are set each year for all contributions), but such a person would begin by contributing Class 2 NICs. Class 4 self-employed earners do not have entitlement.

Class 3 NICs are voluntary payments made if you are not earning enough to pay Class 1 or do not have to pay Class 2. they are used to help protect rights to retirement pension but they are otherwise very limited for benefit purposes.

Class 1 credits can be paid if, for example, a person is ill or is unemployed. Separate rules apply to circumstances when this can be done.

Looking after a sick or disabled person may allow the receipt of Home Responsibilities Protection to protect basic rights to benefits like retirement pensions.

Some married women and widows still have the right to pay reduced liability Class 1 NICs. If a person works over retirement age they no longer pay NICs although their employer continues to pay.

The first way in which benefits may be divided is by looking to see whether they are contributory or non-contributory benefits (see above for details on NICs).

34.3   Major types of welfare benefits

This is in effect the first criteria for claimants.

The following are some of the benefits currently available within the welfare benefit system. Further details can be obtained on individual benefits from the noted leaflet.

34.4   Introduction to benefits

There are a number of categories for benefits which are:

- Benefits for those on low income

  This includes Income Support which is non-contributory and depends largely on the income you have and the allocated allowances for outgoings.

  It includes personal allowances, premiums for particular circumstances and housing costs. There are limits set for each allowance.

Family credit can be paid as a tax-free benefit for working families and does not depend upon NICs.

Housing Benefit is another example and is often paid to those in receipt of Social Fund Payments which help people with expenses difficult to pay out of regular income or benefits payable.

Payments from the Social Fund would be included under 'safety net' payments like maternity payments, community care grants and budgeting loans.

- Benefits for the unemployed

    Jobseekers allowance was a new benefit introduced in October 1996. If sufficient contributions have been paid this jobseekers allowance can be claimed for six months without satisfying a means test. Those not satisfying this criterion may apply for income-based jobseekers allowance.

- Benefits for pregnant women

    Statutory maternity pay is paid to women expecting babies with a maternity allowance paid to those who do not qualify for the former because they have not worked for their employer long enough.

- Benefits for those bringing up children

    This includes child benefit for almost everyone who has a child to look after regardless of income.

- Benefits for young people

    Young people who have just left school or college will find it difficult to obtain benefits that are based on NICs. Since they are guaranteed a Youth Training place or further education they are normally unable to obtain income support.

- Benefits for the sick, injured and disabled

    This includes statutory sick pay and sickness benefit for the long-term sick followed by invalidity benefit for those still incapable of work after six months.

    Severe disablement allowance, disability living allowance and attendance allowance is for those who require additional assistance because of their illness.

There are a number of other benefits designed for specific situations.

- Benefits for those going into hospital, residential or nursing care

    Many of the needs met by the system are met by the NHS when a person goes into hospital or into nursing care.

Benefits are therefore reduced in these circumstances, though usually after a period during which the benefit continues to be paid.

- Benefits for war pensioners

  War disablement and widows pensions may be paid.

- Benefits for women reaching 60 and men reaching 65

  This includes retirement pension paid according to NICs and can be paid after the retirement date even if a person continues to work.

  An extra pension is payable for those over the age of 80.

- Benefits for those who need financial help when a person dies

  Social fund payments can be made if the claimant or partner are already receiving a benefit like income support, family credit or disability working allowance.

  These benefits are sometimes referred to 'passport benefits' since they allow a person to receive another benefit in addition to them.

  Pensions are paid to widows and additional amounts are paid to widowed mothers.

- Benefits for part-time or voluntary workers

  Rights to some benefits will be reduced if a person is working in this capacity.

- Christmas bonus benefit

  This is paid when a person has received some passport benefit like retirement benefit or income support.

- Assistance with national health service costs

  This includes free NHS treatment, prescriptions, sight tests and vouchers for glasses, wigs, and fabric supports.

  Assistance with certain other payments may be made according to the circumstances and the income of the person.

- Social security and medical costs abroad

  Some benefits like child benefit may be affected if a person receiving them goes abroad for longer than few weeks. Other benefits, such as retirement pension, can still be paid if special arrangements are made.

Administration

The Benefits Agency administers benefits like income support, jobseekers allowance, family credit, disability working allowance and the social fund on behalf of the Department of Social Security.

The Employment Service deals with jobseekers allowance claims. Local authorities deal with housing benefit, local education authorities administer education benefits and the Health Benefits Division administers health benefits.

34.5   Appeals

If a person disagrees with a benefit decision they have the right to ask for a Review of the decision and then may appeal to an independent social security appeals tribunal.

Legal aid through the Green Form Advice Scheme may be available to assist a person in preparing for a tribunal hearing but this is not available for appearances at the tribunals themselves since legal aid is not used for this purpose and can only give advice and assistance. The tribunals are not particularly 'formal' and are designed so that the person appearing is enabled to bring their own case.

Reform

On 10 July 1997 the government published the Social Security Bill which makes provisions as to the making of decisions on claims and reviews by officers on the determination of appeals by tribunals. Changes are likely to be effected by statutory instrument and main changes proposed include transferring appeals to a unified 'appeal tribunal' and lessening the use of Social Security Commissioners.

Summary of Part V

Family and Welfare Law

Families involve those who are related by blood or by marriage and may live together (or have done so) and Family law concerns itself with those who have some 'relationship' and were a 'unit' at some time in the past. Usually, 'family' means a husband and wife (or two people in a unit together who live as if they were a husband and wife) and any children in that unit. Society places a value on this unit, but does not legally recognise other units (like homosexual units) in the same way. Family law has regulated this relationship.

Family law

Family law reflects developments in society. Originally, family law was a canon law area regulated by the church. It is not until the last 150 years that Parliament has become involved in regulating the law relating to divorce where the grounds have only gradually been extended. In this time we have also seen the changes in the law relating to family property and the right of parents (particularly mothers) in respect of their children.

The development of family law

See *Hyde v Hyde*. The non-fulfilment of requirements within the definition may cast doubt on the validity of the marriage. However, no longer do we regard marriage as 'for life'. Society has tolerated relationships which reflect marriage although they are not marriage in the legal sense. The commitment that those involved may feel might mean that there are few differences as far as cohabiting couples are concerned; although tolerated and reflected in some legal provisions there are still major differences.

Definition of marriage

These include the legal formalities and the requirements of marriage. Many recent changes have not gone far enough for some, especially unmarried fathers whose recognition under the Children Act 1989 has been one of the most important recognition of cohabitees. Ownership 'rights' have important differences (*H v M* (1992)) for the cohabitee has fewer opportunities to make claims as of right from a partner whereas the married couple have greater claims against each other. However, it is clear that society is beginning, through the use of legal provision, to recognise the existence of cohabiting situations that reflect marriage, particularly those which are long-standing, involve contributions by both parties to the family 'capital', or have children. Parental responsibility

Some comparisons with cohabiting

for the married parents is automatic whereas the unmarried father must use agreement with the mother or s 4 Children Act 1989. The interest in cohabitation agreements has grown in recent years, although there are doubts about the extent to which these are enforceable for they cannot replace existing statutory provision.

Capacity to marry

A person must be 16 or over, single or divorced, of the opposite sex to their intended partner (*Cossey case* (1991)) and it must be a monogamous marriage under English law.

Marriage formalities

These have the aim of regulating the relationship and producing certainty. There are ecclesiastical and civil requirements and failure to comply appropriately may damage the legality of the marriage and could be a criminal offence. There are licence requirements and Banns with residence and notice under the Marriage Act 1949 (as amended) and requirements under the Marriages Act 1994.

Ownership of property

Parties have separate legal personality under the law and can therefore own their own property. This was not always so under English law. Cohabitants have fewer rights over the property of partners than do those who are married to partners. It may be possible to make claims if interests (especially in property like homes) can be established. Married partners have rights accorded to their status and do not have to demonstrate this interest as cohabiting couples must. The position of cohabiting couples has been improved by the provisions in the FLA 1996 (not yet in force). Most problems occur in relationship breakdown or where third parties acquire interests and it is important to establish legal and equitable interests in the property. Most married couples now have joint ownership and these interests are easier to resolve in relationship breakdown than for the cohabiting couple. The Trusts of Land and Appointment of Trustees Act 1996 replaces the trust for sale with a trust for land.

Resolving disputes

There are a number of provisions to assist in resolving disputes and these include s 17 MWPA 1882, s 30 LPA 1925 for declarations of interests. MHA 1983 can establish rights for non-owning spouses and give a statutory right of occupation, now amended (see *Kashmir v Kaur Gill* (1988)) by the FLA 1997.

Equality of ownership is usually implied unless rebutted (*Hoddinott v Hoddinott* (1949)) and the position of gifts is that they are assumed to belong only to the person to whom they were given unless a contrary intention can be demonstrated.

The common law duty to maintain has been 'replaced' by the provisions of ss 2, 6, 7 DPMCA 1978 (for periodical payments, lump sums, regulating agreements to pay and consent order) and s 22 MCA 1973 (maintenance pending suit) plus provisions for liable relatives under SSA 1986 and the Child Support Act 1991 and 1995. The MCA will be amended by those parts of the FLA 1996, when Parts I, II and III come into force.

There are statutory guidelines as amended by MFPA 1984. These would include all the circumstances of the case and income, earning capacity, resources, needs, standard of living, age of parties, duration of marriage, physical and mental disabilities, contribution to family welfare and relevant conduct of the parties.

This is enforced via s 32 with distress, attachment of earnings or imprisonment.

Maintenance can be covered via separation and maintenance agreements and can be supplemented by provisions within the s 15 Children Act 1989 for children.

Financial provision during marriage

This can be found in ss 23 and 24 MCA 1973 as amended by the FLA 1996. There is provision for periodical payments, lump sums, transfer of property. MFPA 1984 means that the court will consider the duration of any orders and other arrangements under the clean break provisions.

Sophisticated arrangements may be made via settlements and variations (*Brown v Pritchard* (1975)) and these can take into account factors noted above under maintenance during marriage see s 25 and 25A MCA 1973 (as amended by the FLA 1996). Orders under these sections can only be made upon decrees of nullity divorce or judicial separation.

See *Suter v Suter and Jones* (1986). Children are a factor but are not 'paramount'.

Clean break provisions are considered and could allow for 'nominal' payments but liable relative provisions and new child maintenance provisions have closed this down.

The Pensions Act 1995 added s 25 B–D to the MCA 1973. This imposes a duty on the court to consider the pension provision of the parties in settling financial provision.

Financial provision upon termination of marriage

See *Re Agar-Ellis* (1883) where the position of wives and children and chattels can be compared to *Gillick* (1985) and the new emphasis on rights not of father, nor of parents, but of the child. Rights of parents (if they exist at all) exist for the benefit of the child rather than the parent. Rights and responsibilities

Parents and children

of parents diminish as the parent approaches adulthood. This is obviously difficult to measure when the law does not necessarily mean a legal adulthood at 18 years but a growing maturity approaching 16 for medical purposes and reaching to the child prior to the age of 18.

Parents

See HFEA 1990 and 'natural' parents and the presumption of parenthood. Blood tie, though, is not the only tie between parent and child and the law recognises the child of the family for many legal purposes. Between parents and children there is parental responsibility for the child's benefit in s 3 Children Act 1989. This was recognised in cases previous to the Children Act 1989. Parental responsibility can be exercised by others as well as parents but note the position of married parents and the unmarried father in s 2(2). The Children Act 1989 permits parental responsibility agreements and provides s 4 and residence order provision giving parental responsibility on a limited basis. Parental responsibility terminates upon a court order, adoption or when the child reaches 18.

Disputes over children

See s 1(5) non-intervention and s 1 welfare principle in the Children Act 1989 which means that there will not be 'intervention' unless essential for the child's welfare since this is 'paramount'. A different order may be given if necessary. There is a welfare checklist in s 1(3) which provides statutory guidelines derived from previous cases. Section 8 orders residence, contact, prohibited steps and specific issue order. Section 11 allows the court to give directions when granting orders.

The state and the child

The state has an interest in the welfare of children and this interest is usually exercised via the local authority.

The Children Act 1989 gives duties to local authorities towards children in need see the general duty in s 17 Children Act 1989. See s 17(10) and (11) where a child is deemed in need if it is unlikely to achieve appropriate physical, emotional, psychological, social and behavioural development without assistance. A range of orders are provided even if the situation does not satisfy s 31 threshold criteria under the Act for care and supervision orders.

Adoption, currently under review, is covered by the Adoption Act 1976 and directions can be given. There are criteria to be met concerning the age of the child and its having lived with prospective adopters. There must be parental agreement (s 16) or this must be dispensed with and the child freed for adoption (see Re W (1971)). The court is concerned with the child's welfare (but this is not the only consideration) and may ask what the 'reasonable' parent would do.

Married and unmarried (single) persons may adopt a child so long as residence and age requirements are met and it is the duty of the local authority or agency to ensure the suitability of adopters.

Section 20 Children Act allows local authority to meet the child's needs by accommodating the child.

Other possibilities are s 31 care (committing child to care of local authority with a limited exercise of parental responsibility) and supervision (assist, advise and befriend the child). For these the child must be under 17 and only the local authority or NSPCC may apply.

Section 36 provides an educational supervision order which can only be applied for by the education authority. Section 43 provides a child assessment order which is useful when an assessment for the child cannot be made or is being obstructed and allows for a limited period for the local authority or NSPCC to make arrangements. Section 44 allows emergency protection orders to be made but is limited to eight plus a possible seven further days with a challenge to the order allowed after 72 hours and anyone may seek such an order. For all orders there is a duty to permit reasonable access between parent and child or the court may be approached to permit.

Grounds in s 31 Children Act 1989 refer to 'significant harm' (see *Re M* (1994)).

The welfare principle applies (but not for s 44).

Domestic violence

The criminal law and the law of tort may be invoked but there are domestic violence provisions within family law. Injunctions and orders are available which can be for the protection of adult victims and for children. There is the inherent jurisdiction of the court but statutory provisions are found in the MHA 1983, DVMPA 1976, DPMCA 1978. See *Richards v Richards* (1983) suggesting that the grounds in MHA 1983 are used. The current provisions are reformed by Part IV FLA 1996, due to come into force in the Autumn of 1997.

The MHA regulated occupation of the Matrimonial Home for the non-owning spouse but the same criteria for orders are used in other provisions for the cohabiting partner.

Wiseman v Simpson (1988) states that the court regarded the ousting or restricting of access to property as a serious matter and will only make an order if there are cogent reasons for the action.

DVMPA 1976 deals with molestation, ouster orders and injunctions to permit entry and remain on the property (see *Davis v Johnson* (1978)).

DPMCA 1978 s 16 can provide an order not to molest, threaten violence against the applicant or a child of the family and can be known as a family protection order.

Cohabitees are more limited in the action that can be taken compared to married partners, and the protection that can be given is limited if the parties are no longer living together.

Enforcement is via fines or imprisonment, but often simply admonishment from court. A power of arrest can be attached but is limited as there must be strong evidence that it is justified. There are plans to reform the law relating to domestic violence as it is seen as complex and lacking in protection for particular groups.

Under FLA 1996 occupation and non-molestation orders can be obtained. A wider group of 'associated' persons may apply, including (ex) cohabitants and other family members. The court will consider all the circumstances of the case, including the welfare of any children involved and a new 'balance of harm' test. Powers of arrest will be attached to orders.

The breakup of the family

Nullity provides method for those not wanting to divorce or unable to do so; see s 11 MCA 1973. If void there never was a marriage at all and if voidable then the marriage is valid until annulled.

There are four grounds in s 11 for void marriages and six grounds in s 12 for voidable marriages. Usually non-consummation of the marriage is the ground relied upon. Section 13 provides bars and defences for nullity.

Divorce is the usual method of ending a marriage. There is only one ground and that is that the marriage has irretrievably broken down (see s 1(1) MCA 1973) but one of five facts must be shown in s 1(2)(a) through to (e) and they cover adultery md intolerability (*Cleary* 1974), behaviour which it would be unreasonable to expect a person to put up with (see *Livingstone-Stallard case* (1974) and the comments on the state of affairs argument), desertion for two years without good cause or 'agreement', living apart for two years with agreement (see *Mouncer* (1972) and *Fuller* (1973)) and living apart for five years where one party does not agree to the divorce (see *Santos* (1972)).

At least one of the parties must recognise that the marriage is at an end.

Defences to divorce include a denial of the ground or facts and s 5 'grave financial or other hardship'. There are bars in that a person must be married for a year and there is a six month 'kiss and make up' rule where living together could be taken into account in deciding relevant periods and behaviour.

Sections 10 (for the examination of financial arrangements) and s 41 (as amended by the Children Act 1989 for the factors relating to the children) can delay the decree absolute.

Judicial separation may be preferable for those with religious objections to divorce or where divorce is not available. Irretrievable breakdown of marriage does not have to be demonstrated although the same facts as are in s 1(2) MCA 1973 are used. The defence might be that the facts have not been made out and bars are available as they are for divorce. Delays through s 10 do not apply, but s 41 does.

Reforms of the legal means of ending a marriage have been passed and ss 1–7 MCA 1973 are replaced by 'divorce over time' in the FLA 1996. Divorce orders and separation orders will replace decrees of nisi and absolute, and judicial separation. General principles of the new provision include the support of the institution of marriage with the assertion that a marriage should be brought to an end with the minimum of distress. A statement of marital breakdown, made after attendance at an information meeting, will precede a regulated period of reflection and consideration providing for financial arrangements and the welfare of children through mediation. Similar ancillary provision with additional pension rights apply but there might have to be changes made to other areas of family law to accommodate this major reform.

Inheritance and family provision

Inheritance and family provision is largely regulated by the Wills Act 1837 and the Inheritance (Provision for Family and Dependants) Act 1975. Through a will property can be left to any person but an individual must make provision for dependants (like partners or children) or the law will have to be used to ensure that reasonable provision (like 'maintenance') is made or the statutory legacy under intestacy applies. Various orders can be made where the will does not provide and there are criteria within s 3 covering the circumstances of the case and the obligations and responsibilities of the persons concerned.

Welfare law

There are questions of the extent to which this is a 'right' or not, but legal entitlements are found largely within SSCBA and SSAA 1992. Entitlements depend upon the qualifying criteria based upon contributions and 'need' with the regulations setting out the detail of the qualifications in relevant regulations attached to the legislation and rates (sometimes criteria) amended annually.

Benefits may be divided into contributory, non-contributory and means-tested benefits depending upon whether their first criteria is the payment of sufficient National Insurance contributions, the circumstances having arisen or the requirement of small means.

The National Insurance system provides for five classes of payments to cover the employed, the self-employed with small and large earnings, and the voluntary contributors.

There is a wide range of welfare benefits covering diverse groups as those with low incomes, those who are unemployed, the young, pregnant women, those with children, the sick and the injured and those who must meet unexpected emergencies.

An appeals system is provided through reviews and the social security appeals tribunal, although this appeals system is currently under review.

PART VI

LABOUR LAW AND THE WORKPLACE

Chapter 35

Employment Law

Labour law and the workplace is really the concern of that area of law called employment law. It has been a contentious area of law for the last 20 years or so, disputes ranging from safety in the workplace to picketing, from rights of part-time workers to productivity and pay rates.

What the syllabus is basically concerned with is the contract area and the termination of the contract, rights relating to the worker, health and safety, provisions for discriminatory action, and the legal position of the trade union. Many of these areas are inter-connected. Some are covered mainly by statutory provision (like discrimination and work) and others by the common law (like aspects of pay, contract, and so on), some areas have elements of both.

There was relatively little regulation about this area of law until some 20 or 30 or so years ago since when there has been legislation about many of the areas with which we are concerned. Examples include the Employment Protection (Consolidation) Act (EPCA) 1978, Sex Discrimination Act (SDA) 1975 and Race Relations Act (RRA) 1976, the Equal Pay Act (EPA) 1970 and the Health and Safety at Work Act (HASAWA) 1974 and the Trade Union Reform and Employment Rights Act (TURERA) 1993.

There have also been many instances of statutory regulation of the collective aspects of the law – that which concerns relationships between workers, their trade unions and employers (and in some instances the government!) and among these could be included the Employment Acts (EA) 1980, 1982, 1988 and 1990, the Trade Union and Labour Relations Acts (TULRA) of 1974 and 1976, and the Trade Union Act (TUA) 1984. The greater the number of statutory provisions, the less likely it is that there is that freedom to personally regulate affairs in the employment arena.

It will also be seen that this area of law operates within a social context which helps the understanding of why particular rules operate in the way that they do and why there are statutory provisions for particular aspects from time to time.

Law in the workplace does not simply 'begin' when a person has got the job. There are legal provisions dealing with job advertisements and the conduct of interviews as well as considerations of discrimination, for example, but some of these are best dealt with under one heading.

For the purposes of the syllabus it is best to begin at what most people see as the beginning!

35.1 The employment contract

The employment contract can be said to consist of elements of the following:

- express terms;

- implied terms;

- terms derived from collective bargaining with the representatives of the workers;

- rules, customs and practice at work;

- statutory provision.

Not all have the same importance for the syllabus and so we will be looking at the main areas of the contract of employment.

Statute does not provide for every eventuality in the employment situation. Consequently, it is essential to look at the provisions of the common law in addition to statutory provision.

A contract of employment may be described as the agreement about the job (subject to statutory requirements) which is a legally binding agreement and contains the terms of the employment. There is only rarely any sense in which this is an individually agreed document for most contracts are not individually negotiated but contain general terms and often refer to other documents. This is 'legal' in that it is not necessary for a contract to be in writing at all to be legally binding.

There are implied and express terms of the contract and unless expressed the law will, if necessary, imply terms into a contract from the circumstances of the situation, often drawing upon similar situations to gain meaning from them.

Implied terms may be used to fill gaps left by the non-inclusion of terms in contracts (ie terms that have not been expressly put into the contract).

This could be an attempt to say what the contract ought to say rather than what it did say, so that a court may be asked to decide what the term ought to be.

Implied terms can be said to be those terms which are included 'because it goes without saying' (see *Luxor (Eastbourne) Ltd v Cooper* (1941)).

What are some of these implied terms? Important common law implied terms of the employee are:

- to obey reasonable orders;

- exercise care at work;

- to maintain honesty and confidentiality and promote the employer's business by not impeding it.

  And of the employer:

- to pay wages;

- to exercise care;

- to cooperate with employees and (possibly) to provide work, although it is possible that this is limited by short-time working and lay-offs which may be regarded by the court as inevitable, especially if the contract actually refers to them.

The rights of the worker are derived from the contract and it is the starting point for decisions on other matters or legal questions. For many workers what is just as important are the conditions of employment which can be derived from collective bargaining.

Employees are entitled to have the terms and conditions of their employment laid down in written terms (sometimes called written particulars) and these must contain:

- the names of the parties to the contract;

- date of commencement;

- continuity of service and could contain (and commonly do);

- job title;

- rate and frequency of pay;

- hours of work;

- sick pay;

- holiday entitlement;

- pension rights;

- notice;

- disciplinary matters.

However, do note that the contract cannot detract from the rights given by statutory provision, and that this may affect the legality of a term in the contract.

A statement of terms and conditions must be given within two months of starting work.

An employee can no longer be directed to other documents, like those concerned with collective agreements, for the details of a contract of employment. TURERA 1993 requires details in the statement. Other documents can be referred to for sickness rights.

There is a limit of 13 weeks after starting work allowed for the employer to provide the written particulars (this is not the same as the contract itself) which gives the basic details of the contract. An industrial tribunal is used for a claim against an employer who does not provide these details as required.

See TURERA 1993 and ss 1–6 EPCA 1978 which cover written particulars.

Note that contracts can be verbal agreements and do not have to be evidenced in writing, but TURERA 1993 will result in the redrafting of many employment documents.

Usually what the job involves is a mixture of verbal and written evidence.

The contract generally might include reference to other documents and to 'custom and practice' operating within the place of work. These are less popular now because workers are expecting to receive written contracts and the vague references to what is customary in a place of work or in an industry might not always fit the pattern of the job.

The EC Directive on proof of an employment relationship (91/533) requires essential aspects of the contract of employment situation to be given to all employees, except where the Member State is able to justify excluding those working less than eight hours a week, or employed for under a month or those whose work is casual. TURERA 1993 goes further in the provision of information. Section 11 Employment Rights Act 1996 permits an employee to complain to the industrial tribunal if provided with no statement or inaccurate or incomplete information.

35.2 Employers, employees and independent contractors

A contract of employment is a contract between an employer and an employee, sometimes referred to in old-fashioned terms as 'Master-Servant' relationships whereby one expert agrees to render services to another person for wages or some other remuneration.

The employee is the person who works under a contract of service or in an apprenticeship the terms of which are written or oral, express or implied.

However, in this area of the law another interpretation could be put on this if the person doing work for another was termed an 'independent contractor'.

The distinction is between contracts of and contracts for employment.

It is important because only an employee will:

- qualify for social security payments;

- get the benefit of the employers duty of care at common law;

- get employment protection rights.

The test of 'control' has been regarded as important here ie who gives directions as to how the job is to be done? The 'control' test can really only be used for simple employment relationships where the employer knows as much about the job as the employee does!

The test of 'integration' has also been used – has the employee been integrated into the organisation and is his work integral to the business? A helpful comparison might be employing a chauffeur and a taxi-driver.

The 'mixed' test currently used seems to be to weigh all the circumstances of the case and decide whether a person on balance is employed on a contract of service or one for services. It is not always very easy to see whether the person is an independent contractor at all.

See *Netherrnire (St Neots) Ltd v Taverna* (1984) where the court said that the employers had to be under a duty to perform some minimum duty (an obligation) for an alleged employer. This test would, however, mean that 'regular' casual workers could be excluded from being regarded as employees if regular work patterns were required to satisfy the test.

The courts have had problems in classifying workers who do not fit into a 'pattern'. Some commentators have suggested that workers ought to be classified as employees with the burden being on those who allege otherwise to demonstrate that they are other than employees. That would give the advantage to the employee.

Two cases provide some assistance:

- *Ready Mixed Concrete (SE) Ltd v Minister of Pensions and National Insurance* (1968)

  Where the ministry claimed that the company was due to pay national insurance contributions for a driver in the company claimed was an independent contractor. The

35.2.1   Employee status?

driver has some independent activities in respect of work including being able to substitute another driver if he was ill, so it was held that he was 'independent'.

- *Market Investigations Limited v Minister of Social Security* (1969)

  A market researcher was able to choose hours of work but was told exactly how to carry out the job.

  Cooke J provided in his judgment a 'list' which could be used:

  (a) control over the work;

  (b) equipment provided;

  (c) financial risk and chance of profit;

  (d) self-description.

  If applied to an individual's situation the list may help to decide if they are employee or an independent contractor.

  It should be noted, however, that the Court of Appeal in *Hall v Lorimer* (1994) did not consider that a mechanistic application of the checklist was 'foolproof', although it did provide good guidance.

35.3 Liabilities and protection for the worker

When we look at the position of the independent contractor it is important to note one of the reasons for attempting to classify the two types of workers in the section above is to use the distinctions in allocating liability in certain circumstances.

The main reasons for the distinction are that:

- An employer may be vicariously liable for the torts (or civil wrongs) of his employees

  Compensation can be paid to employees who incur expenses and liability in the course of their employment so long as they were properly performing their duties at the time. An employer would not be liable for the torts of an independent contractor.

- An employer owes a high duty of care to an employee

  The common law recognises the duty of the employer to take reasonable care of the employee.

- An employee has statutory rights (for example, those under the EPCA 1987) and these rights are not necessarily owed to an independent contractor

  Income tax and welfare benefits may also be different if the worker is regarded as an employee rather than as an independent contractor.

There are a number of ways in which the employment contract may be terminated.

The most obvious ways are not 'dismissal' and do not need much said about them. They involve:

- Death of the employee or employer

  This could involve EPCA 1978 as an act of the employer which has the effect of terminating the employment.

- The contract is 'frustrated'

  This requires an 'outside' change of circumstances which was not foreseen and this has occurred without fault on either side. The cases suggest that long-term absence or an imprisonment might be the likely areas. If frustration is found then there has been no dismissal and no unfair dismissal or redundancy payments rights exist.

  See *Marshall v Harland and Wolff Ltd* (1972) where the factors that ought to be considered by a tribunal were discussed. Factors would include length of employment, time away from work and the position held by the employee.

- The contract was for a 'fixed term' which has now come to an end

  This might be under ss 55 and 83 EPCA 1978 as the lapse of a fixed term contract without renewal

  See *Wiltshire CC v National Association of Teachers in Further and Higher Education* (1980) where the court distinguished between a fixed term contract and a contract for the completion of a task. The latter would be completed by the performance of the task itself.

- The contract comes to an end because the parties agree to it doing so

  This does not usually cause a problem except that there is the possibility that an employee may have been 'misled' in foregoing employment statutory rights (to unfair dismissal), for example, and the courts would be wary of reducing rights in this way.

  It could be used, for example, in early retirement or leaving with a compensation package for some reason.

Termination which is dismissal involves:

- Dismissal by notice to leave your employment

  This is usually a direct dismissal and care needs to be taken in deciding whether any notice (statutory notice or any

35.4   Termination of the contract

more generous provision under the employment contract) is required.

'Instant' dismissal is only justified by a serious breach of the employment contract or if some very serious 'offence' or behaviour occurs.

- Dismissal because there has been a breach of the contract

  This is usually provided for under the terms of the contract.

- A 'wrongful dismissal'

  This occurs where appropriate 'notice' or wages in lieu of notice (instead of working for the period of notice specified in the contract or allowed by statute) are not given and the employee is claiming that the manner of dismissal in that sense was wrong.

There is also a category of dismissal under statutory provisions:

- EPCA 1978 involving an act of the employer which terminates the contract;

- by reason of the conduct of the employer the employee is entitled to treat the contract as being at an end because the employee has been constructively dismissed.

  See ss 55 and 83 EPCA 1978.

  This is often referred to as 'constructive dismissal' and this means that the law will treat some circumstances of leaving the employment as being 'dismissed' because some aspect of the contractual relationship was changed or the employer made it difficult for the employee to continue to perform the requirements of the job. This would then give statutory dismissal rights to those employees. See *Western Excavating (ECC) Ltd v Sharp* (1978) where the court took the view that where an employer is guilty of conduct likely to go the root of the contract which shows that the employer does not intend to be bound by one or more of the terms of the contract then if the employee terminates the contract for this reason then he is constructively dismissed but the conduct must be sufficiently serious to justify this action. The employee must make up his mind soon after the conduct occurs (thus risking losing at the tribunal and then not having a job) and it must have been an essential or fundamental term of the contract.

35.5   Fair dismissal

This is simply a 'good' reason under the law for an employee being dismissed. Refer back to the previous section for guidance.

Cases suggest that the following could be regarded as being fair reasons:

- serious breach of contractual terms;

- a series of less important terms of the contract broken but repeated warnings (especially written warnings) ignored;

- drunkenness on duty (eg of an airline pilot or bus driver) where this is not already covered by the terms of the contract;

- the use of 'bad language' in particular circumstance (there may be occasions where this is not so regarded, like among the workers on a building site!) or some other relevant conduct taken in relation to the employee's job;

- fundamental breach of the contract (like a long prison sentence);

- capability or qualifications of the employee were poor;

- illegality (for the employment to continue);

- redundancy.

There are others but the above are the most common occasions.

It is also a requirement that the employee should have acted reasonably in all the circumstances of the case. In addition to having to give reasons in writing the employer must, for example, offer assistance and training (if appropriate) to the employee rather than dismiss 'on the spot' for a matter which could have been rectified.

Acting reasonably also refers to taking appropriate disciplinary action according to any agreed action in the workplace. If there is a disciplinary code then the employer is required to comply with it.

35.6   Unfair dismissal

The right not to be unfairly dismissed was introduced in 1971 and involves a claim to an industrial tribunal on the basis that the employee has been dismissed for reasons and in a manner suggesting that the circumstances did not justify his dismissal and that he may therefore make a claim against his or her employer. The statutory provisions are found in the EPCA 1978 and the reasons for fair dismissal in s 57. An amendment was introduced by TURERA 1993 which makes it automatically unfair to dismiss an employee for asserting a statutory right.

To claim unfair dismissal the criteria and conditions must apply and the claim made before three months have elapsed. Efforts may be made to 'conciliate' the claim (sometimes by an official from the Advisory, Conciliation and Arbitration

Service) to avoid an actual hearing of the industrial tribunal if this is possible. Before an actual hearing does take place there will be a pre-trial review to either make a final attempt at conciliation, or to identify the issues.

The maximum award is £11,000 plus a basic award if the employee makes out a claim which is upheld by the tribunal.

A claimant must satisfy criteria such as:

*   two years' continuous service except where the dismissal was due to trade union activities, discrimination or non-membership of a union;

*   not over retirement age;

*   and a claim made (normally) within three months of the event taking place.

There are grounds where dismissal is automatically unfair and these are the following:

*   trade union membership or activities;

*   pregnancy as a reason for dismissal;

*   a transfer of the employers undertakings;

*   on the grounds of race or sex discrimination.

An employee may request reason for the dismissal in writing and if employed for at least six months continuously then this must be provided within 14 days. It may contain the 'evidence' for a claim to the industrial tribunal.

What can the employee expect to receive if he 'wins' his case at the tribunal?

*   Compensation (see above)

    For this there is a basic award based upon the employee's age, length of service and weekly pay.

    The compensatory element adds loss of earnings, pensions and other rights which constitutes the amount of money the tribunal considers just in all the circumstances but within the maximum amount.

    Additional awards can be made when an employer refuses to comply with any terms of an order for reinstatement or re-engagement which is an addition to the award unless the employer can show a good reason to satisfy the tribunal that he or she should not take the employee back. This can include an additional number of weeks wages in the case of race or sex discrimination.

    There is a special award where the employee was dismissed for trade union activities and an order for reinstatement or re-engagement was requested by the employee and was not made by the tribunal.

- To have his job back

  See comment above.

- To be re-employed at the place-of-work but not necessarily at the same job

  See comment above.

There are difficulties with the last two because it may not be possible or appropriate for a person to have their job back under the circumstances of an alleged dismissal where there may be statements made about the employees and the employers which might make future working relationships difficult.

35.7   Wrongful dismissal

The conditions for wrongful dismissal are when there has been a breach of the employment contract. Claims are heard at the county court.

There is no maximum award for this and it does not require the employee to have a limit on his or her continuous employment with the employer. There is no age bar to a claim but the court will not normally order that the employee be reinstated if the action is successful.

A claim must be brought within six years from the date of the alleged breach and there is no ceiling on claims which are calculated on the basis of the alleged breach, circumstances of the case and the pay of the employee.

35.8   Redundancy

The job and not the employee are (technically) made redundant. It means that the employer does not require the job to be done any more. Employees are entitled to make a claim for redundancy compensation if their job has been terminated because, for example, the business ceases trading, ceases business in that place or ceases to require the employee to do that job.

Claims can be made if:

- the employee is aged 18–65;

- the employee has been employed for two years' continuous service;

- the employee works for 16 or more hours in the week;

- Special note for part-time workers.

The House of Lords has held that these workers who would have had a five years' service period to comply with if they worked 8–16 hours per week, will now qualify to claim redundancy after a two year qualifying period.

35.8.1   Alternative job offers?

The employer may offer alternative employment and the employee must not refuse this unreasonably.

Reasonable refusal by the employee would include:

- significant loss of pay including overtime and bonuses;
- radical changes in hours of work being involved.

The procedures involved:

- consultation with trade unions, etc with 90 days for 100 or more employees are to be dismissed;
- call for volunteers;
- consideration of re-deployment of workers affected;
- selection according to agreed procedures;
- reasonable paid time off work to seek new employment;
- notification to the department of employment;
- notices of dismissal issued:
- proper calculation of redundancy payments according to the age, wage and length of service of the employees with calculations shown as correct.

Redundancy amounts are calculated by examining:

- the number of years of service;
- the employee's age during those years (amounts of weeks differ according to the agree of the employee); and
- the employee's earnings.

Between the ages of 18–21 years, half a week's pay is multiplied by the years of service.

Between the ages of 22–40 years, one week's pay is multiplied by each year of service.

Between the ages of 41–60 years one and a half week's pay is multiplied by each year of service.

These calculations give the monetary amount due under the law to that worker.

A worker's contract may provide an improved package under its terms.

Reform

Prior to February 1995 a part-time worker working 8–16 hours per week had to work for five years' continuous service to qualify for unfair dismissal and redundancy protection. The Employment Protection (Part-time Employees) Regulations 1995 provide for part-time workers, who are now no longer excluded from rights. Those working less than eight hours per week are unaffected, but other part-time workers (many of whom are women) are now afforded the same rights as full-time workers.

The European influence has recently been felt in this area especially with respect to pregnant women and the armed forces.

35.9   Discrimination – an introduction

Article 119 of the European Community Treaty states that Member States must ensure that the principle of equal pay for equal work is maintained. The Equal Pay Directive (75/117) and Equal Treatment Directive (76/207) deal with implementation of equal pay and equal treatment and the employee can rely upon these provisions under the law whenever they feel that UK law is insufficient.

The SDA 1975 makes it unlawful to discriminate against men and women on the grounds of their sex.

35.9.1   Sex discrimination

Direct discrimination occurs where a person receives less favourable treatment (on the grounds of their sex) than a person of the opposite sex.

The intention of the person doing the discrimination does not matter here.

Indirect discrimination occurs when an employer imposes a term or condition which is such that a percentage of persons of one sex who can comply is considerably smaller than that of the opposite sex. This is only discriminatory if you are able to show that:

- the term cannot be justified irrespective of the sex to whom it is applied;

- it is to a person's detriment when it is applied and they are unable to comply with the term or condition.

Sex might be a genuine occupational qualification:

- for authenticity, eg actors;

- decency and privacy, eg toilet attendants;

- single sex institutions;

  and when employed in a person's home the sex of the employee can be specified for the post and this will not be discrimination.

35.9.2   Race discrimination

The RRA 1976 means that it is unlawful to discriminate against a person on the ground of their race, colour, nationality, ethnic or national origins.

Under the Act the Commission for Racial Equality keeps race discrimination and the legal provisions regarding it under review. Codes of Practice are issued to ensure that employers are kept abreast of the law and what constitutes 'good practice'.

Ethnic origins means a larger group than simply 'race' and the law looks at shared history and cultural traditions to define such groups.

See *Mandla v Dowell Lee* (1983) where the court finally decided that Sikhs were an ethnic group and that there did not need to be an inherited racial characteristic.

Employers must not discriminate against people with respect to making arrangements for job interviews, terms on offer and any recruitment aspects of the job.

Once a person has been employed then they must not be discriminated against on the grounds of race for employment terms, training opportunities, promotion, benefits, and reasons for dismissal.

Employment in a private household is not covered, so this can be specified, although discriminatory advertising for posts will not be permitted.

Race might also be a genuine occupational qualification, eg authenticity, model work, 'authentic' restaurants and services provided for a particular ethnic group where the service provider must be of the same ethnic group for the purposes of the provision.

Direct discrimination occurs when one person treats another less favourably on grounds of race, colour, nationality, ethnic origin or nationality.

The motive is irrelevant but such discrimination is not easy to prove.

Indirect discrimination is when a condition or requirement is applied by an employer and the proportion of persons from one racial group who can comply with it is smaller than the proportion from other groups. The condition or requirement must not be 'justified' irrespective of the racial group of the person to whom it is applied and it is to the person's detriment that they are unable to comply.

Reverse discrimination occurs when there is discrimination in favour of one ethnic minority and this can be against the law, although in certain jobs where it might be helpful to have a person from an ethnic minority it might not constitute discrimination.

Victimisation occurs when a person is treated less favourably on the grounds that he has brought proceedings or given evidence or made allegations of discrimination (so long as they were not malicious and were made in good faith).

Putting pressure on employees to act in a discriminatory manner is also unlawful.

Section 3 SDA 1975 makes it unlawful to discriminate against a married person in employment matters.

35.9.3   Marital status discrimination

However, it is lawful to discriminate against a person because they are single and not married.

At the end of 1995 the Disability Discrimination Act was passed. The main aim appears to be to assist disabled people to lead independent lives and enjoy equal opportunities in employment.

35.9.4   Disability and employment

A person is defined as disabled (under the Act) if they have a physical or mental impairment which has a 'substantial long term effect' on their abilities to carry out normal daily activities. The impairment must last for at least 12 months and may include affects on mobility, manual dexterity, speech, hearing, eyesight, physical co-ordination, memory, perception or ability to concentrate, learn or understand.

It is unlawful for an employer to discriminate against a disabled person applying for a job. A person would be discriminated against if treated less favourably than other employees in terms of taking on that person in employment, terms, training, job opportunities, etc. If an employer cannot show that the treatment is justified then they have unlawfully discriminated.

Employers must take reasonable steps to ensure that a disabled person is not at a disadvantage in the workplace and this may include reallocation of duties, altering work hours or equipment or making adjustments to the premises. Regard must be had to the practicability of making adjustments, cost, disruption, etc.

Discrimination can be justified if the employer is able to show that the disabled person was unsuitable for the employment, training would not assist the employee, or the health and safety of others would be impeded.

A 'National Disability Council' is to be established to advise on measures to reduce disability discrimination. This Council will not have powers of enforcement. A code of practice will be available to employers which will provide guidelines on the operation of the provisions, although small businesses with fewer than 20 employees will be exempt.

If an employer breaches the Act a disabled person who has been a victim of that breach will be able to complain to an industrial tribunal.

35.10   Equal pay

The EPA 1970 laid down the principle of the equality between the sexes in the terms and conditions of the terms of their employment and this was felt most keenly in terms of the issue of equal pay for equal work. These provisions apply to men as much as they apply to women.

Equal pay may be claimed if a person is employed in 'like work' or where the work is 'equivalent work' or it is of 'equal value' to that of a person of the opposite sex in terms of the demand made.

A contract of employment contains an equality clause which is either express or implied and a term of contract can be modified if it results in a situation where one person appears to be treated as 'less' equal than a person of the opposite sex! The clause cannot be altered if it is genuinely due to a material factor other than the person's sex (see later for a fuller explanation of 'material factor').

35.10.1   What is 'same employment'?

Same employment must be the same or associate employer in the UK and there must be common terms and conditions of employment.

35.10.2   What is 'like work'?

Like work applies if the man and the woman are doing work which is the same or of a broadly similar nature and any differences are not of a practical importance.

35.10.3   What is 'equivalent work'?

Equivalent work is when the work done if it can be given an equal value in terms of the demand that are made on the employee and for this purpose there are a number of headings. A job evaluation scheme looks at the skill, effort, decision-making etc of the jobs and a claim for equal pay may be made if it is found that the jobs done by two people of the opposite sex are equivalent.

35.10.4   What is 'material difference'?

Material difference is used as a defence by an employer who wishes to have claim for equal pay by an employee turned down.

In other words, the 'discrimination' must be 'justified' in terms of the needs of the business rather than the sex of the person. Factors such as additional obligations and responsibilities can be a material difference justifying the different rate of pay, for example.

Appropriate facilities must be provided at work, including sufficient toilet and washing facilities appropriate to the number and activities of the employees, including disabled workers' facilities.

'Rest rooms' are a requirement since an employee must provide appropriate facilities which can be regarded as for the 'welfare' of their employees.

The right to a working environment free from hazards is one which is covered by the provisions of the HASAW Act 1974.

35.11   Welfare provisions at work

See Part V on Family and Welfare Law for an introduction to welfare benefits for workers.

35.12   Introduction to state welfare benefits for workers

HASAWA 1974 regulates the requirements for health and safety which are according to the particular requirements for the employment itself.

35.13   Health and safety at work

Charges may not be made for health and safety equipment which the law requires for the purposes of carrying out the job. Additional safety equipment (improved boots, for example, or better goggles when basic goggles are provided) may be charged for, but only if they are shown to be 'additional'.

Detailed requirements under the act apply to hazardous working such as the control of dangerous substances, noise pollution, reporting of injuries and diseases where food products are concerned and requirements relating to the provision of first aid and health equipment.

Claims in the civil courts may be made for injuries which are caused to workers and which are demonstrated to be breaches of employers' liability. Evidence for this could be that acquired under a health and safety inspection. There may also be claims for a breach of statutory duty under, for example, the Factories Act and any regulations made under that Act.

If a worker wishes to take action to claim compensation he must commence the action himself, perhaps with the assistance of his trade union or professional association. The statutory agencies have public duties and the criminal law to enforce, and the civil law here is largely a matter of private enforcement. Lack of legal aid might mean that a worker would be unable to claim at all unless some legal assistance was available.

The same event could result in a criminal action for a breach of the Factories Act 1961 and a breach of the HASAW A 1974. This could result in a prosecution in the magistrates' court and a fine for the employer and even the employee if they have breached the requirements of the Act.

The Health and Safety Executive, a body established to monitor the use of the HASAWA 1974, has the power to inspect the place of work.

Investigations of accidents can take place, and there is an obligation to do this where a serious injury has been caused at work.

In these instances there are three results which can lead to action and they are:

• the issue of an Improvement Notice which requires some aspect of the work process to be improved within a given time limit;

• the issue of a Prohibition Notice which stops work (or an aspect of it) until improvements are made;

• the commencement of a prosecution under the Act which is a criminal offence and for which fines are payable if a breach can be shown.

See the points made about the general position above.

Compensation can be seen under two main headings:

• Welfare provision for injuries at work

This includes sickness benefit and statutory sick pay, invalidity benefit for long-term illness and a range of benefits for those able to work in a reduced capacity.

For those disabled as a result of injury or disease at work there is industrial injuries disablement benefit. Many of the benefits depend upon national insurance contributions and upon just how injured or disabled a person has become.

35.14   Compensation for injuries at work

• Compensation from an employer under the duty of care

The employer owes his workers a duty of care to take reasonable precautions appropriate for the job to ensure that a worker is not injured. There may be statutory duties laid on the employer. These could provide evidence that an injury has been sustained for which the employer ought to pay compensation.

The employment contract may have both express and implied duties which, if breached, could lead to a claim for damages. These may have been included as a result of collective agreements by union activity.

The employer owes a duty of care at common law (*Lane v Shire Roofing Co (Oxford) Ltd* (1995)).

Collective rights at work refers to agreements that have been reached as a result of negotiating and bargaining between trade unions as workers' representatives and the employer. The agreements may be incorporated into contracts and agreements at work as part of the terms of operation.

35.15   Collective rights at work

There exists a right to belong to a trade union and for a trade union to exist unless that right is removed by statutory provision.

Any employee who is a trade union official has the right to time off work (reasonably so) for such activities.

Such duties would include training to be official, membership matters, negotiation or other activities, disciplinary matters at work, etc.

Dismissal due to trade union activities is regarded as unfair dismissal and a claim maybe brought. A case is at present being heard by the House of Lords in respect of 'discrimination' where an employer has attempted to treat non-union employees more favourably than employees who have not agreed to deny themselves the opportunity to belong to a trade union.

35.16   The legal position of trade unions

Under s 15 Employment Act 1982 a trade union can be held vicariously liable for the unlawful industrial action of its membership where such action was authorised by the union.

Industrial action at work is at once a possible breach of the contract of employment and a possible economic tort whereby an employer could make a claim against the person taking the action. However, certain 'immunities' from civil action attract to particular activities where it can be shown that the activity is a genuine industrial dispute. When this occurs there is no liability (within the limits of the provisions) for the trade union organising the activity and the worker will simply not be paid if he does not work!

There are risks, however, and the law is complex, although many areas are outside the syllabus.

35.17   Industrial action, trade disputes and picketing

The Employment Act 1980 limits the activities of 'secondary picketing' and some types of 'sympathetic action' in trade disputes, whereby other businesses not directly involved with the trade dispute are 'protected' from industrial action.

35.17.1   Employment Act 1980

The Employment Act 1982 added to the restrictions of lawful industrial action and ensured that trade unions could, if they breached the provisions, be forced to pay damages. It became unfair dismissal, under this act, to dismiss a worker for non-

35.17.2   Employment Act 1982

membership of a trade union and providing for closed shop ballots every five years.

35.17.3   Trade Union Act 1984

The Trade Union Act 1984 limits the actions of unions in that they must ballot their members every 10 years about political funds, all voting members of trade union executives must be balloted very five years and immunity from damages was removed where trade unions authorised industrial action without first calling a ballot.

35.17.4   Employment Act 1990

The Employment Act 1990 contains provisions about closed shop employment which means that a worker cannot be discriminated on the grounds that they do not belong to a union. Only peaceful and lawful picketing attracts immunity if the action is taken in 'furtherance of a trade dispute' and unions can be liable in tort for the actions of members and officials unless they repudiate those actions in accordance with the Act. There is now no immunity or claim for unfair dismissal claim if all workers were dismissed for taking unofficial industrial action.

Economic torts include:

- inducing another to breach their contract of employment;

- conspiracy to breach contracts and cause economic damage;

- intimidating others;

- interfering with trade, contracts and the business in general.

Statutory immunities are found within s 13 TULRA.

The immunity, though, which is from an action in tort done 'in furtherance of a trade dispute' (see *Express Newspapers v McShane* (1980)) but note that this has been curtailed by legislation since then (see above).

The immunity is lost in given circumstances, like secondary picketing and action without a secret ballot as described in the more recent legislation (see *Hadmore Productions Ltd v Hamilton* (1983)).

Trade unions regard this picketing (picketing a place of work peacefully to persuade others not to enter and work or deliver materials) as being an important aspect of industrial action.

The approach taken by the law is important because there is no positive right of assembly (see provisions under civil liberties with reference to 'positive rights') and there are possible breach of the peace and public order offences where picketing is concerned. Section 15 TULRA defines what can be done as simply peacefully attending the place of work of the worker, or in such a place where there is a trade union official present he or she may attend the place of dispute of members of the union. Secondary picketing (at another place of work) is unlawful under the Employment Act 1980 and the picketing must be at or near the place itself (see *Rayware Ltd v TGWLI* (1989)).

The civil liabilities include:

- economic tort;

- private nuisances;

- trespass

and, since there is no immunity from the criminal law at all, the possible criminal offences include:

- obstructing a police officer in the execution of their duty;

- obstruction of the highway;

- public nuisance;

- Public Order Act 1986 offences as amended by the Criminal Justice and Public Order Act 1994.

Labour Law and the Workplace

There have been many statutes regulating the workplace since the end of the 1960s. The relevant law is contained in statutes regulating a range of activities beginning even before the person begins work.

A contract of employment can be found in a number of documents and reference can be made to collective agreements with trade unions, work rules, disciplinary codes and a contract that the employee has. For many employees and employers the most important terms are express terms (laid out in a document) and implied terms (see *Luxor (Eastbourne) Ltd v Cooper* (1941)) which 'go without saying'. The TURERA 1993 further defines the employment details which must be given to employees.

Contract of employment

Deciding whether the person who is working is an employee or an independent contractor is an issue because legal implications arise in the status. An employee is entitled to certain welfare benefits, statutory rights and duty of care from the employer whereas the independent worker has fewer legal rights and protection. 'Tests' have been used to help decide the category of the worker and currently the most useful one has been the 'mixed' test where all the circumstances are taken into account. However, these tests provide only guidance and may be departed from in given circumstances.

The status of the employee

The problematic areas with the termination of a contract arise when there has been an alleged wrongful, unfair or constructive dismissal. There are reasons which count as 'fair' dismissal, usually when there has been a serious breach of the employment contract. The EPCA 1978 sets out reasons that are 'unfair' although it may depend on the contract and the circumstances of the dismissal itself. A claim for compensation or the job back may be made at the industrial tribunal.

The termination of the contract

Wrongful dismissal often involves the 'manner' in which the dismissal took place and may involve a claim for wages instead of working through a notice period that has not been properly given by the employer.

Redundancy

Redundancy is when the job (not the employee) is no longer required. Claims for redundancy payments are made and are calculated on age, wage and length of service as an entitlement of the employee.

Discrimination

The influence of Europe must be noted with regard to discrimination (see Article 119 Treaty of Rome and the Equal Pay and Equal Treatment Directives).

Both the SDA 1975 and the RRA 1976 concern direct and indirect discrimination and victimisation and there are steps that can be taken in the Industrial Tribunal, as with disability discrimination. There may be 'genuine occupational qualifications' that apply which 'justify' apparent discrimination under the law. Marital discrimination against those who are married (but not the unmarried) is actionable. Recent reform of the law has made it unlawful to discriminate on the grounds of a person's disability, although the provisions permit justification. Equal pay is a requirement where the jobs are rated as being equal (though not necessarily the same) and have no material differences under the provisions of job evaluation.

Welfare provision and health and safety

There are a range of welfare benefits and the employer is expected to make provisions for the safety of his workers, including general provisions for appropriate facilities. There are stringent requirements for health and safety in the HASAWA 1974 which are enforced through inspections, prohibition and improvement notices, and prosecutions. The Health and Safety Executive is also responsible for investigating serious accidents at work. Compensation for accidents may come through the welfare benefit system and through actions for tort in the courts.

Trade unions

There is a right to belong (or not to belong!) to a trade union. This has implications for activities at work where industrial action is concerned. The EA 1980 and revisions thereafter have reduced the protection afforded to trade unions in the past for their support of industrial action by employees who are members of the union. There is a limited immunity for economic torts but there are rules about what activity is covered and secret ballots must be held.

Picketing activities are limited to the place of work and there is no immunity from the provisions of the criminal law.

Index